Managing Sport, Fitness, and Recreation Programs

Concepts and Practices

William F. Stier

State University of New York at Brockport

Allyn and Bacon

Boston ▪ London ▪ Toronto ▪ Sydney ▪ Tokyo ▪ Singapore

Vice President, Editor in Chief: Paul A. Smith
Publisher: Joseph E. Burns
Editorial Assistant: Sara Sherlock
Editorial Production Service: Chestnut Hill Enterprises, Inc.
Manufacturing Buyer: David Repetto
Cover Administrator: Jennifer Hart

A Viacom Company
160 Gould Street
Needham Heights, MA 02494

Internet: www.abacon.com

Between the time Website information is gathered and published, some sites may have closed. Also, the transcription of URLs can result in typographical errors. The publisher would appreciate notification where these occur so that they may be corrected.

Library of Congress Cataloging-in-Publication Data

Stier, William F.
Managing sport, fitness, and recreation programs : concepts and practices / by William F. Stier
p. cm.
Includes bibliographical references and index.
ISBN 0-205-15944-3 (alk. paper)
1. Sports–Management. 2. Sports administration–Vocational guidance. I. Title.
GV713.S75 1999
796'.06'9—dc21 98-27304
CIP

Photo Credits: Photo credits continue on page 384, which should be considered an extension of the copyright page.

Printed in the United States of America

10 9 8 7 6 5 4 3 03 02 01 00

To my loving wife, Veronica Stier,
and our loving family members

Missy Ann
Barbara Ann
Lori Ann
Reba Ann
Mary JoAnn
Missie Ann
Lucy Ann
Samantha Ann
Katie Lee
Joshua
Jessica Bree
Mark
Michael
Patrick
Will III
Mic
Michael II
Jackson William

for loving encouragement and continuing support.

CONTENTS

PREFACE

Introduction—the Purpose of this Book

This book, *Managing Sport, Fitness, and Recreation Programs: Concepts and Practices*, has been written specifically for students in introductory collegiate courses in sport management programs. Readers are given a realistic glimpse into the challenges and opportunities that exist now as well as in the future within the exciting world of sport and sport management.

The purpose of this book is to provide the reader with a comprehensive introduction to the body of knowledge that serves as the foundation for the study of management within sport and sport-related organizations. Specific objectives include assisting the future sport management professional to be capable of

1. developing a beginning philosophy of sport and a philosophy of management (in sport, fitness, and recreation organizations);

2. understanding the relationship(s) between sport, the business of sport, and the management of sport;

3. understanding basic managerial theories and principles as well as concepts of management that form the foundation of sport management;

4. understanding the types of positions, jobs, and career opportunities available in sport management and how one becomes more marketable in the world of sport business;

5. developing essential managerial competencies, survival skills, and leadership attributes appropriate for today's complicated and complex sport, fitness, and recreation organizations.

How the Book Is Organized

The book is divided into three sections. The first (Chapters 1–3) deals with the foundation of sport management and provides an overview of the profession of sport management, including a historical glimpse of sport and sport management. The current status of sport management and professional preparation programs in sport management in this country is examined. A general discussion of career and employment opportunities in the management of sport is provided along with a review of essential skills needed by sport managers in the twenty-first Century. Additionally, the reader is introduced to the process of building a philosophy of sport management and exposed to some of the pertinent theories of management as they relate to sport organizations.

The second section (Chapters 4–6) introduces the reader to the processes and skills involved in successful sport management as an administrator or manager. The reader is then introduced to the areas of leadership, motivation, and decision-making within various types of sport management businesses and organizations. This section also includes treatment of the essential competency of communication in the management of sport as well as conflict management and resolution.

The third and final section (Chapters 7–12) deals with practical and pragmatic issues that exist today and will exist in the future in the world of sport and sport management. The reader is introduced to various strategies and tactics for dealing with the challenges and problems associated with the management of all aspects of sport and sport-related organizations and programs. These six chapters should prove especially helpful for the modern-day sport manager in terms of decision-making and taking specific courses of action.

Unique Features of This Book

A unique feature of this book is the existence of 421 concepts relating to sport management that are strategically located throughout the 12 chapters. These managerial concepts can help the reader appreciate and understand the body of knowledge that serves as the foundation for successful sport management.

The concepts also suggest possible alternatives in terms of decision-making. That is, concepts may serve as "food for thought" for the reader in considering a problem, an obstacle, or a challenge and arriving at one or more acceptable conclusions involving one or more courses of action.

The concepts presented herein are applicable to almost any managerial situation one might face within the areas of sport and fitness/wellness, as well as leisure/recreation programs. These concepts are based on both sound administrative theories as well as practical experiences in the world. Finally, throughout the book are suggestions for handling various situations that the modern-day sport manager might confront.

The author has 26 years of sport management experience in various sport, recreation, and fitness organizations and businesses as well as within colleges and universities. Additionally, he has served as the director of Sport Management/Athletic Administration at the State University of New York, Brockport, since 1990 and as Graduate Director since 1994. This is the author's eleventh book about sport and the management of sport.

ACKNOWLEDGMENTS

I wish to acknowledge the contributions that my wife, Veronica, has made to the completion of this book. To Veronica, who sacrificed so much during the five years it took to research and write this book and whose ever-present support and loving encouragement provided the motivation for its completion, I thank you from the bottom of my heart.

Thanks is also given to the countless sport, recreation, and fitness administrators and staff members with whom it has been my pleasure to work during the past 25 years. I have gained much through my experiences within a wide range of sport, fitness, and recreation organizations and I owe much to my coworkers, associates, and clients. *Special appreciation is given to the late Mark T. Martin, former chairman of the board of directors of CFI, Inc., who served as my early mentor in the world of business.*

I would be remiss if I did not acknowledge the contributions of my undergraduate and graduate students at the State University of New York, Brockport, with whom I field-tested portions of this book during the past three years. I have been blessed with exceptional students in pursuit of their own careers within the world of sport and recreation management and I have learned much from their inquiring minds, challenging questions, and suggestions.

Special thanks should be given to Norman Frisch, graphic designer, and Richard Black, Director of Design and Production, SUNY—Brockport. In addition, I thank Joe Burns who served as my editor for this publication. And, of course, I want to thank the following reviewers of my manuscript for their helpful suggestions and insights: Ming Li, Georgia Southern University; Jeff Messer, Slippery Rock University; Peter Titlebaum, University of Dayton; Jim LaPoint, University of Kansas at Lawrence.

SECTION ONE
Foundations of Sport Management

CHAPTER
1 Understanding Sport Management

Never underestimate the importance of sports promotions.

CHAPTER OBJECTIVES

After reading this chapter you will be able to:

- Explain why the management of sport goes by many names;
- Understand basic terminology in sport management;
- Define the terms *administration* and *sport management;*
- Understand some general principles of management;
- Explain why the management of sport is a business;
- Differentiate between the "art" and "science" of management;
- Justify the need for the formal study of sport management;
- Appreciate the importance, from a historical perspective, of managerial achievements in different societies;
- Indicate why the study of sport management is a recent phenomenon;
- Describe the growth and current status of sport management professional preparation programs;
- Cite areas of controversy surrounding sport management programs in colleges and universities;
- Acknowledge the importance of securing appropriate educational experience within the area of sport management.

Sport Administration—Sport Management: What Is in a Name?

The field of study that the author refers to as *sport management* has been and continues to be referred to by a variety of different names. In fact, the name of the discipline has been the subject of close scrutiny and many debates in its brief history. And the discussion, debate, and disagreement continue today. In reality, there are many terms used interchangeably to describe the profession or the field of study.

Concept 1: The Management of Sport Goes by Many Names.

Such terms as *sport(s)* or *athletic management, sport(s) business* or *administration,* as well as *athletic administration* (among others) have all been in vogue at one time or another or are currently being used. Although there is no consensus in terms of the name of the discipline or profession, the purpose of all the college and university professional preparation programs in sport management remains essentially the same. That is, to prepare future sport professionals—other than teachers and coaches—for managerial careers in the world of sport and sport-related endeavors (Bridges & Roquemore, 1996; Parkhouse, 1996).

Traditionally, the general public has viewed sport management as being associated only with the administration and management (general operation) of competitive sport programs in secondary schools, in colleges and universities, or, perhaps, at the professional level. Yes, sport management is intimately involved with such programs, and much, much more. Today, sport management is in reality a multifaceted domain offering a multitude of opportunities for employment and self-fulfillment in a wide range of sport and sport-related activities, both in the public and the private sectors, as well as in the profit and not-for-profit arenas.

Thus, this book is for those men and women who desire to secure and succeed in responsible managerial and administrative positions within private or public organizations devoted to (1) athletic competitive sports programs—at all levels, (2) health, fitness, and wellness programs, as well as (3) leisure and recreation programs. In reality, the scope of sport management is rather extensive. Chapter 2 presents a detailed look into what comprises the world of sport management in contemporary society.

> **Concept 2:** Administration Is the Management of Human Behavior and the Manipulation of Resources.

Understanding the Terminology: *Administration, Management,* and *Sport Management*

"Administration is the management of human behavior through good leadership skills and the manipulation of resources towards recognized and agreed upon objectives or goals" (Stier, 1996b). One manages, leads, motivates, and guides other human beings. One does not manipulate them. The term *manipulation* carries with it some negative connotations

Fans are attracted to winning programs that provide top-flight competition and entertainment.

when applied to individuals. However, one does manipulate and control tangible objects, such as resources, equipment, supplies, and facilities.

For the purpose of this book the terms *administration* and *management* are generally used interchangeably. Similarly, terms such as *administrators, managers, sport leaders, supervisors,* and *sport personnel* refer to individuals who assume leadership roles and responsibilities within the sport, fitness, or recreation entity *and* who are involved in one or more essential activities related to or associated with managerial responsibilities.

Definition of the Term *Sport Management*

Therefore, for purposes of discussion, one may define successful *sport management* as being the process of striving toward clearly established objectives and goals as a result of working with others and exercising prudent and judicious use of resources and assets—all within the context of a sport or sport-related organization. Being a successful sport manager requires the possession of certain competencies and the use of specific skills in working with human beings, individually, in small and large groups, and as part of informal and formal organizations.

> **Concept 3:** Sport Management Is an All-Encompassing Term Associated with the Management of Sport, Fitness/Wellness As Well As Leisure/Recreation Programs.

Sport management is currently used as an umbrella phrase or term encompassing a large number and variety of sport, fitness/wellness, and leisure/recreation programs and activities. Provided below is a partial list of these specific programs and activities frequently thought of as falling within the purview of sport management (Sawyer, 1993; Stier, 1996a; Ross, Jamieson, & Young, 1997).

1. Amateur competitive athletics
2. Professional sports
3. Sport agencies and league or conference operations
4. Municipal recreation and sports
5. Manufacturing of sporting equipment and supplies
6. Sport merchandising and service organizations
7. Sports news media
8. Health, wellness, and fitness activities
9. General recreational resort and hotel operations
10. Specialized sport resorts and instructional programs

> **Concept 4:** There Are General Principles of Management That May Be Applicable in a Variety of Organizational Structures under Various Settings, Circumstances, and Situations.

General Principles of Management

There are general principles of management that may be applicable in a variety of organizational situations and circumstances. Being able to apply these principles of management and administration can prove to be a significant advantage when faced with the innumerable daily problems and challenges that exist in the world of sport management.

Thus, the reader should strive to develop an understanding and appreciation of these general principles (guidelines). With a thorough grasp of these fundamental managerial principles individuals having responsibility for (1) personnel, (2) programs, and (3) resources will have a realistic and meaningful body of knowledge they can use to make effective and efficient decisions within any sport-related organization (see Figure 1.1).

Concept 5: Management Is Management and Administration Is Administration: Regardless of the Setting, the Principles and Concepts Remain Essentially the Same.

Whether one has administrative or managerial responsibilities within a high school or college, a fitness club, a YWCA/YMCA, a corporate health club, a resort, or a professional team, the principles and concepts underlying sound administrative practices,

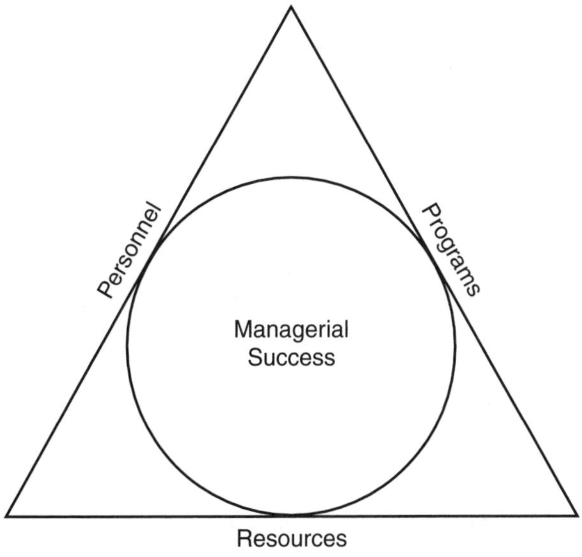

FIGURE 1.1 Areas of Responsibility for Managers

decision-making, and actions remain the same. Administration is administration, management is management, period.

Concept 6: The Management of Sport Is a Business.

The same principles of administration are also applicable whether one is involved in (1) the *business* of manufacturing widgets or sport products, (2) the *business* of providing participatory opportunities or services in sport, fitness, recreational, or leisure activities, or (3) the *business* of providing opportunities or services for spectators at various sport, recreational, or leisure programs or activities.

Concept 7: There Are Very Distinct Understandings, Skills, and Knowledge That Must Be Mastered by the Sport Manager, That Are Specific to the Organization in Which One Is Employed.

Although the concept that administration is administration and that management is management is certainly valid, there still exists the need to possess specific understandings and to develop specific job skills and knowledge relating to the particular organization in which one finds oneself employed. In this respect, there is specific and sometimes unique knowledge that is pertinent and absolutely necessary for a particular sport organization or entity. For example, knowledge of NCAA eligibility rules is a must for an athletic administrator having responsibility for student athlete eligibility within any NCAA institution. However, this knowledge has no relevance whatsoever within a private health club or a public resort facility.

Concept 8: Management Is Both an Art and a Science.

Management is both an art and a science. It is a science because there are fundamental, scientific principles and a body of knowledge underlying and supporting the tasks involved in managing and administering sport. These foundational tenets hold true and are applicable in a variety of settings, at different levels, and under varying circumstances. However, management can also be considered an art, because the actual delivery and implementation of the administrative techniques and managerial strategies and tactics can be significantly affected and, in fact, enhanced, through the creative and innovative utilization of these principles and applications of the knowledge pertaining to management.

The art of management involves the creative application of managerial principles and the creative resourcefulness of those involved in sport management situations. Ingenious adaptations and utilization of these management principles, strategies, tactics, and knowledge is necessary if one is to be a successful sport leader, manager, or administrator.

However, these adaptations should be made in light of the individual's strengths and limitations as well as the setting and circumstances in which one finds oneself (Stier, 1994).

Concept 9: Understanding the Principles of Management Can Facilitate Appropriate and Timely Decision-Making.

One of the objectives of this book is to provide you, the reader, with appropriate knowledge and understanding of the administrative–managerial processes. Such knowledge and understanding will enable you to develop and refine the necessary skills, abilities, and competencies that will facilitate your making wise, fair, appropriate, and timely decisions, and then taking expedient action. It is indeed imperative that decisions be made in light of the existing circumstances, that is, resources and limitations, that currently exist or will manifest themselves in the future (see Figure 1.2).

Why Study Sport Management?

Unfortunately, "historically over 98 percent of all first time managers in all types of organizations are placed in their first supervisory jobs without being trained to manage first" (Bridges & Roquemore, 1992, p. 4). This is truly an unfortunate and deplorable situation. It is unfair to the person to be placed in such a situation. And, all too frequently, it is unfor-

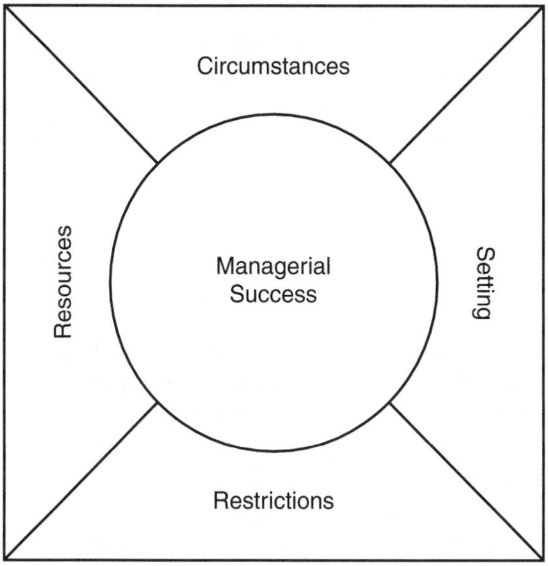

FIGURE 1.2 The Basics of Effective Decision-Making

tunate for the organization, its programs, and others associated with the organization. This horrific practice often hinders progress of the organization rather than facilitates its growth and advancement. However, it reinforces the tremendous need for formal training for those men and women who desire to move into positions of authority involving administrative–managerial responsibilities under the sport umbrella (Stier, 1995; Berg, 1996).

Increased Need for Trained Professionals

It is highly advantageous for those who wish to become actively involved in a sport or sport-related organization to study the management of sport formally for three specific reasons. First, there is an increasing need for professionals trained in the managerial and business aspects of sport (Stier, 1993b). Through a sport management curriculum you will be able to develop essential skills and refine broader and more sophisticated managerial competencies needed in the world of sport. Such skills and competencies will put you in good stead if and when you are in a position to assume managerial responsibilities within the sport organization, either with or without an official title or designation.

Concept 10: The Sophisticated and Complicated World of Sport Requires Managers and Administrators to Be Formally Trained and Educated.

The job demands, both today and in the future, necessitate that you, the sport management professional, possess a depth of knowledge and a broad range of specific competencies. These competencies include, but are not limited to, administrative theory, business practices, communications, computer applications, and law in order to be capable of dealing successfully with changing challenges and problems associated with the business of sport. The mastery of pertinent knowledge and proper utilization of managerial skills can prove most beneficial for your daily survival and your future advancement within any organization.

Nonmanagers Work with Managers–Administrators and Other Nonmanagers

The second reason to study the management of sport is that, if you do not hold the official title of *manager* in your particular position within a sport organization, you nevertheless will work for and with administrators and managers. Knowledge of managerial principles and concepts will facilitate the building of positive relationships with administrators ad managers. In working with managers (bosses), it is especially important that you have an understanding and knowledge of the role(s) of managers.

You need to develop a global perspective of the organization and see the situation from the viewpoint of the administration or management. You need to understand why they act as they do. It is most helpful to have an understanding and appreciation of where (your own) managers or administrators are "coming from." Such knowledge will put you in good stead in your efforts to do your own job within the organization.

> **Concept 11:** The Essential Skills and Competencies for Successful Managers and Administrators Are Also Very Effective for the Nonmanagement Employee or Associate.

Also, as a nonmanager you must be capable of working successfully with others, your peers and the general public. Understanding principles and concepts of good management and demonstrating specific organizational skills and managerial competencies can be most helpful to nonmanagers. You will use such skills, knowledge, and understanding in your everyday tasks—working by yourself as well as with nonmanagerial personnel.

One Needs to Utilize Managerial Skills to "Manage" Oneself

> **Concept 12:** Individuals Assume Managerial and Administrative Duties and Responsibilities at Almost Every Level within an Organization—Even in Entry Level Positions.

The third reason to study sport management is that, in fulfilling your specific job or work responsibilities, regardless of what they may be or at what level you find yourself within the organization, you must "manage" yourself. You must manage your time, prioritize your goals, and complete the tasks for which you are responsible. And, of course, you must exercise good judgment in terms of your daily professional relationships with other people, both inside and outside of the organization. To accomplish these objectives, it helps for you to be professionally trained in the managerial, administrative, and business aspects of sport.

Management and Administrative Achievements in Ancient Times

> **Concept 13:** There Have Been Many Outstanding Examples of Managerial and Administrative Skills since Ancient Times.

Managerial skills and administrative competencies have been demonstrated for eons throughout recorded history. The origins of many so-called modern concepts and practices of management and administration can be traced from ancient civilizations. Whenever formal organizations existed there has been the need for managerial, organizational, and planning skills. In fact, all great leaders throughout history were outstanding managers and organizers. These leaders managed and carried out wars, they managed to construct impressive physical structures and buildings, they planned and managed vast explorations, they developed complex political systems, and they managed and controlled the lives of vast populaces. In three specific areas, (1) architecture, (2) warfare, and (3) political conquest, one can see examples of complex management systems from the earliest time of recorded history. (For a chronological list of when management concepts and methods were introduced, see Appendix A.)

King Solomon: Manager, Organizer, and Leader

The famed biblical ruler, Solomon, directed the establishment of elaborate trade agreements, managed vast construction projects, and negotiated peace agreements in the 10th century B.C. Even before Solomon's time, other ancient rulers utilized wise managerial practices (delegation) by having their servants act as their official representatives, with appropriate authority and power, on behalf of the ruler.

Architecture: The Managerial Challenges of Constructing the Pyramids

The creation of the Pyramids took thousands of individuals decades to build. Such feats took extraordinary skills in terms of logistics, organization, and management. The organizations of armies throughout recorded history are examples of the necessity of great organizational, motivational, and managerial skills.

The Egyptian pyramids are living monuments to the extraordinary managerial ability and organizational ingenuity of the Egyptians. To understand what was then involved in constructing a pyramid, consider that one pyramid covers 13 acres of land, contains some 2,300,000 stone blocks, each weighing an average of 2.5 tons. In terms of manpower alone, it is estimated that over 100,000 workers toiled for over 20 years in the most difficult of living conditions.

In addition to architecture, there are many examples available in Egyptian literature of the early (2160 B.C. to 1788 B.C.) understanding of management principles and concepts. For example, in the Old Kingdom, Middle Kingdom, and the New Empire, the leaders exercised effective control of an extended physical domain through a highly decentralized, and later, centralized governmental structure.

Military Management and Political Organization: Alexander the Great

Military examples of management, administration, and organization can be seen from the earliest times of structured armed conflict. The staff principle was very important in military success as was the involvement of staff planning, coordinating subordinates in delegated tasks. Perhaps the greatest example of successful use of the staff system took place during the reign of Alexander the Great (336 B.C. to 328 B.C.). Alexander the Great conquered the known world through extraordinary administrative skill, exceptional competency, and exquisite timing.

Empire Building: the Romans

Another outstanding example of effective and efficient management was the creation and maintenance of the empire of Rome. At one point, through superior managerial, organizational talents and ruthless use of power, the Romans held control over 50 million human beings. The empire extended from Great Britain in the West to Syria in the East, and included Europe and all of the north of Africa. Mismanagement, or nonmanagement, also led to the eventual breakdown of the Roman Empire and the dissolution of its sophisticated (for the time) way of life.

Sport Activities and Competitions from a Historical Perspective

The planning and the management of sport and sport-related activities is certainly not a new phenomenon (Parks & Zanger, 1990). From a very real and practical perspective, sport management has been in existence from the earliest times of human existence. For literally centuries, throughout written history, individuals and groups have gathered together for informal and/or formal competition in physical activities. And, as a result, there have been individuals involved in the planning, organizing, and supervising of such activities.

Concept 14: The Management of Sport Is Not a New Phenomenon.

The first written accounts of sport competition and organized athletics are found in the *Iliad* and the *Odyssey*. These epic poems depict athletics, games, sport, and dance that became an integral part of Greek life. The descriptions of these games by Homer "are the first literary account of athletics" (Swanson & Spears, 1995, p. 343). In fact, contemporary sport concepts and managerial principles are evident when these games and competitions are clearly described in the poems.

The Ancient Greeks and the Management of Sport

The ancient Greeks excelled in conducting competitive athletic events for their citizens during the 1200 years of the athletic festivals, beginning around 776 B.C. and ending with the banning of the games by Emperor Theodosius I in A.D. 393. Of course, whenever such athletic competitions and sporting festivals were held, there had to be individuals involved in their planning, organization, management, and implementation.

In reality, there were four major athletic festivals, games, or competitions that became an extremely important part of Greek life. These festivals, or competitions, involved athletes from throughout Greece. So much so that wars were stopped, temporarily at least, to allow free passage to the sites of the competition and for the competitions themselves. The four major games were the Olympic (beginning in 776 B.C. in Olympia), the Pythian (beginning in 582 B.C. in Delphi), the Isthmian (beginning in 582 B.C. near Corinth), and the Nemean games (beginning 573 B.C. in Nemea) (Swanson & Spears, 1995).

As a result, extensive and relatively sophisticated stadia and supporting structures (for the time) were constructed for the competitors and spectators. In addition to the sites where actual competitions took place, there were facilities constructed for the training, feeding, and housing of athletes and those who accompanied the athletes. There were also facilities to treat and rehabilitate injured competitors. Finally, there were statues and columns bearing inscriptions about specific athletic contests and individual successful competitors. Such examples of highly organized sport facilities have been discovered at Olympia, Delphi, and at Epidaurus (Yalouris & Yalouris, 1989).

The types of athletic competitions held during the 1200 years of the ancient Greek games included footraces, jumping contests, throwing of the discus and the javelin, wrestling, and boxing. There were also exciting chariot and horse races. Additionally, there was also athletic competition that involved a combination of several of these activities in a competitive event. Two such examples are the pentathlon (involving a footrace, jumping, a discus throw, a javelin throw, and wrestling) and the pancration (a semi free-for-all combination of boxing and wrestling).

History of the Formal Study of Sport Management

Concept 15: The Formal Study of Sport Management Is a Recent Phenomenon.

Prior to 1966 there was no formal study of sport management at the collegiate level. It was not until that year, at Ohio University (Athens), that the first educational program (at the master's level) in the world was initiated in sport management, under the direction of Dr. James G. Mason, who is recognized as the father of sport management. Ohio University was once referred to as the "Harvard of sports management" by then Oakland A's executive vice president Andy Dolich (J. G. Mason, Personal Communication, January 6, 1997).

However, the impetus for this initial educational program started much earlier, 1957 to be exact. It was in that year that Walter O'Malley, then the president of the Brooklyn Dodgers, shared his concern with Dr. James G. Mason, then a professor of Physical Education at the University of Miami, about the lack of formal educational programs for those individuals seeking employment within professional baseball. It took Dr. Mason, who subsequently moved to Ohio University, almost a decade (1966) to establish the first sport management course of study in Athens, Ohio, at Ohio University (J. G. Mason, Personal Communication, May 6, 1997). The second graduate program was implemented at the

University of Massachusetts in 1971 by Dr. Harold J. VanderZwaag, while the third graduate program in sport management was developed in 1972 at Western Illinois University (Macomb, Illinois) under the leadership of Dr. Loren Dittus.

Only six years later, in 1978, there were a total of 20 sport management graduate programs in the United States (Parkhouse, 1978). Additionally, the first 3 undergraduate programs were established at Biscayne College (now St. Thomas University), at the State University of New York College at Brockport, and at St. John's University (Stier, 1993a). In 1982, Lewis indicated that there were a total of 44 graduate and undergraduate professional preparation programs in existence. And, in 1988, the number of undergraduate sport management programs had ballooned to 75, while graduate programs almost tripled to 58 professional preparation programs in the United States (Sports Inc., 1988).

By 1993 there had been literally an explosion of both undergraduate and graduate programs with a total of 193 United States colleges and universities and 14 Canadian institutions of higher education offering undergraduate and/or graduate programs in sport management or athletic administration (NASSM/NASPE, Sport Management, 1993). By 1997, eight doctoral level programs were in existence in the United States, including programs at (1) University of Northern Colorado, (2) The Ohio State University, (3) University of Massachusetts, (4) Florida State, (5) University of New Mexico, (6) University of Connecticut, (7) University of Iowa, and (8) the United States Sports Academy (Daphne, Alabama).

By the year 2000 it is estimated that there will be over 200 professional preparation programs at the graduate and undergraduate levels in this country alone, producing thousands of graduates each year. And, the number of institutions offering such professional preparation programs in sport management continues to grow.

Concept 16: Formal Education and Training Is the Future for Professionals Involved in the Challenging Environment of Sport Management.

Dr. James Mason, father of sport management, being honored at Ohio University.

The trend is clear. Formal education and training is the future for professionals involved in the challenging environment of sport management. The job demands required, now and in the future, of the sport professional in managerial positions "necessitate that individuals possess a depth of knowledge and a broad range of specific competencies in business and in sport to be able to deal successfully with ever changing challenges and problems associated with the business of sport" (Stier, 1993a, p. 1).

This is best achieved through formal and informal education combined with meaningful, practical experience in sport management. Numerous professional organizations have recognized the need for formal training and education of their members in the area of management. Three such organizations that have provided opportunities for their members to experience in-service education are: (1) The National Association of Collegiate Directors of Athletics (NACDA), (2) the College Athletic Business Managers Association (CABMA), and (3) the National Collegiate Athletic Association (NCAA). In fact, the NACDA has had a long history of conducting multiday managerial workshops as part of its *Management Institute,* which is held in conjunction with the organization's annual membership meeting. Similarly, the NCAA has held two management workshops each year in addition to its annual convention.

Reasons behind the Extraordinary Growth of Sport Management Programs

Although the initial sport management program at Ohio University was created in response to a very specific and real need, the same cannot be said of the seemingly extraordinary growth spurt of both undergraduate and graduate programs during the past decade. Parkhouse (1991, p. 6) revealed that "by 1988 only 10% of the programs had been in existence for more than 5 years." By 1990 there had been a 200% increase in the number of sport management programs over the previous five years (NASPE/NASSM, 1993, p. 1).

Most of the early sport management professional preparation programs evolved out of Physical Education departments. Even today the majority of such curricular programs, both at the undergraduate and graduate levels, are administratively housed in Physical Education/Kinesiology/Sports Studies departments (Sawyer, 1993; Ross, Jamieson, & Young, 1997). However, other academic departments also house some sport management programs, most notably departments of business as well as recreation and leisure studies.

There are several reasons behind both the accelerated and sustained growth in the number of sport management professional preparation programs and their positioning within departments of physical education.

1. There has been an effort, on behalf of some institutions, to meet a real and recognizable need for professionally trained administrators and managers within the broad context of sport and sport-related organizations.

2. There has been a recognition and an acceptance of the viewpoint in some academic quarters, resulting from a natural outgrowth of the study of sport, that physical education is a broad-based academic discipline and therefore should encompass sport management as an integral part of its academic curriculum (that is, not be limited to teacher education).

3. There has been a reduction in the number of college students seeking to become physical education teachers. This situation itself places in potential jeopardy the job security of those college/university physical education faculties within the teacher preparation programs (Stier, 1986).

> **Concept 17:** Not All Sport Management Programs Have Been Established for the Right Reasons.

This lack of students pursuing education as a career may be a result of the fact that there exists an overabundance of would-be physical education teachers already seeking positions when there are none. And one of the reasons for the job shortage is that there has been a reduction in requirements for daily physical education classes in many school systems, with the result that fewer physical education teachers are needed.

4. There have been conscious and concerted efforts by professionals within higher education to save the jobs of college physical educators (that might have been in jeopardy due to the lack of students pursuing traditional teacher preparation programs in physical education) by providing an alternative academic career path or option, sport management. This type of situation may very well call into question the accountability of some sport management programs (Arbogast and Griffin, 1989).

5. There have been additional colleges and universities that have joined the sport management bandwagon once they realized that such programs could attract significant numbers of college students. The creation of sport management programs therefore provided a justification for retaining college level physical education faculty who might otherwise have had their positions threatened as a result of a reduction of the number of students pursuing courses within the physical education teacher education tracts or programs.

Consequences of the Expansion of Sport Management Programs

> **Concept 18:** Not All Growth of Sport Management Professional Preparation Programs Has Been Warranted or Welcomed.

Unemployment and Underemployment

The extraordinary growth experienced by the sport management profession, both in terms of the number of professional preparation programs and the number of individuals who are products of such programs, has not been without controversies, challenges, and problems. One of the challenges facing the profession is the matter of the significant excess of sport management graduates seeking employment. The dangers of saturating the job market with highly trained and experienced professionals competing for a limited number of vacancies, many with low wages, are obvious. The reality is that there are more applicants for jobs than there are jobs available.

Concept 19: There Is an Overabundance of Sport Management Graduates Seeking Professional Positions Today.

The consequences have been predictable. First, a high rate of unemployment or underemployment for many of these would-be sport management professionals. Second, a low rate of pay combined, in many instances, with menial or mundane job tasks with few meaningful responsibilities. Third, a high turnover rate among those employed within the sport management arena due to the low pay, menial tasks, limited advancement opportunities, and overabundance of unemployed or underemployed sport management hopefuls.

Additional Areas of Controversy, Challenges and Problems: Daunting Questions

1. Should Sport Management Be an Undergraduate or Graduate Offering?

A problem that continues to haunt the sport management field of study at the professional preparation level is the lack of consistency in the curricular offerings available at the various institutions. That is, at what level should professional preparation programs be offered to the student?

Not a few within the field feel that the subject matter of sport management should be solely a graduate curriculum. These individuals argue that the body of knowledge in sport management is such that it is best broached at the master's and doctoral level following, and based on, an undergraduate degree in the liberal arts. Others strongly argue that sport management must be an undergraduate level field of study. Some within the field would even argue that junior and community colleges should offer terminal degree programs in sport management.

Compounding the confusion is the fact that some undergraduate programs call their sport management programs a "major," while others provide a concentration, others a minor, some a specialization, and still other institutions call their curricular offerings an emphasis in sport management. This lack of consistency in the curricular aspect of sport management programs continues to be controversial and, sometimes, destructive.

2. Are Junior/Community Colleges Usurping the Curriculum of Four-Year Institutions?

There has been some evidence that, in some institutions, most notably at the junior and community college level, the study of sport management has been reduced to the freshman and sophomore levels. In these institutions students barely out of secondary school are enrolled in courses usually made available at the four-year institutions exclusively for juniors and seniors.

Concept 20: Some Sport Management Courses Are Being Offered Too Early within the College Experience.

Again, the need for students to enroll (and thus to justify and save faculty members' jobs) within a college or a specific department—even at the two-year college level—seemingly is the driving force to establish a sport management curriculum that might attract much-needed students.

Concept 21: Junior and Community College Sport Management Offerings Sometimes Cause Problems for the Four-Year Institutions with Undergraduate Sport Management Programs.

Junior and community college programs in sport management create two problems for four-year institutions. The first problem is caused by the graduates of the two-year institutions, those who leave with a terminal degree in sport management and have no desire to continue their education at the four-year institution. They enter the job market with a two-year degree and compete (with lower pay expectations) with graduates from four-year institutions and with students from graduate programs. This further complicates and saturates an already glutted job market.

The second difficulty concerns those graduates of two-year colleges who do pursue their baccalaureate degree in the area of sport management. These students enter the four-year institutions with numerous sport management courses taken during their freshman and sophomore years at the junior college/community college and often expect full transfer credit, even for junior and senior level courses at the four-year institution. Such articulation and transfer problems will only get worse with the continued proliferation of the number of junior college professional preparation programs in sport management.

3. What Department Should House the Sport Management Program/Curriculum

A growing controversy revolves around the question of where in the college/university setting to house the discipline of sport management. Should it be administered by the physical education department? Should it be included within the business department? What about the recreation and leisure department? Or, should sport management be a separate academic field of study, a separate entity altogether?

Some professionals argue that sport management should no longer be housed within the traditional physical education department. "The umbrella of physical education is no longer, and never was, broad-based enough to cover the ever-expanding field of sport management" (Sawyer, 1993, pp. 4–5). Sawyer recommends that sport management curricula be folded into the existing departments of "recreation management or recreation and leisure studies, forming a new, expanded department of recreation and sport management" (p. 5).

Others within the field have made equally convincing arguments for the movement of the sport management curriculum to the department of business or business administration.

The discussion goes on within the profession and will undoubtedly continue for some time in the future.

4. Is Curricular Rigor a Myth or Reality?

Concept 22: Where Sport Management Professional Preparation Programs Are Housed Is Less Important Than the Quality of the Curricular Offerings and the Competency of the Faculty Who Teach in the Program.

One of the challenges facing the field of sport management involves academic sophistication and integrity (Brassie, 1989). Sport management should be more than a bunch of physical education courses clumped together with other courses from other departments in a so-called "package" and, thereby, creating a "sport management" program. A sport management professional preparation program, whether it is called a major, a concentration, an emphasis, or a minor, should be more than merely a collection of physical education courses combined with courses selected from business, communications, sociology, philosophy, computer science, and mathematics.

What are needed are actual courses and classes that are devoted to appropriate and specific content areas within the sport management discipline or field of study. The majority of these courses should be taught by professors with terminal degrees (or, at least, at the master's level) who have had meaningful experiences in the realm of sport management.

Concept 23: Increased Rigor in Curricular Offerings Tends to Increase the Quality of Entering Students As Well As Increase the Competency and Skill Levels of Those Who Graduate.

The American Alliance for Health, Physical Education, Recreation and Dance (AAHPERD) published an article in the *Journal of Physical Education, Recreation and Dance* (JOPERD) (1989, November/December) titled "A Student Buyer's Guide to Sport Management Programs," written by Stan Brassie. This article provided much-needed insight into the quality of sport management programs from the perspective of would-be students. It also provided guidance in terms of curricular offerings and program structure to administrators and teachers alike at colleges and universities with sport management programs.

5. Is There a Lack of Professionally Trained/Educated Faculty and an Overabundance of Self-Taught Faculty?

Related to academic integrity is the question of the qualifications of the faculty involved in administering the program and teaching the courses. Are the faculty members professionally trained as sport managers? Are their degrees in sport management, administration, or management? Do they have successful, meaningful, recent, and relevant experience in some aspect of sport management? Do they possess an adequate knowledge base for the classes that they teach? Are they able and willing to be true scholars within the discipline? Finally, are there sufficient full-time faculty available to teach as well as advise and counsel? Or, is there a sizable number of a program's faculty who are part-timers?

The faculty teaching the college sport management courses and the administrators managing such programs should be professionally trained and educated in the fields of management and sport management. And, ideally, they should possess practical, relevant, and recent experience within the field. However, far too many sport management faculty members are merely self-taught. That is, they have no formal training in sport management at the master's or doctoral levels and/or have neither extensive nor meaningful experiences in the field.

Concept 24: Qualified Faculty Should Be Professionally Trained in Management (of Sport) and Possess Meaningful, Relevant, and Recent Sport Management Experience.

The assigning of faculty who have not been professionally trained and who lack substantial administrative and managerial experience in the field of sport continues to plague our profession, in spite of the tremendous growth in graduates of master's level and doctoral level sport management programs. The presence of self-taught faculty continues to be a major problem on many campuses. This, even in light of the fact that there are more graduates with advanced sport management degrees today than ever before, both at the doctoral and master degree levels. However, while many college faculty have been able to retrain in the sport management field, there continue to be significant numbers of supposedly self-taught, inexperienced teachers involved in the sport management courses and programs.

Conclusions

Whether one experiences success or failure as a professional employed in a sport management position is dependent on many factors, some within the individual's control and many that are not. Nevertheless, in order to have an opportunity to achieve success it is necessary that you, the future sport manager, understand sport as well as the management processes involved in administering a program and working with individuals, groups, and organizations. The time when a potential sport professional could gain access to the world of sport management and thrive professionally without formal training and education, coupled with a willingness to remain at the cutting edge of knowledge and skill, is long gone, if it ever existed.

Today, the consummate professional engaged in some aspect of sport as a manager or administrator needs a wide range of skills, competencies, and experiences, plus the intrinsic motivation necessary to take advantage of those skills, competencies, and experiences. Finally, the sport professional needs to be able to make adjustments, to make changes in light of the circumstances and situations in which one finds oneself. For, the one thing that is certain in the future is that change is inevitable. Nowhere is this more true than in the world of sport and sport management.

REFERENCES

Arbogast, G. W. and Griffin, L. (1989). Accountability—Is it within reach of our profession? *Journal of Physical Education, Recreation and Dance, 60*(6), 72–75.

Berg, R. (1996, November). Head hunting. *Athletic Business, 20*(11), 9.

Brassie, P. S. (1989). A student buyer's guide to sport management programs. *Journal of Physical Education, Recreation and Dance, 60*(9), 25–28.

Bridges, F. L. and Roquemore, L. L. (1992). *Management for athletic/sport administration: Theory and practice*. Decatur, GA: ESM Books.

Bridges, F. L. and Roquemore, L. L. (1996). *Management for athletic/sport administration: Theory and practice* (2nd ed.). Decatur, GA: ESM Books.

Lewis, G. (1982). *Degree programs in athletic and sport administration*. Unpublished report, University of Massachusetts.

NASPE/NASSM. (1993, May). *Sport management program standards and review protocol*. National Association for Sport and Physical Education (NASPE)/North American Society for Sport Management (NASSM). Reston, VA: National Association for Sport and Physical Education.

NASSM/NASPE. (1993, March). *Sport management—Directory of professional programs*. North American Society for Sport Management (NASSM)/National Association for Sport and Physical Education (NASPE) Sport Management Task Force. Reston, VA: National Association for Sport and Physical Education.

Parkhouse, B. L. (1978). Professional preparation in athletic administration and sport management. *Journal of Physical Education, Recreation and Dance, 49*(5), 22–27.

Parkhouse, B. L., Ed. (1991). *The management of sport: Its foundation and application*. St. Louis, MO: Mosby.

Parkhouse, B. L., Ed. (1996). *The management of sport: Its foundation and application* (2nd ed.). St. Louis, MO: Mosby.

Parks, J. B. and Zanger, B. R., Eds. (1990). *Sport & fitness management: Career strategies and professional content*. Champaign, IL: Human Kinetics Books.

Ross, C. M., Jamieson, L. M., and Young, S. J. (1997). *Professional preparation in sports management*. Bloomington, IN: Indiana University Press.

Sawyer, T. H. (1993). Sport management: Where should it be housed? *Journal of Physical Education, Recreation and Dance, 64*(9), 4–5.

Sports Inc. (1988, May 23). A class compendium. p. 3.

Stier, W. F., Jr. (1986). Challenges facing physical education. Alternative career options. *Journal of Physical Education, Recreation and Dance, 57*(8), 26–27.

Stier, W. F., Jr. (1993a, August). Alternative career paths in physical education: Sport management. Washington, DC: *ERIC Digest—Clearinghouse on Teaching and Teacher Education*.

Stier, W. F., Jr. (1993b, July 9). Meeting the challenges of managing sport through marketing, fundraising and promotions. Paper presented at the International Meeting of the World University Games, Buffalo, NY.

Stier, W. F., Jr. (1994). *Successful sport fund-raising*. Dubuque, IA: Wm. C. Brown & Benchmark.

Stier, W. F., Jr. (1995, June 19). The future of fundraising and promotions in international sport competition. Paper presented at the annual convention of the Ontario Hockey Association. London, Ontario, Canada.

Stier, W. F., Jr. (1996a). *Sport management handbook—State University of New York*. Brockport, NY: SUNY–Brockport Press.

Stier, W. F., Jr. (1996b, April 16). Becoming marketable within the HPERD and A profession. Paper presented at the National Conference of the American Alliance for Health, Physical Education, Recreation and Dance (AAHPERD), Atlanta, Georgia.

Swanson, R. A. and Spears, B. (1995). *History of sport and physical education in the United States*. Dubuque, IA: Wm. C. Brown & Benchmark.

Yalouris, A. and Yalouris, N. (1989). *Olympia: Guide to the museum and the sanctuary*. Athens, Greece: Ekdotike Athenon S.a.

DISCUSSION AND REVIEW QUESTIONS

1. Explain the concept of management in general and in terms of sport in particular.
2. Cite examples of sport management being both an art and a science in today's society.
3. Why should those individuals involved in various leadership roles within sport organizations be educated and professionally trained as sport managers?
4. Provide a brief sketch of how managerial skills have been used in various forms and in different societies from the earliest times of recorded history.
5. Summarize several examples of early management of sport.
6. Trace the development of formal professional preparation programs in sport management from their inception to the present time.
7. Differentiate between and explain several of the current controversies within the sport management field.

CHAPTER

2 General Career and Employment Opportunities

Career planning for the sport management professional. Kent academic counselor Cathy O'Donnell advises a Kent student-athlete.

Chapter Objectives

After reading this chapter you will be able to:

- Understand possible opportunities for employment within the field of sport management;
- List numerous specific sport organizations that hire individuals who are professionally trained in the management of sport;
- Explain the interdisciplinary, multidisciplinary, or integrated basis of educating future sport managers;
- Differentiate among the three general components or elements of a professional preparation education program in sport management;

- Justify the importance of field experiences, especially at the undergraduate level, in preparing future professionals in managing sport programs and organizations;
- Provide examples of the positive attributes as well as negative characteristics associated with various types of internships;
- Explain why the internship is viewed as the quintessential culminating experience for sport management students;
- Indicate steps to follow in securing an appropriate internship;
- Understand the importance of networking;
- Cite examples of current curricular standards being used in sport management programs;
- List professional journals important for the modern manager of sport programs.

Sources of Employment

In 1991, a sports executive career recruiter, Mark Tudi, estimated that there existed approximately 4.5 million sport-related jobs at all levels in this country alone. He broke these employment opportunities into six broad categories: (1) marketing, (2) entrepreneurship, (3) administration, (4) representation, (5) media, and (6) other sports-related areas. The number of job opportunities in each of these areas is presented in Figure 2.1 (Markiewicz,

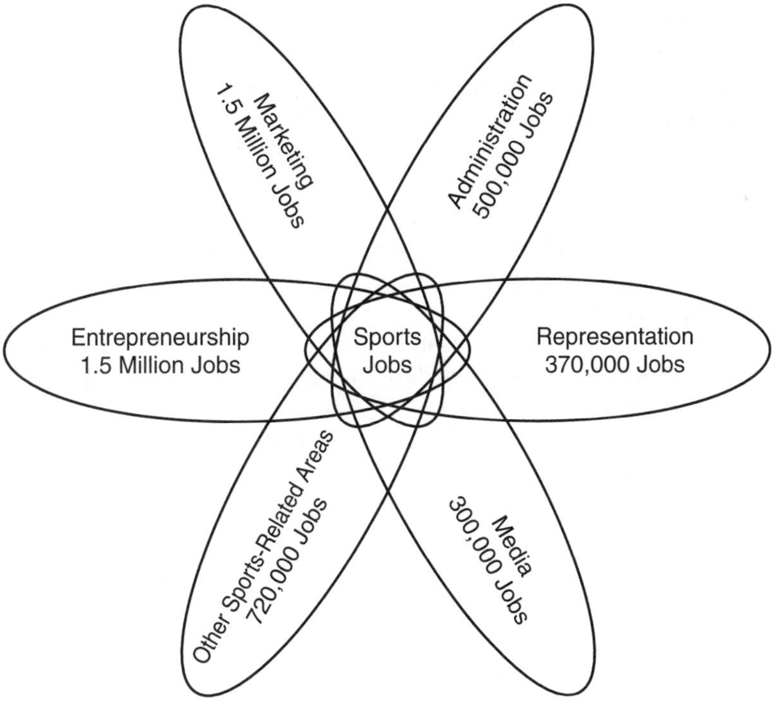

FIGURE 2.1 Types of Job and Career Opportunities in Sports

1991). By the year 2010 the estimated number of total job and career opportunities should be 20% to 30% greater.

> **Concept 25:** There Are Currently More Than Four Million Sport-Related Jobs in the United States, and the Number Is Growing.

Specific Job and Career Opportunities with Appropriate Specialized Training

There are numerous job opportunities in the world of sport (Gleason, 1986). The following is a partial list of general career opportunities for graduates of sport management programs, assuming candidates have successfully completed appropriate general education and specialized training at the undergraduate and/or graduate level (Stier, 1996a).

> **Concept 26:** There Is a Great Diversity of Job and Career Opportunities Available in the World of Sport and Sport-Related Organizations.

1. Amateur, competitive sports, including youth, junior and senior high school, collegiate/university levels
2. Amateur, competitive sports/leagues and conference offices
3. Amateur sport agencies, including the NCAA, NAIA, AAU, and so on
4. Armed services recreation and competitive sports
5. Athletic representation firms
6. City and state sport commissions
7. Corporate and industrial fitness and wellness programs
8. Corporate sport marketing departments (Kodak, Pepsi, etc.)
9. Entrepreneurship opportunities
10. Facility and stadia management, including recreation, intramural, and sport activities
11. Federal recreation/parks, including tourism and travel
12. Fitness, health, and wellness clubs
13. Football bowl organizations, such as the Rose Bowl, Sugar Bowl, Cotton Bowl, and Fiesta Bowl
14. International sport management
15. Law, including representation and agency relationships
16. Municipal sports authorities
17. Nonprofit youth agencies involving recreation and/or sport (such as the YMCAs/YWCAs, Boys Clubs, Girls Clubs, and Catholic Youth Organizations)
18. Municipal recreation organizations
19. Professional sports—individual teams

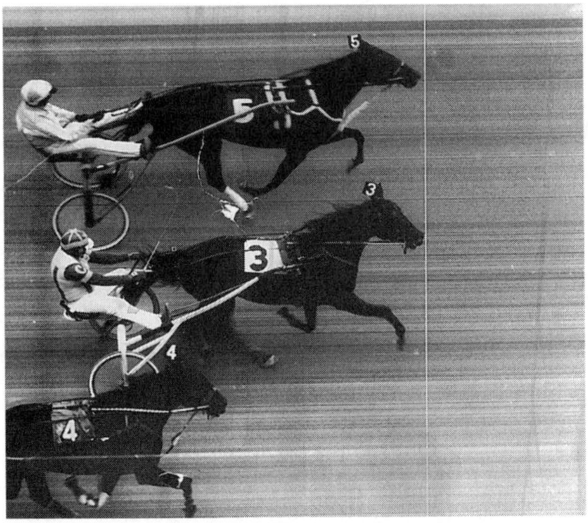

Racing, an exciting sport for the whole family.

20. Professional sports—league offices
21. Proprietary recreation businesses, i.e., "Discovery Zones"
22. Public and private racquet, golf, and aquatic clubs
23. Recreation youth camps
24. Resort and hotel recreation and leisure organizations
25. Special event firms
26. Specialized sport clubs and racquet clubs
27. Sports announcing/broadcasting, in radio and television
28. Sport governing bodies
29. Sports information and media relations at the college, university, and professional level
30. Sport manufacturing
31. Sport merchandising, wholesale and retail sales
32. Sports statistics at the collegiate, professional, media levels
33. Sports writing/journalism, for newspaper, magazine, and book publishers
34. Sport tourism, travel and cruise opportunities
35. Sport marketing agencies
36. Sport promotion, marketing, and event management entities
37. State recreation/parks, tourism and travel
38. Summer sport camps

Sport Management Career Paths

Individuals seeking managerial positions should recognize that there are various paths leading to a variety of different positions in the world of sport, fitness, and recreation. In short, there is no one single method or avenue to managerial positions or authority within a sport or sport-related business or organization.

School-Based Sport Organizations

Until recently, athletic directors within school-based sport programs, such as colleges and universities, came from the ranks of coaches, successful coaches. Usually, however, these individuals had little if any formal training in the management of an athletic department.

Today, however, more and more collegiate athletic directors have had formal training in administration as well as postbaccalaureate educational experiences. While a few ADs hold the doctorate degree, most hold the master's degree and a few have the baccalaureate degree. There is even a movement, especially at the NCAA division I level, toward hiring individuals from the business world who have had successful experiences in the so-called real world of business and management. Advancing up the career ladder today at the college level typically involves assuming an entry-level position and then working one's way up the organizational ladder, gaining valuable experience holding a variety of jobs and assuming different responsibilities, as well as perhaps an advanced degree (or two).

There is a significant difference in terms of educational requirements (expectations) of those individuals who hold the position of athletic director at the NCAA division I and II levels and those who are athletic directors at division III institutions. In the latter case, the athletic directors usually are required to hold at least one advanced degree, and, not infrequently, such institutions advertise that they prefer candidates to hold the doctoral degree.

At the secondary level, the typical athletic administrator is one who possesses the master's degree as well as extensive experience in teaching and coaching. However, even at this level it is increasingly important for the individual to have had some type of formal education and training in management to be seriously considered for the top administrative position of athletic director.

Holders of advanced degrees continue to earn the notice and respect of superiors and employers. This is because possession of such a degree is indicative not only of additional education but of increased skills and competencies as well as a high degree of persistence and dedication. More and more, the advanced degree in today's world of sport business (depending on the situation) could be a master's degree, a masters of business administration (MBA), a law degree, as well as a doctoral degree.

Movement within the Sport Industry

The avenue to an upper level administrative post within the ranks of professional sports varies somewhat, depending on the sport. Having played the sport at the professional level still is important in some circles—again, depending on the specific job and responsibilities accompanying the position. However, demonstrating successful work experience within professional sports, at the entry and middle management levels, is also becoming an important factor in being able to work one's way up the proverbial ladder to a position of greater authority. Being able to demonstrate prior successful experience in related or identical positions (even at a lower level) is advantageous for the upward-bound sport management employee.

There is even a trend for greater movement of highly trained and experienced personnel between and among different professional sports (football, basketball, baseball, ice hockey, soccer, lacrosse, etc.). Being a successful employee in one sport can facilitate one's marketability for a similar post in an entirely different sport.

Expected Pay at Various Levels of Employment in Professional Sports

Pay and other forms of compensation for sport personnel working at the upper echelon of sport organizations and businesses can be very lucrative indeed. However, one does not start at the top. Hence, it is important to realize that in many sports-, recreation-, and fitness-related positions, salary can be minimal, at least at the entry level. And the time spent at the entry level or near entry level can seem to be extremely long in some cases.

Entry-Level Positions in Professional Sports

Entry-level positions in the world of sport often provide relatively low salaries when compared with comparable professional positions in other career avenues, such as teaching. This is especially true in the so-called minor leagues. Many positions in minor league sports involve a combination of salary plus incentives or commission. This is true of many positions in the fitness and wellness arena as well. Many entry-level positions in professional sports as well as in the fitness industry involve some type of selling. And, when there is selling to be done part of the compensation is usually based on commission. Another factor regarding entry-level positions is the matter of job security. There is precious little job protection at the entry and middle management levels within many sport and sport-related businesses. In fact, many organizations do not even have an employment contract for their personnel at the lower level. Instead, these personnel work at the will of the employer.

Concept 27: There Remains Fierce Competition for Sport Management Positions.

Yet, there remains fierce competition for almost all positions within many sport businesses, whether the job involves professional sports, fitness and wellness businesses, school-based sport programs, or any of the other numerous career avenues cited earlier in this chapter. This is because of the nature of the "beast." There are many individuals who have a strong desire to become involved in the business of sport (in some type of managerial role). They are highly motivated to do so, and many are willing to make whatever sacrifices are necessary in order to secure such positions. The law of supply and demand continues to affect the job market at all levels and in every avenue of sport businesses and sport organizations.

For those who have the determination, the motivation, the dedication, the persistence, and the willingness to make sacrifices, increased financial rewards and adequate compensation are often available when the professional employees advance up and within the organization. Greater responsibility generates increased compensation, financial and otherwise.

In evaluating one's career opportunities, it would be safe to say that one needs to acquire an appropriate education, secure meaningful experiences, and be willing to pay one's dues in a variety of tasks if one is to experience success within the world of sport management, regardless of the specific venue that one has chosen for one's life work. One must also be patient and willing to assume meager or less glamorous tasks when first starting out in one's career. Proving one's worth, one's level of competency in the performance of the tasks assumed, is critical in experiencing success within the business world, the business of sport.

Essentials of Sport Management Professional Preparation

Today, in the United States, sport management professional preparation programs are based on an interdisciplinary, multidisciplinary, or integrated approach (DeSensi, Kelley, Blanton, and Beitel, 1990). Examples of such fields of study as physical education, sport, business, computers, psychology, sociology, and communications are all intricately intertwined in the academic preparation of future sport administrators and managers. Sutton (1989) indicates that sport management is a hybrid field of study that encompasses many other disciplines.

Brassie (1989a, p. 27) indicates that "sport management is a broad field serving many different types of work settings. Each type of setting requires a somewhat different preparation: the curriculum should provide flexibility for various options." Institutions of higher education are not in a position in today's society to prepare the student for every single eventuality of the individual's career (Uhlir, 1990, p. 6). What college and university professional preparation programs can do is to provide a firm foundation of general knowledge and specific skills on which graduates—once they are working in the field—can build and expand in light of the different and changing challenges facing them (Murray & Mann, 1993; Stier, 1996b).

Concept 28: Collegiate Professional Preparation Programs Are Based on an Interdisciplinary, Multidisciplinary, or Integrated Approach.

Graduates of undergraduate sport management programs at colleges and universities are usually thought of more as generalists rather than specialists. The graduate level (master's and doctoral) is reserved for those individuals desiring to specialize in one or more specific areas of sport management. However, this does not mean that undergraduate students do not receive specialty training or do not possess a high level of competency in one or more areas. Quite the contrary.

Sport Management Professional Preparation and Undergraduate Curricular Offerings

Generally speaking, undergraduate sport management professional preparation programs involve four basic components: first, a variety of general liberal arts core courses that are required of all undergraduate students; second, cognate or foundation courses related to or supporting sport management; third, specialty or major courses dealing with specific aspects of the management of sport, fitness/wellness, and leisure/recreation programs; and, fourth, some type of field experience, consisting usually of a practicum and an internship.

> **Concept 29:** A Strong, Exemplary Professional Preparation Curriculum Is Based on Offerings Involving the Liberal Arts, Cognate Courses, Theory of Management Courses, and Field Experiences.

General Education Core Courses: Foundation of a Liberal Arts Education

Most undergraduate institutions require a selection of core courses that every student must complete, regardless of the major that student is pursuing. This is the basis of the so-called liberal arts degree that is so highly prized in our culture. These core liberal art classes might be taken from the areas of humanities, social sciences, natural sciences (with and without laboratory experiences), fine arts (with and without a performance component), contemporary issues, computer literacy, and so on.

Specific courses taken by a sport management student can include, but not be limited to, history, political science, foreign language, English, communication, geography, art, philosophy, anthropology, chemistry, physics, African & Afro-American studies, economics, health, psychology, sociology, theater, and so forth. The goal of the general education courses is to provide the student with a broad-based liberal arts education. Such an educational experience would help the person to be a well-educated, well-rounded individual, and one who would be willing and capable of continuing to learn and develop intellectually after graduation.

> **Concept 30:** A Mark of an Educated Individual Is the Ability to Continue to Learn throughout One's Life—Both for the Sake of Learning As Well As to Keep Abreast of One's Field or Profession.

Cognate or Sport Management Foundation Courses

These are classes within a variety of other academic departments that are related to the field of study called sport management and form the foundation of further, more specialized courses for the sport management student. Examples of such courses include, but are not limited to, communications, management and organizational behavior, interpersonal relations, business law, general accounting, ethics, finance, economics, business law, statistics, and the historical, sociological, psychological, kinesiological, and philosophical perspectives of sport (Widdon, 1990; Stier, 1993).

Major or Specialty Courses

The major or specialty courses are frequently referred to as the "core" classes within the sport management curriculum. They are applied courses geared specifically to the discipline of sport management (Brassie, 1989b; Ross, Jamieson, & Young, 1997). Ideally, professors of sport management within the department teach them where the discipline of sport management is housed within the institution.

Concept 31: The Sport Management Core Courses Should Be Taught by Doctoral Faculty Who Possess Real World Experience in the Field.

Examples of such courses include introduction to sport management, sport marketing, sport fundraising, sport sponsorship, sport management theory, public relations in sport, research methods, recreational sports programming, risk management in sport, problems and issues in sport management, facility planning, facility and event management, computer applications to sport, ethics in sport and sport management, sport finance, sport budgeting, sport economics, legal aspects of sport, and the administration of sport, among numerous others. These courses are of such a nature that the instructors should possess the terminal degree as well as have had meaningful and successful real life experience.

Field Experiences

Almost all undergraduate sport management programs offer some type of field experiences (Sutton, 1989; Verner, 1993; Marston, 1993; Ross, Jamieson, & Young, 1997). Generally speaking, there are two types of field experience commonly associated with sport management, a practicum and an internship. Both are very important for the modern sport management student in providing the individual with a glimpse into how sport and sport-related organizations and programs operate. Additionally, depending on the student and the student's skills, such field experiences can enable the individual to demonstrate specific skills and competencies while upgrading and expanding one's knowledge base.

Typically, a practicum is a preinternship, part-time field experience in which the student is physically at a sport management site. The practicum could involve any site including professional sports, fitness clubs, wellness programs at large corporations, collegiate athletic programs, and so on. The practicum provides students the opportunity to experience, on a limited basis, what it is like to work in the real world within some type of sport management setting, under the direct (on-site) supervision of a professional in the field.

The practicum is normally taken while the student is actively taking cognate and/or specialty courses within the sport management curriculum. Usually, the practicum experience or practica experiences (if more than one such experience is provided) are part of a regular course. However, on some campuses the practicum experience is offered as a stand-alone class.

Concept 32: Both Practica and Internship Experiences Provide the Sport Management Intern with Meaningful Real Life Experiences and Skills.

The culminating field experience for sport management students usually involves a full-time commitment, either for an entire semester or a quarter (Campbell & Kovar, 1994). Some internship experiences are for two semesters or three quarters and a limited number of internships involve a 12-month commitment of the student intern (Cunnen & Sidwell, 1993).

The number of credits given to students involved in the internship experience ranges from 3 to 15 semester hours. During the internship the student is usually enrolled in no other coursework and has no other major commitments. The student intern is expected to demonstrate the competency level of a beginning, first-year professional and provide meaningful assistance to the organization and staff where the individual is interning.

Evaluation of the Student Intern

The intern is evaluated both by an on-site supervisor and a college or university faculty member (Bell & Countiss, 1993). In some instances, the college supervisor/faculty member periodically travels to the site of the internship to personally supervise and oversee the intern. However, in many programs, a campus faculty or supervisor does not personally visit the student intern at the site unless there is a definite problem. Rather, the student intern is evaluated only by the on-site supervisor (for whom the intern works). In this situation, the college supervisor oversees the intern from a distance, via phone and mail.

Another common practice is to require interns to maintain a diary or journal of their involvement and accomplishments that they periodically share with the campus faculty member assigned to them (Campbell & Kovar, 1994). Even when the intern is not visited by a representative of the college or university there is usually periodic communication by phone between the intern and the college as well as between the on-site supervisor and the college representative.

The Exit Interview for Intern Candidates

Another practice that has been utilized quite successfully on some campuses is to require an exit interview for would-be interns (Stier, 1996b). This individual interview is held prior to the semester in which a student will begin the field (internship) experience. The exit interview consists of the future intern being interviewed by a group of four to six practicing professionals within the world of sport management.

The interview questions are geared to determine the level of competency of the student and whether or not the student should be given permission to undertake the internship in a subsequent semester. If the responses to the questions reveal that the student is not ready to undertake the internship, then remedial courses as well as independent work are required prior to beginning the internship. On some campuses this exit or pre-internship interview helps the student become familiar with the interview process, a factor that is critical in successful job-hunting following the internship.

Problems with the Internship or Final Field Experience(s)

Concept 33: Not All Internship Experiences Are Created Equal.

Not all is well with the internship concept. In fact, a number of controversies have involved the internship experience in recent years. The location of internship sites is absolutely essential for the sport management programs and for the students who are nearing the completion of their formal sport management education and training. This fact, coupled with the large number of students seeking internships, both undergraduate and graduate, creates potential problems or challenges for the colleges preparing interns, for the interns themselves, and even the organizations accepting interns.

The Availability of Suitable Internship Sites

There is always the question of whether or not there are sufficient numbers of suitable internship sites available, sites that will provide adequate culminating, on-the-job training, for interns (Ruder, 1993). With the significant number of students seeking quality, high visibility internship sites it is sometimes difficult to adequately match interns with the available sites that are the students' first choices, or even second and third choices. The quality of the learning experience associated with any internship site is the major challenge facing both the potential intern and the college or university sport management program that is preparing the student for a career in the management of sport.

Concept 34: Sport Management Internships Have Three Possible Consequences, and Two of Them Are Negative.

Woody Hayes, former football coach at The Ohio State University, was credited with saying that there were three things that could happen when a team attempted a forward pass, and two of them were negative. Well, sport management is a lot like football in that regard. There are three possible consequences associated with an individual's internship experience, and two of them are negative.

First, the host site can take advantage of the intern and abuse the individual by making the intern work "25 hours" a day in performing all types of tasks and duties. Whether these tasks are menial, mundane or, on the other hand, rather sophisticated, the point is that the intern is taken advantage of as a form of cheap labor.

A second possible negative scenario involves the host site (supervisor) literally ignoring the intern by giving the individual almost nothing to do as part of the internship experience, and what is assigned to the intern is mundane and meaningless. Both of these scenarios are negative and defeat the purpose of the culminating internship or field experience.

Concept 35: The Intern Should Be Given Meaningful Responsibilities and Tasks Commensurate with the Individual's Skills, Abilities, Capabilities, and Training.

The third consequence (and the one positive outcome) of an internship involves the intern being assigned appropriate, meaningful, and adequate work responsibilities and tasks, commensurate with the intern's capability, willingness, and training, so as to provide the intern with a meaningful learning experience. This type of learning experience will also provide to the intern's supervisors ample opportunities to evaluate the abilities and accomplishments of the student intern.

The meaningful sport management internship experience also helps the intern to master new skills or refine and broaden existing competencies while demonstrating to the supervisors how effective and efficient the intern can be on "the firing line"—in the real world. Finally, such a superb internship experience will expedite the person's chance for a full-time sport management position in some appropriate organization or company following the conclusion of the internship or field experience.

Concept 36: A Secondary, but Nevertheless Significant, Objective of the Internship Experience Is to Help the Student Intern Secure Full-Time Employment Following the Internship—Somewhere.

The ideal concept behind the internship is that such an experience not only will help the student intern develop, enhance, and refine skills and competencies, but will also aid the intern in securing full-time employment at the conclusion of the internship in some suitable and appropriate organization. Sometimes the site where the student completes the internship might do the hiring because the competency level of the student intern would be well known to that organization. Other times the student cannot be hired at the internship site because of a lack of a vacancy there. Nevertheless, a strong recommendation on the intern's behalf to other organizations (especially those in the same business, association, or league) might provide the job-seeker with an advantage over other applicants who do not possess such a strong, recent, and relevant recommendation.

Viewing the Student Intern as Cheap Labor

In recent times it seems that some organizations are only too happy to accept interns, but not for the right reasons. Granted, most interns are usually highly motivated and relatively competent, possessing appropriate skills and experience. Plus, the interns are also, simply put, cheap or free labor. This is because the vast majority of internship experiences are nonpaying. In fact, in some instances, selected organizations that accept interns do so in lieu of hiring someone to fill that particular role and assume those responsibilities.

Concept 37: Relatively Few Internship Sites Offer Meaningful Pay to the Intern—Usually the Experience Is for No Pay at All.

Even though there are some organizations that do pay or provide a meager stipend for their interns, these are relatively few and far between. Nevertheless, some organizations, such as the NCAA, do provide stipends, but reserve them exclusively for women and minorities. White males need not apply for these paid internships. Other organizations provide unrestricted stipends, some more financially beneficial than others.

Some Interns Are Used by Organizations as Replacements or Substitutions for Full-Time Employees

A disturbing trend that is being seen more and more among some segments of the sport industry is the advertisement for so-called internships that involve stipends involving cash payments or some combination of cash and free room and/or food for individuals willing to assume specific duties. The problem is that a full-time employee really should assume these duties and responsibilities. In this situation the organization is replacing, or not hiring, a full-time employee because of the availability of a temporary intern. The organization can accomplish this at a fraction of the cost and with absolutely no long-term obligation for the intern's employment.

Concept 38: Interns Must Not Be Placed (or Left There) in a Situation Where They Will Be Misused, Abused, or Neglected.

At the conclusion of an internship, such an organization merely replaces (recycles) one intern with another at a low salary (stipend) and the cycle is repeated again and again. In this scenario the intern has little chance of securing a position with the organization when the internship is over simply because the organization is going to secure the services of another intern, with little or no obligation.

And, in some instances, the type and caliber of work assigned to the intern is not advantageous for the intern by any stretch of the imagination. In fact, it may even be counterproductive for the intern because the intern has, at the conclusion of the internship, no meaningful experiences, no significant accomplishments to point to while seeking a full-time position.

Concept 39: An Internship Can Be Viewed As a Double-Edged Sword.

The internship experience is a double-edged sword. On the one hand the colleges and universities are totally dependent on sport and sport-related organizations to provide their students with meaningful internship experiences. On the other hand, however, some of these same internship sites, these same organizations, companies, and corporations, have little incentive to hire the interns once the field experience is concluded.

This is because there is always another skilled and highly motivated student intern lurking just around the corner "begging" for the opportunity to work for nothing, 14 hours a day, seven days a week, for an entire semester, or even longer. The large number of professional preparation programs in sport management, especially at the undergraduate level, exacerbates this situation.

Concept 40: Every Internship Has the Potential for Being a Positive and a Negative Experience for the Intern.

All internships have the potential for success and failure, for good and for bad, for the student. It is imperative that those involved in the professional preparation of future sport managers be alert to potential situations that might misuse and abuse interns. In the final analysis, the following question needs to be answered: Does the internship experience provide meaningful learning experiences for the intern, opportunities for students to demonstrate their competencies and range of skills to others, and aid them in the search for an appropriate full-time position?

In other words, are the assignments given by the organization to the intern made because they are helpful to and are in the best interest of the intern? Or, are the assignments made merely because the organization needs cheap work completed? It is indeed a thin line that colleges that prepare interns, as well as organizations that accept interns, must walk.

Characteristics of an Ideal Internship

Concept 41: An Appropriate Internship Experience Can Benefit the Intern, the Host Site/Organization, and the College/University.

When the internship experience is such that the student intern is able to learn, to expand one's capabilities, as well as to contribute meaningfully to the host organization, the best of all worlds exists. The student intern benefits because of this opportunity to learn, to increase skills, to mature, and to demonstrate a high level of competency. The host site benefits because the organization is able to take advantage of a highly motivated intern who is able and willing to provide significant contributions to the organization, at a most reasonable cost. And, the college or university that has prepared the student for the internship benefits by developing and reinforcing its reputation as an institution with a quality sport management program. Every institution that offers such a program desires for its graduates to be successful. Such success tends to breed success by attracting and retaining quality faculty and students to the program.

Concept 42: The Internship Experience Is Deemed to Be the Quintessential Culminating Experience for Sport Management Students.

In reality, the internship is important, very, very important. In fact, it is deemed to be the quintessential culminating learning experience for the sport management student (NASPE, 1987). It is probably not an exaggeration to say that no other single learning experience is as important or has more significant impact on the student in terms of knowledge and mastery of subject matter as well as on potential job placement than the final field experience or internship (Ebersole, 1996).

How to Go about Securing an Appropriate Internship

Concept 43: There Are Many Factors That Must Be Considered When Evaluating a Potential Internship Site.

What should an appropriate internship experience consist of? First, it should be a place where the intern is able to further enhance one's knowledge base. The student should be able to learn on the job. The ability to refine and further develop competencies and master skills is critical to the success of the intern, both at the internship site and later when employed by a sport organization.

Second, the student should have appropriate support as well as critical feedback and guidance from the staff at the internship site as well as from the college or university faculty. Third, it is also essential for the intern to have opportunities to visibly demonstrate, in the real world of the internship site, one's dedication and commitment, one's knowledge, one's abilities and aptitudes, and one's competencies in getting jobs and completing tasks in an effective, efficient, and acceptable fashion. Being judged by others to have performed in an exemplary fashion as an intern by the on-site and college-based staff is critical, because exceptional performance as an intern generally generates positive recommendations from one's supervisors, recommendations that are absolutely critical in successfully entering the job market.

Concept 44: Would-Be Interns Should Select a Site That Is Similar to the Type of Organization Where They Would Like to Secure Full-Time Employment.

Naturally, the internship should be in, or closely related to, the area or segment of the sport management profession in which the student wishes to gain employment. To do otherwise is simply a waste of one's time, if not actually counterproductive. It would indeed be foolish for a student to complete an internship at a locally owned health club or a racetrack if that same individual wished to secure full-time employment within a professional football organization in the area of marketing.

It is absolutely essential that the student secure the very best internship opportunity possible. Good internship sites don't just happen. They don't normally fall into the lap of the student. It takes great effort, dedication, old-fashioned work, some networking, and a little bit of luck for the student to be able to find a meaningful internship site successfully.

One word of warning to those students contemplating accepting any offer for an internship. Would-be interns need to take time to evaluate carefully every facet of the potential internship experience. Don't make the mistake of falling in love with the potential site or organization because of its name, its size, or the caliber or reputation of the organization. Carefully scrutinize every aspect of the would-be site, looking at the people who are involved, the type of tasks one would be involved in, the range of responsibilities one would be given, the opportunities for further professional growth, and, finally, the full-time job prospects there and elsewhere following the successful conclusion of the internship. Only when these assessments have been completed should the prospective intern make a decision.

Students should begin to look at potential internship sites as early as their sophomore, and certainly by the beginning of the junior, year. This involves examining different aspects of the sport management profession, assessing the advantages and disadvantages of taking a job, and possibly choosing a career in a specific segment of the business of sport.

Searching the Available Literature for Information on Sport and Sport-Related Organizations

Once a student has decided the segment or area of sport most personally suitable to work in, it is necessary to initiate some research into specific groups, individuals, organizations, and associations. Such publications as *Sports Market Place* (Lipsey, 1996, January) and *The Sports Business Directory* (Moss, 1996) are just two examples of directories that provide a great deal of information about a wide range of sport organizations, including the names of individuals holding specific jobs within each organization.

If one is to begin an internship in the fall semester, letters of inquiry should be sent out some 12 months earlier. To whom should the letter be sent? It is best to have a specific individual to address in the letter. To secure the name, try calling the organization and requesting the name of the individual who is in charge of interns. There may be more than one, depending on the specialty of the intern, or, one person may handle all intern requests.

> **Concept 45:** One Must Be Assertive, Professionally Assertive, if One Is to Be Successful in the World of Sport and Sport Management.

Don't be put off by being informed that there is no person with responsibility for interns. Try and find the name of the person who has responsibility for the general area in which you wish to intern. For example, if you are interested in marketing, then obtain the name of the marketing director. Also, don't be discouraged if you are told that the organization or company has never taken interns. Secure the name of the person(s) you want to write to and attempt to create your own internship. Just because an organization has never had an intern doesn't mean that you cannot be the first one. Don't be bashful, be assertive, but be professionally assertive.

The Introductory Letter Seeking an Internship

The introductory inquiry letter (one page) should include pertinent information about you and why you are seeking an internship with this particular organization. If you know that a paid internship is not available, indicate that you are seeking an unpaid internship. Make explicit you are not seeking a paid internship. To do otherwise might cause some recipients to think you are looking for a paying position and may dismiss your letter out of hand.

Concept 46: Résumés Should Be Personalized, Informative, and Be No More Than Two Pages in Length.

Along with the letter provide an updated, personalized, one-page résumé. Usually, résumés should be one page in length. However, in unusual instances, the résumé may be two pages. This occurs when the individual's experience warrants more than one page. Don't leave off important and informative data just because the résumé would be two pages.

However, be careful lest you merely pad your résumé with unnecessary information. Personalize the résumé, so that the recipient knows that you are definitely seeking a specific position in that organization. The letter accompanying the résumé may request general information about a possible internship opportunity, an official application for an advertised internship, or a personal interview.

The Use of the 3-D Résumé

In recent years the use of a 3-D résumé has become more common. The 3-D résumé includes one or more physical objects or devices, such as a videotape, a CD-ROM, a film, an audiotape, copies of news releases and/or printed programs created by the candidate. These tangible objects can provide great insight into the candidate's experiences, skills, and potential professional growth. Just as an artist might show paintings or a singer might provide an audiotape to reveal one's skills, so too might a sport management candidate submit three-dimensional objects as part of the résumé package.

Subsequent Follow-Up Phone Calls

Following personal letters of inquiry the future intern should follow up with personal phone calls to determine whether the application has been received and whether any other information might be needed. Also, a request for an interview might be made. Again, if you desire an interview, indicate that you are willing (if you are) to cover all travel expenses associated with the interview.

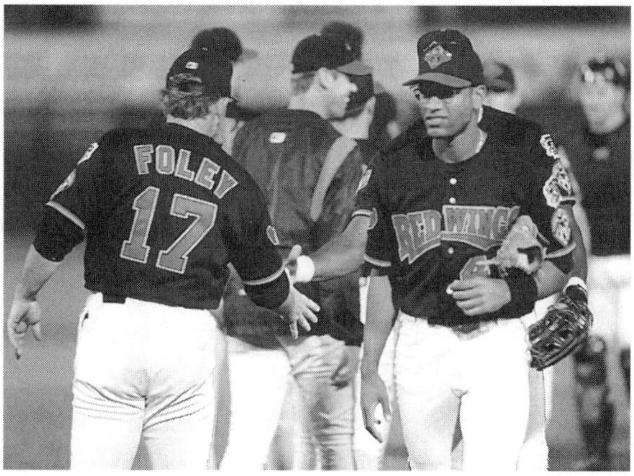

Rochester Red Wings manager Marv Foley congratulates team members after another victory.
Barbara Jean Germano, Photographer.

Maintaining Contact with the Potential Internship Sites

After the student has initially contacted those organizations where one might want to intern it is important to remain in contact with the various organizations' intern coordinator or some other appropriate individual. It is important that one or more people at the potential site be aware of and periodically reminded of your sincere interest. However, don't be a pest, be professionally assertive. Personal letters and phone calls can be most effective, both from the would-be intern as well as from professors and other people of influence.

Expenses Involved in Seeking the Internship and during the Internship

In today's marketplace, if there are travel expenses involved in traveling to the organization for an internship interview, the costs are almost always paid by the candidate. There are just too many applicants willing to pay such costs for organizations to have to pay them.

If you are some distance from the location of the internship site, provide information that transportation and housing will not be a problem. For example, indicate that you have funds for renting an apartment or a room close to the site if selected as an intern. If you have a relative living in the area and you could live there while serving as an intern, mention this fact. If you are attending a college or university a great distance from the organization where you desire to intern but your family lives near the internship site, share this fact.

The reason is simple. Many organizations don't want to be hassled with any potential problems involving living accommodations of their interns. In reality, there are just too many colleges and universities in close proximity to ideal internship sites. These organizations, without too much work, can accept quality interns who can live at home and commute to the intern site. As a result, make it easy for the organization to accept you without having to provide for your needs. Most of them just won't do it because of the multitude of quality internship candidates seeking sites.

Visiting the Potential Internship Site Prior to Accepting the Position

If at all possible, and you have the necessary finances and time available, attempt to visit the internship site prior to accepting the position, if it is offered. Plan on visiting with those individuals with whom you will be working. Such personal contact is often very revealing and can also help you get a jump start on your activities once you do report ready for duty—with "bells on."

Networking: Dropping Names of Heavy Hitters or Centers of Influence

Don't hesitate to network. Networking involves keeping in touch with individuals and keeping them abreast of where you are, what you are doing, and what your goals are for the future. The more important these individuals are, the more influential they are, the better. That is why the terms *heavy hitters* and *centers of influence* are used to denote those individuals who are viewed with respect and admiration by others within the community.

> **Concept 47:** Networking Is an Important Key in Securing Internships As Well As Full-Time Employment.

These are the individuals who have influence over others and are able to get things done due to their contacts, prestige, reputation, image, position, and/or charisma. Timely and effective communication is at the heart of networking. People need to have your name in the back (or front) of their brain. They need to know what you are all about and what you have done and what you are currently engaged in. They need to have developed a positive image of you, your abilities, and your competencies.

Network with your professors. Network with your former and current employers. Network with people you know (and who know you) in and out of the sports world. If you (or your parents, relatives, friends, or their acquaintances) know of individuals within sport organizations, use them to open doors for you. Drop their names (with their permission, naturally) in your initial communications with the potential internship sites. Ask your contacts to communicate, on your behalf, directly with their friends or acquaintances within the sport organization.

Networking is vital in finding out about potential internship sites as well as in securing an internship. Networking is also indispensable in securing full-time employment. Now is not the time to be timid, bashful, or fainthearted. Be bold, be assertive, but professionally so.

Identifying One's Network of Contacts, Colleagues, and Associates

To assist you in identifying your current networking contacts, see Table 2.1 (Stier, 1995). In the left column, under the category "People I Know in the Sports Profession" place the

TABLE 2.1 Identification of One's Networking Contacts in Sports

People I Know in the Sport Profession	People in Sports Who Know Me or Know of Me	People in Sports Who Would Give Me a Professional Recommendation
1.	1.	1.
2.	2.	2.
3.	3.	3.
4.	4.	4.
5.	5.	5.
6.	6.	6.
7.	7.	7.
8.	8.	8.
9.	9.	9.
10.	10.	10.
11.	11.	11.
12.	12.	12.
13.	13.	13.
14.	14.	14.
15.	15.	15.

names of those individuals you personally know who are either involved in some fashion with the world of sport or who have contacts with sports people or organizations, even though they themselves might not be associated with the sport world.

In the middle column, under the heading "People in Sports Who Know Me," place the names of individuals associated with the sports arena (or who know people who are) and who know you, know something about you, your competencies, and your activities. Under the right column, "People in Sports Who Would Give Me a Professional Recommendation," write the names of individuals in sport (or who have contacts with people in sport) who would feel comfortable providing you with a positive professional recommendation.

Naturally, you will have the largest number of names in the left column and the least number of names in the right column. The objective is to begin now, as a student, to fill up all three columns so that you begin to have a significant network of contacts that you know, that acknowledge knowing you, and who feel comfortable providing both written and verbal recommendations on your behalf.

Increasing One's Contacts, Expanding One's Network

You need to make other people aware of you, your qualities, and your potential. There are many ways to accomplish this. One is to become professionally involved in a variety of volunteer activities, even as a student. Another is to attend workshops and clinics and interact with other professionals in the field. Don't hesitate to introduce yourself to others. Yet a third way is to actively seek out current professionals and communicate with them.

And, if you work your way through college, take jobs that are related to your future career activities. Secure part-time positions in the sports field or in business. While a job at Arby's or McDonald's is acceptable, a job working for a specific sport organization will carry more weight in terms of being applicable to your aspirations.

Concept 48: It Is Never Too Early or Too Late to Begin to Network.

It is never too early (or too late) to start developing one's contacts, one's network of professional associates and colleagues. Now is the time to begin to work deliberately and consistently on expanding one's network of contacts. Networking is essential not only for one's internship search but also for all subsequent job searches. As the saying goes, "Today is the first day of the rest of your life."

Current Curricular Standards for Sport Management Programs

In the last decade, there has been a growing concern in some quarters of the profession about the lack of consistency and the quality existing within the sport management curricular offerings among the large number (200+) of colleges and universities in the United States. There is a need for accountability in every profession (Arbogast & Griffin, 1989). As a consequence, there have been several attempts to provide guidance in curricular matters for those colleges and universities preparing future professionals in fitness and sport management positions.

Accreditation Activities within Higher Education

Accreditation is nothing new for colleges and universities in this country. In fact, as early as 1913 the North Central Association of Colleges and Secondary Schools initiated the general process of accrediting colleges and universities. This effort was made possible by the institutions voluntarily joining together to meet agreed-on standards and criteria in an effort "to demonstrate that institutional quality was commensurate with the standards for membership" within that association (Uhlir, 1990, p. 6).

Specialized accreditation for specific curricular offerings or programs had existed even prior to that point in time. For example, there were very specific standards identified and utilized by the American Medical Association in approving and accrediting specific medical educational institutions and their graduates or practitioners (Uhlir, 1990).

Concept 49: There Has Been Concern in Recent Years about the Lack of Consistency in Sport Management Professional Preparation Programs.

In the area of fitness and wellness, the document, *Standards for Programs Preparing Undergraduates for Careers in Fitness,* was published in 1988 by the National Association for Sport and Physical Education (NASPE, 1988). This publication sought to specify the standards that colleges and universities should use to judge the preparation of professionals for jobs and careers in the fitness arena.

Two years earlier, 1986, a sport management task force was created by the National Association for Sport and Physical Education (NASPE) for the purpose of developing curricular guidelines for both undergraduate and graduate sport management programs. The guidelines were promulgated the following year in the document *Guidelines for Undergraduate and Graduate Programs in Sport Management: Membership Report* (NASPE, 1987). And, in 1989 this task force evolved into a joint committee made up of NASPE members and individuals representing the North American Society for Sport Management (NASSM). Over the next four years input was solicited from professionals throughout the nation actively involved in the field of sport management via surveys and meetings held at national conferences.

Approval and Accreditation of Professional Preparation Programs in Sport Management

Four years later, in May of 1993, a milestone was reached when the National Association for Sport and Physical Education (NASPE) and the North American Society for sport management (NASSM) cooperatively published the approved standards and protocol for the accreditation of both undergraduate and graduate sport management curricula. This 41-page publication included information (standards) needed for institutions to prepare for sport management program review at the undergraduate, master's, and doctoral levels.

> **Concept 50:** Approval and Accreditation of Sport Management Professional Preparation Programs Is a Rather Recent Phenomenon.

The publication also provided a general overview of the accreditation review and the timelines for the program review, and established a comprehensive list of minimum competency areas for the baccalaureate level, for the master's level, and for the doctoral level. The competency areas for the undergraduate sport management professional preparation programs are:

1. Behavioral dimensions in sport
2. Management and organizational skills in sport
3. Ethics in sport management
4. Marketing in sport
5. Communication in sport
6. Finance in sport
7. Economics in sport
8. Legal aspects of sport

9. Governance in sport
10. Field experience in sport management
(NASPE/NASSM, 1993, pp. 3–6)

Concept 51: The Creation of Approval Procedures and Criteria Indicate a Strengthening of the Sport Management Profession.

Two years later seven institutions in this country had received approval for their sport management programs. In the spring of 1995 the National Association of Sport and Physical Education (NASPE) announced the names of the seven programs that had been approved by the sport management program review council (SMPRC) (NASPE, 1995). There was one institution at the doctoral level, three at the master's level, and three at the undergraduate level. Only Temple University (Philadelphia) received approval at all three levels. Georgia Southern University received approval at the undergraduate and the master's levels. Other programs approved included the University of Louisville's master's program and the undergraduate program at the University of New Haven.

Professional Journals Dealing with Aspects of Sport Management

One measure of the importance and impact of the management of sport in our society can be determined by the number and type of professional and trade publications that deal with various aspects of the management of sport, fitness/wellness, and leisure/recreation arenas. In this respect, the growth of sport management as a distinct body of knowledge took a giant step when, in January of 1987, *The Journal of Sport Management* became a reality (Stier, 1990).

This publication was the first scholarly, refereed journal, dedicated to the exclusive study of sport administration or management. There have been and continue to be other journals and periodicals that address specific issues associated with the management and organization of sport. However, these publications are either not exclusively devoted to sport management or they are not refereed (Stier & Stier, 1992). (A refereed publication is one that utilizes a blind review as part of the selection process of the articles that appear within the publication.)

Concept 52: There Are Numerous Professional Journals That Deal, at Least in Some Respect, with the Management and Organization of Sport.

Examples of publications that are refereed and periodically carry articles devoted to some aspects of sport management include, but are not limited to, the following:

1. *Academic Athletic Journal*
2. *Aethlon: The Journal of Sport Literature*

3. *Annual of Applied Research in Coaching and Athletics*
4. *CAHPER Journal, Canadian Association for Health, Physical Education and Recreation*
5. *International Journal of Physical Education*
6. *International Journal of Sport Psychology*
7. *Interscholastic Athletic Administration*
8. *Journal of American Fitness Association*
9. *Journal of Applied Sports Science Research*
10. *Journal of the International Council for Health, Physical Education, Recreation, Dance and Sports*
11. *Journal of Leisure Research*
12. *Journal of the National Intramural Recreation Sports Association* (NIRSA)
13. *Journal of Park and Recreation Administration*
14. *Journal of Philosophy of Sport*
15. *Journal of Physical Education, Recreation and Dance* (JOPERD)
16. *Journal of Sport Behavior*
17. *Journal of Sport and Exercise Psychology*
18. *Journal of Sport History*
19. *Journal of Sport Management* (NASSM)
20. *Journal of Sport Sciences*
21. *Journal of Sport and Social Issues*
22. *Journal of Sports Psychology*
23. *Journal of Teaching in Physical Education*
24. *Palaestra: The Forum of Sport, Physical Education & Recreation for the Disabled*
25. *Parks and Recreation*
26. *Physical Education Review*
27. *The Physical Educator*
28. *Play and Culture*
29. *Quest*
30. *Research Quarterly for Exercise and Sport*
31. *Sociology of Sport Journal*
32. *Sport Marketing Quarterly*
33. *The Sport Psychologist*
34. *Sport Science Review*
35. *Strategies*
36. *Women's Sports and Fitness*

A partial list of nonrefereed magazines that either are exclusively devoted to administrative and managerial areas of sport or that periodically carry such articles include:

1. *American Fitness*
2. *American School & University—Facilities, Purchasing and Business Administration*
3. *Athletic Administration*
4. *Athletic Business*

5. *Athletic Management*
6. *The Chronicle of Higher Education*
7. *Club Industry*
8. *Corporate Fitness and Recreation*
9. *CoSida Digest*
10. *Educational Resources Information Center* (ERIC)
11. *Fitness Management*
12. *Health Values: Achieving High Level Wellness*
13. *Interscholastic Athletic Administration*
14. *JUCO Review (Journal of the National Junior College Athletic Association)*
15. *Lawn & Landscape*
16. *NCAA News*
17. *Runners World*
18. *Scholastic Coach*
19. *Sport Marketing Letter*
20. *Team Marketing Report*
21. *Texas Coach*

The number of professional journals and trade publications that devote at least some of their pages to some area of sport management speaks well to the growing professionalism of the discipline. (A list of sport organizations, with their addresses, can be found in Appendix B.) It reveals that increased emphasis is being placed on the study and evaluation of the numerous areas or components that go to make up the field commonly referred to as *sport management*. It also indicates that there is a significant need on behalf of practitioners as well as scholars to read such journals in order to remain current in the field.

Conclusions

There is a multitude of job opportunities for the would-be sport manager. To be competitive in the sport job market today and in the future it is necessary to possess formal training and education, including meaningful field experiences. The internship experience is a critical part of the formal education of any future sport manager. Many of the strategies and tactics that are utilized to secure meaningful internships can also be used in the pursuit of paid positions on graduation.

REFERENCES

Arbogast, G. W. and Griffin, L. (1989). Accountability—Is it within reach of our profession? *Journal of Physical Education, Recreation and Dance, 60*(6), 72–75.

Bell, J. and Countiss, J. (1993). Professional service through sport management internships. *Journal of Physical Education, Recreation and Dance, 61*(1), 45–47, 52.

Brassie, P. S. (1989a). A student buyer's guide to sport management programs. *Journal of Physical Education, Recreation and Dance, 60*(9), 25–28.

Brassie, P. S. (1989b). Guidelines for programs preparing undergraduate and graduate students for careers in sport management. *Journal of Sport Management, 3*(2), 158–164.

Campbell, K. and Kovar, S. K. (1994). Fitness/exercise science internships: How to ensure success. *Journal of Physical Education, Recreation and Dance, 65*(2), 69–72.

Cunnen J. & Sidwell, M. (1993). Sport management interns—Selection qualifications. *Journal of Physical Education, Recreation and Dance, 64*(7), 91–95.

DeSensi, J., Kelley, D., Blanton, M., and Beitel, P. (1990). Sport management curricular evaluation and needs assessment: A multifaceted approach. *Journal of Sport Management, 4*(1), 31–58.

Ebersole, P. (1996). What's a liberal arts degree worth? *Democrat & Chronicle,* Oct. 7. Rochester, New York, pp. 1, 2.

Gleason, T. (1986, February). Sport administration degrees: Growing to fill a need/supply overwhelms demand. *Athletic Administration,* 9–10.

Lipsey, R. A., Ed. (1996, January). *Sports Market Place.* Phoenix, AZ: Sportsguide.

Markiewicz, D. A. (1991, July 30). More fans line up for careers in sports. *USA Today,* 7-B.

Marston, R. (1993). Developing professionalism at the undergraduate level. *Journal of Physical Education, Recreation and Dance, 64*(7), 36, 37, 40.

Moss, A., Ed. (1996). *The sports business directory.* Bethesda, MD: E. J. Krause & Associates.

Murray, M. & Mann, B. (1993). Is our professionalism showing or slipping? *Journal of Physical Education, Recreation and Dance, 64*(7), 30, 31, 35.

NASPE (National Association for Sport and Physical Education). (1987, February). *Guidelines for undergraduate and graduate programs in sport management: Membership report.* Reston, VA: National Association for Sport and Physical Education.

NASPE. (1988). *Standards for programs preparing undergraduates for careers in fitness.* Reston, VA: National Association for Sport and Physical Education (NASPE).

NASPE. (1995). The freshman class of approved sport management programs. *NASPE News.* Reston, VA: National Association for Sport and Physical Education, p. 11.

NASPE/NASSM. (1993, May). *Sport management program standards and review protocol.* Reston, VA.

Ross, C. M., Jamieson, L. M., and Young, S. J. (1997). *Professional preparation in sports management.* Bloomington, IN: Indiana University Press.

Ruder, K. (1993). Being professional now. *Journal of Physical Education, Recreation and Dance, 64*(7), 29, 35.

Stier, W. F., Jr., (1990) Wanted: Athletic directors as Renaissance leaders. *Athletic Director, 7*(3), 8.

Stier, W. F., Jr. (1993, August). Alternative career paths in physical education: Sport management. Washington, DC: *ERIC Digest—Clearinghouse on Teaching and Teacher Education.*

Stier, W. F., Jr., (1994). *Successful sport fund-raising.* Dubuque, IA: Wm. C. Brown & Benchmark.

Stier, W. F., Jr. (1995). *Successful coaching—Strategies and tactics.* Boston, MA: American Press.

Stier, W. F., Jr. (1996a). *Sport management internship handbook—State University of New York.* Brockport, New York: SUNY Brockport Press.

Stier, W. F., Jr. (1996b, April 16). Becoming marketable within the HPERD and A profession. Paper presented at the National Conference of the American Alliance for Health, Physical Education, Recreation and Dance (AAHPERD), Atlanta, Georgia.

Stier, W. F., Jr. and Stier, M. M. (1992). Alternative considerations for the would-be writer. *Journal of Physical Education, Recreation and Dance, 63*(9), 68–72.

Sutton, W. A. (1989). The role of internships in sport management curricula: A model for development. *Journal of Physical Education, Recreation and Dance, 60*(7), 20–24.

Uhlir, G. A. (1990). Professionalism—The role of the college and university. *Journal of Physical Education, Recreation and Dance, 61*(8), 6.

Verner, E. (1993). Developing professionalism through experimental learning. *Journal of Physical Education, Recreation and Dance, 64*(7), 41–44.

Widdon, S. (1990). Graduate dual preparation programs in business and sport management. *Journal of Physical Education, Recreation and Dance, 61*(3), 96–98.

DISCUSSION AND REVIEW QUESTIONS

1. Review the various types of jobs and career opportunities available in sport management.
2. Outline the essential elements of sound undergraduate professional preparation sport management programs.
3. Speculate as to how you might prepare yourself for a suitable internship experience.
4. Cite the three possible outcomes of sport management internships and how you might go about insuring that your internship experience is a successful one.
5. What are the characteristics of an ideal internship?
6. Illustrate (and provide examples of) how networking can be an effective technique for both securing an internship and actual employment.
7. Outline the current efforts in approval and accreditation of sport management professional preparation programs in the United States.
8. Review various professional journals and cite five such publications that hold particular interest for you in terms of your current career plans in the area of sport management.

CHAPTER

3 Philosophy and Theory of Sport Management

A packed stadium—a sign of sound support.
James Dusen, Photographer.

Chapter Objectives

After reading this chapter you will be able to:

- Understand how one's philosophy is a reflection of one's beliefs, values, and attitudes;
- Articulate your current philosophy of life;
- Describe various administrative styles;
- Express your ethical beliefs in light of your professional responsibilities;
- Differentiate between various views of management thought and management theories;
- Trace management thought from ancient times to the present;
- Define what a theory is and articulate various theories as they relate to management and leadership styles.

Developing a Philosophy

Concept 53: Managers Need to Develop Appropriate Philosophies.

All professionals in every field of endeavor or discipline need to develop and refine their philosophy or philosophies. "Each administrator has a philosophy, whether or not he or she realizes it" (Tillman, Voltmer, Esslinger, & McCue, 1996, p. 16).

Concept 54: A Philosophy Is a Reflection of One's Beliefs, Values, and Attitudes.

What exactly is a philosophy? *Webster's New Collegiate Dictionary* defines a philosophy as "most general beliefs, concepts, and attitudes of an individual or group." An individual's philosophy may be thought of as how that person views any given situation. A philosophy is a reflection of a person's personality, beliefs, attitudes, and values. Most importantly, one's philosophy has a tremendous effect on the decisions made and the actions performed by an individual.

A philosophy is a result of and is influenced by one's formal and informal education, training, environment, skills, and knowledge as well as by life's experiences. In short, a person's philosophy is affected "by the sum total of all that affects and touches the individual" (Stier, 1995, p. 40).

Concept 55: One's Philosophies Are Not Stagnant; They Evolve in Time as a Result of Experiences, Education, and Training.

A person's philosophy is not stagnant. Rather, it is flexible. It can change, imperceptibly or significantly. It can shift in an abrupt fashion or it may change through an evolutionary process. This flexibility is necessary in order for an individual to be able to grow as a professional and to remain current, competent, and up-to-date in the modern world, a world full of change and changes.

A Single Philosophy or Multiple Philosophies?

A sport manager needs to be concerned with more than a single philosophy. In reality, there are three distinct, but related, areas that form the foundation of a philosophical perspective for the modern-day sport manager. These three philosophical dimensions are: (1) a philosophy of life itself, (2) a philosophy of one's profession, and (3) a philosophy of management or administration.

Concept 56: Administrators Need to Develop a Philosophy of Life, of One's Profession, As Well As a Philosophy of Management.

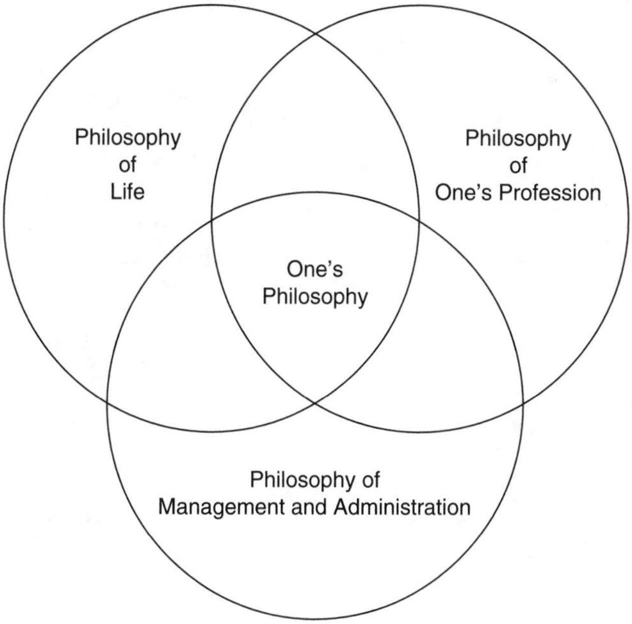

FIGURE 3.1 Multiple Philosophies

A Philosophy of Life

In the most simplistic view, a philosophy of life is made up of one's personal values, opinions, and beliefs. It can be thought of as the way an individual views one's own life as well as the lives of others on this planet—within the society of humankind. A person's philosophy of life helps define who and what that individual is and reflects one's value system as a member of the greater society of all human beings.

A well-thought out, sound philosophy of life helps one serve as a meaningful member of and contributor to society, as a citizen of the world. It deals with the purpose(s) of life, the value of life, and how one deals with and relates to others. In short, it serves as the foundation for how one lives.

A Philosophy Relating to One's Profession

As a professional one also needs to develop and refine a philosophy of one's own profession. In some cases the profession might be that of education, in which case it is imperative that a sound, defensible *philosophy of education* be conceived. For some people the profession might be that of fitness and wellness, and these individuals would need to forge a reasonable and thoughtful *philosophy of fitness/wellness*. For still others the profession could be amateur/professional sports or recreation and leisure, and so forth. In these scenarios professionals would need to develop a *philosophy of sports* or a *philosophy of recreation and leisure*.

Sports are for everyone.
James Dusen, Photographer.

When developing or expressing a professional philosophy, one should be able to answer the question of "what do I think concerning—" about any number of things or situations within the particular professional domain. For example, what do you think about the value of education? What is the purpose of public or private education? What do you think about amateur or professional sports? What should be the priorities in a school-based sports program? What are the values of recreational activities? What do you think about the financial base of education or sports? What is the value of exercise? What role should government play in fitness and wellness programs? How should specific programs be financed and promoted? What do you think about different types of exercise? What about the ethics of specific strategies and tactics associated with selling and marketing? The answers to these and innumerable other questions would be indicative of the sport manager's professional philosophy.

A Philosophy of Management

The third philosophical dimension is that of management itself. The administrator needs to develop a philosophy of management (administration) within the confines of the specific professional arena or organization in which the person is involved. This philosophy of sport management is rooted in the formal historical study of management and in modern theories of management, as well as the individual's own professional and personal experiences.

The professional sport manager needs to come to grips, philosophically speaking, with such areas as motivation, leadership, communication, decision-making, evaluating, budgeting, directing, staffing, planning, organizing, problem-solving, prioritizing, coordinating, reporting, recording, facilitating, and so on. The sport manager needs to be conscious of how one's philosophy, how one's philosophical perspective, can play an important, significant, and ongoing role in the individual's efforts to manage the behavior of other people and to manipulate resources toward appropriate objectives and goals.

Concept 57: Successful Managers Are Able to Effectively Articulate Their Philosophy of Life, of Their Profession, and of Management.

It is very important that the sport manager not only possess a philosophy of life, of the profession, and of management, but also be able to consistently, effectively, and efficiently communicate these philosophies to others, because other individuals, groups, and, in some instances, the general public, need to understand from "whence the manager is coming." Others need to understand the philosophy and thinking of the sport manager. They need to understand the decisions and actions of the manager. Without such sharing of one's philosophies (and rationale for actions) there are tremendous opportunities for miscommunication, partial communication, or even failed communication between individuals, both inside and outside of the sport organization itself.

A person's philosophies should be consistent in terms of value systems, priorities, goals, and relationships with others. Because one's decisions and actions are the direct result of one's philosophies, it is important that consistency be the watchword when it comes to making decisions and taking action in real life situations.

Styles of Management

Depending on one's philosophies, one's experiences, one's training, one's perceptions, it is possible for a sport manager to exhibit one or more different styles of management. Typically a sport manager can exhibit a variety of managerial styles during one tenure in an organization.

Concept 58: A Person's Style of Management May Shift from One Paradigm to Another Depending on the Situation and the Circumstances.

In fact, the manager can exhibit different management and leadership styles at different times and in different situations. Such a shift can occur within the same week or during the same day. It depends on the specific situation and the existing circumstances (including historical implications) in which the individual is involved.

Some situations may call for the sport manager to be a dictator. Others may require that the manager assume the role or style of a benevolent dictator, while still other circumstances might indicate that the laissez-faire (or permissive) style would be most

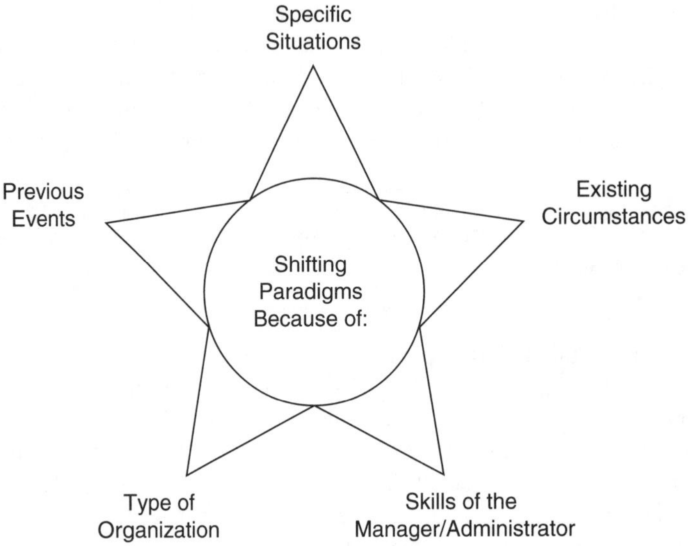

FIGURE 3.2 Factors Affecting Administrative Styles

productive. The important point is this: different managerial styles may be more appropriate at different times, depending on the talents and experiences of the sport manager, the current situation or circumstances, the type of organization itself, and what has taken place previously (see Figure 3.2).

The Authoritarian or Autocratic Administrator

The autocratic administrator is one who controls and manipulates almost every aspect of a situation. The individual is a dictator in the truest sense of the word. Subordinates are viewed as inferior. They are dominated and restricted in their actions and communication by the controlling and repressive actions of the autocratic manager. They are to listen, obey, and follow directions.

Autocrats or dictators control situations by imposing their will on others. *Intimidation* and *manipulation* describe the atmosphere existing within an organization controlled and dominated by an authoritarian or autocratic administrator. Fear and apprehension are quite prevalent within the organization because any action or voice not in tune with the autocratic administrator is subject to discouragement, if not outright censure.

The Benevolent Dictator

While there is still the element of control by the benevolent dictator, this type of administrative style has the manager doing the controlling, the leading, the subjugation, because the manager feels that he or she knows what is best for others. As a result, this manager acts in a benevolent or parental fashion in determining the most appropriate course of action and how it will be accomplished. There is no sense of malevolence in the intent or motivation of such an administrator. Rather, the benevolent dictator acts much as a kindly patriarch or matriarch for one's "children" so that the youngsters' needs are met. Nevertheless, this manager makes the major decisions, sets the tone, and controls the climate for the organization (Stier, 1995).

The Pragmatic Administrator

The pragmatic manager is one who is driven by "doing what it takes to get the job done." *Expediency* describes this style of administrator. Politically astute, this individual is willing to take risks in trusting others. There is willingness to give responsibilities to others, and to delegate tasks to others if such action will result in objectives realized and goals reached. The emphasis in this type of management style is directly related to the objectives and goals associated with the organization.

The Democratic Administrator

The democratic administrator insures that input is consistently secured from a wide range of subordinates. Although the final decision rightly rests with the administrator or manager in charge, this does not discourage the individual from seeking counsel, opinions, ideas, and suggestions from others. The atmosphere established by a democratic manager is such that individuals feel comfortable in having opportunities to play a bigger part in the organization. Relationships between democratic managers and nonmanagers are noted for their openness and the free exchange of ideas.

Concept 59: Democratic Administration Does Not Mean Management by Committee or Management by Popular Vote.

However, one would be mistaken to assume that the democratic style of management removes the need for the administrator or manager to make decisions. Quite the opposite. There can be a democratic style of governance within the organization but the final decision, in terms of major decisions, certainly must rest with the person in charge—in this case, the manager or administrator. Although democratic administrators frequently utilize a participatory approach to management, this does not preclude the administrators from making final decisions. Democratic administration is not management by committee or management by popular vote.

The Humanistic Administrator

This type of manager possesses true empathy and sympathy with others, both in and out of the organization. The humanistic manager interacts with others as true individuals, as human beings, with sincere dignity. Such relationships involve demonstration of compassion and understanding of the needs of others. This type of manager deliberately attempts to get to know others as important individuals. The cornerstone of the treatment of others is the *Golden Rule:* Treat others like one would like to be treated by others. Humanistic managers acknowledge their own strengths and weaknesses as well as the strengths and weaknesses of others. This type of manager recognizes that people are human, that they are fallible, capable of making mistakes and errors as well as making appropriate decisions and performing in a suitable fashion.

The Laissez-Faire or Permissive Administrator

This type of administrator can be recognized for the freewheeling atmosphere of the workplace, where there is very little structure or organization. This type of administrator often fails to assume an active role in many of the important aspects of the organization. Often criticized as the lazy person's method of managing (if this style is the predominant approach to management), the permissive style is identified by the presence of few parameters in terms of how things should be planned, accomplished, or implemented.

The manager allows others to perform many of the tasks and to assume many of the responsibilities that might rightfully be within the purview of the administrator. The "head person assumes a very low profile and allows the organization to operate on its own" (Horine, 1991, p. 9). The laissez-faire manager allows others to do as they see fit without many checks and balances in place. Symptoms of this type of managerial approach include an overabundance of delegating and infrequent, if any, follow-up and supervision.

The Empowering Administrator

The administrator who seeks to empower others within the organization in effect facilitates others in the performance of their specific tasks. This type of administrator attempts to provide others with ample opportunities to express their individuality and to demonstrate their competency. The empowering administrator is trusting and allows others to assume responsibilities, to assume important roles, and to carry out significant tasks. Such administrators are not afraid to delegate suitable tasks or to entrust responsibilities to others. Quite the opposite. The empowering manager will deliberately seek ways to facilitate the professional growth and expansion of subordinates by allowing freedom, within limits, in the performance of their duties.

Ethical Behavior and Social Responsibilities in the Management of Sport

Closely aligned with one's philosophy of life, of the profession, and of management are the areas of morality and ethical behavior. Managers are consistently faced with making decisions, many of which revolve around moral or ethical issues. Appropriate, just, and right decisions are the responsibility of the manager, the leader. One leads through example.

The world we live in can be a challenging one in terms of ethical or right (just) behavior. Similarly, the sport or sport-related organization in which one works can also provide significant challenges in terms of what is right and just and what is improper and aberrant in the areas of ethics, integrity, decency, and morality.

Administrators must have the highest of morals. They must be guided by the highest principles of good conduct and right choices. Their integrity must be beyond reproach. The responsibilities, temptations, and challenges facing managers in the twenty-first century are such that individuals with great integrity are needed, individuals who are able to make appropriate and right decisions in the face of extreme pressure, coercion, and urgency.

In many, many situations, the right decision may not be the easy decision. On the contrary, being able to withstand the onslaught of outside and inside pressures, the ability to resist the "easy way out," and the willingness to take risks for the sake of justice, fairness, and legitimacy, equitableness, and righteousness is sorely needed.

Concept 60: Managers Must Be Able to Assume Great Risks in Terms of Making Right Decisions, or "Get Out of the Kitchen."

Sport managers are in a position to play a major role in social responsibility. Every citizen has such an obligation. However, the sport manager is in a unique position in terms of making decisions, taking actions, and implementing programs that can have an impact on society. This responsibility should not be taken lightly. The impact of many decisions by managers are far-reaching, extending beyond the artificial boundaries of the sport organization itself.

Concept 61: It May Not Be Just, It May Not Be Right, It May Not Be Fair, but It Happens.

In many instances, managers "need to take a stand" in terms of doing what is right. Not everything in this world is just or fair. In reality, "things may not be just, they may not be right, they may not be fair—but they happen anyway." That is unfortunate indeed. Courageous administrators will be willing to assume risks to insure that appropriate, just, and fair decisions are the norm rather than the exception to the rule in terms of their areas of responsibilities.

A Glimpse of the History of Management Thought and Theories

There are several advantages of viewing the history of management thought as well as the history of earlier managerial efforts. Such a review not only provides a glimpse into past practices and how we got to where we are today but it also helps us in our current and future efforts to serve as sport managers successfully. It also aids in our efforts to more effectively and efficiently develop a working philosophy and understanding of sport management. Finally, it helps to identify various strategies and tactics that might be appropriate and applicable in a variety of settings if one is to experience success as an administrator or manager. (For a list of those who made significant contributions to the history of managerial theory, see Appendix A.)

Concept 62: Good Theory Results in Good Practice.

It is also advisable to review the applicable and more common managerial theories as they relate to the management of "sport" and all that that term encompasses. Doing so enables the practitioner to more successfully integrate both practice and theory in the day-to-day operations of the sport organization in which the individual is involved. A management aphorism holds that good theory results in good practice. Today's sport manager needs to be a student of history and of management in order to keep theory and practice in proper perspective as one attempts to prevent, react, and solve problems and challenges.

Management Thought in Ancient Times

Management is certainly not a twentieth-century concept. On the contrary. The current status of management thought and the level of managerial practice have obtained their present status and position in our society through the efforts of a large number of individuals, groups, and cultures throughout the centuries.

Concept 63: Management Is Not a Twentieth-Century Concept.

Management as a separate process was initially verbalized during the time of Socrates (400 B.C.) and Plato (350 B.C.). However, even then, the principles and concepts of management were not part of any type of scheme or grand design. This was not accomplished until many centuries later. Nevertheless, major contributions to what has become modern management thought, ideas, practices, and theories can be traced to the contributions of the early Greeks, who played a major role in providing the basic foundations for Western civilization. For example, the origin of the scientific method of investigation had its origins in Greek thought.

Similarly, numerous individuals, cultures, and societies in ancient times have played significant roles, as previously pointed out in Chapter 1, in the development of rather sophisticated and significant management practices, strategies, tactics, and techniques. These achievements were in the areas of (1) architecture, (2) warfare, and (3) political organization. Examples of superior managerial achievements included King Solomon (trade agreements, large construction projects), the Egyptians (the pyramids), Alexander the Great (military management and political organization), as well as Roman society (empire building) (*The history of management thought,* 1974). Numerous other contributions have been consistently made throughout history (see Appendix A).

Significant Changes in the Eighteenth Century, and Their Impact on Individuals, Management Thought, and the Structure of Organizations

Beginning in the early 1700s, a number of separate developments took place in Europe that had significant impact on managerial practices and thought at the time and for centuries to come. The first of these important developments was the growth of cities. It was this tremendous expansion of humanity within a limited geographical area that so drastically altered the so-called rural makeup of society at the time.

The second development involved the application of the principle of specialization, in terms of individual skills and competencies. The extensive use of the printing press was the third development that had a significant impact on the common citizenry. The fourth development that rocked civilization to its basic foundation and would have a profound impact on all society was the beginning of the Industrial Revolution in England.

As a result of these and other occurrences or developments there gradually emerged a whole new generation of managers, administrators, organizers, planners, and leaders. These individuals, within a variety of organizations, began to look at the then-present challenges from the perspective of how to get things accomplished effectively and efficiently.

English Industrial Revolution: 1700–1785

Between 1700 and 1785 the English Industrial Revolution saw England dramatically evolve from a rural country to the so-called workshop of the world. In fact, England was the first European nation to successfully make the adjustment from a rural agrarian society to a society based on industrial commerce. This transition was not without hardships and challenges and sacrifices, for both individuals and the country. It should be emphasized again that many of the management strategies employed in the 1700s in reaction to these sweeping changes were not totally new. In fact, many of the managerial ideas, strategies, and tactics used in the eighteenth century can be traced to much earlier times.

Concept 64: The Interpretation and Utilization of Management Strategies and Tactics Evolved during the English Industrial Revolution.

However, this fact does not detract from the significance of the managerial efforts at the time. Although a large number of management strategies, techniques, and tactics utilized in the 1700s were not totally new, their interpretation, application, and utilization in meeting the new challenges and problems of society during the English Industrial Revolution (1700–1785) were unique. And, indeed, there were new concepts, strategies, techniques, and tactics employed as well to meet new obstacles and challenging problems.

Society in the eighteenth century had quickly become a constantly changing and more complicated world to live in. There was a need to rethink how members of the society would meet the challenges that were emerging during these rapidly changing times. As a result, there was a shift in the management process itself that involved how people viewed themselves as members of the society, how they viewed others, and their perception of the work process itself and the organizations that evolved.

Scientific Management Efforts in the United States

Up to this point, development and application of scientific management production techniques had taken place for the most part in England. Soon there were similarly significant advances across the sea—in the United States. For example, in the latter part of the 1700s,

Eli Whitney initiated the system for the milling machine that was used to smooth and shape both wood and metal. This development became the foundation of modern factories. Eli contributed greatly to the foundation on which the early pioneers of scientific management built their discipline.

> **Concept 65:** Eli Whitney Had a Major Influence on the Thinking of Early Pioneers of Scientific Management.

Eli was also involved in interchangeable parts manufacture for making muskets for the government, at a considerable profit. Similarly, he also developed an extensive cost-accounting system in which every component and every process carried its own dollar value. Finally, he used a form of quality control in his Mill Rock factory. In fact, Whitney invented a score of modern machines (including the cotton gin) that made large-scale enterprises possible, and profitable.

Management Thought in the United States during the Nineteenth Century

The 1800s brought about a wealth of literature on management and management processes in the United States. Economists at this time thought and wrote about (1) managerial concepts, (2) functions of management, and (3) applications of management theory. Early writers dealt principally with fundamentals. No unified management theory was developed at that time. The important point is that individuals were at least attempting to make an effort—a beginning—to think critically about management, about managers, and about the process of management.

With the advent of the American Civil War (1860) a new industrial era began in the United States. This was caused by the (1) expansion of mechanical industries, and by the (2) abolition of slave labor. Financiers such as J. Gould, J. P. Morgan, and Cornelius Vanderbilt built up large business organizations (*firms*) and these organizations had a tremendous influence on the development of the U.S. economy throughout the nineteenth century. During this period, the United States's most dramatic enterprise, the railroads, grew in importance and stature.

Beginnings of "Scientific Management": 1880–1898

It is generally acknowledged that the modern management movement began around 1880. In fact, the term *scientific management* was first used during this time. Between that time and the early or mid-1920s, management thought exploded with different ideas, theories, systems and strategies, and techniques, all related to ways of looking at management and the management process.

> **Concept 66:** Management Thought Exploded between 1880 and the Mid-1920s.

During the latter part of the nineteenth century, U.S. business was undergoing significant changes. The west was being settled and "civilized." Large businesses and organizations were creating a schism between management and the workers (labor). And, finally, there emerged a new and important group of people in society, the managerial class.

These managers became involved with solving problems associated with bigness and consequently moved from the area of the "big business" concept to the area of "things within the business or firm." For example, they became concerned with processes, the location of equipment and plant layout, production techniques, incentive systems, and so forth. Management was also becoming *things* oriented instead of *firm* oriented as it had been in the past. Finally, management began to evolve away from the brush fire mentality (crisis management) to more of an anticipatory style (planning) of management.

The result was that a manager was treated with greater respect and esteem, and the subject matter of management was beginning to be recognized as a significant field of study by both academics and those involved in the business of management. In reality, management as a separate discipline or area was coming into its own, at least in a small, but nevertheless, significant way.

In addition, people became interested in exchanging ideas and information about the processes and problems of management, which resulted in numerous publications dealing with management. Numerous meetings and conferences were also held to discuss the challenges and problems facing organizations, workers, and management. As a result, the groundswell to consider management as a separate entity or field of study grew in momentum. In fact, during this time management was recognized as a teaching curriculum at a leading university for the first time.

Exciting and succsessful teams, coaches, and athletes play a major role in garnering news media coverage and fan support.
Tom Wolf, Photographer.

Concept 67: Insightful Thinkers Examined Management from the Scientific Perspective.

At this time there also emerged a group of visionary thinkers studying the concept of management and organization from a scientific perspective. These individuals provided significant and far-reaching contributions to management thought, not only for their time but for the present as well. In fact, in examining the development of today's managerial concepts, principles, theories, and strategies, it becomes necessary to look at the specific contributions and thoughts of a number of outstanding leaders in modern management thought (see Table 3.1).

School of Scientific Management

Concept 68: Frederick W. Taylor Is Credited as Being the "Father of Scientific Management."

Because of the efforts of Frederick W. Taylor, the school of scientific management became a reality. His accomplishments were many and varied. For example, managers were encouraged to utilize the processes of planning, organizing, and controlling. Stopwatch studies of workers' performance were conducted. The work site was organized so that working conditions were standardized in an effort to make standards of worker performance possible and meaningful. Feasible standards were established per person or per machine hour. Accountability was a key element in Taylor's view of management.

Frederick Taylor also emphasized the importance of good supervision of an employee and the working conditions. The supervisor was relieved of the "whip persuasion role" and provided with incentives to offer workers to increase their individual productivity. Supervisors became specialists who facilitated productivity and accountability. Finally, Taylor attempted to devise ways in which workers would be identified for specific jobs in light of each worker's skill and potential for performing the task(s).

Early practitioners of scientific management were indeed pragmatists. They were not reluctant to tackle problems on the basis of urgency or need. As a result, the most urgent problems or challenges naturally received the greatest attention. Consequently, some of the problems that were dealt with initially centered on such production questions as:

1. What is a fair day's work?
2. How long should a worker take to do a given job?
3. What is the best location for a plant?
4. How should workers be supervised?
5. What is the best way to select a worker for a job?

Taylor served as both a flashpoint and a foundation for those who followed him and adhered to his concepts of scientific management. There were a large number of individuals—

TABLE 3.1 Major Pioneers in Early Scientific Management Thought

Contributors (approximate times)	Contributions
Henry Towne and Henry C. Metcalfe (1886)	**1.** Unified system of management rather than the usual hit-or-miss practices employed in earlier times; **2.** Called for managers to form professional organizations; **3.** Encouraged the publication of journals devoted to management; **4.** Exchanged findings and views with others.
Frederick W. Taylor (1900)	**1.** Developed the idea of scientific management, "Father of Scientific Management"; **2.** Establishment of uniform job procedures; **3.** Job selection by qualification; **4.** New roles for supervisors; **5.** Time–motion studies.
Frank B. Gilbreth (1900)	**1.** Science of motion study; **2.** "Father of Work Simplification"; **3.** Process charts and flow diagrams.
Lillian Gilbreth (1900)	**1.** "First Lady of Management" (1878–1972); **2.** Psychology of the workplace; bridged the gap between people and things; **3.** Motion studies.
Henry L. Gantt (1901)	**1.** Gantt Chart (daily balance chart) of output time; **2.** Humanitarianism in employee treatment and pay; **3.** Teaching and training employees; **4.** Service as an objective.
Hugo Munsterberg (1910)	**1.** Created field of industrial psychology; **2.** Initiated system of tests and measurements of psychological differences between employees.
Harrington Emerson (1910)	**1.** Broader focus on the organization structure and its importance; **2.** Emphasis on the objectives of a firm and their relation to its organization; **3.** Emphasis on use of experts, staff, consultants, and the like; **4.** Twelve principles of efficiency.
Harlow S. Person (1911)	**1.** Gave academic recognition to scientific management; **2.** Emphasized total scope of management, lifting it from a movement dedicated to the stopwatch and speedup.
Henri Fayol (1916)	**1.** Concept of universality of management; **2.** First comprehensive theory of management; **3.** Need for teaching management in schools and colleges; **4.** Need for better leadership in management.

(continued)

TABLE 3.2 Continued

Contributors (approximate times)	Contributions
Oliver Sheldon (1923)	**1.** Emphasis on social aspects of management; **2.** Social responsibilities of managers; **3.** Conceptualization of (philosophy of) management, bringing it to a higher theoretical level; **4.** Management as a separate, distinct function in industry that revolved around a given set of principles that could be analyzed and studied.
Elton Mayo (1927–47)	**1.** Hawthorne studies: attitudes and reactions of groups under varying conditions (Western Electric's Hawthorne Works); **2.** Importance of psychological and social factors on productivity; **3.** Effect of "morale" on productivity; **4.** Experimental rather than theoretical research.
Mary P. Follett (1930)	**1.** Contributed to the study of leadership; **2.** Individuals can be trained to be leaders; **3.** Importance of education for managers/leaders; **4.** Examined motivating desires of individuals and groups; **5.** Importance of group dynamics and human behavior.
James D. Mooney (1931)	**1.** Scaler principle (1926): superior and subordinate relationships arranged in an heir apparent fashion; **2.** Classic treatise on the nature of and creation of the organization, *Onward Industry,* 1928; **3.** A tight engineering approach to management; excluded human side or social aspects of management.
Chester Barnard (1938)	**1.** A behaviorist; **2.** Great influence on understanding organizations; **3.** Logical analysis of organization's structure; **4.** Theory of cooperation and organization; **5.** Description of the executive process; importance of the competent executive.

associates, contemporaries, and followers—who subscribed to his general scientific management philosophy. Many of them went on to refine the then current thinking relating to organizations and management, while others developed their own versions of the science of management. Still others made significant contributions to the overall scientific study of management. Some of these individuals include, but are not limited to, the following: Harlow S. Person, Hugo Munsterberg, Henry L. Gantt, Harrington Emerson, and Henri Fayol. All played a part in extending the knowledge we now have of "management" as a distinct field or body of knowledge.

Impact of Early Leaders in Managerial Thought

These and other leaders, within a matter of a few decades, played a very real and important role in elevating the management process, as well as the study of management, to a recognized profession based on scientific knowledge. Their contributions serve as a firm foundation for the further study and expansion of knowledge relating to management by current and future professional managers and scholars.

Managers in the olden days made decisions and initiated actions because they believed that what had worked before should solve their current problem. However, the modern-day manager utilizes the analytical approach to preventing and solving problems, because the proponents of scientific management followed the practice of discovering the facts and making decisions in light of these facts. When faced with challenges, these individuals would seek the best way to approach the problem today. Because sound management is based on facts, on data, and on scientific reasoning, what has worked before in other situations and under different circumstances might not be either applicable or appropriate in today's organization, in today's setting, and under today's circumstances.

Management Thought Following World War II

Management thought just before, during, and immediately following World War II was somewhat confused. As a result, there was an effort by a large number of practitioners and scholars after the war to bring some semblance of order to the mass of theories that had grown up since the initiation of Taylor's scientific management.

Beginnings of a Philosophical Approach to Managerial Thought

One of the factors that distances modern-day management from earlier management efforts is the philosophical approach to managerial thought. This philosophical perspective evolved gradually and represents a significant change from the earlier mechanistic thinking associated with management. Today, the realm of values and value judgments play an important role in management and management thought, and there is a great deal of emphasis placed on group dynamics, the social dimension of groups.

Schools of Management Thought That Evolved in the Twentieth Century

During the course of the twentieth century there evolved, under the leadership of various researchers and students of management and organizations, several schools of management thought. The major schools of management thought (*The history of management thought,* 1974) include:

1. *The Traditional or Scientific School of Management Thought*
Sometimes referred to as the Classical School, this perspective of management thought resulted from systematic observations of how things are produced. The emphasis was on

specific techniques, such as time studies, the layout of plant equipment, "time and motion" studies, division of labor, organizational structure, the effect of various wage incentives, and production planning and control. There were efforts to research and analyze various elements of the operation of the "shop" or the plant in an effort to determine their impact, effectiveness, and efficiency. Frederick Taylor was the single most important and influential individual within the Traditional School.

2. *The Behavioral School*
This school of thought was based on the interpersonal relationships that exist within the workplace or organization. The centrality of the individual became the focus of this school of management thought. It was recognized that organizational goals and objectives could be achieved through the efforts of individuals. Consequently, the behaviorists concentrated early on the motivational factors of individuals and groups. The area of group dynamics became an important field for study with close examinations of individual drives, group interactions, and relations. Eclectic in their approach, proponents of the Behavioral School incorporate most of the social sciences, including psychology, sociology, social psychology, and anthropology, in their efforts to examine management and the organizational process.

3. *The Management Process School*
As the name suggests, this theory of management is based on the processes involved in managing or administering. Management is viewed as management, regardless of the type of organization. Management is universal in its perspective. Proponents of this theory of management examine and study the functions of a manager, the processes of management (see Chapter 4).

4. *The Quantitative School*
Emerging after 1940, the Quantitative School represents a scientific effort to take advantage of knowledge from a wide range of different disciplines in studying and examining organizations and in solving problems associated within them. Supporters of the Quantitative School would rely upon experts, operating in closely integrated research teams, from various academic disciplines (utilizing their scientific tools and resources) in attempting to come to a conclusion or to solve a particular problem of management or within an organization.

Theories, Principles, and Concepts of Management and Leadership

"A theory is accepted principles devised to analyze, predict, or explain the nature of behavior of a specified set of phenomena. Theories are tested by research" (Parkhouse, 1991, p. 32). A more thorough definition is provided by Jensen (1992, pp. 11, 12):

> A theory is one step beyond an assumption or hypothesis. It is a guide, which has some evidence in its support, but is still not validated. Theories are useful in education in the formulation of administrative practices. Sometimes, a theory gradually evolves into a standard procedure, a policy, or a principle after sufficient evidence has been accumulated to support it. In other cases, theories become discarded because attempts to prove their validity and

usefulness are unsuccessful. Theory can be viewed as a starting point for the development of facts, policies, principles, and laws. Administrative theory precedes administrative practice and nurtures it.

McGregor's Theory X and Y Motivational Leadership Styles

Douglas McGregor, while a professor at MIT, wrote the book, *The Human Side of Enterprise* (1960). He investigated the ways workers were viewed by their managers and superiors. He expressed the belief that there are two styles of motivational leadership in light of the needs and capabilities of workers. He referred to one style as Theory X and the other as Theory Y.

In Theory X, workers are thought to be lazy, lacking in ability and motivation with a significant amount of distaste for work. They need to and want to be told what to do, when to do it, and how to do it. Workers do not desire responsibility, instead preferring security, sanctuary, and safety. As a result, workers need to be controlled. They are to be coerced and threatened if they are to perform at an acceptable level in terms of effectiveness and efficiency (Tillman, Voltmer, Esslinger, & McCue, 1996, pp. 42, 43).

Horine (1995, p. 21) describes the manager who subscribes to the Theory X line of management thinking as requiring "a tight authoritative structure to supervise employees directly (called the 'scalar principle'), and the staff as needing to be consistently pressured to maintain adequate performance."

However, the opposite side of the leadership coin is expressed in Theory Y. Those who subscribe to Theory Y believe that workers not only truly enjoy their work but that they desire responsibility and independence. Additionally, employees are viewed as self-motivated and self-directed. They need less supervision and direction and can operate successfully and continually at a high performance level with a less rigid and less threatening organizational structure. In short, workers can be productive, efficient, and effective with less direct control, less supervision, and with a less restrictive environment.

Theory Z

William Ouchi coined the term *Theory Z* in his book, *Theory Z: How American Business Can Meet the Japanese Challenge* (1980), in which he closely examined various "cultures" within organizations. This theory has elements of highly successful Japanese business management tactics and strategies adapted to the U.S. scene with its own particular organizational climate and culture (Tillman, Voltlmer, Esslinger, & McCue, 1996). Key concepts of this theory revolve around the need for trust, loyalty, openness, and positive relationships between management and workers; the benefits of having educated workers; the need for workers to have the best interest of their organization at heart; as well as the need for inspirational and visible leadership on the part of management (Plunkett & Attner, 1994).

Theory Z stipulates that not only management but workers should be in a position to have an understanding and knowledge of the resources available to the organization as well as the problems and challenges facing it (Horine, 1995). Problem-solving should be a cooperative venture, with both workers and administration working together for the common good (the organization) in solving the problem(s). To this end it is necessary that workers play an integral role in the establishment of the objectives and goals of the organization or program. Workers who have a say in the establishment of objectives/goals tend to work harder to realize them.

Quality Circles

The essence of Quality Circles is that productive, effective, and efficient performance of the workforce (as well as change) is best when it comes from within rather than being imposed from the outside. To accomplish this, quality circles involve small groups of individuals, all working on similar tasks and toward common objectives, who meet on a regular basis. The periodic meetings are held to address common problems and challenges within the organization and to suggest ways to address them.

Frequently, in an effort to facilitate the group interaction, increase two-way communication, and foster trust, an outside leader is often utilized. The objective is to prevent and solve problems, problems that face those individuals who face similar tasks and have similar responsibilities. The process goes on through frank and democratic discussion. The method involves "give and take," a willingness to accept the ideas of others as well as to be open (being a risk-taker) in one's dealings with others. This participatory style of management can be traced to Japanese industry, which has used it successfully for many years.

Total Quality Management

The "customer is always right" concept is an important facet of Total Quality Management or TQM. TQM, as a management style or principle, involves educated, motivated, and caring employees/workers whose primary goal is quality in all that they do. Customer satisfaction is critical to the TQM concept. Developed by a U.S. businessman, W. Edwards Deming (1900–1993), TQM was popularized in Japan following World War II. In that country, businesses that implemented this stratagem experienced tremendous financial success (Mawson, 1993).

In recent years, TQM has received equal acclaim here in the United States in a wide range of businesses, both service- and product-oriented. Even in the realm of education TQM has its strong proponents as many of the principles or concepts are applicable in the not-for-profit sector. Crucial to using TQM to do business are 14 essential principles or concepts (U.S. Office of Personnel Management, 1991). These principles are presented in Box 3.1.

Similar in some ways to quality circles, TQM involves employees working together for the common good of the organization, i.e., maintaining quality in all that the organization and the workers are involved in *and* meeting the needs of the customers. Teamwork and quality control are key concepts in TQM. Care and respect for the organization, coupled with a desire to provide for quality service and quality products for the customer, remain essential elements within TQM. However, the greatest challenge with TQM is attempting to change human behavior. TQM is not about mastering technical skills. Rather, it is the change in how one perceives one's own role within an organization and how one perceives others, including the all important "customer" (Hillkirk, 1993).

BOX 3.1

Fourteen Principles of Total Quality Management (TQM)

1. Establish a constant organizational purpose or role in satisfying customers
2. Commit to the new quality control philosophy
3. Cease inspection of the final product or service, but seek improvement in the process instead
4. Disregard the cost in securing the best quality in organizational resources
5. Continually improve the process of providing goods and services through statistical analysis of performance data
6. Institute training and development programs for employees
7. Select leaders who enable people to excel rather than directing or punishing worker behavior
8. Drive out employees' fears about asking questions, seeking assistance, or making mistakes, or they will continue to do things wrong or not at all
9. Eliminate barriers between organization work units to eliminate conflicting competition, or one unit may cause performance problems for another
10. Eliminate organization slogans and targets for workers, and let them create their own
11. Eliminate numerical quotas, because they do not account for quality or methods
12. Encourage pride of workmanship by acknowledgment of intrinsic excellence and elimination of management's standards of performance
13. Encourage retraining and self-improvement through education in new methods, teamwork, and statistical techniques
14. Take action so the organization's management and all employees can create the new quality system

Employee empowerment is a key concept with TQM. They are encouraged to seek out problems and difficulties and then to solve or eliminate them. Deming is quoted as saying that "People are entitled to joy in their work and a sense of ownership" (Hillkirk, 1993, p. 1-B). TQM involves attempting always to improve in one's efforts, using hard data for important decision-making, attempting to satisfy one's customers, all the while working with others in a wholesome, teamlike atmosphere and involving everyone in the effort to achieve such goals. If TQM is to work, it is important that both management and employees fully understand the concept of TQM and adopt the concepts or principles underlying it. TQM is not a "quick fix" for an ailing organization or business.

Management by Objectives

Management by objectives, or MBO as it has become known, is a popular method of viewing the planning process. In order to experience success managers and employees work in a collegial fashion and establish agreed-on objectives. Everyone then manages, administers, and works in light of these objectives. Peter Drucker (1954) became famous after the release of his best-selling book, *The Practice of Management,* in which he introduced his theory of management by objectives.

Managerial objectives, in order to be meaningful, must be realistic and obtainable. If they are not, then the objectives can prove to be a hindrance to the motivation of those working within the organization. However, an important element in the practice of management by objective is the cooperative interaction among those individuals (managers and employees) who are affected by the objectives, criteria, or expectations. MBO aids in the analysis of objectives and goals. Although the process can indeed be time-consuming, the outcomes are frequently worth the extra efforts (Clegg & Chambliss, 1982).

Maslow's Hierarchy of Needs Theory

This theory attempted to identify and differentiate between various types of needs of individuals on a hierarchical basis (see Figure 3.3; Davis, 1994). These five different needs, in the order of importance, are: (1) basic safety and physiological needs (food, shelter, warmth, rest, and sex); (2) security or safety needs (protection against danger, illness, property and income loss, and uncertainty); (3) social needs (belonging, acceptance, friendship, and understanding); (4) self-esteem needs (pride, achievement, self-respect, and status); (5) self-actualization needs (self-fulfillment, self-satisfaction, and self-realization).

According to this theory individuals are naturally concerned first with the needs on the low end of the hierarchy before being concerned with those needs at the top. In other words, human beings are first and foremost concerned with insuring that their physiological needs are met before being able to be concerned with other needs, such as those associated with self-actualization or self-esteem. Once those needs at the lower end of the hierarchy have been met, then individuals can concentrate on needs higher in the hierarchy.

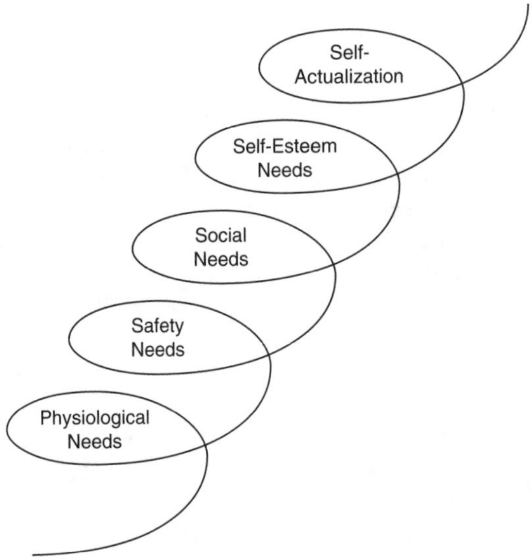

FIGURE 3.3 Maslow's Hierarchy of Needs

McClelland Motivation Theory

This theory supports the position that there are three essential "motivators" for workers. The first is the need for high achievement by individuals. The second is the need for affiliation, and the third is power, power over individuals, processes, and things. Davis (1994, p. 103) observes that "McClelland's research points out that the best managers rate high in their need for power and low in their need for affiliation."

Preference–Expectancy Theory

In his book, *Work and Motivation* (1964), Victor Vroom described Preference–Expectancy theory, theorizing that motivation is connected to what he refers to as "preference" and "expectancy." In this concept, rewards are intricately interwoven with specific, identifiable behavior and particular work performance. *Preference* relates to what an individual would like to occur, while *expectancy* "is the subjective probability of what will happen if certain behavior patterns are followed" (Bridges & Roquemore, 1992).

Motivational Reinforcement Theory

This theory of motivation in management deals with the connection between positive reinforcement and desired behavior (Skinner, 1976). The reinforcement can take the form of various types of rewards, including verbal appreciation, recognition, encouragement, and the bestowing of honors and accolades, as well as tangible prizes and compensation such as raises, promotion, and increased responsibilities. Positive reinforcement, when associated with specific types of behavior, tends to motivate and encourage that behavior. Negative reinforcements, on the other hand, tend to discourage those behaviors.

Conclusions

Competent sport managers need to be well-grounded in various philosophies of life, of their profession, and of management. Having a well-grounded personal and professional philosophy aids in making timely and appropriate decisions. It is also important for sport managers to understand how different administrative styles can affect working relationships with others as well as the workplace climate. Finally, understanding the historical perspective of management thought, as well as the various managerial theories, can aid the inexperienced as well as the experienced manager in the world of sport business.

REFERENCES

Blake, R. R. and Mouton, J. S. (1978). *The new managerial grid.* Houston: Gulf Publishing.

Bridges, F. L. and Roquemore, L. L. (1992). *Management for athletic/sport administration: Theory and practice.* Decatur, GA: ESM Books.

Clegg, C. C. and Chambliss, G. (1982). Management by objectives: A case study. *Journal of Physical Education, Recreation and Dance, 53*(4), 45–46.

Davis, K. A. (1994). *Sport management: Successful private sector business strategies.* Madison, WI: Wm. C. Brown and Benchmark.

Drucker, P. (1954). *The practice of management.* New York: HarperCollins.

Hillkirk, J. (1993, July 26). Manufacturers take quality lead. *USA Today,* p. 2-B.

Hillkirk, J. (1993, December 21). World-famous quality expert dead at 93. *USA Today,* pp. 1-B, 2-B.

The history of management thought: A study guide for administrative core, Unit 1. (1974). Brockport, NY: State University of New York Press.

Horine, L. (1991). *Administration of physical education and sport programs* (2nd ed.). Dubuque, IA: Wm. C. Brown Publishers.

Jensen, C. R. (1992). *Administrative management of physical education and athletic programs.* Philadelphia, PA: Lea & Febiger.

Mawson, L. Marlene. (1993). Total quality management: Perspectives for sport management. *Journal of Sport Management,* 7(5), 101–106.

McGregor, D. (1960). *The human side of enterprise.* New York: McGraw-Hill.

Mooney, J. D. (1931). *Onward industry.* New York: Harper & Brothers.

Ouchi, Wm. (1981). *Theory Z: How American business can meet the Japanese challenge.* Reading, MA: Addison-Wesley.

Parkhouse, B. L., Ed. (1991). *The management of sport—Its foundation and application.* St. Louis, MO: Mosby YearBook.

Plunkett, W. R. and Attner, R. (1994). *Introduction to management* (5th ed.). Belmont, CA: Wadsworth Publishing Company.

Skinner, B. F. (1976). *About behaviorism.* New York: Random House.

Stier, W. F., Jr. (1995). *Successful coaching—Strategies and tactics.* Boston, MA: American Press.

Tillman, K. G., Voltmer, E. F., Esslinger, A. A., and McCue, B. F. (1996). *The administration of physical education, sport, and leisure programs.* Boston: Allyn and Bacon.

U.S. Office of Personnel Management. (1991). Federal Quality Institute. Federal total quality management handbook: *Introduction to total quality management in the federal government.* Washington, DC: U.S. Government Printing Office.

Vroom, V. H. (1964). *Work and motivation.* New York: John Wiley and Sons.

DISCUSSION AND REVIEW QUESTIONS

1. Describe your philosophy of life.
2. How would you describe yourself, at the present time, in terms of operating in a particular style? Why?
3. Why should you, as a sport manager, vary your administrative style at different times and in different situations? Provide examples.
4. Cite some significant occurrences that have taken place in earlier times and have had a profound influence on modern-day managerial thought and practice.
5. Explain how McGregor's theory X and Y might have an effect on a sport manager's administrative style.
6. If you, as a sport manager, wanted to follow the tenets of Total Quality Management, provide examples of decisions you might make and actions that you might take that would be consistent with TQM.

SECTION TWO

The Processes of Sport Management: Developing Competencies

CHAPTER

4

The Processes, Roles, and Competencies of Sport Managers

Image is very important for any sport program.

CHAPTER OBJECTIVES

After reading this chapter you will be able to:

- Describe the basic processes of management;
- Explain the different types of jobs and positions available within a variety of sport and sport-related organizations;
- Specify 10 responsibilities typically assumed by sport managers;
- Be familiar with specific computer software applicable to sport businesses;
- Understand the importance that perception plays in dealing with people and in businesses;

- Acknowledge the importance of being a Renaissance person as a sport manager;
- Define the Diamond Concept of Management;
- Appreciate that graduating from a college in sport management is only the first step in a long process of developing competency in the management of sport.

The Essential Processes of Management

Seven essential processes for managers (leaders) were identified by Gulick and Urwick in 1937: (1) planning, (2) organizing, (3) staffing, (4) directing, (5) coordinating, (6) reporting, and (7) budgeting. These processes became known by the acronym POSDCoRB. Later, three additional processes were identified: (1) recording, (2) facilitating, and (3) evaluating (Stier, 1994). And, in 1995, yet another essential process with which every manager must be involved was identified, that of prioritizing. As a result of these additions, the acronym stands for 11 essential managerial processes, PPOSDCoRRFEB (see Figure 4.1) (Stier, 1995, p. 158). Each of these processes is described briefly below and is dealt with in greater detail in subsequent chapters.

Planning

Everyone with management responsibility should be involved in the process of planning. Planning prevents the manager from "flying by the seat of one's pants" (Stier, 1995, p. 158). Planning can involve personnel, goals and objectives, and tactics and strategies, as

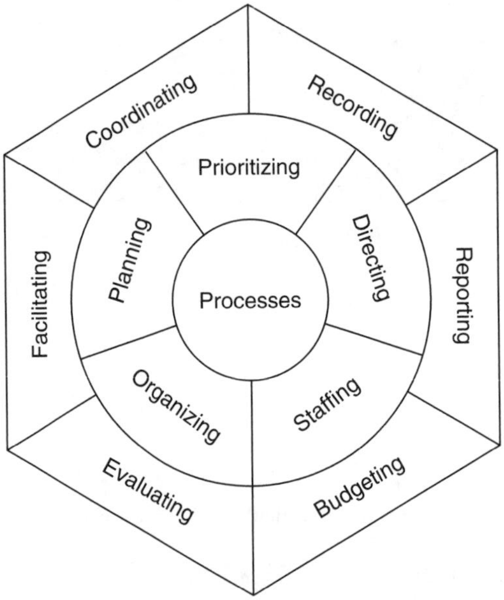

FIGURE 4.1 The Processes of Management

well as resources. Planning also involves establishing goals and assessing where one is and where one wants to be.

Planning may be thought of as both "everyday planning" as well as "strategic planning." Everyday planning, as the name implies, deals with anticipating what needs to be done on a day-to-day basis. Strategic planning implies a more complex type of planning associated with a longer time frame, a more structured approach as well as a larger perspective of the objectives and goals being sought. Lumpkin (1997, p. 38) defines strategic planning as "a formal, continuous process of making decisions based on internal and external assessments." A ten-step approach to strategic planning was proposed by Bryson (1995, p. 23):

1. Initiate and agree on a strategic planning process;
2. Identify various organizational mandates;
3. Clarify the organizational mission, priorities, and values;
4. Assess the external and internal environments of the entity in an effort to identify its strengths, weaknesses, opportunities, challenges, and limitations;
5. Identify the essential strategic issues that the entity faces in the pursuit of its mission;
6. Formulate strategies to manage these issues (5 above);
7. Review and adopt the strategic plan(s);
8. Establish an effective and efficient organizational vision;
9. Develop an effective and efficient implementation plan and process;
10. Continually review, assess, and reevaluate the strategies implemented as well as the actual strategic planning process itself.

Concept 69: Always Plan for the Worst-Case Scenario, in an Effort to Prevent Problems from Happening.

In order to prevent the "management by crisis" syndrome, sport managers must be concerned not only with the present but with the future as well. Adequate planning frequently prevents many problems from occurring and often reduces the negative consequences of those problems that do arise. Managers, as part of their planning process, should anticipate the worst-case scenario and then plan to prevent it from happening or plan to mitigate the negative consequences of its occurrence.

Concept 70: Learn from the Mistakes and Successes of Others, and Plan Accordingly.

When planning, be sure to learn from others, both from their successes and their failures. Managers do not have sufficient time in a lifetime to learn only from their own mistakes. They must avoid pitfalls associated with their managerial responsibilities and one way this can be achieved is to learn from the experiences of others, both through personal observation and from professional reading and study.

Fans can play a major role in the excitement associated with sport.
David Steele, Photographer.

Prioritizing

It is very important that sport managers be skilled in prioritizing those tasks and responsibilities that face them. Simply put, *prioritizing* means recognizing that there are some tasks that are more important than others and that some tasks must be completed before others. Prioritizing can be associated with tasks, objectives, goals, individuals, and resources.

> **Concept 71:** Time Is One of the Most Important Resources Available to the Manager; It Must Never Be Wasted.

Prioritizing is closely associated with time management. Because time is one of the most important resources available to the manager, it is imperative that it not be wasted. To waste time, or any other important resource or asset, is a cardinal sin for the administrator or manager. Time is one thing that is not replaceable. When it is gone, it is gone forever. Prioritizing one's time is an essential element of skilled management.

Organizing

Every manager must be personally and professionally organized as an individual, as a professional, and as a leader of others. In addition, successful managers are capable of organizing others, as individuals and as members of small and large groups.

Concept 72: Highly Skilled Sport Managers Must Be Personally and Professionally Organized As Well As Capable of Organizing Others.

Finally, one's organization must be thoroughly structured so that all components within the entity are operating at peak efficiency in an effort to reach agreed-on objectives and goals. Being a skilled organizer means that the individual is aware of available resources and is capable of using these resources or assets where they will be best utilized.

Staffing

Because management involves working with human beings, it is essential that the sport manager be highly competent in staffing the organization with highly qualified staff, both paid employees and volunteers. Staffing involves the assignment of qualified individuals to specific tasks or responsibilities. It also involves the total area of personnel management, which includes all actions, from the initial solicitation of potential employees, the interview process, eventual hiring, training, assigning, assessment, promotion, and pay raises to eventual outplacement from the organization.

Concept 73: Staffing Involves Working with Both Paid Employees As Well As Volunteers.

Staffing is a very important and essential process, one that the competent manager will pay the closest attention to at all times. Staffing can have tremendous impact on the organization and its ability to adequately function and realize its mission(s). A significant number of the problems found within organizations can be traced to difficulties with individuals working within that entity. Most of these problems can be prevented if proper steps are taken within the staffing (personnel) process.

Directing

Directing involves making others aware of what needs to be done, what needs to be accomplished. Sport managers must be capable of directing the energies and efforts of others toward activities that will result in positive results. Directing also includes advising others in a variety of different areas as well as overseeing the activities of people as they perform their responsibilities. Managers can provide direction for both individuals as well as small and large groups and for the overall organization.

Coordinating

Tasks, people, and objects need to be coordinated if the sport manager is to be successful and organization's goals are to be realized. Like the proverbial juggler who must keep three, four or five different bowling pins or balls in the air, the skilled sport manager must be willing and able to juggle many things at the same time. The sport manager must coordinate the activities of many people, numerous activities, and innumerable objects, all the while keeping in sight the eventual goal of the organization.

Concept 74: In Today's Complex Sport World and Complicated Society the Process of Coordination Is Absolutely Essential.

The administrative process of coordination in today's complicated society and complex world of sport is so important that it is doubtful that effective and efficient sport management is possible without it. Sport and sport-related activities have become too big, too complex, not to require an exceptional level of coordination in their implementation. From the seemingly simple tasks associated with the conduct of a high school conference track championship meet to the more complicated tasks involved in the New York City Marathon, there are innumerable tasks, "things," and people to be coordinated. If proper coordination is lacking, the result is often a catastrophe.

Reporting

An important and ongoing process within any organization is that of reporting. This means keeping others informed of what is taking place. This involves keeping abreast a wide range of individuals, not the least of whom is one's immediate superior.

Concept 75: In Sport Management One Must Always Keep One's Superiors Informed of What Is Taking Place; Don't Surprise Your Superiors.

Not all reporting involves keeping your boss(es) abreast of important developments and information. There are numerous other instances in which a sport manager must be able to report facts, information, intentions, and opinions to others (individuals and groups). However, the most important person or persons to whom the sport manager must keep up-to-date is one's immediate superior(s). Surprising one's boss(es) is not the way to make friends and influence people.

Recording

Keeping timely and appropriate records is closely associated with adequate reporting. Without accurate records it is more difficult, if not impossible sometimes, to be able to make appropriate reports to others. The types of records that should be kept will vary with the type of organization and the specific responsibility that the sport manager has assumed. However, financial records, records of accidents, contracts, names of donors, names of ticket holders, are only a few that might be appropriate in any given organization.

Concept 76: Appropriate and Accurate Records Provide a Historical Snapshot of What Has Taken Place, and Can Guide Future Decision-Making and Actions.

One of the reasons why keeping accurate and timely records is so important is that such data enables managers and leaders to make correct assumptions and appropriate decisions for the future. Without such data, the sport manger is indeed "flying by the seat of the pants" and is often forced to rely on anecdotal information rather than hard data.

Facilitating

Sport managers are facilitators in the sense that they frequently operate in the help or assist mode. One role of any sport manager, regardless of the type of sport entity one is involved with, is to help others do their tasks, to help others accomplish their jobs, to enable others to achieve their objectives.

Concept 77: Managers Must Remain in the Help Mode as Facilitators of Others within Their Organization.

Toward this end, managers need to assume an unselfish attitude when working with others, especially those for whom they are responsible. This ability to help one's staff, whether they are paid or volunteers, is part of the leadership function. This process of facilitation can involve, but not be limited to, the removal of specific obstacles and allocation of additional resources, as well as opportunities for additional education and training.

Evaluating

Evaluating encompasses three dimensions. First, assessing one's own capabilities, abilities, and accomplishments. Second, evaluating the efforts, effectiveness, efficiency, and results of others, both in and outside of the organization. And, third, evaluating the progress of the organization or entity itself as well as its programs and activities.

Concept 78: The Process of Evaluation Is an Ongoing One.

The process of evaluation should not usually be a one-shot deal. Rather, evaluation is an ongoing process in which periodic and consistent measurement is taken of how either an individual is performing or how well an organization itself is operating. Both subjective and objective criteria may be used in the evaluation process, although most personnel evaluations now include at least some element of objective measurement.

Budgeting

Planning for income and expenses is only part of the budgeting process. Accounting for how the money is collected and how it is spent are both important elements of budgeting. Two key words associated with the budgeting process are (1) *accountability,* and (2) *security.* Managers in charge of budgets are held accountable for the handling of the monies as well as for the security of the funds. Finally, in some situations the general process of budgeting might also include the responsibility for generating sources of additional revenue (such as fundraising).

Concept 79: Problems with the Budgetary Process Can Have Disastrous Consequences for the Sport Manager.

So important is the budgetary process that any problem, any weakness discerned with any area of the budget, is reason to suspect the competency of the manager whose responsibility it is to oversee the budget itself. The budget is a powerful tool. Having responsibility for a sizable budget is a major responsibility and gives to the individual with this responsibility significant power. However, to make critical errors with any aspect of one's budgetary responsibilities is often the "kiss of death" in the world of management.

Essential Responsibilities of Sport Managers

Managers today face many and varied responsibilities in their roles as administrators and leaders. Many of these responsibilities are generic to and are assumed by the "manager" regardless of the type of organization one is employed in or the level of management the individual occupies within the entity.

Concept 80: There Are Essential Responsibilities That Sport Management Professionals Assume Regardless of Their Position or the Type of Organization.

Some of the responsibilities associated with being an effective and efficient manager include being a

1. Leader
2. Problem-solver
3. Motivator
4. Communicator
5. Disciplinarian
6. Risk-taker
7. Decision-maker
8. Teacher/educator
9. Counselor/confidant
10. Delegator

What Sport Managers Do

"Making things happen, getting things done, and achieving results is what effective management is all about" (Sattler & Doniek, 1995, p. 52). However, it sounds much easier than in reality it is, especially in modern-day organizations.

Those employed in sport do a lot of different things. Depending on their specific situation, they can be involved in a wide range of different tasks in the performance of their jobs. Naturally, the type of things that people do within an organization will depend on the organization and their job descriptions (Stier, 1988).

Concept 81: Sport Managers Can Be Involved in a Wide Range of Different Job-Related Tasks.

Listed below is a comprehensive list of the types of jobs and job-related activities that are available within various categories of sport and sport-related organizations and businesses, both nonprofit and profit entities. The categories of sport organizations and businesses have been defined broadly and arbitrarily and the list is not meant to be definitive. Nevertheless, it should provide the reader with an understanding of the range of positions (jobs) available under the umbrella of sport management as well as the general types of tasks that individual employees actually perform within each of these types of organizations.

1. College athletics (institutions within NCAA; NAIA; NCCAA; NSCAA; NJCAA): Event management, compliance/eligibility, facility management, budgeting and finance, operations, promotion, corporate and group sales and sponsorships, publicity, public relations, marketing, fundraising, tickets, transportation, sports information and media relations, academic counselor, concessions operations, game operations, and so forth.

2. Professional sports (NFL; NBA; WNBA; NHL; MLB; CFL; Arena Ball; World Basketball League; U.S. Basketball League; Major League Lacrosse League): Operations, security, sales, tickets and box office, personnel, marketing, promotion, public relations, publicity, media relations, corporate and group sales and sponsorships, event management, camp operations, game operations, concessions, souvenir/merchandise sales, transportation, budgeting, finance, and business operations.

3. Sport agencies and governing bodies (Olympics; USOC; NCAA; NAIA; NCCAA; NJCAA; National High School Federation, various state high school state athletic associations; various officials' organizations; AAU; National Sporting Goods Association): Budgeting and finance, scheduling, personnel, promotions, media relations, marketing, public relations, operations, tickets and box office, and so on.

4. Municipal and state recreation entities and federal parks (city recreation departments; county recreation departments; state recreation departments; federal parks): Promotion, publicity, personnel, sports and activity programming, grounds and facility management, budgeting, operations, scheduling, and so on.

5. Manufacturers of sporting equipment and supplies (Nike; Adidas; New Balance; Nautilus; Adidas; Etonic; Rawlings; L. A. Gear; Voit Sports; Reebok; Champion): Sales, marketing, promotions, camps, budgeting, operations, inventory, supervision, personnel, and so forth.

6. Merchandising and sales of sporting equipment and supplies (Locker Room Sports; Lady Sport Locker; Champs Sports): Sales, sales and marketing and sales training, promotions, advertising, marketing, inventory, budgeting, personnel, inventory, store management, and operations.

7. News media (daily and weekly newspapers; national publications; television stations; radio stations): Announcer, broadcaster, research and statistics, sales, writing, interviewing, marketing and promotions, operations, personnel, reporting, and technical operations.

8. Health, wellness, and fitness clubs (Gold's Gym; Bally's; Jewish Community Centers): Sales, operations, budgeting and finance, front desk operations, facilities, fitness assessment, fitness programming, sports coordinator, merchandising, personal training, and membership orientation.

9. Resort and hotel facilities (Hilton Hotels; Westin Hotels; Circus Circus; Radisson Hotels; Disney World and Disney Land; Ritz Carlton Hotels): Sales, operations, scheduling and programming, personal training, sports coordination, activity instruction, private lessons, promotions, inventory, publicity, media relations, customer relations, and so forth.

10. Specialized resorts and facilities (Vail; Steamboat Run; Sun Valley): Sales, marketing operations, instruction, personal training programming, promotions, publicity, individual and group sport instruction, media relations, facilities, and customer relations.

11. Facility/Arena/Dome Management (municipal arenas; institutional facilities; educational arenas—such as the Rochester (New York) War Memorial, Buffalo's Marine Midland Arena, Cleveland's Gund Arena, the University of South Dakota's Dakota Dome, and Pittsburgh's Civic Center): Advertising, sales, operations, scheduling, publicity, concessions, media relations, facilities, and customer relations.

Factors That Determine Success or Failure of the Sport Manager

Generally speaking, there are four general factors that have a significant effect on an individual's effectiveness within any sport or sport-related organization (see Figure 4.2). It is advantageous to have an understanding of how these factors can have an effect on one's ability to serve successfully as a sport manager, because such knowledge can be an aid to those who must negotiate the organizational maze and climb the corporate ladder of sports and sport-related entities.

The first of these factors is the individual's skill. It is important that the professional bring a wide range of personal and professional skills and competencies to the workplace. The second factor involves prior experience. What type of experiences has the manager been involved in and in what type of organizations? What has been the scope of the experience? Were the experiences meaningful, relevant, and significant? Was there substance to the experience? What part or role in the experience did the individual play? Were the experiences successful or were they failures? Did the individual learn from the experiences?

> **Concept 82:** With a Wide Range of Experiences the Sport Manager Frequently Does Not Have to Reinvent the Wheel When Facing New Challenges.

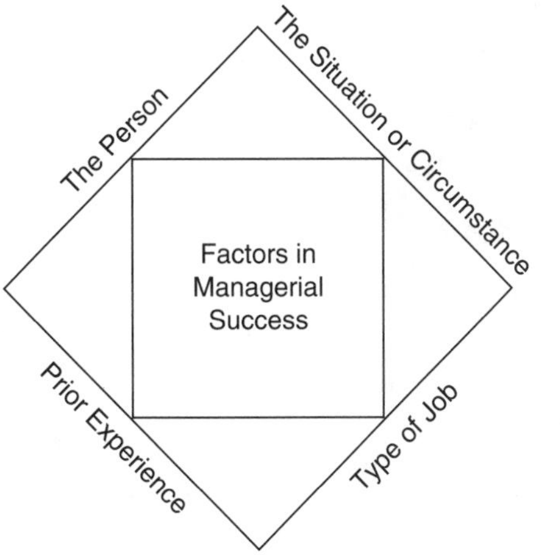

FIGURE 4.2 The Diamond Concept of Management

One of the advantages for a person with a wide range of meaningful experiences is the ability to learn from them. One is able to grow professionally and personally from experiences, both good and bad. Thus, experience—successful as well as unsuccessful—can help the sport manager in future situations and circumstances by applying the general principles and concepts learned to new circumstances and making appropriate and timely decisions.

The third factor that can have a significant impact on a person's success or failure in any organization is the type of job. What type of position or job is it? What skills and competencies are required to do the job, to accomplish the tasks, and to complete the mission? What is the level of the position? What type of organization is it? Is it a health club, a high school, a big-time university, a professional sport setting, a Fortune 500 corporate health facility? The type of job as well as the level of the position can have immeasurable impact on the effectiveness and efficiency as well as ultimate success of the manager.

The fourth and final factor that can affect the effectiveness of any manager is the situation or circumstance surrounding the job or position. Is the situation such that what is needed is a manager to maintain the status quo? Is the job or organization in desperate need of a turn-around artist? Are the circumstances such that drastic expansion and growth (change) is on the horizon and a true visionary is needed? Is there a financial crisis looming? Is there a political morass hidden in the wings?

Being successful as a sport manager in any job or position, in any type of organization, requires that the professional employee have an understanding of all four of these factors. The person not only must possess specific skills and competencies but also should have had meaningful experiences. In addition, the individual must discern the requirements of the job or position itself and determine whether there are any special circumstances or situations that may affect the likelihood of success in that position.

Teams in northern climates face challenges from the weather—special indoor practice facility of the New York Buffalo Bills.
Scott Berchtold, Photographer.

Skills and Competencies of Sport Managers

> **Concept 83:** Managerial Success in Sport Management Is Dependent on Possession of Skills and Competencies.

Success as a manager or administrator is dependent on efficiently utilizing specific techniques and employing special tactics that have proven to be effective in management and organizational situations. An aphorism in the world of management is that there are three distinct types of managers: Those who make things happen, those who watch things happen, and those who are left wondering what happened (Stattler & Doniek, 1995).

As a would-be effective, efficient, and successful manager, one needs to be able, capable, and willing to develop specific managerial skills. There are a number of general skills and competencies that all successful managers and administrators seem to demonstrate to one degree or another. These skills need to be demonstrated by almost all sport management professionals. In fact, these fundamental managerial skills are highly prized regardless of the specific type of organization in which one is employed or the type of position one holds.

> **Concept 84:** Regardless of the Specific Management Job One Holds or the Type of Sport Organization One Is Associated with, the General Skills and Competencies Needed Are Very Similar.

If you become a sport manager or administrator there are at least 10 very specific competencies and skills that are very important for continual success within the sport entity. Being an effective and efficient manager is a difficult assignment. Not everyone can be successful. It takes dedication, skills, competencies, and commitment. Studying the management of sport can help one develop these necessary skills, competencies, and attributes.

The 10 Essential Administrative Skills

Katz (1955) identified three essential attributes or skills of administrators: technical, interpersonal, and conceptual. Basic skill, dedication/commitment skills, and image skills are three additional categories of managerial skills identified by Stier (1994) as being necessary for sport managers. A year later Stier (1995, p. 165) added "the essential skills of adaptability, leadership, professionalism, and vision if the professional sport manager is to be a well-rounded, talented, able, and conscientious professional" (see Figure 4.3).

Basic Skills

Basic skills are those competencies that any well-educated member of this society would possess. Men and women involved in sport management should be able (1) to think logically, (2) to write skillfully and creatively, (3) to speak clearly and convincingly, (4) to listen attentively, (5) to be well read in terms of both professional and general literature, (6) to be knowledgeable as well as appreciative of the arts, and (7) to be generally proficient as a contributing member of both today's and tomorrow's society. Those individuals who possess basic competencies "are able to comprehend, analyze, synthesize and interpret accurately and in a timely fashion what they hear, observe, and experience" (Stier, 1995, p. 166).

Concept 85: The Sport Manager Should Not Be Distinguishable from Other Professionals within Our Society by One's Lack of Basic Skills, by the Lack of Basic Competencies, That Would Be Expected of Any Reasonably Intelligent and Educated Professional.

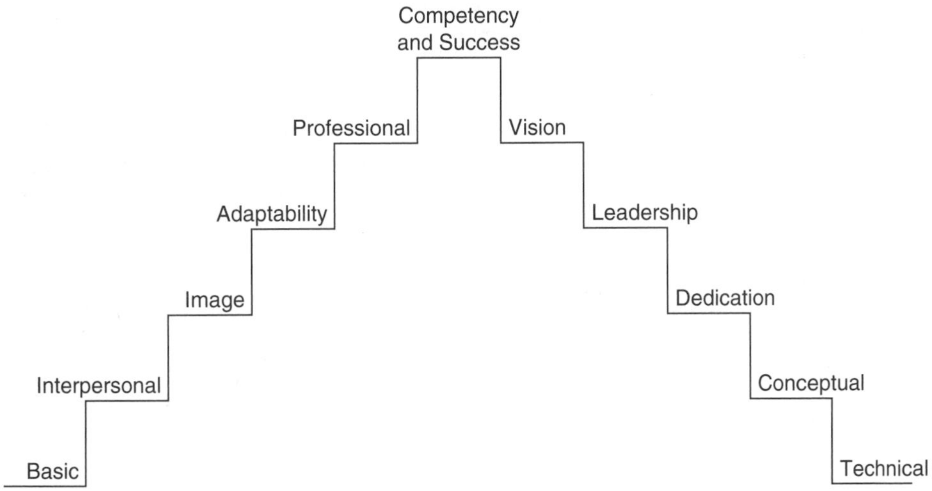

FIGURE 4.3 Ten General Administrative Skills for Sport Managers

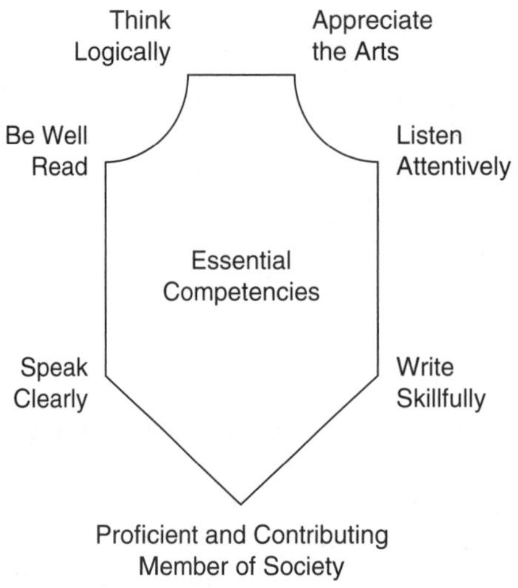

FIGURE 4.4 The Need for Essential Skills

Sport managers usually interact with a wide range of individuals in the conduct of their business, so it is imperative that they possess an adequate repertoire of basic skills that enable them to deal with and relate to others in an acceptable, appropriate, and all too often, sophisticated fashion (see Figure 4.4).

Technical Skills

There are numerous technical skills that must be mastered by the modern sport manager. With society and business so intertwined with the technological age it is obvious that computer competency is an absolute must for anyone desiring to make a career in the business of sport.

Specific Computer Competencies. Although the computer skills needed by sport managers today depend on their responsibilities, there is general agreement that to be deemed computer literate in the twenty-first century one needs to be competent in the following areas:

1. Word processing, utilizing software such as Microsoft Word, Lotus Word Pro, WordPerfect;
2. Database, utilizing software such as Microsoft Access, Lotus Approach, Wall Data Salsa for the Desktop;
3. Spreadsheet, utilizing software such as Microsoft Excel, Lotus 1-2-3, Corel Quartro Pro;
4. Presentation, utilizing software such as Microsoft PowerPoint, Astound, Scala MultiMedia MM200, or Corel Presentations;

5. Desktop publishing, utilizing software such as Adobe PageMaker, Microsoft Publisher, QuarkXPress, Broderbund Print Shop, I publish, or Adobe FrameMaker;
6. Photo editing, utilizing software such as Adobe Photoshop;
7. Graphics and drawing, utilizing software such as *Visio* Standard, CorelFlow, *CorelDraw, Micrografx* Graphics, Adobe Pagemaker, and QuarkXPress;
8. Illustration and design, utilizing Adobe Illustrator, MetaCreations Expressions, or Macromedia FreeHand;
9. Professional image editor, utilizing Adobe Photoshop, MetaCreations' Painter, or Paint Shop Pro;
10. Communications, being able to utilize e-mail, fax, the Internet, and the World Wide Web (WWW) (with a browser such as the Netscape Navigator, Microsoft's Explorer, or Shockwave Flash Plug-in);
11. Search engines, utilizing HotBot, Infoseek, Yahoo, or Excite;
12. Business accounting, utilizing software such as Intuit QuickBooks Pro, Peachtree Complete Accounting, or M.Y.O.B. Accounting;
13. Illustration and image editing, using Adobe Systems Photoshop for Windows, Adobe Systems Illustrator, or Fractal Design Painter;
14. Personal finance, utilizing Quicken Deluxe, Microsoft Money, or Turbo Tax Deluxe;
15. Project manager, utilizing SureTrak Project Manager, Microsoft Project, or Project Scheduler;
16. Personal Information Manager, utilizing Lotus Organizer GS, Starfish Sidekick, or Microsoft Outlook;
17. Personal image editor, utilizing Microsoft Picture It, Kai's Photo Soap, or Adobe Photo Deluxe;
18. System utilities, utilizing Symantec Norton Utilities, Helix Nuts & Bolts, or CyberMedia Oil Change;
19. Antivirus software, utilizing Symantec Norton AntiVirus, McAfee VirusScan, or PC-cillin;
20. Web page publisher, utilizing Microsoft FrontPage, NetObjects Fusion, or SoftQuad Hotmetal Pro.

Additionally, there are special software packages that are integrated and provide the user with several software applications bundled together. For example, applications for word processing, database, spreadsheet, presentation and communication are bundled together into one package with all of the software applications integrated so as to be used together.

1. Microsoft Office Professional, containing (among other applications) Microsoft Word, Access, PowerPoint, Excel, and Schedule;
2. Lotus SmartSuite, containing (among other applications) Lotus 1-2-3, Lotus Word Pro, Freelance, Approach, and Organizer;
3. Coral Office Professional, containing WordPerfect, Quartro Pro, Presentations, Flow Chart, ATT World Net, Starfish Software, Internet Sidekick, Inso Quicm, and View Plus.

There are also graphics suites that "are to designers what office suites are to businesspeople" (Graphics suites, 1997, January). Graphics suites typically include draw and paint programs, graphics utilities, and a great deal of clip art. Three outstanding graphics suites include:

1. Micrografx's ABC Graphics Suite 95
2. Corel Graphics Pack
3. CorelDraw

Finally, there are several software packages created specifically for sport management applications. One of the first examples of such a software package was the Paciolan system created by Paciolan Systems. This software package includes applications for a variety of tasks facing the modern sport manager, such as ticket office operations, accounting and budgeting, and fundraising. In fact, 85 of the 107 division I-A intercollegiate athletic programs in this country utilize the Paciolan software system.

The University of West Virginia's graduate program in sport management, under the leadership of Dr. Dallas Branch, was the first (1992) institution in the United States to utilize the complete Pociolan software system as part of its professional preparation program for future sport administrators at the master's level. In 1996 Ohio University's master's program, under the direction of Dr. Keith Ernce and Dr. Andy Kreutzer, became the second institution to incorporate this software system in the preparation of future sport managers (Werfelmann, 1996).

Concept 86: The Type of Technical Skills to Be Mastered Is Dependent on the Type of Job One Has and One's Duties and Responsibilities.

There are numerous other technical skills that one might need to develop competency in depending on the person's specific responsibilities and duties. These include, but are not limited to, the following areas: ticket operations (box office), legal aspects (contracts), telecommunications (phone systems), audiovisual equipment, risk management, fitness assessment, teaching/training, statistics, scoreboard operations, facilities and grounds, security, sales, broadcasting, budgeting and finance, scheduling, personnel, marketing, promotions, fundraising, transportation, concessions operations, inventory, and repair of specialized equipment.

Interpersonal Skills

Sport managers deal with people, both inside and outside of the sport organization, and in dealing with people one must be highly skilled in working with and relating to a wide range of individuals as well as small and large groups of people. Doing so requires expertise and experience in interpersonal skills. More professional employees in sport fail because of their inability to demonstrate competency in interpersonal skills than for any other single reason (Stier, 1986).

Concept 87: Sport Managers Should Strive to Develop Positive Working Relationships with Everyone, both In and Outside the Sport Entity.

Possessing interpersonal skills enables one to work productively (efficiently and effectively) with others; to gain their confidence, trust, respect and loyalty; to motivate others; as well as to lead others. Because sport managers must work with and through people, those who demonstrate greater skill in doing so will typically experience more sustained success than those who do not.

Conceptual Skills

Conceptual skills refer to the ability to understand the bigger picture of any situation. The opposite of showing conceptual skill is for an individual to operate as if possessing tunnel vision. Many managers need to be detail persons, some more so than others. However, they simultaneously must be capable of viewing any given situation in light of a more global (total) perspective.

Professionals must not have blinders on and be concerned only with their own world or "fiefdom." They need to be cognizant of the whole "kingdom" if they are to be truly team players with the good of the organization as their major concern.

Concept 88: Don't Lose Sight of the Ultimate Objective or Mission of Your Organization because of Your Involvement with Your Own Specific Job or Task(s).

Too frequently young or inexperienced employees within a sport organization fail to demonstrate conceptual competency. They fail to take the "big picture" into consideration and get hung up and focused only on their own immediate area of responsibility or sphere of influence. They are concerned only with their immediate tasks, their present challenge. Less frequently, this type of poor judgment is displayed even by experienced personnel.

Adaptability Skills

Administrators and managers need to be adaptable. This is important because of the nature of the beast, the nature of people, the nature of sport, the nature of organizations. The ability to adapt, the ability to remain flexible, is a very important competency for any sport manager.

Concept 89: Things, Organizations, and People Change; Anticipate Such Changes and Be Adaptable, Be Flexible.

Seemingly everything changes as time goes on. Progress is made. Problems are solved. Rules change. Expectations are altered. Resources shift. Innovations (technological) are made. Society evolves. Needs fluctuate. Goals are refined or replaced. Managers must be capable of changing with the times and adapting to the existing situation, whatever it might be. No one would attempt to manage or administer sport organizations today exactly as they were administered just a generation ago. That is because of the differences today in any number of factors that can have a significant impact on the sport organization, its employees, and its customers.

Leadership Skills

Sport managers must be leaders. They must be capable of managing the behavior of other individuals and guiding them in their actions. They must be able to motivate others to action.

Concept 90: Leadership Competency Must Be Earned: It Is Not the Result of Merely Holding the Title of Manager or Boss.

Leadership is a skill developed and earned. One demonstrates the ability to lead, one does not lead merely because one holds the title of *manager.* The mark of a good leader is the ability to have people to do things and to get things accomplished. Competent managers lead through example as well as by giving directions or orders.

Dedication/Commitment Skills

It is not easy, by any stretch of the imagination, to be a successful sport manager or administrator. One must be personally and professionally committed to being a sport manager. One must be dedicated to the tasks at hand. Dedication simply means being willing and able to do what it takes to get the job(s) completed in terms of effort, time, and sacrifice. It also means that one's spouse (and children, if any) are willing to share this commitment and dedication.

All too frequently one must make sacrifices if one is to fulfill one's responsibilities and successfully complete one's duty. This is the point at which one's family comes into the picture. Sport managers need to have an understanding with their spouses and children in terms of the amount of time, effort, and sacrifice their jobs might entail. Being dedicated and committed to one's job or profession, however, does not mean that one must sacrifice one's family or one's family life.

Being dedicated does mean that one is committed to seeing one's tasks completed on time and at an acceptable level of quality. Being dedicated doesn't mean just working long hours or working "hard." It does imply putting in sufficient hours and enough work that one's responsibilities are fully met, and in a timely fashion. It does imply that one must work "smart," one must expend quality effort and spend quality time on task.

Concept 91: Effort Alone Doesn't Count; Results Count.

It is not merely a matter of how hard one works. It is never a matter of merely putting in many hours each day. Rather, success as a sport manager is dependent upon actually doing the job and completing the tasks in an acceptable fashion while meeting the deadlines. One shouldn't equate effort with results or competency.

Professionalism Skills

Sport managers need to be professional. They need to demonstrate those skills and competencies that mark or define professionals in our society. One such criterion is being current in one's field. Because there is so much change taking place in our society and in the world of sport and the world of business, sport employees must remain at the cutting edge in terms of knowledge and skills.

Concept 92: Sport Managers Need to Remain at the Cutting Edge of Their Discipline.

Managers cannot remain competent for long without making a conscious effort to remain up-to-date in their professional reading and by attending workshops, conferences, clinics, and lectures. It is absolutely necessary that today's sport managers remain at the cutting edge in the world of sport, in the world of business, in terms of the latest techniques, strategies, and knowledge applicable to their area(s) of responsibility.

Toward this end, managers need to consistently read the latest professional journals and books in the areas of business, sport, and sport management. Just as a physician, a dentist, or an accountant needs to remain at the forefront of the knowledge base, so too does a sport manager need to keep up-to-date in terms of knowledge, techniques, and strategies needed in the world of sport business.

Image Skills

Sport managers need not only to be professional and competent but they also need to look the part. They need to be viewed by others as competent, qualified, and knowledgeable professionals. They need to present the image of a professional in our society.

Concept 93: Perceptions Are as Important as Reality When Being Viewed by Others.

Image has to do with how one is received or viewed by others. This is closely associated with how one dresses, how one presents oneself, and how one acts. An important concept related to image is that of perception. How one is perceived by others is most important. If a sport manager is perceived by another as being unprofessional or acting in a less than professional manner, then that sport manager is indeed unprofessional in the eyes of the person holding that opinion. Even if the perception is faulty, for the person holding that opinion the perception is very real indeed.

A number of witty administrative definitions were provided by David Peltier, dean of Arts and Sciences at Ohio Northern University (author unknown, mimeograph copy, 1983) (see Table 4.1). These statements are "tongue in cheek" interpretations or perceptions of terms commonly utilized by managers within different organizations.

> **Concept 94:** Sport Managers Need to Be Competent, Caring, Experienced, Knowledgeable, and Trained Professionals, and Give That Impression to Others.

Sport managers need to be concerned with the image that they project, with the perception of themselves that others have of them. Such professionals live in a fishbowl in terms of being visible to others, both inside and outside of the sport organization. Sport managers need to project an image that will reinforce the perception that they are competent, caring, experienced, knowledgeable, and trained because one needs, in fact, to be all of these things.

Vision Skills

Competent sport managers need to possess vision. They need to be able to look to the future and anticipate how individuals, programs, organizations, and technologies might be changed or altered. Because so much in our society is changing it is most helpful if the manager can anticipate and even facilitate such change in a positive fashion in terms of one's own organization or program.

> **Concept 95:** Vision Skill Is Needed in the Sport Management Profession Lest We Blindly Go Where No One Wishes to End Up.

Anticipating change and how such change might affect, both positively and negatively, one's program and one's organization is a highly prized ability. There are numerous examples of individuals, groups, and organizations attempting to glimpse the future so as to be able to meet the challenges and needs of the future successfully.

Examples of Efforts to Look into the Future

Two such efforts in the area of curricular planning for sport management occurred in the fall of 1994 and again in the fall of 1995 at the State University of New York—Brockport. In the fall of 1994 a national conference was held in Brockport dealing with The Future of the Physical Education Profession—Survival or Extinction. At this four-day conference leaders from throughout the United States and Canada met to discuss and examine the

TABLE 4.1 Administrative Definitions (author unknown)

It is in progress: So wrapped up in red tape that the situation is almost hopeless
We will look into it: By the time the wheel makes a full turn, we assume that you will have forgotten about it too
A program: Any assignment that can't be completed by one telephone call
Expedite: To confound confusion with commotion
Channels: The trail left by inter-office memos
Coordinator: The guy who has a desk between two expediters
Consultant: Any ordinary guy with a briefcase who is more than 50 miles from home
To activate: To make copies and add more names to the memo
To implement a program: Hire more people and expand the office
Under construction: Never heard of it
Under active consideration: We're looking in the files for it
A meeting: A mass mulling by master-minds
A conference: A place where conversation is substituted for the dreariness of labor and the loneliness of thought
To negotiate: To seek a meeting of minds without the knocking together of heads
Reliable source: The guy you just met
Informed source: The guy who told the guy you just met
Unimpeachable source: The guy who started the rumor originally
A clarification: To fill in the background with so many details that the foreground goes underground
We are making a survey: We need more time to think of an answer
Note and initial: Let's spread the responsibility for this
See me, let's discuss: Come down to my office, I'm lonely
Re-orientation: Getting used to working again
Give us the benefit of your thinking: We'll listen to what you have to say as long as it doesn't interfere with what we have already decided to do
We will advise you in due course: If we figure it out, we'll let you know
To give someone the picture: A long confused and inaccurate statement to a newcomer
Forward for your consideration: You hold the bag for awhile
Approved, subject to comments: Re-do the thing
Spearhead the issue: You be the goat
Point up the issue: To expand one page to fifteen pages
The issue is closed: I'm tired of the whole affair
Let's plan our strategy: I want to tell you what to do
A coffee break: When, and where, all the decisions are made
Open-door policy: A platitude meant to pacify the multitudes
A raise: Increase in pay to help you keep up with the federal minimum wage law
We want you to utilize staff and resources fully: Everyone is going to have to work harder
I'm glad you raised that question: What are you trying to do? Embarrass me?
After every factor was explored in depth: That's the only reason we're going to give

current status in physical education as well as sport management and allied academic areas in an effort to determine what the future of these academic entities might be.

These leaders, both practitioners and educators, sought to gain insight in terms of the future for physical education, sport management, and related disciplines and consider what might be done to insure their survival in the twenty-first century. Strategies were also examined that might insure the survival and healthy growth and development of physical education, sport management, etc. (Stier, Kleinman, & Milchrist, 1995, October).

Concept 96: Visionaries Not Only Attempt to Anticipate the Future but Facilitate the Change Process As Well.

The following year another four-day national conference was held in New York. The purpose of this second conference was different as evidenced by its name, The Future of the Profession—Developing a Vision. At this gathering leaders from Canada and the United States sought to arrive at a vision or visions of what physical education, sport management, and other academic areas might be well into the next century. The visionaries at this conference sought ways to facilitate the changes affecting our profession and our programs that will take place in the future. They also examined how to guide the curricular offerings within sport management, physical education, and related areas into possible new configurations, relationships, and alliances.

All good leaders and managers are visionaries in some sense of the word. They anticipate the future. But they do more. They also plan for the future. They prepare for the future. In fact, true visionaries help shape the future (Massengale, 1995).

Mastering the Skills and Competencies Needed in Sport Management

Can the managerial skills and competencies needed by sport managers be taught? Can they be learned? Or, are successful sport managers born with the skills and competencies necessary for success in the world of sport?

Concept 97: Managerial Skills and Competencies Can Be Taught/Learned.

The answer is simple. Managerial skills and competencies may indeed be taught (Staffo, 1990). Through formal and informal educational efforts as well as through meaningful and pertinent managerial and organizational experience, individuals can significantly enhance their managerial abilities. Would-be managers can indeed become more efficient, more effective, more successful, in a variety of leadership roles, through deliberate efforts to learn, to broaden their knowledge base, and to develop both general and specific skills.

That is why numerous colleges and universities offer curricular options (preservice educational opportunities) in management as well as sport management. That is why literally thousands of businesses, including sport and sport-related businesses, provide in-service educational opportunities to their managers and would-be managers. That is why there are thousands of management consultants who conduct workshops and clinics and deliver speeches and lectures on numerous aspects of management.

Being a Renaissance Person

The Renaissance Sport Management Professional

Sport managers should strive to be Renaissance people (Stier, 1986, Spring). In reality, there are two essential aspects to being a true renaissance individual. First, there is the matter of sport management competencies. The sport management professional needs to be very knowledgeable in a range of areas and possess a variety of skills and competencies associated with the management of sport and sport-related organizations. Additionally, this person should also become an expert or near expert in one (preferably two) areas within the sport management field.

Concept 98: Sport Management Professionals Should Strive to Be Renaissance Persons, Highly Competent in Most Areas and an Expert or Near Expert in at Least One Area, Preferably Two.

An example will suffice. An employee in a minor league (AA) baseball operation might be placed in charge of the concession and souvenir operations. This responsibility requires the individual to possess very specific skills, aptitudes and expertise. However, this same individual must understand, at least in a general way, the overall operation of the organization.

Concept 99: A Bane of Sport Management Professionals Is to Possess Limited Skills, Experience, and Expertise.

Additionally, this person must also be somewhat knowledgeable in a wide range of other areas (tickets, grounds, public and media relations, promotions) within that specific baseball organization, and generally knowledgeable in terms of professional baseball and professional sports. The competent sport management employees must not be limited in their perspective or possess skills that are so specific or limited that they are incapable of successfully assuming other responsibilities within that organization or even another entity (Stier, 1990).

The Renaissance Citizen of Our Society, of the World

The second aspect of a sport manager being a Renaissance person involves a more global concept and centers around being well read and knowledgeable in a wide range of areas outside the very specific sport management domain. For example, a truly educated individual in our society must be knowledgeable in politics, literature, history, political science, sociology, psychology, music, dance, science, and other fields.

In other words, the sport management professional, if the person is to be truly educated in our society, today as well as the future, must possess a wide range of knowledge and demonstrate a high degree of specific skills and competencies, not only in the limited domain of sport management but also in the larger, more global perspective of being a citizen of our society, a citizen of the world.

One reason that sport management professionals, now more than ever, must possess more global skills, understanding, and knowledge as they move up the career ladder is that they will deal with a wide range of individuals, groups, and organizations in the conduct of their sport management business. These sport management professionals will find themselves personally and professionally involved with doctors, lawyers, salespeople, farmers, civil servants, teachers, and business persons as well as "bakers" and "candlestick makers." The sport manager needs to be able to work with and relate to a wide range of individuals, groups, and organizations in the performance of their own jobs.

As a consequence, today's and tomorrow's sport management professional must be a well-educated individual, both in terms of general education and knowledge of our society as well as the specialized knowledge, skills, and competencies associated with the world of sport management. Sport management professionals need "to exist within the real world, within our society, and must be able to represent themselves as well-rounded individuals who are bright, articulate, intelligent, educated, and refined" (Stier, 1995, p. 163).

Willingness to Learn

Another very important component of being competent as a professional within the world of sport management is being able and willing to learn. The new graduate of a college sport management program has only begun to master the skills and obtain the knowledge needed during that person's professional life. In fact, it is this ability to learn that is so highly prized today by all businesses and organizations in our fast-paced society. And it will continue to be so in the future.

Concept 100: Graduating from Any Sport Management Program Is Only a Beginning of a Lifelong Learning Process.

Yes, of course the sport management graduate will possess specific skills. But this same graduate will have to continue to learn and master additional skills on the job, throughout that person's entire professional career. If not, the career will become stagnant and others will pass that individual on the career ladder.

For example, although any sport management graduate will be expected to be computer-literate, this does not mean that the individual will be competent in the specific software application used by a new employer. Many organizations and companies use specific computer applications, and the recent graduate may be unfamiliar with that software package. However, this same graduate also possesses basic computer competencies and can learn and master the new or different software package within a reasonable amount of time.

> **Concept 101:** Sport Managers Must Continue to Learn, to Master, and to Refine Managerial Skills and Competencies.

This ability to learn is most highly prized for two simple reasons. First, no undergraduate curriculum can begin to prepare the student to be competent in every single dimension, every aspect, of the sport management arena. There is simply too much to learn in too short a time. Besides, the undergraduate professional preparation program, by definition, is supposed to prepare generalists. More specialized knowledge may be mastered at the graduate level or on the job (in-service training).

> **Concept 102:** Change Is Inevitable; Change Is the Watchword for Sport Management Professionals.

The second reason why the ability to learn is so highly valued by employers is that seemingly "everything" in our society is changing at a very rapid pace, and it will continue to do so, perhaps at an accelerated pace in the future. New ideas are being explored. New knowledge is being discovered. New products are being developed all the time. New applications, new techniques, new strategies are being studied, evaluated, and, frequently, implemented. Change is the watchword of tomorrow. If one is not able to keep up with the changes in our profession, in our society, one is simply left behind or "out in the cold."

Future Directions of Sport Management

The future of sport, of sport business, and sport management will be closely associated with advances in technology and a continued expansion of knowledge. Some of the areas in which tremendous growth will continue to occur will be in computerization and technology, facility and arena management, health, fitness, and wellness sport services, private lessons and instruction, recreational activities, competitive sports, sport merchandising, and sales. There will also be continued growth in the number of sports and sport-related activities, both in terms of actual participation and in terms of spectators. Finally, there will be increasing growth in terms of sport consumers in terms of services, products, and knowledge/information (see Figure 4.5).

Conclusions

Managerial employees in sport, recreation, and fitness programs should be effective in implementing the 11 processes (PPOSDCoRRFEB) of management in a variety of situations. In addition, there are specific skills that competent managers, regardless of their

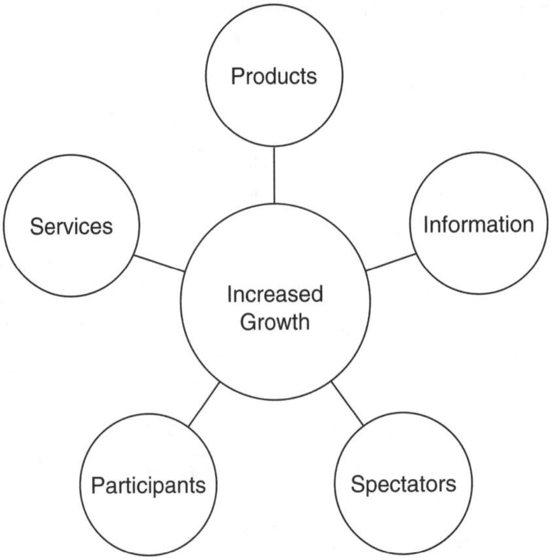

FIGURE 4.5 Potential Growth in Sport and Sport Management

position or the type of organization in which they work, should demonstrate in the course of their day-to-day activities. Most managers within the sport world assume a variety of responsibilities at various times. Truly exceptional managers are considered to be Renaissance persons in that they are experts in one or more specific areas while retaining general knowledge in many areas. It is especially important that modern managers be at the cutting edge in terms of technology.

REFERENCES

Bryson, J. M. (1995). *Strategic planning for public and nonprofit organizations.* San Francisco: Jossey-Bass.

Graphics suites have it all. (1997, January). *PC World,* p. 162.

Gulick, L. and Urwick, L. (Eds.). (1937). *Papers on the science of administration.* New York: Institute of Public Administration.

Katz, R. (1955). Skills of an effective administrator. *Harvard Business Review, 33*(1), 34–35.

Lumpkin, A. (1997). Strategic planning in health, physical education, recreation and dance. *Journal of Physical Education, Recreation, and Dance, 68*(5), 38–40, 46.

Massengale, J. D. (1995). Visionary leadership and the physical educator. *The Physical Educator, 52*(4), 219–221.

Sattler, R. P. and Doniek, C. A. (1995, October). Quantitative analysis for a better bottom line. *Fitness Management, 11*(11), p. 52.

Staffo, D. F. (1990). Should administrators be specifically trained for positions in HPER-Athletics? *Journal of Physical Education, Recreation and Dance, 68*(2), 62, 63, 78, 79.

Stier, W. F., Jr. (1986, Spring). Athletic administration: Athletic administrators expect qualities, competencies in coaches. *Interscholastic Athletic Administration, 12*(3), 7–10.

Stier, W. F., Jr. (1988, January). Competencies of athletic administrators. *The Athletic Director, 16*(2), 3.
Stier, W. F., Jr. (1990, July). Wanted: Renaissance athletic directors. *Athletic Director, 7*(3), 34–35, 42.
Stier, W. F., Jr. (1994). *Successful sport fund-raising*. Dubuque, IA: Wm. C. Brown & Benchmark.
Stier, W. F., Jr. (1995). *Successful coaching: Strategies and tactics*. Boston, MA. American Press Publishers.
Stier, W. F., Jr., Kleinman, S., and Milchrist, P. A. (1995, October). The future of physical education—Survival or extinction. *ERIC—Resources in Education*. ED383644. p. 10.
Werfelmann, J. (1996, July). *Interface, 8*(4), p. 2.

DISCUSSION AND REVIEW QUESTIONS

1. Explain the roles that the processes of management play in the management of sport entities.
2. Which of the processes of management (PPOSDCoRRFEB) seem to be the most important for you as a future sport manager? Why?
3. Select one of the 10 essential responsibilities of a sport manager and illustrate how this particular responsibility can play an important role in your efforts to serve as a sport manager in a hypothetical business situation.
4. Identify a general employment situation and specify several specific job opportunities that you might wish to pursue as a career. Why?
5. What are the four factors that affect a sport manager's effectiveness in any sport-related entity?
6. Specify computer applications (software) that might be of significant use in a sport management employment situation in which you might find yourself in the future. Be specific.
7. What, in your opinion, is the most important skill or competency of sport managers? Justify your position.
8. Explain how a sport manager should be a Renaissance person both personally and professionally.

CHAPTER

5 Leadership, Motivation, and Decision-Making

Athletic clubs and fitness centers are major players in the fitness industry.
Read Photography, Cedar Rapids, Iowa.

CHAPTER OBJECTIVES

After reading this chapter you will be able to:

- Understand the concept of leadership as it relates to business organizations;
- List the traits of effective leadership;
- Explain why not all managers are leaders;
- Differentiate between formal authority and acknowledged leadership;
- Cite the challenges of being a leader;

- Illustrate the strategies and tactics of responsible leaders;
- Identify three leadership styles;
- Define motivation as it pertains to managing sport in a complex society;
- Specify the differences between intrinsic and extrinsic motivation;
- Describe negative and positive motivational strategies;
- Be familiar with the terms *feedback* and *criticism* in terms of motivation;
- List motivational techniques, strategies, and tactics;
- Comprehend effective and efficient decision-making within a sport organization;
- Understand the basis of effective and efficient decision-making;
- Appreciate the role of decision-making in problem solving;
- Explain the importance of making exceptions;
- Justify the delegation of some decision-making to subordinates.

Leadership within Sport Organizations

Jack Welch, chairman/CEO of General Electric, and one of the most highly recognized and honored leaders of Fortune 500 companies, was selected as Manager of the Year in 1991. However, in an interview he indicated that he is not so sure that he wants to be referred to as a "manager," because people sometimes mistakenly think of a manager as one who merely "controls rather than facilitates, complicates rather than simplifies, acts more like a governor than an accelerator" ('Manager of year', p. 2-B).

As the highly effective and revered leader of General Electric, Mr. Welch wanted to make sure that his activities as leader of the corporation reflected the positive elements associated with the modern view of leadership within organizations and businesses. The goal of a modern-day manager, a true business or organizational leader, is to be able to increase the effectiveness and efficiency of the organization or business.

Concept 103: To Be an Effective Sport Manager One Must Be a Leader.

Sport managers "need to assume a dynamic leadership role" in advancing their organization (Ross & Young, 1997, p. 22). Managers, by the very nature of their role, must be able to work with people, including paid staff, volunteers, members of various constituencies, and the general public. Being successful in business, sport or otherwise, requires the same essential skills, qualities, and characteristics (Success is the same, 1988, September).

The ability to be an effective and efficient leader is an essential ingredient for the modern sport manager or administrator. In today's and tomorrow's complex sport business (profit or nonprofit) it is essential that the modern manager be a skilled leader, motivator, and decision-maker (Judd, 1995). Henry Kissinger is reported to have said that the task of management (managers) is to take *people* from where they are to where they have not been. To accomplish that, it is necessary to lead (direct), motivate (influence), and make effective and efficient decisions (to act) in critical situations.

Leadership Defined

Leadership is a universal phenomenon among human beings (Smither, 1988; Lewis, 1993). Although there are many different definitions of leadership, they all have several things in common. First, effective leaders are very good in working with and dealing with people. Second, competent leaders are able to establish appropriate goals for the organization and programs. Third, capable leaders successfully influence, guide, and direct the actions of others. Fourth, skilled leaders are successful in having goals realized. In short, most people view a person as a leader who is able to get other people to do things that will lead to a realization of some important and significant objective or objective.

Concept 104: An Effective Leader Gets the Job Done through People.

Leaders must have a constituency. This implies that leaders are involved with people (within an organization, group, or loose affiliation) who view or recognize the person as the leader. Leaders have commanding influence on others and the ability to (1) coordinate people, (2) influence and persuade people, (3) delegate responsibility, (4) guide (show) others in action and direction, (5) motivate (guide) others to action, and (6) have others do things they want done (Krause, 1981; Vick, 1989; Woyach, 1993).

Goal-Setting

Leaders (sport managers) need to be concerned with three types of goals. First, there are personal goals of the individual assuming the role of the leader. Second, there are professional goals of the leader. Third, there are the business goals of the organization within which the leader works. It is the ability to recognize and officially identify a wide variety of appropriate objectives and goals and to work towards them (with and through people) that distinguishes the true leader within any organization. True leaders guide and point the way, they get things done, they get people to work together toward a common objective(s) or goal(s).

Tactics for Effective Leadership

Michael Hammer, author of the 1992 best-selling book *Reengineering the Corporation* and the re-release of the book, *The Reengineering Revolution,* stated (only slightly in jest) that leaders should be one part visionary, one part motivator, and one part leg breaker (Balog, 1995, p. 1-B). A more useful list of tactics for effective leadership was presented by Dressler (1977, pp. 270–271):

1. Know and train yourself, study techniques of good leadership and develop your own personality to be more effective in light of your experience, training, and job.
2. Know and control your styles of leadership.
3. Know and support your people (their strengths/weaknesses) and respect differences.
4. Adapt to the characteristics and demands of each situation.

5. Act like a leader, be energetic, dress like a leader, look like a leader, think like a leader.
6. Delegate but don't abdicate, train subordinates but keep important decision-making jobs to yourself.
7. Build a strong team and encourage teamwork; use participatory techniques and develop cohesion, respect, and collegiality among team members.

Absence of Leadership

What happens when there is no leadership? Or, when there is inadequate leadership? The lack of leadership means a lack of direction, a lack of motivation, a lack of decision-making, and a lack of cohesion among those individuals working within the organization. The end result can be confusion, difficulties, problems, chaos, and, of course, the failure to realize objectives and goals (Imundo, 1991).

Formal Authority versus Acknowledged Leadership

There is a difference between what is referred to as *formal authority* and *acknowledged leadership* within the workplace. Authority can emanate from outside the individual and may be bestowed by another, like a title. Leadership comes from within the individual who is perceived as the leader. A person may be given power and authority to do something. Acknowledged leadership is when someone is perceived as a leader, not necessarily because of having been given a title or a specific responsibility, but because of who and what that person is and what that person can accomplish.

Concept 105: Not All Managers Are Leaders; All Leaders Are "Managers" of People.

Managers are different from leaders. Not all managers are leaders. However, all leaders are "managers," in the sense that leaders get things accomplished through (managing) people. Managers are appointed and, although they have a legitimate right to have the title of *manager,* they must still earn the respect of those with whom they work and interact (subordinates, peers, and others) in order to be perceived as leaders.

Leaders and the Exercise of Power

Leaders are authority figures and as such can potentially wield significant power. Managers have formal power and authority due to the position they hold. Leaders have power because subordinates and others willingly comply with their directions (Smither, 1988, p. 359). There are several sources of power (influence) that form the basis for effective leadership and frequently outstanding leaders exhibit power from any combination of the following sources:

1. **1.** Reputation power: being influential because of impressions created by one's image/reputation;
2. **2.** Knowledge (skill) power: abilities enable one to exert influence and get things accomplished;
3. **3.** Experience power: based on one's previous experiences;
4. **4.** Referent or charismatic power: power emanating from one's personality;
5. **5.** Coercive power: being able to reward and punish;
6. **6.** Legitimate power: conferred by higher authority.

Developing Skills as a Leader

People are not born leaders (Imundo, 1991). Rather, individuals can be trained, can be educated, to be leaders and managers. In fact, Staffo (1991) recommends that would-be administrators should be specifically trained for responsible administrative positions in sport.

> **Concept 106:** Leaders Are Made, Not Born.

An individual can become a better leader, a more competent manager, by working toward that goal. One needs to experience appropriate training in the areas of leadership and management. Formal education can facilitate this learning process. Also, practical experience in leadership and managerial roles are essential if one is to enhance one's skill level. Thus, practice being a leader, practice being a manager of people in everyday situations. Become involved in volunteer activities that involve leadership roles.

Desirable Traits of Competent Sport Managers and Leaders

What makes a good leader? What makes for an effective leader? What are the traits (distinguishing characteristics or qualities) that are usually present in outstanding leaders in any organization? While many leaders exhibit common traits or characteristics, there is no single trait, characteristic, or quality that automatically identifies a leader or qualifies one to be a leader.

> **Concept 107:** There Is No Single Distinguishing Trait that Automatically Makes One an Effective Leader.

Numerous authors and authorities have voiced opinions regarding skills and characteristics that leaders should possess or demonstrate from time to time in the conduct of their business. Some of the more important skills for an effective leader, according to Flamholtz and Randle (1987), are decision-making, recruiting employees and volunteers, day-to-day leadership and supervision, personnel development, time management, delegation, and planning. Other important elements of leadership are enthusiasm, self-confidence, patience, strength, ability to inspire, to motivate, and to generate faith, loyalty, trust, and confidence among subordinates (Vick, 1989; Staffo, 1991).

Of course, effective leaders also need to be capable and willing to solve problems, resolve conflict, compromise, mediate, negotiate, build teamwork (coalition-building) among subordinates and peers, be excellent communicators (and listeners), and display a high achievement drive. In short, leaders need to be competent and caring persons, willing to be responsible for others (Lewis, 1993; Stier, 1998a).

Visionary Leaders

Leaders are frequently visionaries (Hoyle, 1995). Being a visionary implies being able to work in a future timeline, to be able to anticipate things that others might not be so capable of discerning. Being a visionary implies skills and willingness to establish appropriate long-range goals, in which goals are actually dreams with deadlines. Being a visionary also involves motivating others to follow, accept, or share the dream of the leader. For example, Ray Kroc's vision for McDonald's restaurants included the visionary commitment to quality, service, cleanliness, and value. These words might very well be attributed to sport organizations interns of their goals for their customers, patrons, or constituencies (Competitive edge, 1990, p. 20).

Leaders Are Risk-Takers

Frequently, leadership involves being intuitive in terms of taking into account changes that are taking place or have taken place in society, in institutions, in organizations, and among workers (Renesch, 1992). Being a leader almost always involves making difficult and challenging decisions. Being an effective leader means that one is willing to take risks and to be viewed in an unpopular or negative light. Lets face it, being a leader is not easy. Far from it. Being a leader is difficult, challenging, frequently frustrating, and often involves risk, both personal and professional. Leadership demands courage and grit by the individual attempting to lead, direct, influence, motivate, and make decisions. It should be noted that being a leader makes it almost impossible to please everyone all of the time. Table 5.1 illustrates in a humorous fashion this challenge.

Being a Responsible Leader: Strategies and Tactics

There are numerous techniques, strategies, and tactics that have proven, in some situations and under certain conditions, to be helpful to managers who are in a leadership role.

Projecting the Image of a Leader

Leaders look and act the part. It is very important that managers project a professional appearance (image and actions) that is usually associated with leaders. Leaders are as leaders do (and look). If one is to be perceived as a leader then one must act and look the part.

TABLE 5.1 The Challenges of Being a Leader

The Leader	
1. If a person begins on time	one is a tyrant
2. If a person waits for late-comers	one is too tolerant
3. If a person requires constant attention	one is a despot
4. If a person does not care	one makes himself foolish
5. If a person assumes the spokesperson's role	one becomes a bore
6. If a person yields	one becomes unnecessary
7. If a person calls for silence	it is an abuse of power
8. If a person permits disorder	one fails in authority
9. If a person is firm	one takes himself too seriously
10. If a person is good-natured	one does not maintain one's rank
11. If a person expounds one's own ideas	people are perforce against you
12. If a person asks for a choice	one is irresolute
13. If a person is dynamic	one is worked up
14. If a person remains cautious	one is inefficient
15. If a person does everything oneself	one is conceited
16. If a person delegates	one is lazy

Adapted from "The Club President," *The Rotarian,* July 1982, by J. P. Guillon, Rotary Club of Marmande, France. Translation by Wallace Flint, Rotary Club of Hilton Head Island, South Carolina, USA.

ABWA

Wise and experienced managers practice leadership by *administering by walking around.* This means that one leads by being involved. One leads by being seen as being involved. One leads by being an integral part of the organization and its programs. One cannot hide in one's office or be aloof and be an effective leader, at least not for long. Many managers practice ABWA by physically walking around and among the "troops" as they work. This is done in an effort to find out firsthand what is going on within the organization.

Being Able to Do the Job

Being viewed as competent, as capable and worthy of the trust of subordinates, peers, and others, is an important goal. Part of being perceived this way involves being able to do one's job as a manager in an acceptable manner. Being able to produce, to be successful, as a manager will instill trust and confidence in others, essential elements for being a successful leader.

Leading by Example

Managers who are leaders tend to lead by example. This pertains to every facet of life within the organization. Leaders demonstrate their own quality by being able to do that which they expect of others in terms of professionalism, competency, dedication, and image.

Enabling (Empowering) Each Person to Reach His or Her Potential

Competent leaders (managers) are able to create situations in which others can accomplish their specific objectives and goals within the organization. Part of the leader's responsibility and obligation toward subordinates is to see that they reach their potential or near potential, at least with respect to their job responsibilities within the sport organization or business.

Being Reasonable—Not a "Stress Inducer"

Good managers are able to influence others in a positive manner without undue pressure on or stress for them. Good leaders are reasonable in their expectations of others and in their judgment of what can and cannot be accomplished within a specified time frame. The manager who gives others (and oneself) ulcers is what is called a "stress inducer." Such a manager actually impedes progress within the organization with such behavior. Stress can significantly degrade the organizational climate and can impair the workers' capacity for quality performance.

> **Concept 108:** Crisis Management Is No Management at All and Reflects an Absence of Planning and Organization.

Quality managers exhibiting good leadership skills practice stress management so that they and their subordinates (as well as peers) do not have to operate under severe adverse stressful situations or circumstances. Part of this effort involves keeping emergency projects or tasks to a minimum, and not giving employees too many tasks to perform or projects to complete in too short a time period. As stated elsewhere in this book, "crisis management" is not quality management. It is the absence of management and results from a lack of planning and organization.

"Satisfying" Both the Boss and One's Subordinates

> **Concept 109:** Most Leaders (Managers) Walk a Tightrope between Their Subordinates and Their Superiors.

When one occupies a leadership role, it is often necessary to walk a tightrope between one's superior(s) and one's subordinate(s). In many sport organizations the manager (especially at the middle management level) is responsible *for* the actions of subordinates while simultaneously being responsible *to* one or more superiors. It is important that the leader be perceived to be competent and working in the best interest of the organization and the program, by both subordinates and superiors. Thus, being able to represent oneself in such a fashion is an important skill or ability for the individual who is in this type of situation.

Concept 110: There Are No Universal Traits of Leaders.

Just as there are no distinguishing traits that automatically make a person an effective leader, there are no universal traits that all leaders possess. Leadership is truly an individual matter. Many traits, characteristics, qualities, and skills are possessed by acknowledged leaders. But these vary among individuals to such an extent that one is not able, with certainty, to say that possessing any of these will automatically make one a leader or that all leaders possess any single skill or quality.

The Leadership Process—Different for all Situations and Circumstances

The way in which a person leads, that is, exhibits skills (acts, conducts oneself, performs) as a leader is a *leadership style*. Leadership styles vary among people, just as there are many different skills that different leaders possess. *There is no one single best style or process of leadership*. No particular leadership process or style is right for all employees, in every situation and all circumstances (Chung, 1984; Woyach, 1993). Different people use different techniques, strategies, and tactics in their efforts to be leaders, and success depends on the individual leader and the others involved as well as the situation and circumstances that exist at the time.

Concept 111: Leadership Styles Vary Depending on the Situation and Circumstances.

Leadership styles "are prismatic in that they may change from situation to situation, or be described completely differently by various individuals with whom they interact" (Lewis, 1993, p. 2). Leaders can have many styles, many backgrounds, many abilities, but almost all leaders relate to and work well with other people (Chelladrai, 1990). A leader's style will reflect that person's personality, experiences, education, and training as well as the type of sport organization and the specific circumstances in which one finds oneself. Also, effective leaders do not act in the same behavioral style all the time. Different situations and circumstances call for different styles, and wise leaders know when to adjust their style, strategies, and tactics.

Three Identifiable Leadership Styles

In 1939 three different leadership styles were identified (Lewin, Lippitt, & White): (1) authoritarian, (2) democratic, and (3) laissez-faire. Democratic is viewed as being supportive while authoritarian is more directive. Laissez-faire has been traditionally viewed as the least effective of these three global descriptive terms. Again, leadership style can change in light of the circumstances and situation as well as the type of people involved. When the task at hand involves mere routine directions perhaps an authoritative style of leadership might be effective. However, in a more creative and challenging situation, leaders might choose a more participatory technique.

Motivation of Personnel within Sport Organizations

Managing Sport in a Complex Society

Today's sport managers are often faced with working in increasingly complex organizations. One of the reasons why managing in the twenty-first century will be different than in decades past is that the "diversity of today's workforce presents managers with a problem of considerable magnitude" (Green, 1992, p. 1). The employees and volunteers associated with sport businesses and organizations are different than in years past. Personnel, paid and otherwise, have different needs. They have different "hot buttons" in terms of motivation. They need to be treated as individuals within the workplace in order to take advantage of their skills and capabilities and maximize their effectiveness and efficiency. Managers must be capable of adjusting and adapting to these and other changes if they are to be effective.

Concept 112: Managing (Leading) within a Complex Society Can Be a Daunting Process.

There have been many changes in the twentieth century in terms of management thought and how motivation is viewed within businesses and organizations. The typical employee and volunteer today is a much more complex individual than in the past. Society itself is more complex. There are more pressures on managers, subordinates, and the organizations themselves. And subordinates have greater stressors (problems, aspirations, and needs) affecting their personal and professional lives and the lives of their family members. As a result of all of these changes, personnel are more demanding, more mobile, and less loyal, resulting in significant turnover.

Concept 113: The One Certainty in the Future Will Be Continued Change.

Perhaps the only thing that is certain in the future is that the future will continue to bring about change. Back in 1919, Fred Taylor, as part of his machine theory or economic man theory, postulated that money equals motivation. Today, we recognize that money is not the best motivational tool for all situations. Quite the contrary, the organizational climate or atmosphere plays a much more important role in the motivation of professionals engaged within an organization.

Motivation Defined

Many practicing professionals view a motivated individual as one who looks and acts motivated. People who are motivated are excited about the job, the challenge, the opportunities that their job, their involvement, their program presents. A motivated person thinks about and fantasizes about the tasks at hand. Such a person is frequently goal-oriented, -directed, and -driven to go beyond what is normally expected of someone in that position. In short, a motivated individual is excited about and really cares about the job and the responsibilities associated with the position.

Motivation is the force that moves people to act, to perform their jobs (Smither, 1988; Petri, 1996). Motivation can involve the changing of a person's behavior and/or the reinforcement of that person's behavior. Organizational motivation involves any external stimulus that influences, persuades, or directs the behavior of human beings. Such stimuli can include actions of individuals, policies of businesses, as well as working conditions or environments within the business or organization (Chung, 1984). A "motivational system" within an organization includes everything that is done (consciously or unconsciously) and everything that exists within an organization that influences, directs, or affects behavior within that entity (Gellerman, 1992, p. 21). Thus, motivation can be conceptualized around three factors: (1) the person initiating the motivating action, (2) the person being motivated, and (3) the situation or circumstances affecting the organization and individual being stimulated or affected.

Concept 114: Motivated Personnel Don't Necessarily Perform Well.

Although motivation is an important facet of any sport organization, it would be a mistake to think that motivated employees and volunteers always perform better. This is not true. There are numerous anecdotes as well as documented cases in which highly motivated personnel failed to perform to satisfaction. There is a difference between being motivated and being competent. If the individual is already competent and then is also highly motivated, the likelihood of superior performance is enhanced. However, it is not always a foregone conclusion that motivated employees always necessarily perform well (Green, 1992, p. 5).

Intrinsic and Extrinsic Motivation

Motivation can come from within as well as from the outside (Lawler, 1994). When a person is motivated from within it is said that the person is self-motivated or is *intrinsically motivated*. When an individual does things because that person wants to do them, because that person likes to do them, these motives are intrinsic or from within. Motivation emanating from outside the individual, from others or from the work environment or climate, is referred to as *extrinsic motivation*. Thus, when a subordinate does something because the boss tells the person to do it, we have external motivation. The reason for doing something originates from outside of the individual.

Concept 115: Managers Can Choose from Positive or Negative Motivational Techniques.

Positive and Negative Motivation

Motivation can also be thought of as either positive or negative in nature (Boyett, 1991). Positive motivation includes some type of reward or pleasurable consequence, i.e., the "carrot" approach. Negative motivation involves just the opposite, some type of unpleasant consequence or punishment, i.e., the "stick" approach. Motivation can also be physical as well as psychological in nature.

Examples of positive motivation include being praised, receiving positive feedback or criticism, an increase in salary, greater fringe benefits, a larger office, more job security, additional training or education, and so on. Negative motivation can be negative criticism, being ignored, having excessive demands made of oneself, fear of being fired, demoted, or not rehired, being embarrassed, losing privileges, receiving negative performance reviews, and so on.

Fear can have an especially debilitating effect on subordinates. Although fear can be somewhat effective in the short term, in the long run the use of fear to motivate is counterproductive, both in terms of the employee and the organization. Although employees may accept (take) such abuse from superiors, their production levels frequently drop in direct proportion to the amount of fear (abuse) heaped on them by others. People dislike being placed in a position of being fearful. If possible, such abused employees simply leave the organization.

Motivation for the Manager and Subordinates

Concept 116: Fear Is a Poor Motivator of People in the Long Run.

Motivation should be examined from two perspectives, from the vantage point of the manager and that of the subordinate. Not only do sport managers need to be motivated as leaders and doers but they need to be concerned with the degree to which their subordinates, both paid and volunteer, are motivated in their roles and with their responsibilities within the business or organization. Peter Drucker, considered by many to be a guru of management, characterizes motivation as an equation (see Figure 5.1). In this equation **M** stands for **motivation** (stimulation to action), **P** stands for **probability** (the perceived probability that the person can actually do the task or the job), and **V** represents **Value** (the benefits that can be derived from the action for the person) (Young, 1991).

M = P times V

FIGURE 5.1 Peter Drucker's Formula for Motivation

Can People Really Be Effectively Motivated?

There are many professionals who feel that it is not really possible to motivate people. They believe that all people are already motivated, at least to some extent. People are already predisposed to do some things and not do other things. Thus, the reasoning goes, managers need to redirect and focus this already existing motivation toward an appropriate end for the good of the organization.

Other experts and experienced practitioners are of the opinion that individuals can indeed be motivated, directed, and influenced to act in a predetermined fashion. These professionals hold to the belief that people can be encouraged and induced to act in a specific manner, to perform at a certain level, and to achieve identifiable objectives and goals through a variety of motivational strategies and techniques, allowing for individual differences and a variety of circumstances.

Motivation: Determining the Motives of Others

One cannot study motivation without seeking to determine the motivation of others. Weiner (1992) suggests that almost everyone functions as motivational psychologists because human beings continually seek to find out why other people think and act as they do. Motives of others are important as they shed light on the reasons why they act in a specific manner. If people are already motivated or included to act it is easier for the manager to lead them in a specific direction. Because people within organizations often have complex and competing forces tugging at them and their time, it is important for sport managers to have an insight into what stimulates others to act or not to act in any number of ways in a variety of situations and circumstances (Lawler, 1994).

Concept 117: Sport Managers Should Be Cognizant of Motivational "Ghosts."

When sport managers become involved with personnel it is wise that they become aware of the past history of the organization insofar as how people were previously treated (and reacted) within the organization. There may have been a variety of motivational tactics and strategies used as well as other factors in existence that might have caused lasting (negative and/or positive) impressions on the personnel. Current management must be aware of such lingering effects, referred to as motivational "ghosts." These motivational "ghosts" can have long-lasting and significant effects on individuals that can be much stronger than current motivators (Gellerman, 1992, p. 281).

Importance of Motivation within the Workplace

The concept of motivation is very important in terms of the overall health of the sport organization as well as the ability of the organization to reach its goals. When contemplating the hiring of new personnel, managers need to consider how motivated the potential employee is as well as the person's abilities (skills and competencies). In many instances motivation can serve as a predictor for potential success as an employee or subordinate.

Lack of Motivation

Lack of motivation can result in poor performance, indifference, absenteeism, confrontation, personal use of business facilities and equipment (copy/fax machines, computers, telephone, and office machines), turnover, and eventual failure. When there is insufficient motivation among personnel the entire interpersonal relationship climate suffers and with it the capability of the entity to function properly.

Concept 118: Managers Should Be Situationally Sensitive When Motivating Others.

Managers need to be sensitive to the situation and circumstances in which personnel work (Hoyle, 1995). Toward this end managers should exhibit flexibility and choose motivational styles to suit different situations and circumstances. Motivation can also be enhanced if leaders are able to change, adapt, or alter the circumstances and situation in which subordinates perform and work.

Staffing the Sport Organization: The Use of Motivation

Concept 119: The Use of Honey Is More Effective than Vinegar in Dealing with Personnel (McGarvey, 1991, p. 132).

Ultimate organizational success is dependent on the individuals who make up the organization. Thus, staffing is a matter of great concern for any organization. If competent and motivated personnel are hired by the sport business, the likelihood of success for the business is much greater than if less skilled people were selected. Success in staffing is dependent on four factors. First, selecting appropriate people. Second, getting these individuals aboard the organization. Third, nurturing, developing, training, and motivating these employees so that they are truly competent as staff (preventing the "warm body syndrome," Hanley, 1996). And fourth, retaining quality personnel as members of the organization's team (Loyle, 1997; Plummer, 1997).

Playing the Turnover Game

Concept 120: Success Equals Motivation, Persuasiveness, and Communication.

The key to attracting *and* retaining quality personnel is motivation. To motivate, one must be extremely skilled in communicating (see Chapter 6). One of the big challenges facing management in the world of sport is that of attrition, the loss of quality staff. This "turnover game" is a contest that competent managers must win.

Why People Leave Their Positions

A 1994 survey conducted in New York City by the national outplacement firm of Challenger, Gray & Christmas, involving some 1000 individuals, revealed that the leading reason that employees sought to leave their current positions and find a different (new) job was due to the fact that they disliked their current boss. In other words, these employees were willing to relocate simply because they perceived their boss or supervisor or superior to be incompetent as a supervisor/manager/leader/motivator (Most look, 1995).

> **Concept 121:** Happy and Satisfied (Motivated) Employees Tend to Be Better and More Efficient Workers.

The second reason, as revealed by this same study, for employees to seek a job change was that they felt underutilized in their job. In other words, their managers (leaders) failed to take advantage of their skills, motivation, and competencies. As a result, these employees were unmotivated, dissatisfied, and ungratified to the extent that they wanted a change. The lack of sufficient money was a far distant third in terms of reasons why these employees wanted to find a different company to work in.

Enjoying Quality Personnel while They Are on Staff

Over the long run it is far better to have excellent personnel on staff and then lose them to another organization (hopefully, a bigger, better entity with greater responsibility and authority) than not to have had them at all. The alternative is to have less competent people within the organization who are not attractive to other businesses or organizations. If subordinates are treated with the respect that they deserve, provided with the support and assistance (education and training) they need, and motivated appropriately and in a timely fashion, managers may not have to replace them as frequently.

> **Concept 122:** It Is Better to Have High Quality Staff and Lose Them to Other Organizations than to Have Mediocre Staff Whom No Other Organizations Would Want to Hire.

Besides, what better motivational ploy (to use with potential employees) than to say that previous personnel, who were loyal, hard-working, and extremely competent, are employed in even better positions in larger businesses with greater responsibilities and authority. For many potential and current staff members the possibility or likelihood for further professional growth can be a truly motivating prospect.

> **Concept 123:** Many People Are Motivated with the Prospect of a Better Position, More Responsibility, and Greater Authority in the Future.

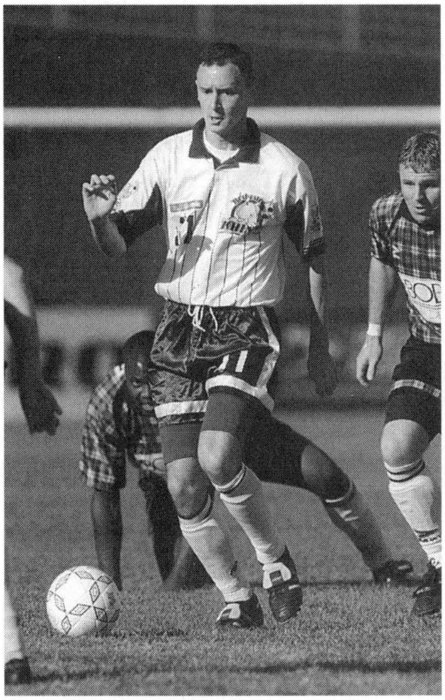

Moving through the "traffic" for the game-winning score.
James D. Lathrop, Photographer.

Job Satisfaction "Motivators"

Any number of factors within a sport organization can motivate individuals. One of the more important motivating factors or "motivators" revolves around their job satisfaction. There are seven specific job satisfaction "motivators," which include having opportunities for: (1) important areas of responsibilities, (2) increased recognition in the performance of one's tasks, (3) potential professional growth, (4) significant achievement(s), (5) professional advancement, (6) the continued enjoyment and satisfaction of the work itself, and (7) the challenge posed by the job, the tasks, and the responsibilities.

Concept 124: Cross-Train Subordinates to Give Them Diversity in Experience, Increase Their Marketability, and to Keep Them from Being Bored.

Managers should consider allowing their personnel to cross-train in different areas of responsibility within the organization. This can be a very effective motivational ploy in that such involvement can prevent boredom from setting in among these individuals. Another advantage is that such a broad range of experiences helps make the individual employee a more highly prized employee for the sport organization. Cross-training, changing jobs, or redesigning responsibilities for a subordinate also makes the individual more marketable as a potential employee for other businesses. As such, being allowed to increase one's marketability can be a significant motivational factor for some personnel.

Working with Volunteers

Concept 125: Volunteers Need to Be Motivated through Means Other than Money.

Volunteers are dedicated and interested individuals who donate their time, services, skills, and talents to the sport organization for no monetary compensation. Of course these people receive rewards or "payment" in other ways. There are almost as many different reasons why people volunteer their time to help a sport organization as there are people. Some of the reasons (potential motivational hot buttons) include, but are not limited to, the following:

1. A desire to be close to the sport organization;
2. A desire to be associated with the people who are involved in the organization, i.e., athletes, coaches, administrators, and so forth;
3. A desire to give something back to the sport or a sport organization;
4. The experience becomes an "ego trip" for some individuals;
5. They have an abundance of free time and want to spend it in a worthwhile fashion;
6. The experience of helping out a worthwhile organization in some way gives them pleasure;
7. A desire to make a difference by offering a specific skill or experience that will prove beneficial to the sport organization.

Motivating Volunteers

Concept 126: Volunteers Need to Be Trained and Motivated.

Volunteers need to be motivated just as much as any paid staff member does, but volunteers need to be motivated in different ways than the full- or part-time staff member because of their unique situation: They are not paid for their services or contributions. Money, never a good motivator of personnel, is not even a factor for the volunteer, for the obvious reason (Plummer, 1997).

Although volunteers might receive, from time to time, some kind of token reward for their efforts, contributions, or accomplishments on behalf of the sport organization, they receive no significant monetary compensation for their allegiance, assistance, or contributions to the organization. Therefore, motivation of these individuals hinges on making the volunteers feel worthwhile, making them feel that they are making a contribution, enabling them to enjoy themselves, to take pride in their activities, and making them aware that the organization and other people associated with the sport entity appreciate all of the efforts and assistance provided by volunteers.

Working with and Motivating Employees

When working with subordinates it is important to stimulate and motivate their behavior consciously in those areas that will result in better performance (Perlson, 1990, p. 10). Toward this end it is important to: (1) be clear in asking for specific performance levels, (2) use positive reinforcement (feedback) for those behaviors that are acceptable and desirable, (3) build positive professional relationships with others, (4) try to understand the point of view of others (walk in their shoes), (5) model the behavior that you desire in others, (6) expect a high level of performance, and, (7) appropriately reward competency.

The Use of Feedback and Criticism

A technique that can be very effective in motivating subordinates is the use of constructive, positive feedback. Not to be confused with negative criticism, constructive feedback is making recipients aware of how well they are performing (Wakin, 1991). The emphasis is on making improvement on those areas needing improvement and/or providing positive reinforcement for those areas of performance that are already at a high level. An important facet of providing meaningful feedback (and positive criticism) is selecting the right situation and environment to communicate one's feelings to the person.

Concept 127: Don't Embarrass or Humiliate Others When Providing Feedback.

Criticism, when used judiciously, can be positive in nature by pointing out how an individual could improve or elevate one's performance level. Criticism, to be effective, should be objective in nature and not personal. When used in a negative vein, criticism can be threatening, stifling, humiliating, and destructive. Thus, the emphasis should be on remaining in the "help mode" so that the subordinate can improve and become a more effective contributor to the overall mission of the sport entity.

Concept 128: Praise Given Publicly Can Be Doubly Effective.

An essential part of feedback is providing praise rather than criticism. Criticism for its own sake is counterproductive. When faced with the opportunity to praise someone or the way a task was performed, consider the following factors (Blanchard, 1989, p. 48). First, inform the person that you intend to compliment him or her. Second, do so as soon as feasible after the person's outstanding performance. Third, tell the person specifically what act or performance warranted the praise or compliment. Fourth, let the person know how proud or how good you feel because of what the person accomplished or did. Fifth, allow the praise to sink in, to register with the person. Sixth, encourage the individual to continue to perform at this level. And, seventh, by vocal or physical means demonstrate that you are sincere and honest in your comments.

Motivational Techniques

People are motivated for any number of reasons. The challenge facing sport managers is to discern what the needs of each subordinate are and then to coordinate or synchronize the motivational wants and needs with the needs, goals, and mission(s) of the organization or business. Just as there are different leadership styles, there are also different motivational styles. Thus, it is important for the modern sport manager to be flexible in one's motivation style depending on the situation.

Concept 129: To Motivate Another Find Out What that Person's Hot Buttons Are, and Push Them.

Managers need to find out what makes Jimmy or Jeannie "run," what motivates subordinates and peers. What are the other person's hot buttons, the motivating "triggers" that will induce or stimulate the individual to action? Remember, not all people are motivated in the same way. And, of course, managers should never assume that others are motivated in the same way that they are. To do so would be foolish and self-defeating.

One way to go about finding out the person's hot buttons or "triggers" is to ask the person, talk with the individual, carefully listen to what the person says and how it is said, and, finally, observe closely how a subordinate behaves, acts, and reacts in a variety of different situations.

There are any number of specific motivational strategies and tactics espoused by various practitioners and scholars. Young (1991, p. 36) provides six such strategies for motivating employees:

1. Communicate candidly and show others that you care about them and that they are both needed and appreciated—through positive motivation;
2. Empower employees by getting them involved in the business and the process of planning and decision-making;
3. Develop staff and volunteers professionally through in-service education, thus providing opportunities for others to develop skills and experiences (professional growth);
4. Show appreciation through approval, praise, public recognition, and other forms of positive reinforcement;
5. Manage ethically, honestly, and impartially; don't have favorites; create a trusting environment;
6. Promote workplace wellness in an effort to help alleviate stress; sponsor wellness and health programs (smoking cessation, fitness, stress reduction, etc.) for employees (Sattler & Doniek, 1995).

Motivating and Rewarding Employees within the Fitness and Wellness Industry

Eleven free or low-cost employee rewards for the fitness and wellness industry were recently highlighted in an article in *Club Industry* (Staff management, 1997).

1. Make the reward or praise of the subordinate public.
2. Offer perks, gift certificates (local merchants trade outs), or free items to the employee.
3. Give the "token money bonus," usually a brand-new, in mint condition, 2-dollar bill (or whatever the market will bear).
4. Prepare a memo and provide praise in writing to make it personalized; handwrite it or sign in color ink.
5. Award time off some afternoon or morning or allow the person to leave early.
6. Implement an in-house reward and recognition system whereby employees get points for good deeds, for going beyond the call of duty.
7. Award blue ribbons, simple blue ribbons, to a staffer to signify a job well done.
8. Provide a variety of benefits to deserving employees, perhaps involving a payroll deduction plan.
9. Make special phone calls to outstanding personnel, after hours, to congratulate them and to show your sincere appreciation.
10. Utilize an "employee of the month" reward system with a plaque displayed for all to see.
11. Take outstanding personnel, along with other peers, out to lunch to show respect for the prized employee and to acknowledge superior performance.

Concept 130: Motivational Techniques Need Not Be Overly Complicated or Expensive; Sometimes the Simplest Tactic Can Be Very Effective.

Money is no longer a great motivator in most situations. That is, money is not a universal motivator of people. Of course it depends on the person and situation, but money ceases to be a major motivator of personnel once employees are recipients of a decent living wage.

Concept 131: Money Is Not the Cure-All Motivator in Business.

Stated another way, money is not what makes a person happy on the job, but the absence of a fair and just compensation system can make the individual dissatisfied. Money can be a significant matter when the job is menial or routine, when it is boring, and when the salary is minimal. Money is of concern when the compensation is insufficient to provide a decent living wage. In this sense, the person's basic survival needs might not be met by such a minimal wage scale.

The Organizational Culture, Climate, and Working Environment

An organization's culture is described by Whetten (1984) as a set of beliefs, assumptions, values, and norms that are shared by the members in terms of how things are (or should be) done within a group. The culture, climate, or environment within the organization can go a long way to facilitate or hinder employee performance. And employee morale can be significantly affected by motivation. Morale decreases when the needs of the individual(s) are not being met. And the climate and environment of the workplace can affect motivation. Morale, in turn, has a direct relationship to performance, absenteeism, and turnover.

Managers must remember that it is to their advantage to create an environment in which workers feel motivated and even empowered. The successful business environment today is one that attracts and retains quality personnel who enjoy the challenges posed by a positive and rewarding work environment, one that fosters creativity and self-development (Young, 1991).

Concept 132: A Positive Work Environment or Climate Facilitates Employee Performance and Motivation.

The importance of a positive work environment, one in which individuals developed and worked together in teamwork, was highlighted in the General Electric studies done during the 1930s. In fact, the term *Hawthorne Effect* describes how workers were motivated not by outside, extrinsic elements, but by a psychological environment in which teamwork and self-esteem played major roles. The workers in this study continued to improve their performance because of their social dimensions and interactions. The group dynamics were such that positive reinforcement, mutual encouragement, and self-esteem became significant "motivators," and the result was increased performance. Losoncy (1995) emphasizes the importance of managers using encouragement and a pleasant work environment (physically and psychologically) to motivate personnel.

These results are supportive of numerous other studies that show that it is the work environment that is important insofar as the satisfaction level of personnel is concerned and in terms of their overall level of competency, efficiency, and effectiveness (Stier, 1987). Management must provide a healthy work atmosphere or environment. People need an environment in which they have good relations with their superiors and their peers. *They need to have an environment in which they are appreciated, supported, and nurtured, both by their peers and by management.* They need to be helped, guided, directed, and counseled.

Additionally, individuals are more productive and satisfied in an environment in which they are challenged and can experience a sense of accomplishment, a sense of importance, a sense of being an important and integral member of "the team." They need to be adequately utilized and to feel that they are properly utilized in terms of their abilities and skills. They need to be involved in the important processes within the sport firm and feel that they have a part in the overall success of the organization. They need to be given opportunities to spread their wings and to soar, to take risks, to be at the cutting edge. And they need to take pride in themselves, their work, their contributions, their organization, the programs and activities associated with the firm, and in their potential to be even better contributors to the organization and the team in the future.

Team Building

It is essential that management strive to build a team concept among all personnel (paid and volunteer) within the sport organization (Beck & Yeager, 1994). Administration involves getting things done through people. And motivation enables people to get things accomplished. Henry Ford is credited with the saying that while coming together is a beginning, keeping together is progress, and working together is success. Thus *teamwork* is essential for the smooth running of any organization, business, or program.

Ken Blanchard, author of *The One Minute Manager,* reveals that leaders or managers need to be and be seen as motivators, motivators of teams comprised of personnel ready to compete. He emphasizes that the competition is not among and between one's own workers or staff. Rather, there is teamwork among the organization's personnel and competition in the marketplace against other organizations and personnel (Balog, 1995, p. 2-B). Thus, it is important to develop the best team approach to management that one can if one is not only to survive but prosper in the competitive sport marketplace in the twenty-first century.

It is important to train the team members in order that they become highly effective. If personnel within the sport organization work as a team, things will happen. There is strength in numbers. Membership on the team should be voluntary, not mandatory. Invited individuals should be those people with whom other members of the team can work effectively and efficiently. Be sure to create clear goals and establish reasonable responsibilities for individual team members and for the group as a whole. Finally, be sure and reward both individuals and the team as a whole when performance warrants it (Eng, 1997, 5-E).

Decision-Making within Sport Organizations

Effective and Efficient Decision-Making

A maxim in management states that effectiveness is doing the right things and that efficiency is doing things right. Success is the result of doing the right things for the right reasons (Moore, 1990). In terms of decision-making, arriving at a correct or acceptable decision involves doing what is right for the correct reasons, based on one's fair assessment and interpretation of available information in light of one's philosophy, experience, and training.

Concept 133: Sport Managers Are Judged on Their Decisions.

Leadership and decision-making are intertwined in that good leaders make good decisions and good decisions are the result of good leadership (Heller, 1992). And, for sport managers/leaders, there are literally hundreds, if not thousands, of decisions that they must make on a daily basis.

Many of these decisions are of a mundane nature. However, others are of a far greater magnitude. Sport managers, supervisors, and leaders must have the ability to make good and wise decisions relative to the sport organization itself, the programs and activities sponsored by the entity, and the personnel associated with the business. Managers must exercise sound judgment and mature thinking in making correct, timely, and appropriate decisions, decisions that facilitate the work of others, coaches, athletes, support staff, volunteers, and members of the public.

Concept 134: The Ability to Make Appropriate and Timely Decisions Is a Mark of a Superior Decision-Maker (Manager).

Types of Decision-Making

Decision-making involves a sequence of events: (1) use of good judgment, diagnosis, and evaluation, (2) determination or action, and (3) implementation (Beach, 1997, p. 14). Arriving at a decision means making a bundle of interconnected activities revolving around getting information, weighing various options, receiving input from others, and then arriving at a determination of some type of action or no action at all (Guzzo, et al., 1995, p. 4). Decision-making can be an individual matter or it can revolve around a team approach to determination (Hirokawa & Poole, 1996).

Individual versus Group Decision-Making

Team or group decision-making is significantly different from individual decision-making. In *individual* decision-making the "buck" stops on the desk of the person making the decision. This is true even if input or consultation took place prior to arriving at a decision. In this instance, accountability and responsibility is quite evident—it rests with the manager or leader who made the final decision. One of the worst things a manager can do is to blame decisions that are the purview of the administrator on others, such as subordinates or (worse yet) on committees, even if there was interactive participation with subordinates.

Concept 135: Competent Managers Are Capable of Making Hard Decisions (The Buck Stops at their Desks).

In terms of *group* decision-making (such as with committees) there is the matter of the unique chemistry involving the group and the individuals comprising the group. The potential for social interactions within a group helps make decision-making different and, in some instances, more challenging than individual decision-making. Nevertheless, those involved in the team approach to decision-making often become highly motivated because they really feel part of the process. Additionally, the combined thinking, assessments, and contributions of the group members can prove to be instrumental in arriving at superior decisions. One of the problems in group decision-making is that consensus is often difficult to achieve. Additionally, accountability, in terms of responsibility for the decision, is often more difficult to determine with group decisions.

The Basis (Criteria) of Effective Decision-Making

Decisions can be arrived at on the basis of objective and/or subjective criteria. Objective criteria include tangible facts, documentation, and authenticated evidence. Subjective decisions are arrived at on the basis of the person's prior experiences, education, philosophy, feelings, and intuition. Yet, these "judgment calls" are just as defensible as decisions based on cold, hard facts (Stier, 1998b).

Decision-Making and Problem Solving

The majority of a sport manager's decisions are made in order to prevent a potential problem, solve a problem, or to resolve a problematic situation. Both objective criteria and subjective criteria should be taken into account in arriving at a timely and appropriate decision. Timely and accurate facts as well as one's prior experience, coupled with adequate knowledge, make for better decisions.

The challenges that confront sport managers when faced with difficult decisions are many. Some of these difficulties include the fact that time is frequently important. Also, all too often adequate information, facts, or data are not available (Baird, 1989). There is outside pressure as well as internal pressure put on the decision-maker to act, to act now, and/or to act in a specific manner. Uncertainty is another big concern.

There is uncertainty in terms of the consequences of various decisions. The uncertainty of the whole situation in which the decision(s) must be made can complicate the entire process (Heifetz, 1994). The complexity of the situation is another factor that can muddy the waters (Bacharach and Hurby, 1991). Finally, the people who are involved and the power that they wield are additional factors that can complicate matters for the sport manager.

Concept 136: Making Decisions Is Like Playing in a Chess Match.

When contemplating various solutions to any problem it is essential for the sport manager to look at alternatives in terms of possible consequences. In this sense, making decisions and solving problems can be likened to playing chess. Just as chess players think two, three, four, or more moves in advance—anticipating the consequences of each of their potential moves on the board—the sport decision-maker must likewise think of possible consequences of various decisions and actions. There are always choices and alternatives for the decision-maker. It is a matter of closely examining and evaluating these alternatives in light of consequences down the road that distinguishes the competent decision-maker from the incompetent.

Good Decision-Makers Are Made, Not Born

Just as leaders are made and not born, effective decision-makers are made (Guzzo, Salas, & Associates, 1995). This simply means that one can learn to make good decisions as a sport manager. Formal training or education coupled with experience in making decisions will help the sport manager become more proficient in exercising the skills involved in decision-making.

Decision-Making Involves a Real Element of Risk

> **Concept 137:** It Takes Courage to Make the Big Decisions in Critical Situations.

Decision-making is not for the faint of heart. It takes courage, it takes guts, to make many decisions. This is especially true when the decisions are not popular or when they adversely affect people. It is always true *in critical situations* when much is at stake and the consequences (positive or negative) can be significant (Stier, 1990). It is this ability to make sound and defensible decisions, decisions that are fair, just, and equitable, that makes the sport administrator so valuable for the organization or business.

Risk-taking is part of every sport manager's job. However, a key element for the sport administrator is knowing what are acceptable risks and what risks are unacceptable. This is especially true in the area of decision-making.

Making Exceptions

Many of the decisions of sport administrators will fall under the category of "making exceptions," exceptions to policy, exceptions to procedures, exceptions to practices. Yet, these decisions can all be valid and justified. As stated earlier, one of the reasons why there is a need for trained, educated, and skilled sport administrators is because organizations cannot always be "run by the book."

> **Concept 138:** In Some Instances Sport Administrators Must Decide to Make Exceptions to the Standard Operating Procedures.

There are times (many times) when individual administrators must make decisions, make exceptions, in order to expedite the process, to move forward, to make progress, and to do the *right thing*. The decision to make an exception also falls under the category of risk-taking by the very nature of the act. But extenuating situations call for deviation from the normal, standard methods of operating within the organization.

Delegating Decision-Making

The ability to delegate is an important skill in a good sport manager (Imundo, 1991; Tegper, 1995). Today, no person can do it all by oneself; the emphasis is on the team approach. *Collegiality, cooperation,* and *collaboration* are current buzzwords in the management of sport businesses and in business in general. Thus, it is important to decide which responsibilities can be successfully delegated to subordinates so that others can make decisions under your general supervision.

> **Concept 139:** Managers Should Not Attempt to Kill a Flea with a Howitzer.

There are several advantages of delegating tasks to others. First, this frees up time for managers and administrators to devote to more important and critical areas for the health and well-being of the organization or program (Horine, 1996). Second, delegating tasks to subordinates enables them to upgrade their skills and to demonstrate their increasing level of competency. Third, delegating tasks can facilitate the creation of a team atmosphere among those subordinates involved.

It is important that sport managers not squander their time, efforts, or skills doing tasks that could be done successfully by subordinates. The key concept is simple: Organizations should expend *the appropriate amount* of resources to get any job done or task accomplished, *and no more*. Organizations that waste personnel resources while accomplishing tasks when it is possible to complete the tasks with less are ineffectual at best and incompetent at worst. Managers who fall into the trap of "killing fleas with a howitzer" are wasting valuable resources, resources that could well be allocated to other important areas and tasks.

Concept 140: Administrators Have the Responsibility to Decide What Tasks Should Be Delegated to Subordinates.

There are two very important things for sport managers to remember when delegating tasks to subordinates. First, although administrators may well delegate tasks to others, it is impossible to delegate one's own responsibility for these same tasks totally. Second, one should never delegate responsibility without also providing that person with the authority and power necessary to carry out the tasks.

Delegating Some Tasks while Retaining Ultimate Decision-Making Responsibility

Some areas of responsibility within an organization can be more easily delegated than others. For example, in the area of budgets or financial affairs, some delegation of tasks is appropriate and even mandatory. However, this does not mean that the administrator in charge of this area abdicates the ultimate responsibility for the decisions made.

Concept 141: Some Decisions May Be Delegated while Others Should Not.

In the case of a university athletic director, the day-to-day responsibility for financial affairs—record keeping, data collection and reports—might very well (and probably should) be delegated to a budget clerk or an accountant. However, when it comes time to make important decisions relative to the budget (allocation of funds, priority changes, significant expenditures, etc.), it should be the responsibility of the administrator in charge to make these critical decisions.

Different Types of Delegation

There are different degrees of delegation in terms of the amount of freedom the person has who has been delegated specific tasks. For example, an athletic director (AD) at a major

Everyone "pitching in" after a rain delay—teamwork is an essential ingredient in sport management.

university delegates the task of coaching the football team to the head football coach. In this situation, the AD leaves it up to the discretion of the head coach to do the (coaching) job without undue influence. Although the head coach is responsible to the athletic director, the athletic director will not (usually) be telling the head coach how to conduct his business of coaching the team. A second kind of delegation can be seen when a health club manager (GM) or owner delegates to the sales manager the task of selling memberships for the health and fitness club. In this situation, the GM or owner is saying to the sales manager, "do the job and check with me periodically to keep me informed of your continued progress."

A third type of delegation takes place when the president of a professional football team assigns the care of the field to the head groundskeeper and instructs this individual to perform the tasks normally associated with keeping the field in tip-top shape. In this situation, there will probably be no need for any direct communication unless there are problems or questions.

The last type of delegation involves a sport administrator who is in charge of media relations and who delegates to a new college graduate the task of designing the front cover of the media book for the athletic team. In this case, the administrator doing the delegating might well indicate to the inexperienced staffer that "you decide how you would do it and run your ideas past me before any final decisions are made."

Survival Tips for Decision-Makers

Maureen Dowd, former White House correspondent, described seven survival tips involving decision-making in business (1991). These suggestions are just as appropriate for sport managers as they are for politicians and business people. This is because, in a very real sense, managers, supervisors, and administrators in sport organizations are politicians and also businesspeople. It is the nature of the beast.

1. Don't make enemies you don't have to.
2. Don't start believing you are indispensable.
3. Don't confuse what is good for you with what is good for the boss (or the organization).
4. Don't forget that you are not the boss.
5. Don't start blaming the boss if you get into trouble.
6. Don't unilaterally announce you are going to run things, rather than letting the boss announce who will run things.
7. Some must pay the price when the status and the reputation of the organization (or of the boss) begin to plummet, and anyone who has maintained a high profile will be a prime target.

Decision-making is a learned skill, an acquired competency. Managers become better in making decisions through experience, their own and the experiences of others. Decision-making is not without perils and risks. However, it can be extremely rewarding, both personally and professionally, because individuals who are adept at making appropriate decisions, who are not afraid of biting the bullet, who get the job done in critical situations are in high demand. As a result, those sport managers and administrators who can show a track record of effective and efficient decision-making have a leg up on those would-be professionals who fail to demonstrate a proficiency in this important area within the world of sport business.

Conclusions

Sound sport management is dependent on leadership, proper motivation, and timely and appropriate decision-making. Part of being an effective leader is being able to assume reasonable risks and to solicit loyalty from one's staff and one's constituencies. Being able to use a variety of motivational techniques (both intrinsic and extrinsic) in light of differing circumstances enhances the effectiveness of the leader, the sport manager. And, of course, sport managers need to be willing and able to make decisions, decisions of all kinds. Decision-making ability and a willingness to delegate appropriate tasks to others are two key elements that are trademarks of the successful sport manager. Leadership skills, motivation skills, and decision-making skills can all be learned and improved on by sport managers who are willing to work to enhance their professional competency level.

REFERENCES

Bacharach, M. & Hurby, S. (Eds.). (1991). *Foundations of decision theory: Issues and advances.* Oxford, England: Basil Blackwell.
Baird, B. F. (1989). *Managerial decision under uncertainty: An introduction to the analysis of decision making.* New York: John Wiley & Sons.
Balog, K. (1995, May 17). Coaches find fans in management. *USA Today.* p. 1-B, 2-B.
Beach, L. R. (1997). *The psychology of decision making: People in organizations.* London, England: Sage.
Beck, J. D. W. & Yeager, N. M. (1994). *The leader's window.* New York: John Wiley & Sons.

Blanchard, K. (1989, March). It pays to praise. *Today's Business,* p. 48.

Boyett, J. H. (1991, February). Iron hand or kid gloves? *Entrepreneur, 19*(2), 20–21.

Chelladurai, P. (1990). Leadership in sports: A review. *International Journal of Sports Psychology, 21,* 328–354.

Chung, K. H. (1984). *Motivational theories and practices.* Columbus, OH: Grid.

Competitive edge—Winning strategies from a pro. (1990, September). *Entrepreneur, 18*(9), 20.

Dowd, M. (1991, December 8). Survival tips within the political world of business. *Democrat & Chronicle,* p. A-3.

Dressler, G. (1977). *Management fundamentals.* Reston, VA: Reston.

Eng, S. (1997, August 25). How to build a better team. *Democrat and Chronicle,* p. 5-E.

Flamholtz, E. G. and Randle, Y. (1987). *The inner game of management: How to make the transition to a managerial role.* American Management Association.

Gellerman, S. W. (1992). *Motivation in the real world.* New York: Penguin Books.

Green, T. B. (1992). *Performance and motivation strategies for today's workforce.* Westport, CT: Quorum Books.

Guzzo, R. A., Salas, E., and Associates. (1995). *Team effectiveness and decision making in organizations.* San Francisco: Jossey-Bass.

Hanley, M. (1996, February). Develop employees. *Fitness Management, 12*(2), 32, 34.

Heifetz, F. A. (1994). *Leadership without easy answers.* Cambridge, MA: Belknap Press of Harvard University Press.

Heller, F. (Ed.). (1992). *Decision-making and leadership.* Great Britain: Cambridge University Press.

Hirokawa, R. Y. and Poole, M. S. (Eds.). (1996). *Communication and group decision makers* (2nd ed.). Thousand Oaks, CA: Sage.

Horine, L. (1996, June/July). Deciding to delegate. *Athletic Management, VIII*(4), 13.

Hoyle, J. R. (1995). *Leadership and futuring: Making visions happen.* Thousand Oaks, CA: Corwin Press.

Imundo, L. V. (1991). *The effective supervisor's handbook.* New York: American Management Association [AMACOM].

Judd, M. R. (1995). A gender comparison of competencies (traits) important for success in a college athletic administrator. *The Physical Educator, 52*(1), 8–13.

Krause, R. (1981). *Recreation leadership and supervision: Guidelines for professional development.* New York: Saunders College Publishing.

Lawler, E. E., III. (1994). *Motivation in work organizations.* San Francisco, CA: Jossey-Bass.

Lewin, K., Lippitt, R., and White, R. K. (1939). Patterns of aggressive behavior in experimentally created 'social climates.' *Journal of Social Psychology, 10, 271–299.*

Lewis, A. (1993). *Leadership styles.* American Association of School Administrators. Arlington, VA.

Losoncy, L. E. (1995). *The motivating team leader.* Delray Beach, FL: St. Lucie Press.

Loyle, D. (1997, March). Nobody's perfect. *Club Industry, 13*(4), 27–28, 30, 32, 34.

'Manager of year' shuns 'managing'. (1991, July 16). *USA Today,* p. 2-B.

McGarvey, R. (1991, May). Positive criticism. *Entrepreneur, 19*(5), 130–132, 134–135, 137.

Moore, R. B. (1990). Why take fifteen years to become an overnight success? *Learning 2001,* pp. 6–7.

Most look for new job to escape boss, survey says. (1995, January 2). *Democrat & Chronicle,* p. 3-A.

Perlson, M. R. (1990, May). The game of management. *Rochester Business Magazine, 6*(6), 10–13.

Petri, H. L. (1996). *Motivation theory, research, and applications* (4th ed.). Pacific Grove, CA: Brooks/Cole.

Plummer, T. (1997, October). Staffing for success. *Fitness Management, 13*(10), 31, 33–36, 39–40.

Renesch, J. (Ed.). (1992). *New traditions in business: Spirit and leadership in the 21st* century. San Francisco, CA: Berrett-Koehler.

Ross, C. M. and Young, S. J. (1997). Research: The key to the future of recreational sport management. *Parks & Recreation, 32*(8), 22–29.

Sattler, T. P. and Doniek, C. A. (1995, December). Worksite wellness for the health of it. *Fitness Management, 11*(13), 18, 20, 22.

Smither, R. D. (1988). *The psychology of work and human performance.* New York: Harper & Row.

Staff management. (1997, February). *Club Industry, 13*(2), 35–36.

Staffo, D. F. (1991). Should administrators be specifically trained for positions in HPER-Athletics? *Journal of Physical Education, Recreation and Sport, 62*(2), 62–79.
Stier, W. F., Jr. (1987). Competencies of athletic administrators. *The Bulletin, the Connecticut Association for Health and Physical Education, Recreation and Dance Journal, 33*(2), 4–6; Reprinted in *The Athletic Director* (AAHPERD), January 1988, p. 3.
Stier, W. F., Jr. (1990). Wanted: Renaissance athletic directors. *Athletic Director, 7*(3), 34, 35, 42.
Stier, W. F., Jr. (1998a, April 8). Marketability in the 21st century. Presentation at the national convention of the 1998 American Alliance of Health, Physical Education, Recreation and Dance, Reno, Nevada.
Stier, W. F., Jr. (1998b). *Successful coaching: Strategies and tactics* (2nd ed.). Boston, MA: American Press.
Success is the same in business or sports. (1988, September). *Athletic Business, 12*(9) 30–32, 34, 36.
Tegper (1995). *Effective delegation skills.* West Des Moines, IA: American Media.
Vick, C. G. (1989). *You can be a leader: A guide for developing leadership skills.* Champaign, IL: Sagamore.
Wakin, E. (1991, August). Give employees feedback, not criticism. Make sure feedback will have a positive effect, will do some good. *Today's Office, 26*(3) 22, 23.
Weiner, B. (1992). *Human motivation: Metaphors, theories and research.* Newburg Park, CA: Sage.
Whetten, R. W. (1984, November/December). Effective administrators: Good management on the college campus. *Change, 16*(8), 38–45.
Woyach, R. B. (1993). *Preparing for leadership.* Westport, CT: Greenwood Press.
Young, B. B. (1991, January). Motivating your employees. *Athletic Business, 15*(1), 35–38.

DISCUSSION AND REVIEW QUESTIONS

1. Why do sport managers need to be leaders?
2. Elaborate on tactics that a sport manager can utilize to be an effective leader.
3. Provide examples of the use of formal authority (or power) and acknowledged leadership within a sport entity.
4. Explain why there are or are not universal traits of leaders.
5. Is money a good motivation for employees? Explain.
6. Cite examples of intrinsic and extrinsic motivation as used by sport managers for their employees.
7. What are job satisfaction motivators? Provide examples in the sport workplace.
8. Outline a strategy for motivating both paid employees and volunteers.
9. Illustrate with an example why some decision-making and problem solving is like playing a game of chess.

CHAPTER

6 Communication and Conflict Resolution

Technology and sports—a marriage of necessity.

CHAPTER OBJECTIVES

After reading this chapter you will be able to:

- Appreciate the importance of communication in sport business;
- List the seven components of communication;
- Describe the hindrances to effective communication;
- Illustrate how feedback can lead to efficient communication;
- Value the importance of listening in the communication process;
- Differentiate between horizontal and vertical organizations;
- Cite examples of proper use of the chain of command;
- Reveal sources and signs of conflict within an organization;
- Describe techniques and strategies for preventing or managing conflict;
- Understand the role of stress and stress management in the overall health of a sport organization;
- Realize the values and shortcomings of the committee process.

Chapter 4 pointed out that possessing interpersonal relationship skills is very important for the sport manager. An integral element of interpersonal skills is the ability to communicate. Closely associated with communication competencies is the ability to deal with conflicts—preventing conflicts, managing conflicts, as well as resolving them.

Concept 142: The Ability to Communicate Is an Essential Element of Interpersonal Relationships.

Essentials of Communication

Communication is more than merely talking to someone or telling a person something. Communication can be thought of as a process in which information, facts, or concepts are passed from one person to another by means of some medium or instrumentality (Stier, 1998). Communication involves one or more of the following: writing, speaking, reading, observing, and listening (Helitzer, 1995). Many of the problems associated with communication (or lack thereof) stem from an overemphasis on the attempt at delivery and insufficient attention to the message itself, its reception, and its understanding by others.

In order for communication to take place there must be four essential elements present. First, there must be a *sender,* someone who sends or attempts to send a message. Second, there must be an *actual message* that is conveyed to another. Third, there is the matter of the *medium* used by the sender to transmit the information. Fourth, there must be a *potential receiver,* someone who is the intended or unintended recipient of the communication effort.

Concept 143: It Takes Two to Successfully Communicate.

The Sender

Communication is not possible without someone initiating the attempt (Bridges & Roquemore, 1996). The sender of communication (*message*) can be a single individual, several individuals, a group, or an organization or business (Bucher & Krotee, 1993). However, this does not mean that all communication is necessarily deliberate. In fact, messages emanating from individuals or organizations can be classified as deliberate, accidental, or incidental.

Deliberate communication, as the term implies, denotes intentional conveyance of a message to another or others. This type of communication allows the sender adequate time to consider all aspects of the message, the medium, and the potential effects the message and messenger might have on the intended receiver(s). Thus, intentional communication should be the most effective and efficient because the sender has time to consider all aspects or ramifications of the communication. However, this is not always the case, obviously. Just because one has time to consider and plan what and how to communicate does not necessarily mean that the communication will be successful.

Accidental communication is that which takes place without preplanning. It is communication without anticipation. It happens without conscious effort on the part of the sender. Nevertheless, there is a message that is sent and received, whether planned or not.

Sports are a big news item today.

Incidental communication takes place when the message received is incidental or collateral to the main message included within the communication. Incidental communication is contingent in nature, but can potentially be very important—for both the sender and receiver.

Both accidental or incidental communication messages can have far-reaching consequences for the sport manager and the sport organization. The fact that these messages are not necessarily planned in advance has nothing to do with whether they are received or how others receive them.

The Essence (Content) of the Message

Concept 144: The Purpose of the Communication Determines the Medium and Timing of the Effort.

This concept refers to the type of message and the purpose for which it is to be conveyed. Why is a particular message being conveyed? What is in the message or the communication attempt? What exactly is the purpose? Is the message one of general information? Is it motivational in nature? Is it essentially a persuasive communication? Is the purpose educational? Does the communication attempt to solicit information of some type? Or, is the communication an effort to motivate others, to a particular course of action, perhaps?

The purpose of the message can significantly affect other elements of communication. Specifically, how the communication is to be conveyed to others, when and where it is to be conveyed, and the actual form the communication takes.

Efforts at communication can range from the simplistic to the complicated and anywhere in-between. Frequently, the content of the message will dictate the sophistication level of the effort, although not always. Simplistic communication efforts are sometimes the most effective, both in terms of effort expended and the likelihood of the message being received and understood.

Concept 145: Some of the Most Effective Communication Efforts Are also the Simplest.

The Medium

How the communication is conveyed or transmitted can sometimes be as influential as the message itself. In this respect the medium (the method) can be as much of a message as the actual content of the communication effort. There are numerous communication formats or mediums. It is important that the appropriate medium be utilized in light of one's situation or circumstances. In today's technological society sport managers are not limited exclusively to pen and paper and the printed word but may take advantage of radio, television, telephones, the World Wide Web, e-mail, and so on.

Concept 146: The Medium Can Sometimes Be the Message—the Format Can Be as Important as the Message.

The significant advances in the area of printed materials developed and produced by high tech computers (and various software packages) and printers have raised the level of the "playing field" of communication to a very, very high (sophisticated) level. It is imperative that the modern sport manager be knowledgeable and experienced in these modern forms of communication. However, this does not mean that one can neglect the old fashioned way of communicating, by speaking to others.

Not all communication attempts need to be verbal (Davis, 1994). Nonverbal communication can be equally effective. Examples of such communication efforts include the printed word, computer messages, one's physical actions, and body language. Body language and the physical image that one presents to others are examples of communication that can convey a variety of messages. Often, but not always, these messages (especially with body language) are without the conscious thought or deliberate intention of the individual sending the communication. Nevertheless, body language is still a viable means of sending messages, deliberately, accidentally or incidentally.

Concept 147: The Absence of Communication Can Be a Form of Communication.

Even the absence of formal communication can be, in itself, a form of communicating. In fact, failure or refusal to communicate can send important messages to others. That is why sport managers must be careful not to be incommunicative, especially when faced with problems or in times of crisis. Such a posture is seen as a sign of weakness and even incompetence.

The Recipient(s) of the Message

All the communication efforts in the world are for naught if a receiver is not able and willing to receive the same. Thus, it is very important to consider the abilities, experiences, and characteristics of the person(s) to whom the message is conveyed. What are the distinctive characteristics of the recipient(s)? Are the persons adults? Young adults? Children? What are their backgrounds in terms of sports? How knowledgeable are they in the area of sports and/or your sport organization?

Concept 148: Know Your Audience before Communicating a Message.

One of the common problems that sport managers or administrators experience in the area of communication is that they fail to take into consideration who their intended audience might be. The message must be compatible with the recipients in terms of appropriateness, timeliness, and the level of knowledge required to understand the communication.

No one would attempt to deliver a formal speech to a large group of individuals without first ascertaining the makeup of one's potential audience in terms of the individuals' background, experience, and general knowledge of the speech's subject matter. The same care should be taken in terms of one's communication efforts with others, both individuals and groups. The concept is simple: Think before you speak, think before you write, think before you act. Everything a person does or fails to do, everything about an individual has the potential of sending various messages to others and these messages can leave lasting impressions, either positive or negative.

Concept 149: Think before You Speak, before You Write, before You Act.

Hindrances to Communication Attempts

The ability of the recipient of any message to correctly interpret what the sender intended to communicate is paramount to any successful communication (Stier, 1994, p. 61). Failure to successfully translate and understand what the sender intends can be traced to any number of factors (see Figure 6.1). For example, many words are subject to different interpretations or misinterpretations. The various interpretations may be traced to any number of factors, including different social/economic backgrounds (and cultures) of the people involved, their personal and professional experiences, and their formal education. Also, some words are just less precise in terms of their meanings than others. Careful choice of words, phrases, and sentences is a first step to clear and understandable communication.

Other factors that can play a role in making it difficult to decipher and understand a message include words that are taken out of context, varying circumstances surrounding the communication effort, the timing of the communication, the age, sex, or political dif-

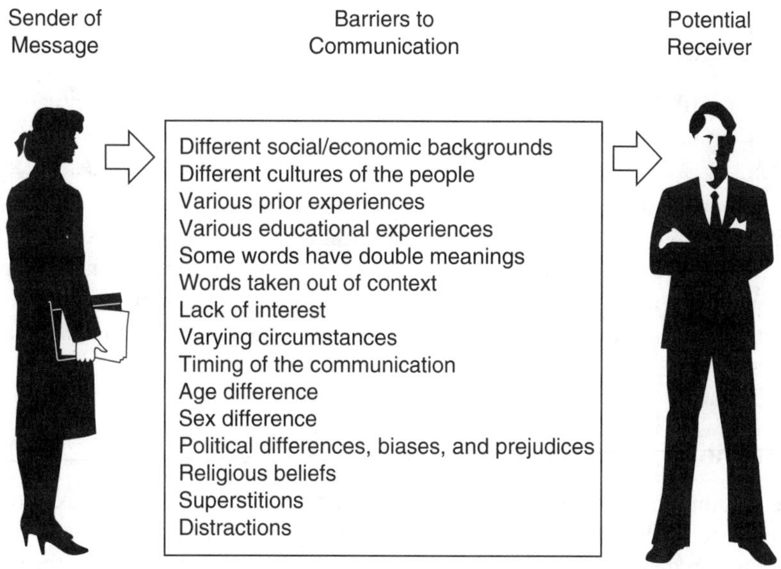

Sender of Message
Barriers to Communication
Potential Receiver
Different social/economic backgrounds
Different cultures of the people
Various prior experiences
Various educational experiences
Some words have double meanings
Words taken out of context
Lack of interest
Varying circumstances
Timing of the communication
Age difference
Sex difference
Political differences, biases, and prejudices
Religious beliefs
Superstitions
Distractions

FIGURE 6.1 Factors That Play a Part in Hindering Communication

ferences between the sender and the receiver, lack of interest by the recipient, biases and prejudices, religious beliefs, superstitions, as well as distractions such as noise (Zeigler & Bowie, 1983; Horine, 1995).

The Components of Successful Communication

Jensen (1988) identified several ecomponents that make for successful communication: (1) content, (2) clarity, (3) credibility, (4) context, (5) continuity, (6) consistency, and (7) channels of communication. Stier (1998) adds an eighth component, that of continuance (timing).

Content

Concept 150: "Fluff" Can Significantly Impede Communication.

The content of the communication effort must be accurate. If the communication involves inaccuracies or fluff there is great potential for confusion in the interpretation of the message. Thus, unnecessary elaboration, enhancement or embellishment of the facts—while seemingly defensible or even necessary to the sender—can sometimes have severe negative consequences in terms of the acceptance of the communication. Any communication that is based on inaccuracies (or exaggerations) tends to undermine the credibility of the sender and the actual message.

Clarity

Concept 151: Keep Messages Brief and to the Point; Brevity Facilitates Clarity in Communication.

The communication must be absolutely clear lest misunderstandings develop. Keeping the communication effort short and simplistic frequently helps in this regard. Keeping sentences short frequently aids in making messages clear and to the point, whereas unnecessary verbiage tends to overcomplicate matters for the recipient of the communication. Sport managers should strive to be crystal clear in their attempts to convey a message to others.

Credibility of the Messenger

The credibility of the sender of the communication has a significant role to play in the acceptance of the message. People tend to accept facts, information, and opinions from those whom they have confidence in, from those whom they trust. Thus, the individual initiating the communication attempt must be believable. And, to possess such credibility means that the person must have a track record, a reputation, for truthfulness, for honesty, for frankness, and for sincerity.

Concept 152: To Be Viewed as Credible One Must Have a Track Record of Truthfulness, of Candor, of Frankness.

This points out the advisability, if not the necessity, for the sport manager to develop trusting relationships with others if one's communication efforts are to be fully effective. Part of this building of trust or credibility involves being a good communicator, speaking

Working with the news media is an essential element of sport.

with authority, clarity, and credibility. One builds trust and credibility by being honest and forthright with others and being viewed as such.

Context of the Message

In order for a communication attempt to be effective, it is essential that the context or environment in which the message takes place be conducive to its being received and accurately interpreted. This refers to the situation in which the communication is attempted. It also refers to the timeliness or the circumstances that might have an adverse effect on the sending or the receipt of a particular message. Finally, there is the matter of the appropriateness of the message in light of the intended audience. Is the intended recipient capable of understanding the true meaning of the message under the circumstances in which the message is conveyed?

Continuity

In any communication effort(s) the ideas conveyed must be presented in a coherent fashion in order to be understood. Messages that contain disjointed concepts, disorganized facts, or irrelevant information only tend to confuse the communication effort. When communicating one should attempt to have the essential elements of the message flow smoothly together so as to be easily understood and less prone to misinterpretation. In other words, there should be organization or structure associated with verbal and written interaction.

Consistency

Consistency also refers to proper organization and structure of the communication effort but specifically addresses whether the words, information, and ideas are consistent. Lack of consistency can easily create confusion on the part of the audience. Thus, it is important that words and concepts be chosen carefully and utilized in a consistent and compatible fashion so as to present an intelligible and comprehensible message.

Channels

Without adequate means of transmitting a message, all efforts to convey ideas or information are for naught. Thus, choosing an appropriate method of channeling the message is most important. Whether the communication effort is to be made verbally (in a one-on-one situation), in written form (letter, pamphlet, signs, posters, newspapers, magazines) or electronically (phone, computer, etc.), the concept is the same. The method of distributing the message must be appropriate for the audience and the situation or circumstances that exist at the time.

Continuance of Communication Efforts

Continuance of communication refers to the time factor of such efforts. In the area of timeliness, the following factors should be considered. First, when is the most appropriate time (timeliness) for a particular message to be conveyed? Second, how long should each message be? Third, what should be the duration of the total communication effort (all messages combined)? Fourth, what should be the interval between communication efforts?

Concept 153: Timing Is an Essential Component of Effective Communication.

Sport managers, in this era, need to pay particular attention to the matter of timeliness in their communication efforts. The total effectiveness and efficiency of communication attempts can be significantly enhanced or hindered by the time factor. And knowing one's audience is a necessary prerequisite for evaluating the timeliness of the communication effort. Experience, coupled with common sense and an awareness of the essential principles of communication, will put the individual sport administrator in an excellent position to engage in meaningful dialogue with others, both individuals and groups.

One-Way versus Two-Way Communication

All communication efforts involve either a one-way attempt at conveying a message or a two-way interaction or dialogue. The type of communication (one-way versus two-way) to be attempted will determine, for the most part, the method (the medium) of conveying the message, and the timing of the attempt, as well as the actual format. For example, in one-way communication the sender of the message is doing just that, sending a message without anticipating any response from the audience (an individual or many individuals). It can involve a person-to-person situation in which an individual tells something to someone. It can also be more of a long-distance effort (involving a written or electronic message). Typically, one-way, deliberate communication is suitable for distributing factual information to large numbers of people, information that does not need a direct or immediate response. For example, advertisements, promotional flyers, and signs are all examples of one-way communication efforts (Graham, 1994).

Concept 154: Being Able to Think on One's Feet Is a Mark of an Effective Communicator in Two-Way Communication Settings.

In contrast, two-way communication involves interaction between the sender and another person, persons, or groups of individuals. In this situation communication flows both ways, back and forth, between two or more parties. Such communication is fluid. It is dynamic. It can be evolving in nature. It is frequently immediate. It can also be simplistic in nature or very complicated, elaborate, and involved. Typically, but not always, two-way communication involves verbal (voice or electronic) interaction. Less frequently, but yet commonly, it also involves the written or printed word.

Two-way communication places a great degree of responsibility on the participants to think on their feet and to react appropriately in response to what is being communicated to them. It is this ability to react to and respond or counter with an appropriate message or exchange of ideas that marks the successful sport manager. Taking time and expending the effort to understand what the other person is attempting to convey is an important element in developing competency in two-way communication. Part of this process involves being

Communicating with the general public—keeping the public informed.

aware of the background and motivation of the person with whom one is communicating or conversing with. Similarly, being able to be flexible in one's thinking and beliefs as well as communication strategies can facilitate one's communication efforts.

Importance of Feedback in Communication

> **Concept 155:** Without Adequate Feedback Meaningful Communication Efforts Are in Peril.

Feedback is vital to good communication. Feedback involves obtaining some type of reaction to one's efforts at sending a message. Without feedback one is unable to discern whether the message is being or has been received and correctly deciphered or interpreted. Good communication is just more difficult without some type of feedback. On the other hand, feedback, if utilized correctly, can greatly enhance communication.

The importance of feedback within a sport management setting can be seen when a manager delegates a task to a subordinate. It is important to seek some type of feedback in terms of verbal or physical cues from the person to whom the responsibility has been given. Does the person indicate understanding of the assigned task(s) in some fashion? If feedback is forthcoming from the subordinate, how does the sport manager know that the person truly understands what needs to be accomplished? If the supervisor doesn't obtain adequate feedback there is always a risk of miscommunication or misunderstanding with disastrous consequences.

Verbal and Nonverbal Feedback

Feedback is important both in verbal or written communication. Feedback is necessary, or at least helpful, in being able to judge the effectiveness and efficiency of one's communication efforts. Feedback can take the form of verbal acknowledgment (cues) that a message was received and understood, or that it was not. Feedback can also involve physical or body language that can convey as much if not more than verbal or written communication.

> **Concept 156:** Feedback Is Important in Both One-Way and Two-Way Communication Efforts.

Feedback is essential if one is to make suitable and oftentimes necessary adjustments, corrections, or improvements in communicating with others. Without meaningful feedback one is almost working in the dark or being blindfolded. Without feedback one cannot know with certainty how one's message is being interpreted, or if it is being received at all. Without adequate feedback, the sender of the message is at a decided disadvantage. With such feedback, however, the sender is in a much better position to structure, adjust, and time subsequent messages specifically to the intended audience. The end result is better communication, communication that adequately and appropriately conveys a message that is clearly understood by the recipient(s).

Even in one-way communication, such as in the distribution of advertisements or written materials to various constituencies or the general public, it is important to gauge the reactions of the individual(s) to whom the message(s) was (were) sent. For example, sport managers involved in promotion and public relations need to ascertain the effectiveness of their communication efforts relative to a specific promotional or publicity campaign. This type of feedback is very important in order to gauge adequately the effectiveness of prior communication (promotional and publicity) attempts.

Listening—An Essential Ingredient for Meaningful Communication

Typically, when one considers the concept of communication, the emphasis is on the person doing the communicating, the speaking, the writing. However, it is important not to forget about the art of listening. It does take two to complete the communication process. All communication efforts are wasted if there is no one listening, no one hearing, no one understanding or comprehending the message that is being sent.

> **Concept 157:** It Takes Work, It Takes Effort, to Be an Effective, Proactive Listener.

Effective communicators insure that they have a receptive audience prior to initiating communication. It is like talking over the phone. No one would speak into a phone unless they knew that someone was at the other end listening or that an answering machine was connected and ready to record any message that is left. Similarly, in real life situations, sport managers must insure that there is a person who is a receptive listener, ready, willing, and capable of understanding what is to be communicated.

Similarly, competent sport managers need to practice the art and science of being good listeners (Harris, 1994; Armstrong, 1997–1998). Just because one is a manager or administrator doesn't mean that one need not be a careful and diligent listener. To the contrary, being an excellent listener (and being perceived as such by others) can facilitate communication in two ways. First, if one really works at being a careful listener and an insightful interpreter of what another person is sharing, one is more likely to better understand and comprehend what the message is and why the sender is transmitting it. The result is that the listener is in a far better position to subsequently respond or act on the basis of the message(s) received than if the original message had been somehow garbled, misinterpreted, or misunderstood.

Concept 158: Careful Listening Reduces Misunderstandings and Misinterpretations.

Second, when an individual is perceived by another (or others) to be an *active listener,* this person is viewed with great respect and as having credibility. Thus, the resultant level of communication can often be significantly enhanced in such situations.

Potential Communication Constituencies

There are any number of differing individuals and organizations with whom the sport manager might be involved in terms of communicating. Figure 6.2 depicts some of these potential communication "partnerships," depending on the type of sport organization or business in which the professional is engaged. In reality, there are innumerable potential communication partners (individuals, groups, and organizations) with whom sport personnel must be capable of working and communicating as part of their job responsibilities. Similarly, there are countless situations and incalculable circumstances that can affect communication efforts.

Informal Communication: The Grapevine

Sport managers should pay special attention to what is commonly referred to as the "grapevine" within an organization. This refers to information communication channels that exist within any organization. Some would categorize the grapevine as the "rumor mill." Members of management should strive to remain in touch with the grapevine so as to be conscious of information being shared via this method and to be capable of using it to distribute appropriate messages or information. Sport administrators should not ignore this

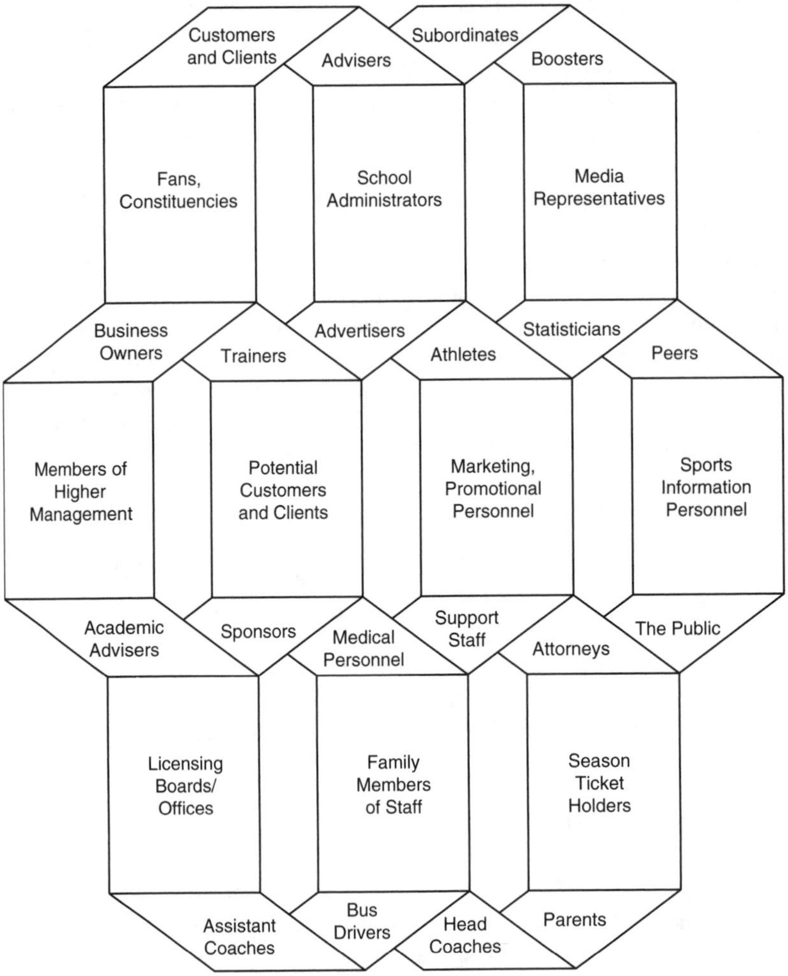

FIGURE 6.2 Communication "Partnerships"

form of internal, informal communication. Such a posture would be a severe mistake because such communication channels will exist and will be utilized by members of the organization whether management approves or not. It is better to recognize such channels and to be aware of the communication attempts utilizing the same.

Line and Staff Organizational Charts

Every sport organization has a formal structure, a structure made up of its personnel (Mason & Paul, 1988). Personnel comprise both line and staff positions. An organizational chart (see Figure 6.3) can illustrate the duties and responsibilities of and the relationships

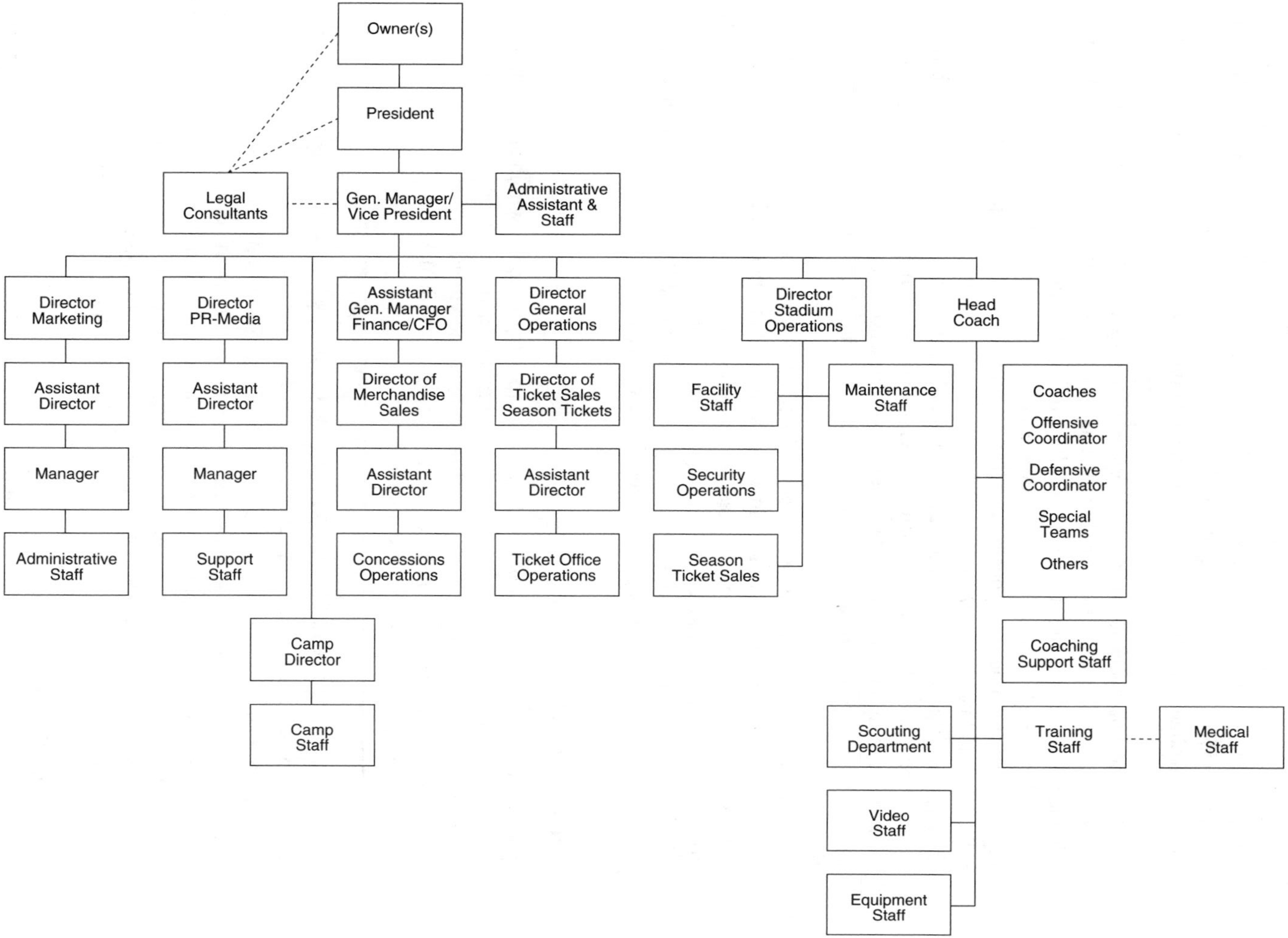

FIGURE 6.3 Organizational Chart of a Professional Football Organization

between the various members of the organization. An organizational chart can illustrate the relationships between different employees, in both line and staff positions, as well as indicate their general areas of responsibility. The structure of an organization, revealed by such a chart, can either facilitate or hinder communication among various employees and departments.

Those employees who are in line positions have direct responsibility for making decisions and assuming tasks that are directly related to the organization's primary mission(s) (Tillman, Voltmer, Esslinger, & McCue, 1996, p. 25). In a professional sports organization the coaches and general manager are examples of line personnel. Those individuals assuming a staff position have responsibilities primarily for providing support, advice, and counsel to those individuals who are line personnel. Again, in a professional sport organization the equipment personnel, the public relations office, the legal department, as well as the business or financial office, represent staff employees. When examining an organizational chart one can differentiate between a staff and a line position in that the former is represented by being placed on a horizontal position and connected to a staff position by a dotted line (see Figure 6.3).

In a professional sports organization the coaches would be considered line personnel because they are involved in the primary mission of the organization, i.e., preparing the team for competition. The employees who are involved in arranging for transportation, communication, accounting, medical, and the like, are all working in staff positions. Those who hold staff positions work in support of (and provide advice to) the personnel involved in line positions, in the primary activities of the sport entity.

Chain of Command

The concept of *chain of command* refers to the reporting structure within any organization. Viewing an organizational chart one is able to see that each subordinate "box" (representing one or more staff members) reports directly to an individual (represented by a "box" on the chart). This reporting to the next higher individual within the hierarchy of the organization is referred to as the chain of command.

Concept 159: One Should Not Jump the Chain of Command.

Within any organization it is deemed inappropriate, except in extremely unusual situations or circumstances, for individual personnel to "jump the chain of command" and bypass one's superior in an effort to communicate with an individual at a higher level within the organization. An example can clarify the situation. A groundskeeper for a professional baseball team would not normally bypass an immediate superior and go directly to the general manager to complain about one's immediate superior. This jumping of the chain of command would be deemed highly inappropriate unless there are very unusual and extenuating circumstances.

This does not mean that communication of a social nature or of a nontechnical or business nature cannot be consummated by a subordinate with an individual to whom the subordinate does not normally report or work with. It does mean, however, that there are

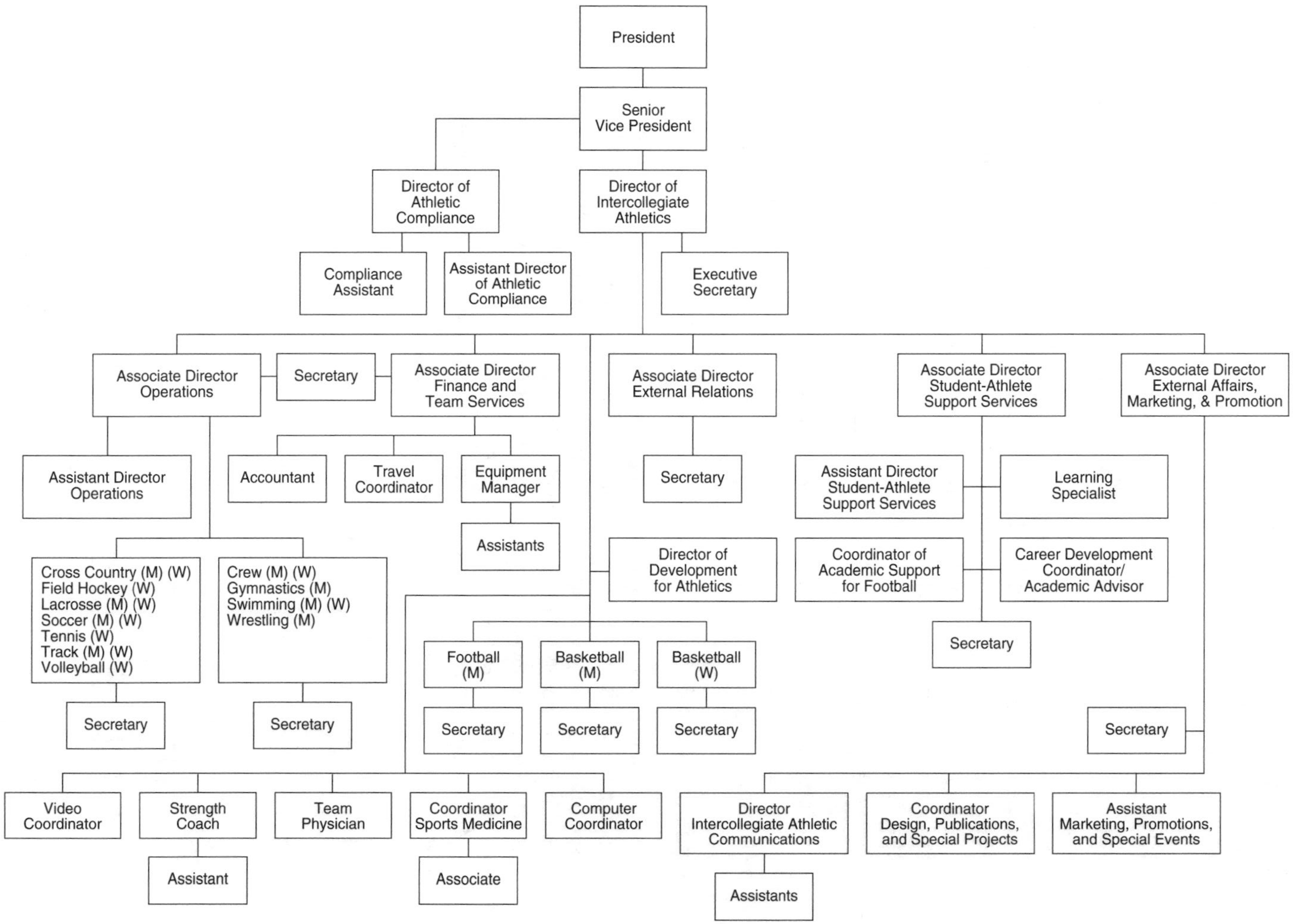

FIGURE 6.4 Organizational Chart of a NCAA Division I Athletic Program—Vertical (Tall) Organization

specific lines or avenues of communication within any organization that employees are expected to utilize in the normal course of business. These normal reporting and communication channels comprise the chain of command.

Horizontal versus Vertical Organizational Structures

Organizational structures can also be conceptualized or described as being either horizontal or vertical. Horizontal (or tall) organizations are characterized by having many layers between the top of the organization and the bottom. Figure 6.4 is an example of a sport organization with a horizontal or tall organizational structure in that there are numerous levels between the lower echelon and top management. The organization or business represented by this chart has very definite reporting channels for its employees but the chain of command involves numerous levels through which official communication must travel before it reaches members of the higher administration or senior management.

Figure 6.5 illustrates a horizontal (flat) organizational structure. As can be seen there are relatively few levels between the top and bottom personnel positions within this organization. The absence of a multitude of layers of personnel facilitates communication between and among the employees, especially between those personnel located at the bottom of the organizational structure (the rank and file) and those within the upper tiers.

Span of Control

Span of control refers to the number of divisions or departments any single administrator is responsible for within the organization. If an administrator is saddled with too many responsibilities, being accountable for an inordinate number of different divisions, departments, or areas (not to mention personnel), that administrator is susceptible to becoming ineffectual in one or more areas of responsibility. In short, an administrator in such a position can become spread so thin as to be unable to perform effectively all the duties and responsibilities that accompany such a wide span of control, over so many different and diverse areas (and personnel).

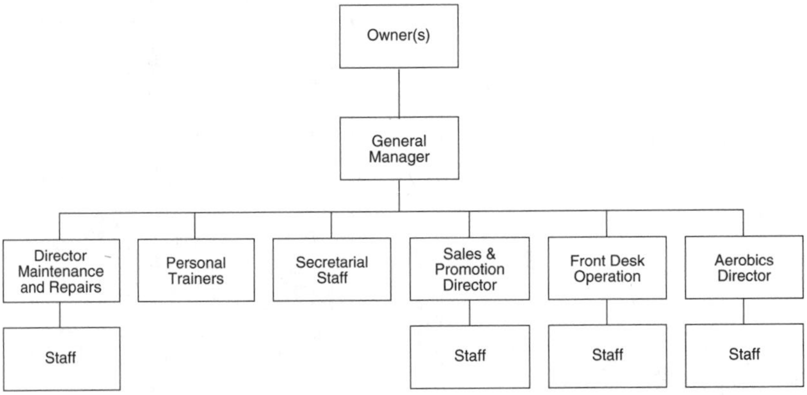

FIGURE 6.5 Organizational Chart of a Fitness Club—Horizontal (Flat) Organization

Generally speaking, it is recommended that individual managers or administrators not have more than seven to nine major departments, offices, or areas reporting directly to them. Of course, the ideal number could be less. What is appropriate for a specific sport organization or business depends on a number of factors, including but not limited to: (1) the complexity or elaborateness of the subordinate departments or offices, (2) the number of employees involved in the subordinate divisions, and (3) the sophistication of the tasks or responsibilities assumed by these divisions, departments or offices.

Organizational Conflict and Tension

Sport managers are naturally concerned with the organizational climate of their business or entity. An important element of organizational atmosphere or ambience is the absence or presence of destructive conflict. Conflict can be either positive or negative. Conflict within organizations happens (Sattler & Doniek, 1997), because people are involved. When there are people involved, working together, there is always the potential for conflict.

The presence of conflict between or among individuals as well as groups can serve as a motivational factor for the organization and/or result in professional growth for the individuals involved. Conflict can also facilitate growth within the organization itself. On the other hand, some types of conflict, if not addressed in time, can become so unsettling,

Fans—an essential component of competitive sports.
James Dusen, Photographer.

so unnerving, as to have the sport organization, or its divisions or its personnel, become dysfunctional to such an extent that day-to-day operation is impeded.

Concept 160: The Absence of Conflict Does Not Necessarily Mean that the Organization Is Healthy.

On the other hand, the absence of conflict within the entity is not necessarily a positive sign. Some conflict can be healthy. In fact, some conflict is probably necessary for the general health and professional growth of the employees as well as the organization.

Sources of Conflict

There can be many sources or causes of conflict among personnel, among employees and among volunteers (Sattler & King, 1998). Some of the causes of conflict stem from human beings. People can be the source of conflict because of (1) inadequate communication, (2) clashes of personality, and (3) how they treat others, (4) programs, (5) priorities, (6) procedures, (7) standards, (8) practices, (9) administrative or managerial decisions, (10) scarce resources, (11) ambiguous jurisdictions or overlapping areas of responsibilities, (12) organizational size and structure, and (13) the use, misuse, or abuse of power.

Concept 161: Personality Clashes or Friction Can Be a Source of Organizational Conflict.

Conflict Is Often a Power Issue

Conflict is often a power issue between different individuals or factions within an organization. Such conflict frequently arises when there is inadequate or ineffectual leadership within the organization, regardless of the level. It can also occur when there is a lack of specificity in terms of areas of responsibility, authority, and jurisdiction. These types of conflict can be avoided or the negative fallout can be greatly diminished by the presence of appropriate policies, practices, procedures, and priorities within the sport entity. Again, leadership is the key to both conflict prevention and conflict resolution.

Conflict Prevention/Management Resolution

The Proactive Approach in Dealing with Conflict

The best way to deal with destructive conflict within any organization is to prevent it from occurring in the first place. This is the *proactive approach*. Naturally, this is much easier said than done. It is simply impossible to prevent conflict totally. It happens in spite of the best efforts of management and employees. However, the negative consequences of conflict situations can be greatly diminished, mitigated, or at least satisfactorily managed in some instances. The essential elements in preventing conflict situations include excellent communication efforts and excellent planning, coupled with the ability and willingness to work with and to understand (the motivation of) others.

Concept 162: Negative Consequences of Conflict Can Be Mitigated with Preplanning and Attention to the Needs of Others.

The Reactive Approach in Dealing with Conflict

Dealing with the problem situation that has developed as a result of a conflict is the *reactive approach.* Although frequently necessary, dealing with a problem created because of some type of conflict is troublesome from two perspectives. First, one must deal with the source of the conflict itself. Second, it is necessary to deal with the consequences of the conflict whether they be hurt feelings, damaged communication channels, distrust, anger, loss of motivation, jealousy, or any other negative attribute or characteristic. The worst thing that management can do in a conflict situation is to do nothing. This approach usually exacerbates an already bad situation.

Recognizing Signs of Conflict

Of course one has to recognize that a conflict situation exists before it is possible to deal with it. If one is unaware that a conflict situation is or could be a significant problem, one can hardly take steps to address the situation adequately. Once management is aware of conflict existing in the workplace, both managers and employees must be ready, willing, and capable of dealing with the conflict situation in order to prevent further discord, friction, and hostility.

Conflict is like a disease, a disease that is both contagious and ravenous. Left untreated, organizational conflict has the potential for seriously disrupting the day-to-day operations as well as to impede progress at all levels severely. Negative attitudes, distrust, jealousy, and resentment are just some of the negative results of conflict left untreated and should be avoided or prevented if at all possible (Yukelson, 1993). If the situation (involving causes, consequences, and peoples' feelings) is not dealt with in a forthright, timely, and decisive manner, the consequences can be severe, including disruption of day-to-day operations and the eventual failure of the ultimate mission of the sport entity.

Techniques for Preventing and/or Managing Conflict

One of the most important things for sport managers to remember is that they must keep their conduct, their communications efforts, at the highest professional level possible. They should never be judgmental in their actions or in their communication efforts, verbal or nonverbal. Their comments should be descriptive and not judgmental. Administrators do not help a conflict or hostile situation by becoming personally involved, by taking things personally, by reacting as if the difficulties are a personal affront to their professional abilities.

Concept 163: In Dealing with a Conflict Situation, Keep It Professional, Not Personal. Communication Efforts Should Be Descriptive rather than Judgmental.

Cooperation and Understanding

In all situations involving dissension and discord there is a need for understanding and cooperation. People act the way that they do because they have a reason or reasons. These reasons may be sound, may be logical, and justifiable. Or, they may not be any of the above. Nevertheless, it is important for the supervisor to attempt to understand the rationale behind the action or inaction of those involved in the conflict. Thus, it helps to be able to walk in the other person's shoes, to look at things through the eyes of those intimately involved in the conflict or stressful situation. By doing this one is in a better position to diffuse the situation based on an understanding of the root causes of the problem, the conflict.

Involvement of Personnel in the Management Process

Involving personnel in many aspects of the management process, especially in planning and decision-making, can pay big dividends in preventing and managing personal and organizational conflicts. Staff members who have actively participated in the setting of goals, individually or as members of groups, become part of the process within an organization. They have something at stake because they were part of the process (Zander, 1982).

The establishment of clear expectations on behalf of employees can pay big dividends in conflict prevention and management. Clearly defined roles and responsibilities of staff also play a very important role in management, especially in terms of group cohesiveness (Copeland & Wida, 1996). Cohesiveness among personnel is an important goal of management. In fact, cohesive groups are more likely to resist disruptive behavior. They are also more likely to work together and to share responsibility for the consequences (Brawley, Carron, & Widmeyer, 1988).

Concept 164: Organizations Must Insist on Civility among All Personnel—without Civility There Is Anarchy.

The presence of conflict doesn't necessarily imply a lack of civility among an organization's personnel. On the contrary. Management must insist that all employees and volunteers, at all levels throughout the business organization, are professional and civil in their interactions with one another, even in light of professional disagreement or conflict. Lack of civility in combination with a negative organizational climate can result in chaos and mob rule. Yes, there is such a thing as civilized or professional conflict.

General Techniques of Conflict Management and Resolution

Bridges & Roquemore (1996) described four tactics commonly used in resolving conflicts within organizations. The first is *conciliation,* which involves a third person working with two dissenting groups or individuals. The conciliator's role is one of defusing the situation while attempting to establish goodwill between all of the parties. "If conciliators are selected from each of the conflicting groups, they may be called *linking pins* because they can present the views of their group and hear the views of the other group or groups" (p. 346).

Concept 165: Competent Managers Must Take a Proactive Approach in Dealing with a Potentially Destructive Organizational Climate.

The second method of resolving conflict is to attempt to *mediate* the disagreement. This involves a third, impartial individual whose job it is to bring the two warring groups together to deal with their conflict. The third method is to *arbitrate* the problem situation: Both groups agree to have an outside, independent, and impartial person listen to the pertinent evidence and facts and then render a decision that is binding on both parties. The fourth and last method delineated is the *negotiation* tact. In this situation an individual in authority, a manager or supervisor for example, seeks to arrive at a fair, just, and acceptable decision (perhaps a compromise) regarding the dispute. The goal is to render a decision that will resolve the disagreement or conflict among the personnel without losing the productivity of these employees.

Negotiation is a skill that sport managers should be familiar with since they will be working with people almost on a daily basis. In fact, Patterson (1996) indicates that we are negotiating all the time, every day, in most of our interactions with others. Additionally, there are predictable responses that one can anticipate when involved in the negotiation process. In negotiating with others, especially in attempting to create a win–win situation for all parties, attitude and temperament are most important. Finally, two essential elements that are the linchpins of negotiation are information/data and the factor of time. One must be in possession of adequate and accurate information. Information is the foundation of wise decision-making. Time is important because successful negotiation takes time. There is also the matter of the timeliness of negotiation processes, sharing information, asking questions, listening, and so on.

Specific Strategies and Tactics of Conflict Management

Other specific strategies for dealing with conflict management, both in terms of preventing conflict and resolving or managing conflict within an organization, include: (1) staff meetings and open forum gatherings, (2) use of committees, (3) cracker-barrel sessions, (4) open telephone lines, (5) suggestion boxes, (6) periodic operational reviews, (7) in-service educational opportunities, and (8) maintaining an open-door policy.

Concept 166: The Use of Committees Can Be a Two-Edged Sword.

One word of caution should be mentioned in terms of committees. The use of committees can be a two-edged sword. On the one hand, if used correctly and judiciously, committees can facilitate communication and foster group cohesion while contributing to effective decision-making. On the other hand, ineffectual committees can prove to be devastating in terms of creating conflicts and ill will among the employees as well as between the employees and management. Management should use committees judiciously lest they be viewed as a substitute for managerial decision-making.

It is also important that management judiciously utilize the periodic operational reviews. These reviews have managers or supervisors going to various work sites or areas and entering into a dialogue with employees in an effort to learn firsthand about the everyday challenges, problems, and potential conflict or friction within the entity. However, just as the use of committees can be viewed as a negative, these operational reviews can similarly be viewed as unnecessary prying, snooping, and interfering efforts by distrusting and suspicious employees and subordinates.

Stress and Stress Management

Stress can play an important role in organizational conflict both for members of management and for the rank and file. Being able to manage stress on a personal basis is very important for the health of the organization as well as for the health of the individual employee. Thus, it behooves management to provide the means (time, opportunity, education, tools, etc.) to all employees for adequate stress management.

Concept 167: Management Must Take Assertive Steps to Alleviate Inappropriate Stress Experienced by Employees and Administrators.

Working in a business is a very competitive and stressful experience. Working in a sport-related business can be very, very stressful. Managers and nonmanagers alike need to be knowledgeable in terms of managing their stress and need to have the time and tools with which to combat the effects of negative stress. Thus, stress management strategies and tactics can play a significant role in dealing with organizational and personal conflict, both in terms of preventing conflict and in managing conflict when it does occur.

It is a responsibility of members of management to provide a healthy and positive physical and psychological work environment for employees and volunteers. Doing so will facilitate interpersonal relationships and positive communication among and between employees and will go a long way toward preventing unacceptable and debilitating conflict within the organization.

Communicating with Unhappy, Dissatisfied or Irate Customers

An important facet of communication as well as stress management is successfully dealing with the sport organization's customers or constituencies (Hart, Heskett, & Sasser, 1991).

This is especially important when dealing with unhappy or irate customers, patrons, or fans. It is estimated that for each dissatisfied "customer" there are least 10 other individuals with whom the unhappy camper has shared the real or perceived problem with the sport entity. Of course, when there is a problem or difficulty between the sport organization and the customer it is "always" the fault of the sport organization in the eyes of the customer (and the customer's relatives, friends, and business associates). This is why it is so important to be able to deal with customers, patrons, and fans in an effective and expedient fashion.

Concept 168: Unhappy Customers Not Only Go Away Disgruntled but Often Try to Get Even as Well.

An important part of the process of handling complaints (real or perceived) from constituencies is to deal with the problem immediately and to convey to the individual(s) that you are there to help resolve the problem or conflict. Also, allow the dissatisfied patron to express oneself as long as it does not involve abuse of staff. However, this does not mean that the sport manager becomes a "whipping post" for the abusive customer. The content and form of the conversation (communication) must be kept at a professional level. When it descends to abuse or misuse then the customer has stepped out of bounds and needs to be so informed. No one should be treated with disrespect, by customers, patrons, fans, or any other category of people.

In essence, it is imperative to take a proactive professional approach in dealing with the confrontational situation, all the while maintaining eye contact and exhibiting confidence in one's job. It is also most important to understand all of the extenuating factors that are involved in the situation. This may involve taking detailed notes. Managers who create the image that they really do care about the customer's problem or conflict and that they are trying to do all in their power to address and resolve the situation lay the foundation for a suitable resolution to an otherwise ticklish situation. If managers are not able to resolve the situation, to the customer's satisfaction, it is necessary that this fact be explained, including why it cannot be resolved to the customer's satisfaction (8 Steps, 1993).

The Necessity of Being an Effective Communicator

Communication is an essential competency for sport managers because it is one competency that every employee will need to deal with in day-to-day operations regardless of the type of business or organization in which one finds oneself (Parkhouse, 1991). Communication skills are so essential because so many other skills are dependent on being able to communicate clearly to a wide range of individuals, groups, and organizations. Failure to develop sophisticated communication skills (verbal and nonverbal) places the would-be sport manager at a severe disadvantage in the twenty-first century. As has been pointed out, the lack of adequate communication is one cause of conflict within the organization. Thus, those individuals who are highly skilled in communication are in a position to prevent many problems related to conflict prevention, management, and conflict resolution.

Concept 169: Competency in Communication Forms the Basis for Other Essential Skills of Sport Managers and Leaders.

Human beings are social animals. As such the ability to clearly communicate is indispensable if they are to not only survive within the organizational structure but also grow and prosper. Being able to relate to, communicate with, and work within a group setting is an absolute requirement for the modern-day sport manager or administrator. Without adequate grounding in communication skills (sending/receiving/deciphering) the prospect of success as a member of management within a sport organization is severely limited.

Conclusions

Successful sport management is dependent on sound communication practices. The structure of the organization has a definite impact on communication channels within the entity. Understanding the communication process and the strategies and tactics that are supportive of good communication will put the sport manager, at every level, in good stead. However, mere awareness of communication techniques is not enough. Sport managers need to put such knowledge to actual use in the real world. The importance of feedback cannot be overstated in terms of becoming an effective communicator. And, of course, communication, both verbal and nonverbal, is an essential ingredient in conflict resolution. Although conflict resolution is an important and sometimes imposing challenge facing the sport manager, the ability to prevent conflict from taking place or reduce its negative impact is a quality that cannot be overemphasized.

REFERENCES

Armstrong, W. H. (1997–1998, Winter). Learning to listen. *American Educator, 21*(4), 24–25, 47.

Brawley, L. R., Carron, A. V., and Widmeyer, W. N. (1988). Exploring the relationship between cohesion and group resistance to disruption. *Journal of Sport and Exercise Psychology, 10,* 199–213.

Bridges, F. J. and Roquemore, L. L. (1996). *Management for athletic/sport administration: Theory and practice* (2nd ed.). Decatur, GA: ESM Books.

Bucher, C. A. and Krotee, M. L. (1993). *Management of physical education and sport.* St. Louis, MO: Mosby Year Book.

Copeland, B. W. and Wida, K. (1996). Resolving team conflict: Coaching strategies to prevent negative behavior. *Journal of Physical Education, Recreation and Dance, 67*(4), 52–54.

Davis, K. A. (1994). *Sport management: Successful private sector business strategies.* Madison, WI: Wm. C. Brown & Benchmark.

8 steps for handling complaints. (1993, October). *Club Industry, 9*(8), 43.

Graham, P. J. (1994). *Sport business: Operational and theoretical aspects.* Madison, WI: Wm. C. Brown & Benchmark.

Harris, R. M. (1994, May). Articulate listening. *Successful Meetings, 43*(6), 116.

Hart, W. L., Heskett, J. L., and Sasser, W. E. (1991, April). Surviving a customer's rage. *Successful Meetings, 40*(5), 68–70, 72, 75, 76, 79.

Helitzer, M. (1995). *The dream job—$port$—Publicity, promotion and marketing* (2nd ed.). Athens, OH: University Sports Press.

Horine, L. (1995). *Administration of physical education and sport programs* (3rd ed.). Dubuque, IA: Wm. C. Brown.

Jensen, C. R. (1992). *Administrative management of physical education and athletic programs* (3rd ed.). Philadelphia: Lea & Febiger.
Mason, J. G. and Paul, J. (1988). *Modern sports administration.* Englewood Cliffs, NJ: Prentice-Hall.
Parkhouse, B. L. (Ed.). (1991). *The management of sport: Its foundation and application.* St. Louis, MO: Mosby Year Book.
Patterson, J. G. (1996). *How to become a better negotiator.* New York: American Management Association.
Sattler, T. P. and Doniek, C. A. (1997, March). The art of negotiating: Attitude is everything. *Fitness Management, 13*(4), 37.
Sattler, T. P. and King, J. M. (1998, January). Understanding organizational and personal conflict. *Fitness Management, 14*(1), 20, 22.
Stier, W. F., Jr. (1994). *Successful sport fund-raising.* Dubuque, IA: Wm. C. Brown & Benchmark.
Stier, W. F., Jr. (1998, April 8). *Marketability in the 21st century.* Presentation at the national convention of the American Alliance of Health, Physical Education, Recreation and Dance, Reno, Nevada.
Tillman, K. G., Voltmer, E. F., Esslinger, A. A., and McCue, B. F. (1996). *The administration of physical education, sport, and leisure programs.* Boston, MA: Allyn & Bacon.
Yukelson, D. (1993). Communicating effectively. In J. Williams (Ed.), *Applied sport psychology* (pp. 122–136). Mountain View, CA: Mayfield.
Zander, A. Z. (1982). *Making groups effective.* San Francisco: Jossey-Bass.
Zeigler, E. F. and Bowie, W. (1983). *Management competency development in sport and physical education.* Philadelphia: Lea & Febiger.

DISCUSSION AND REVIEW QUESTIONS

1. Describe the essential elements for effective communication to take place.
2. Differentiate between deliberate, accidental, and incidental communication and provide examples within a sport entity.
3. Elaborate on the various types of hindrances that a typical sport manager might encounter when dealing with employees, with volunteers, and with constituencies or the general public.
4. What can employees working within a horizontal organization do to enhance communication efforts across departments as well as within the chain of command?
5. How can a sport manager go about soliciting feedback in terms of communication so that the individual is aware of the effectiveness of the communication effort?
6. Why is conflict a power issue? Explain how conflict among personnel within a sport entity might be prevented or resolved. Provide examples.
7. Set the stage for role-playing by creating a situation in which you, as a sport manager, must deal with a subordinate and you wish to initiate communication that is descriptive rather than judgmental.
8. Cite examples for which the use of committees would be justified. Also, cite examples for which the use of committees might not be warranted.
9. What are the implications that some unhappy customers not only go away disgruntled but also, frequently, attempt to get even? Provide specific examples of what sport managers might do in light of this tendency.

SECTION THREE

Practical and Pragmatic Aspects of the Management of Sport

CHAPTER

7 Budgeting and Sound Financial Management

Successful sport programs attract loyal fans.

CHAPTER OBJECTIVES

After reading this chapter you will be able to:

- Appreciate the importance of the budgeting process for the success of the sport management organization;
- Understand how proper budgetary planning and implementation can prevent many problems from occurring;
- Characterize the essential elements of a sound budget;
- Describe the total budgetary process from planning through implementation;
- Differentiate between a fiscal year and a calendar year budget;
- Explain the purposes of an audit of the budget and the budgetary process;
- Outline the various methods of budgeting;
- Define various terms such as *formula budgeting, zero-based budgeting, bids,* and *quotes;*
- Provide examples of different methods of accounting;
- Outline the purchasing process;
- Read and understand a sample budget used within a sport organization;
- Understand the importance of accountability in sound fiscal management.

The Importance of Effective Budgeting for Sport Organizations

The process of budgeting, with all of its various components, is an all-important element in the arsenal of the modern sport manager. Indeed, many sport managers, at different levels and in a variety of sport organizations, do indeed have significant roles to play in the overall budgetary process. The purpose of the budgetary process is to facilitate the realization of the organization's goals and objectives *through fiscal responsibility, sound business practices, effective decision-making, and prudent financial management.*

> **Concept 170:** One's Sphere of Influence Is Greatly Enhanced by the Degree to Which One Has Financial Authority and Responsibility.

Some individuals have more direct responsibility in financial matters than others. Nevertheless, regardless of the degree of responsibility, the fact remains that all would-be sport managers must be knowledgeable about the overall budgetary picture as well as competent in the basic day-to-day financial operations of the sport entity.

> **Concept 171:** The Person Who Controls the Budget Possesses the Power.

Because the financial aspect of any sport or sport-related organization is so important, managers must recognize how important it is to demonstrate sound financial management consistently in the conduct of their duties and responsibilities. Individuals who have a degree of control over finances and financial decision-making wield great power, exert influence, and command authority. Thus, it is imperative that sport leaders possess financial acumen and retain financial decision-making powers if they are to be effective and efficient managers.

Concept 172: Leaders in Sport Organizations Should Usually Not Relinquish Total Budgetary Decision-Making to Others—Effective Leaders Retain Control over Their Budget and Financial Decisions.

One usually never relinquishes the budgetary decision-making power within one's financial domain. Yes, it is perfectly permissible and even expected that managers will delegate to subordinates specific tasks and responsibilities relating to the budget; however, the ultimate decision-making within the budget arena remains with the manager or leader of that unit or area.

There are numerous individuals involved in the budgetary process and financial arena within any sport organization. Various staff and line personnel, coaches, directors, coordinators, bookkeepers, and assistants could all be involved, in some way or another, in the financial arena of the organization. Some provide information. Others collect data. Still others provide recommendations. But it is the manager or leader who makes the final decisions based on the financial data and recommendations provided by the support personnel, assistants, and others. It is this decision-making power that is the distinguishing factor between a high level administrator and a person filling a support or advising role.

Concept 173: One's Expertise in Budgeting and Fiscal Management Provides Insight into the Sport Manager's Level of Competency in the Eyes of Others.

Because the budgetary process is so important to the general health and welfare (and to the very survival) of the organization, the financial skills of the sport leader will have a decided impact in terms of how this sport manager is viewed by others, both in and outside of the sport organization (Olson, 1986, April). Ineptitude in things financial or relating to the budget or the budget process can spell disaster in terms of the manager's image, up and down the organizational chart as well as in and out of the organization.

Concept 174: Budget Competency and Sound Fiscal Management Are Equally Important for Profit As Well As for Not-for-Profit Organizations.

Every sport organization needs to be concerned with fiscal responsibility and sound business practices, policies, and procedures. This is true for both profit and not-for-profit businesses and organizations. The need to develop and follow a sound budget and to make effective and efficient fiscal decisions is essential for every business and organization.

Concept 175: Many Problems and Challenges Facing Sport Organizations Can Be Significantly Reduced or Prevented Entirely with Astute Financial Decision-Making Coupled with Sound Budgetary Practices.

Many of the problems facing sport organizations, now and in the foreseeable future, revolve around financial challenges or are fiscally based. However, many of the problems evolving from the financial aspects of any given sport business can be better addressed and the negative impact lessened, if not avoided entirely, by wise fiscal management and decision-making in advance of or in anticipation of such financial crises. One of the goals of sound financial management is to prevent fiscal problems or at least minimize the negative consequences or fallout that results from such problems. This can be accomplished by wise decision-making, by insightful anticipation, and by judicious accurate prediction of the future based on the available information and data and coupled with meaningful and relevant experience.

Concept 176: Sound Financial Decision-Making and Budget Construction Depends on Accurate Data and Information.

Sound fiscal responsibility involves more than merely having a well-thought out and accurate budget, although that is very important. Fiscal responsibility implies timely decision-making in all matters financial. However, decision-making must not be made in a vacuum. Financial decisions are made in light of existing circumstances and situations as well as best projections of what the foreseeable future might be. This requires a great deal of information, data, and recommendations to be made available to the ultimate decision-maker and those who serve as advisers and counsel to the decision-maker. Without appropriate and accurate budget information and financial data, sound fiscal decision-making is often not possible.

Concept 177: The Budget Can Present an Accurate Snapshot of the Current Financial Situation of the Organization As Well As a Glimpse of the Future of the Entity.

The Budget: Definition, Purpose, and Functions

A budget is a written statement of anticipated income and expenses over a period of time, usually a 12-month period. The use of the budget instrument is important in planning for the future, in implementing in the present, and in reviewing past activities.

Concept 178: Budgets Consist of Statements of Anticipated Income and Expenses over a Specified Period of Time.

The budget document should be viewed as a means to an end—a tool. In light of the definition of administration provided in Chapter 1, the budget is a tool that enables sport leaders to manage individuals and manipulate resources better toward previously agreed-on goals and objectives within a specified time frame.

Concept 179: The Budget Is a Tool, a Means to an End.

Budgets serve as a guide for current as well as future decisions and action on the part of the sport leaders. Budgets facilitate the planning necessary for the organization itself as well as for the individuals and the programs within the organization. Budgets help individuals make appropriate and timely decisions based on the financial climate and current circumstances that affect the organization. And, of course, budgets enable individuals to keep track of the current financial health and well-being of the organization and all of its components. The wise use of budgets enables managers to take a proactive stance in viewing the financial health of the entity by predicting possible future occurrences in terms of income and expenses, all the while providing for various scenarios should differing futures come to pass.

Essential Elements or Components of a Budget

The essential elements of any budget consist of (1) anticipated income, (2) anticipated expenses, and (3) cash reserve, if any. Other components that customize or make budgets different from one another include the time factor (calendar or fiscal year) as well as whether the budget is a reflection of the entire organization or merely depicts the financial picture of a component or part of the entire entity.

The Calendar Year versus the Fiscal Year

Budgets reflect the financial picture of a program or an organization over a specific period of time, usually 12 months. These 12 months can span a calendar year or arbitrarily determined fiscal year. In unusual instances the budget cycle or term might be 24 months or even longer. In the case of the budget based on the calendar year, the financial year starts on January 1 of any given year and concludes on December 31 of that same year. However, using the calendar year as the time frame for the budget cycle is not required. Many organizations, for any number of reasons, choose not to operate on a calendar year. Instead, a specific fiscal year is chosen based on a starting date at any time of the year. For example, a fiscal year might begin on June 1 and end 12 months later on May 31.

Departmental Budgets versus the Budget for the Entire Organization

A budget can take many forms. Budgets can also be simplistic in nature or they can be very complicated. The type and size of the organization as well as whether the budget reflects the financial situation of the entire entity or merely one subcomponent of the organization will determine the degree of sophistication of the budget document as well as the process by which it is developed and finalized.

Overall Organizational Budget

A budget that illustrates how the entire organization will attempt to spend the dollars available to it as well as how the entity will secure the necessary financial resources with which to support its planned expenditures is called an *overall organizational budget.* Such a budget, reflecting the anticipated financial income and expenses (plus any cash reserve) for an entire organization, will naturally be more encompassing and complicated and detailed than a budget constructed for a small department or component within the organization.

Departmental Budgets

In an academic institution, for example, there is an overall budget for the entire college or university. This overall budget is in turn made up of numerous departmental budgets. For example, there would be a separate budget for Public Relations and Development, another for the Department of Political Science, another for Biology, another for History, and one for Intercollegiate Athletics.

The intercollegiate budget, in turn, may be made up of numerous other subbudgets. These subbudgets within the athletic department budget could include a budget for the football team, one for the field hockey team, another for the softball team, the cross country team, and so on.

Types of Budgets

There are different types of budgets that organizations may utilize to help facilitate financial planning and implementation. For example, there is the *operational budget,* which deals with the expenses (costs of doing business) associated with the daily operation of the entity throughout the budget year. The *personnel budget* deals with the costs of employees within the organization. Some organizations break down their expenses into a *capital expenditure budget,* which forecasts how much is anticipated to be spent on large ticket items such as constructing a building or making major rehabilitation efforts to an existing facility. If there are going to be major (and expensive) equipment purchases in the next budget cycle some organizations will have a separate *equipment budget* for the entire entity.

Differentiating Equipment from Supplies

Supplies refer to those consumable items that have a very short useful life. Typically, supplies are thought of as wearing out or existing for less than a year or so. *Equipment,* on the other hand, consists of those items that have a longer usefulness. Three to five years or even longer may comprise the life of equipment. *Capital expenditures* are those which involve a significant amount of money coupled with a very long life span (15–20 years and more) in terms of usefulness. For example, the addition of facilities, modification of or alterations to existing facilities, and the purchase of certain kinds of major equipment can all be thought of as capital expenditures.

Creating a Budget: The Budget Development Process

Creating a budget for a sport organization does not have to be a complicated, tedious, and time-consuming process. In fact the budget development process or cycle can be streamlined and facilitated by being aware of some basic concepts and following several time-tested suggestions.

1. *The budget document should be prepared well in advance of the start of the upcoming fiscal or calendar year.*

Planning for future purchases through the creation of a budget frequently places sport managers in a position of anticipating expenses and income many, many months in advance. If the sport organization is on a fiscal year running from September 1 through August 31, it will be necessary to begin work on the budget document well before the September 1 date. For school-based athletic departments the budget process can *begin* as early as October or November for the fiscal year beginning the next September 1. This means that the budget document being prepared is being worked on some 12 to 16 months in advance of when parts of the budget will actually be implemented.

This time factor can have significant repercussions in terms of the type of decisions that must be made by various staff members. For example, the anticipation of actual income and expenditures this far in advance is sometimes rather challenging (Olson, 1986).

Concept 180: Being Able to Predict Expenses Is Very Important When Constructing a Budget.

It is very important to obtain accurate estimates of future expenditures so that when you actually order the items the real costs will be within the range you had expected and planned for. However, it may be difficult to *project* many expenses due to the lead time at which the budget document is actually constructed. For a budget constructed to cover the period of August 1, 2000 through July 31, 2001, it will be necessary to begin building the budget document as early as October or November 1999. This necessitates that actual expenditures that will be made in June or July of 2001 will have to have been anticipated as early as December 1999, some 18 months in advance.

2. *The budget process is initiated by examining the organization's and/or program's objectives, goals, and mission.*

It is important to remember that the budget is a reflection of the mission, goals, and priorities of the organization or the program. One must not lose sight of the established objectives, goals, and mission(s) of the entity for which the budget is being prepared. The budget is a tool that makes it possible for the organization to realize its mission(s) by meeting its objectives and goals.

3. *Information and data must be obtained relative to the needs, strengths, and resources of the organization and/or program.*

The type of information and data can include, but not be limited to, input from vendors, previous budgets, inventory of equipment and supplies, future commitments of the program, cost estimates, and so forth. There is a definite need for accurate financial data before intelligent decisions can be made for the upcoming budget (Lederman, 1993). Today, with the presence of computers and appropriate software, data collection and analysis is available to a greater extent than ever before.

Concept 181: Take Advantage of Technology such as Computers in Obtaining, Evaluating, and Comparing Information and Data.

Essential to this collection of data is to examine the resources already at hand, what needs to be replaced, and what needs to be secured for the first time. This necessitates adequate inventory records.

4. *Solicit the input, knowledge, and expertise of others in the collection and evaluation of information and data as well as in the construction of the budget document itself.*

Seeking input, ideas, and suggestions from others is only prudent for the sport leader developing a budget. No person would want to play the role of the Lone Ranger when it comes to the development of a sophisticated budget. Take advantage of the knowledge and experience of others, both inside and outside of the organization. Learn from others with specialized knowledge and skills.

Concept 182: An Intelligent Individual Doesn't Know All of the Answers, Only Where to Find the Answers.

5. *Review the data collected and analyze the pertinent available information in terms of what was done previously, what is required now and in the foreseeable future.*

This may necessitate looking at previous years' budgets as well as past expenditures and current costs of items and making projections in terms of anticipated income and anticipated costs and expenditures. Making good financial decisions and recommendations for the future are only possible with good, appropriate, and accurate information and data. It is the analysis of this information and the decision-making that follows such an examination that will determine the quality of the budget itself as well as future financial decisions based on the budget document.

6. *In the preparation of the budget document, follow the stipulations and requirements set forth by the organization or one's superiors.*

Follow directions (standard operating procedures—SOPs) of your boss/organization in the construction, development, and presentation of the budget. Use the appropriate forms in the construction, preparation, and presentation of the formal budget document. Utilize appropriate formulas and other financial limitations (mileage and other travel costs, for example) when developing the budget.

Concept 183: Padding One's Budget in Anticipation of One's Request Being Cut Is Poor Financial Management and Diminishes One's Credibility.

To pad one's budget request is to deliberately overstate the amount that you are requesting in anticipation of your request being reduced or cut. The thinking is that if one asks for more than one needs and if the possible cut comes then one might end up with what one really needs. This assumes that one's budget request will always be cut.

Concept 184: Program and Departmental Administrators Are Hired to Make the Decisions in Terms of Budgeting—Don't Force Superiors to Assume Budgetary Decisions at the Program or Department Level.

On the other hand, the superior who is in charge of the budget looks at the individual submitting the budget request suspiciously and anticipates that the budget request has a lot of "fat" in it and is severely padded. Knowing that the budget request is padded with a great deal of "fat," the "powers that be" cut the request. This places the superior (the college president, for example, in a school-based sports program) in the position of determining how much is needed for the sports program, and making decisions that are properly the job of the AD.

7. *The budget document must be accurate, feasible, and realistic.*

Always double- and triple-check the budget document to make sure that it is accurate and free of errors or omissions, however slight. The image and reputation of the administrator presenting the budget is at stake in the eyes of the board and/or superiors within the sport organization who will examine the document. It should be error free.

Concept 185: The Budget Should Correctly Reveal the Financial Situation of the Organization at a Particular Point in Time.

Because important decisions, some having far-reaching implications, will be made as a result of looking at the budget, it is imperative that the document be a workable document. This means the budget must be feasible, reasonable, and realistic, while revealing the current financial situation of the organization.

8. *Submit the completed budget documents to a select few for critical analysis prior to making the formal presentation to the board or one's superior(s).*

Allowing select individuals to review the completed budget document prior to the actual formal presentation to the board or one's superiors provides opportunities to make last minute corrections. It is far better to catch errors or oversights at this point than to be embarrassed in a formal presentation by having a mistake pointed out or by being faced with a question that one can't answer.

There is a decided advantage in allowing one of the individuals who happens to be on the board that will receive and review the budget document to view an advance copy of the budget. The advantage is that this individual, having reviewed and "passed" on the document, can become a "ringer" (inside supporter) in the meeting(s) where the document is being discussed. Naturally, the person to whom the advance copy is given should be a stout supporter of one's program as well as an influential and well-respected colleague of the other members of the board.

Concept 186: The Budget Document Must Be Easily Understood and Interpreted.

If the first cardinal sin of budget preparation is having one or more errors in the document, the second cardinal sin is creating a budget document that is confusing and difficult to understand. First and foremost, use a simple format and concise language. Don't hesitate to include detailed footnotes in the appendix of the document to answer any questions that might crop up or to clarify any potentially confusing situation. Footnotes in a budget document are an extremely helpful tool to explain, clarify, and interpret potentially confusing, unusual, or unexpected elements of the document to the layperson as well as to the sport business expert.

The ideal goal of the budget presenter is that there should be no unanticipated questions created by the budget document itself. The document should be self-explanatory. It must be remembered that many of the individuals who will sit in judgment of the budget document may not be professional accountants or even knowledgeable business people. They may not be familiar with sport, with the business of sport or with financial documents, including budgets. The document itself must be comprehensible for those nonsport-oriented individuals.

9. *When making the formal budget presentation, anticipate questions and be ready with accurate and timely responses.*

Be prepared to answer confidently and accurately questions during the budget presentation session in a pleasant, helpful, and professional manner. Never become irritated or provoked by unreasonable or stupid questions put to you by members of the review board, even if the person(s) should have known the answers. It may be advisable at one specific meeting to distribute the budget document to those in attendance and then to make a short formal presentation related to the document itself. Then, at a second meeting scheduled for just such a purpose, allow general discussion on the document as well as questions from the group.

Concept 187: Don't Take It Personally When Questioned about the Budget Recommendations and Requests.

When presenting the budget document to superiors or to a review board, the purpose of such a meeting is twofold: First, to inform and educate the individuals to whom the budget is being presented; second, and most importantly, to gain approval from these individuals for the implementation of the budget. These two objectives can rarely be accomplished without a great deal of discussion involving a multitude of questions and answers and the sharing of ideas, opinions, and suggestions. Don't cut off your nose to spite your face by becoming antagonistic toward those individuals asking the questions or expressing concerns or reservations.

10. *The final step in the budget approval process, after the formal approval of the document, with any changes, by the appropriate individual or board, is the actual implementation of the budget itself.*

Because the budget is a tool designed to facilitate the work of the sport leader or manager, it remains only for the sport manager to implement the budget during the upcoming fiscal or calendar year.

Concept 188: Budgets Are Not Written in Stone—Flexibility Is Still the Watchword as Time Progresses and Events Take Place.

Professional soccer—a sport that is ever growing in popularity.
James D. Lathrop, Photographer.

Inevitably there will be changes, some small and some not so small, in the anticipated income and planned expenses within a sport organization. One simply can't anticipate everything regardless of how hard one tries or how much experience one has. The only thing that is certain is that nothing is certain. Consequently, one should anticipate that the working budget document may have to be adjusted at different times during the budget year to take into consideration events and occurrences that were not and could not have been foreseen. Being able to make suitable and timely adjustments or changes is the responsibility of the person in charge of the budget. Such is life in sport and in business.

11. *An audit of the budget is conducted following the conclusion of the budget year.*

The budget cycle is complete when the fiscal or calendar year comes to a close and an audit of the past year's fiscal activities is conducted. This culminating fiscal activity brings to a close the budget cycle that began, in some cases, 18 months earlier. The audit, as stated elsewhere in this chapter, serves two purposes: to insure that generally accepted accounted procedures and practices were followed by those responsible for the budget; to assist the sport manager in becoming an even more proficient and competent fiscal manager and leader.

Methods of Budgeting

Line-Item Budgeting

Budgets that utilize the *line-item method* of categorizing income and expenses are very common in the sport business world. Elements of most budgets utilize some aspect of the line-item concept in differentiating the various types of income and expense accounts on the budget document. In such a budget each class or type of expense and income is categorized

TABLE 7.1 1990–91 Planning Budget for Intercollegiate Athletics

(in comparison with Planning Budgets for 87–88, 88–89, 89–90)

Revenue/Expense Summary

ANTICIPATED REVENUE:	*1987–88*	*1988-89*	*1989–90*	*1990–1991*	
Mandatory Athletic Fee	—0—	—0—	212,800.00	205,000.00	(a)
Brockport Student Govt.	105,000.00	125,000.00	—0—	—0—	(b)
*State Funds	22,500.00	23,200.00	23,100.00	28,335.00	
Temp. Ser. Officials	18,278.00	18,400.00	—0—	—0—	
Brockport College Fund	11,000.00	—0—	—0—	—0—	(c)
Roll-over (estimated)	11,813.80	12,000.00	7,500.00	30,000.00	(d)
Gate Receipts	12,000.00	12,000.00	2,500.00	5,000.00	(e)
All-Events Tickets	6,000.00	3,500.00	—0—	—0—	(f)
FOBA	3,675.00	6,300.00	10,100.00	8,300.00	(g)
**Maurauders	1,300.00	—0—	—0—	—0—	
Entry Fees	680.00	1,200.00	400.00	300.00	
***Bus Subsidy			4,500.00	—0—	
	192,246.80	201,600.00	260,900.00	276,935.00	

ANTICIPATED EXPENSES:	*1987–88*	*1988–89*	*1989–90*	*1990–91*	
Teams (Table 7.2)	134,000.00	140,900.00	154,650.00	176,945.00	(h)
Post Season	6,000.00	6,000.00	6,000.00	6,000.00	(i)
Admin. & selected team expenses (Table 7.3)	41,025.00	42,900.00	41,750.00	48,910.00	(j)
Training Supplies	7,000.00	7,000.00	9,000.00	9,000.00	
Contingency/Miscellaneous	4,221.80	4,800.00	15,000.00	10,000.00	(k)
***Outside Bus Expenses			4,500.00	—0—	
	192,246.80	201,600.00	230,900.00	250,855.00	

RESERVE ACCOUNT					
Reserve	—0—	—0—	30,000.00	26,080.00	(l)
Anticipated Expenses & Reserve			260,900.00	276,935.00	

*Exclusive of personnel (team physician/PA/athletic staff) and plant management costs (salaries, utilities, supplies, etc.)

**IFR account with Recreation

***"Wash"

Prepared by: William F. Stier, Jr., Ed.D., Athletic Director, SUNY–Brockport

TABLE 7.2 1990–91 Planning Budget for Intercollegiate Athletics

(in comparison with Planning budgets for 86–87, 87–88, 88–89, 89–90)

Team Budgets (BSG, STATE, AND SOFT FUNDS)

	1986–87	*1987–88*	*1988–89*	*1989–1990*	*1990–91*	
Baseball	5,005.50	4,300.00	6,400.00	5,800.00	6,800.00	(m)
Men's Varsity BB	5,578.60	6,500.00	9,450.00	9,550.00	9,200.00	
JV Basketball	1,713.85	1,800.00	1,450.00	1,850.00	1,990.00	(n)
Women's Varsity BB	5,763.50	6,000.00	8,000.00	8,300.00	9,880.00	(o)
Cross Country	2,689.75	2,500.00	2,100.00	2,150.00	3,600.00	(p)
Football Varsity	22,281.55	23,000.00	23,400.00	19,050.00	27,600.00	(q)
"B" Football	1,560.50	1,600.00	1,800.00	2,500.00	2,300.00	
Gymnastics	4,070.50	3,300.00	4,500.00	4,500.00	5,830.00	(r)
Field Hockey	5,852.75	5,000.00	5,100.00	7,900.00	9,150.00	(s)
Ice Hockey	15,298.00	23,000.00	23,850.00	23,100.00	26,850.00	
Men's Varsity Soccer	6,010.50	6,500.00	6,550.00	6,500.00	9,680.00	(t)
Women's Varsity Soccer	6,370.50	7,000.00	6,600.00	6,150.00	5,550.00	
Softball	4,937.50	5,000.00	6,500.00	8,800.00	7,100.00	
Tennis	2,317.45	2,100.00	1,300.00	2,100.00	2,250.00	
Swimming—Men	3,380.00	4,700.00	2,550.00	6,200.00	5,800.00	(u)
Swimming—Women	3,414.55	4,800.00	2,550.00	6,400.00	5,800.00	(u)
Track—Indoor	4,297.25	6,200.00	6,300.00	8,050.00	8,400.00	(v)
Track—Outdoor	3,399.40	5,700.00	5,500.00	6,550.00	7,135.00	(w)
Volleyball	5,909.45	6,600.00	7,550.00	6,600.00	8,580.00	(x)
Wrestling	8,117.85	7,000.00	7,550.00	10,400.00	10,700.00	
"B" Wrestling	1,002.75	800.00	400.00	400.00	700.00	(y)
Football Cheerleading	556.00	300.00	300.00	400.00	400.00	
Basketball Cheerleading	617.80	300.00	300.00	400.00	400.00	
Trans. Contingency	2,000.00	—0—	—0—	—0—	—0—	
Equipment Contingency	—0—	—0—	900.00	1,000.00	1,250.00	
	122,145.50	134,000.00	140,900.00	154,650.00	176,945.00	(z)
		9.71% increase	5.15% increase	9.75% increase	14.4% increase	

Prepared by: William F. Stier, Jr., Ed.D., Athletic Director, SUNY–Brockport

or classified on a different line identified as a specific item of expense or income. Tables 7.1, 7.2, and 7.3 illustrate the line-item concept in budgeting.

In Table 7.1 the expenses are broken down into different categories, including a line-item called *Teams* ($179,945). These figures are, in turn, broken down (Table 7.2) into 23 different team expenses plus the transportation contingency and equipment contingency

TABLE 7.3 1990–91 Planning Budget for Intercollegiate Athletics

(in comparison with Planning Budgets for 87–88, 88–89, 89–90)

Administrative and Selected Team Expenses

STATE FUNDS	*1987–88*	*1988–89*	*1989–90*	*1990–91*	
Temp Service	500.00	600.00	600.00	1,500.00	(aa)
Supply and Expense (S & E)					
Dues	7,050.00	7,315.00	7,500.00	8,035.00	(bb)
Supplies	2,000.00	1,500.00	2,300.00	3,000.00	(cc)
Copier expense	2,200.00	1,385.00	2,200.00	2,700.00	(dd)
Storehouse	2,000.00	2,000.00	2,000.00	2,500.00	
Phone	3,500.00	3,500.00	3,500.00	3,500.00	
Postage	2,000.00	2,000.00	2,000.00	2,000.00	
Central Duplicating	2,000.00	2,000.00	2,500.00	3,100.00	(ee)
State Auto Recharge	500.00	2,400.00	500.00	2,000.00	
Team Programs	N/A	500.00	—0—	—0—	(ff)
sub-total:	22,500.00	23,200.00	23,100.00	28,335.00	
SOFT FUNDS	*1987–88*	*1988–89*	*1989–90*	*1990–91*	
Insurance	6,000.00	6,500.00	—0—	—0-	
Team Programs/Schedule Cards	3,500.00	—0—	—0—	1,000.00	
Printing, frames, photos, film	300.00	300.00	300.00	300.00	(gg)
Books/Publications	300.00	350.00	350.00	375.00	
FOSA	3,675.00	6,300.00	10,100.00	8,300.00	
Travel					
MACDA, ECAC, NCAA, SUNYAC	2,400.00	2,400.00	2,500.00	3,400.00	(hh)
State (NYSWCAA) & local	350.00	350.00	350.00	400.00	
Equipment	2,000.00	2,000.00	2,000.00	2,000.00	
Generic uniforms/wk-st & teams	—0—	1,500.00	1,250.00	1,200.00	(ii)
Supply and Expense (S & E)	—0—	—0—	1,800.00	2,000.00	
Computer, printer	—0—	—0—	—0—	1,600.00	
sub-total:	18,525.00	19,700.00	18,650.00	20,575.00	
Total:	41,025.00	42,900.00	41,750.00	48,910.00	

Prepared by: William F. Stier, Jr., Ed.D., Athletic Director, SUNY–Brockport

accounts. Each of these team expense categories are in turn differentiated, in a line-item format, in Table 7.4. In Table 7.4 on page 183, the actual expenses of individual teams can be seen to be classified according to the categories of (1) *meals and lodging,* (2) *fees,* (3) *transportation,* (4) *equipment and supplies,* (5) *officials,* and (6) *other.*

Incremental Budgeting

Incremental budgeting involves adding to or taking from the previously year's budget a specific increment, a certain percentage, 2 percent or 4 percent for example. In some instances the incremental budgeting approach gives a specific percentage, an increment, to the total sport program within the overall budget. For instance, in a school-based sports program, all of the sport teams within the athletic program might be given a 2.5 percent rate of increase over the previous year's allocation. The problem with this budgeting approach is that it fails to take into account real needs or special needs of individual sports or subprograms within the athletic program.

Zero-Base Budgeting (ZBB)

Peter A. Pyhrr and a team of financial visionaries within Texas Instruments conceived *zero-base budgeting* in 1969. Some years later, in 1973, Jimmy Carter, then governor of Georgia, became a proponent of this system and, with the help of Peter Pyhrr, implemented the ZBB as the official budgeting tool for the state government. "The most important difference is that ZBB avoids the practice of considering last year's budget as the base, thereby avoiding the question of how much will be required to continue with a particular function" (Jensen, 1992, p. 129).

Zero-base budgeting is based on the requirement that organizations and their programs must justify their *total need* for budgeted resources, not merely their request for an increase (Dirmith & Jablonsky, 1979). Jimmy Carter was a big proponent of zero-base budgeting both as President and as governor of Georgia because this process required managers to justify the cost-effectiveness of their operations (Carter, 1977).

Formula Budgeting

Another technique or method utilized in constructing a budget is the use of formulas. A simplistic example of formula budgeting in sports can be seen when the amount to be expended for a specific line-item (away-game travel) is determined by using a formula that automatically determines the dollar amount for that expense item.

For example, seasonal expenses for each team's away contests can be determined by following a very simple formula involving (1) the cost per miles driven (37¢ per mile for the team bus, for example), (2) the number of individuals (players and coaches) comprising the travel team, (3) the number of meals to be consumed by each person, (4) the dollar allocation for each meal, including breakfast, lunch, dinner, and after-game snack, and (5) the dollar allocation for hotel accommodations (if needed) for the traveling squad.

> **Concept 189:** Formula Budgeting Is Effective if Prior Decisions Have Been Made Relative to Establishing Guidelines or Parameters that Predetermine Maximum Costs in Specific Instances or for Specific Purchases.

In the above example it is necessary that advance decisions be made or policies established regarding (1) what opposing teams will make up the away schedule, (2) the cost per mile traveled, (3) the number of individuals comprising a travel squad, (4) the maximum number of people to stay in each hotel room, (5) the number and types of meals to be consumed, and (6) the maximum amount of money to be spent for each type of meal to be consumed. Once these decisions and policies are known, all that is needed is for someone (a budget clerk or a secretary) to follow the policies and to plug the correct numbers or figures into the formula.

That is, once the staff member has determined the number of miles to be driven to each away site (from a master list of miles to each opponents' city), the number of individuals comprising the travel party for each game (from the policy handbook of the department), the number of meals to be consumed and the number of rooms needed for each away contest (also determined by reviewing the policy handbook of the department), it is a simple matter to merely plug the appropriate figures in the formula. The result is the total dollar expenditure for each away contest for all away contests for the entire season for that particular sport.

Concept 190: In Most School-Based Athletic Budgets the Only Discretionary Expenses Fall under the Category of Equipment and Supplies.

In many sport budgets the planning of expenditures is actually determined by following decisions and policies that have been made well in advance. In fact, in some sport budgets, especially school-based programs, the major discretionary expense category is that of "equipment and supplies." The reason for this is that the other major expense categories are all predetermined by earlier policy decisions or scheduling decisions. Once a home and away schedule has been determined, the major expenses of any individual team are likewise determined by merely filling in the formula categories as cited above. The result is that the amount of discretionary money to be spent for any individual sport is in equipment and supplies.

Concept 191: Maintaining Accurate Inventory Records of Current Equipment and Supplies Is Quintessential for Accurate Budgeting and Financial Decision-Making.

Even in this category the amount needed to be expended is greatly affected by what the inventory of equipment and supplies reveals. Thus, it is very important that accurate records be kept regarding the items of equipment and supplies as well as their current condition and expected useful life span.

PPBES: Planning, Programming, Budgeting, Evaluating System

Originally known as PPBS (Program Planning Budgeting System), this system of budgeting was devised in 1949 to be based on three factors: (1) function, (2) activities, and (3) objectives. Some five years later (1954) the Rand Corporation devised a performance-based budget for use by the military–industrial complex. Early proponents of this type of budgeting were the Ford Motor Company and the DuPont Corporation. Later, Robert

McNamara, a former Ford Motor Company executive, brought the PPBS system to the Defense Department. The results were impressive both in fiscal expediency and in elimination of financial waste. By late 1965 all departments and agencies of the United States federal government were utilizing the budgeting system by presidential decree. When the process of evaluation entered this budgeting concept the acronym evolved to the current day PPBES (Butcher & Krotee, 1993).

As the name indicates, PPBES budgeting involves establishing programs and activities to coincide with objectives and goals previously planned, and then budgeting and allocating resources to meet the needs of these programs. Finally, an assessment is necessary to determine the degree, if any, that the budget allocations allow the programming aspects of the organization to facilitate the realization of the established objectives and goals (Haggerty & Patton, 1984; Apostolou & Crumbley, 1988; Horine, 1995).

Methods of Accounting

There must be an understandable and orderly system of keeping track of all monies, both expenses and income. Financial accounting enables the sport leader to ascertain, based on hard data, a snapshot of the financial status of the organization as well as any program or subset within the entity itself. Proper accounting makes it possible to track and determine whether purchases were made for the purpose they were intended and authorized as well as to determine whether expected income was indeed received and deposited to the correct account(s).

> **Concept 192:** One Goal of Accounting Is to Determine Whether or Not Funds of the Organization Have Been Misused, Stolen, Lost, Misplaced, or Otherwise Unaccounted For.

Cash System of Accounting

The cash system of accounting treats expenditures as actual expenditures only when the money is materially spent, that is, when the money is physically sent (by check, etc.) to the person or organization owed the debt. On the other hand, anticipated income is not recorded on the books (income ledger) until the money is actually "in hand."

"The cash accounting system tracks income as cash is received and expenses as payment is make. The tracking of transactions is related to the disbursement or receipt of cash regardless of the time period in which the commitments are made" (Railey & Tschauner, 1993, p. 206).

Accrual Accounting

In accrual accounting, expenses and income are recorded in the organization's financial records or "books" when they are incurred on behalf of the organization or program, regardless of when the money is actually forwarded to the person or entity. Accrual accounting presents a far more accurate picture of the financial state of any organization or program than the cash accounting procedure (Parkhouse, 1996).

Some sport organizations choose a very conservative approach to accounting by utilizing a combination of both the cash and accrual accounting methods. In this hybrid accounting strategy all income is treated on a cash basis while all expenditures are dealt with on an accrual basis. In this scenario, any income expected or owed to the sport organization would not be recorded as actual income in the financial records (income ledger) until the money was actually in hand, physically in possession of the organization or program.

However, in terms of expenditures, when an expense is committed to, the appropriate funds are *encumbered* on the books. That is, they are earmarked as future expenditures (for a very specific purpose) even though the money may not physically leave the company's coffers for many months to come. Nevertheless, these same funds, on the books of the sport organization, are treated as if they have indeed already been spent and are not available for use by any other program or segment of the sport entity. In reality, such monies have been earmarked (encumbered) for expenditure and are merely temporarily residing in the organization's asset account until the "check is put in the mail."

Purchasing and Receiving Equipment and Supplies

When initiating purchases it is imperative that steps be taken to insure that the items ordered are the items that one needs and that they are actually received from the vendor. It is a given that accurate records are retained in all aspects of the ordering and purchasing process.

> **Concept 193:** Insure that All Equipment and Supplies Are Delivered to a Central Receiving Location and Check the Invoice Against the Original Order Form.

It is very important that all items of equipment and supplies are properly protected once they have been received by the sport organization. This can be accomplished by safe and secure storage combined with accurate inventory control. However, it is also important to provide security for items ordered as these items are delivered. Toward this end it is advisable that all equipment and supplies be delivered to a central receiving location and checked to insure that the items shipped or delivered are indeed what had been ordered and that the individual items are in good condition.

Ethical Decisions Regarding the Purchase of Equipment and Supplies

Well-managed sport organizations have well-established and publicized policies guiding the ordering and purchasing process to prevent unnecessary items from being ordered, to prevent misappropriation of equipment and supplies, as well as to deter the acceptance of "kickbacks" from vendors.

Concept 194: Accepting Kickbacks or Gifts from Prospective Vendors Is Wrong, Unethical, and Dishonest.

Some vendors advertise that orders totaling at least a specific amount of dollars qualify the person submitting the request for any number of prizes or premiums, depending on the exact amount of the order. Proper ethical behavior dictates that involvement in such kickback schemes is not acceptable under any conditions. Purchase requests or recommendations should be made on the basis of real need without any consideration of any reward or compensation being given to the person initiating the request.

Petty Cash

Petty cash accounts are a necessary element of the purchasing efforts of most organizations. However, at the same time, such petty cash accounts can also create many problems if they are not managed and supervised properly.

Petty cash accounts are kept for small purchases when it is neither appropriate nor possible to go through the normal purchasing process to secure the item or items. Typically, departments keep a petty cash fund of $100 to $250 dollars on hand. Out of this money, purchases may be made on an emergency basis when there is insufficient time to go through the more formal and time-consuming ordering procedures established by the organization. Once any of the petty cash is expended, the receipt for the item(s) secured is processed through the normal accounting procedures in an effort to replenish the petty cash account.

Concept 195: A Petty Cash Account Should Be Utilized to Handle Small Purchases in an Emergency Situation when It Is Not Possible or Advisable to Utilize the Normal Budgetary Process.

It must be strongly emphasized that the petty cash account is not to be consistently utilized as a means of paying for goods and services. Rather, it is to take care of the unusual situation or challenge that presents itself. However, overuse of the petty cash account is a sign of a lack of planning and managerial competency.

Bids and Quotes

The purpose of bids and quotes is to encourage competition and to reduce the costs of the organization employing the bid–quote process. Those organizations that are state entities utilize the use of bids and quotes to help ensure that the public's money is utilized in the most cost-efficient manner possible (Bidding at all costs, 1995). Ideally, the use of bids should enable the administrator of a public sport or recreation organization to secure goods and services at the lowest possible price. The use of bids and quotes is not limited to public organizations. Private, for-profit entities can also benefit from the use of bids and quotes in securing services and goods for their programs.

Definition of the Bidding Process

The bidding process involves a written solicitation from potential vendors for a specific service or item (good[s]) for a specific price (a bid) based on a very exacting set of specifications. For example, if a sport administrator is seeking a certain type of paper, the individual would provide specifications outlining the type and quality of paper desired, its dimensions, color, weight, material, and so on. The bid specs might also include a date by which the paper would be made available as well as specific delivery requirements.

The potential or would-be suppliers must be able to provide the item or service (or in some cases, the "equivalent") and submit a bid for the right to provide said item or service to the organization at a specific dollar amount. Usually, the lowest bidder wins the right to provide the item or service to the organization or entity seeking the bid. However, in many instances organizations may not be required to accept the lowest bid. In this situation, the individual purchasers may have to make an argument to a higher authority as to why they are recommending acceptance of a higher bid.

The bidding process typically requires that the specifications provided by the organization be in written form and that the solicitation of potential bidders be written. The submission of bids by potential or would-be vendors must also be in writing.

Items "On Contract"

Some states have some items and services "on contract." This means that the state has already gone out and secured the lowest bids on specific items and services from numerous vendors. Subsequently, when public organizations and state employees at their jobs seek items that are on contract, the state already has identified specific vendors from whom the item(s) must be purchased by the various state entities (schools, colleges, parks, hospitals, prisons, police agencies).

In New York state the Bureau of the Budget organizes a meeting of experts from various state agencies in Albany periodically. At this meeting the various items that are usually purchased and used by different state entities are examined to determine which specifications would be necessary for different agencies or organizations. For example, many different agencies or organizations might want to purchase basketballs (colleges, parks, prisons, hospitals) but there might indeed be different needs by each agency in terms of quality and costs. Basketballs purchased for colleges might be of higher quality and cost more than those purchased for use in prisons.

Concept 196: Not All "Equivalents" Are Equal—Beware of the Would-Be "Same As" Claim.

Not everything that is labeled "equal to" or "equivalent to" is truly the same as the item which is being sought. There are numerous (horror) stories about companies or organizations that sought a specific item or its equivalent only to find, when the lowest bidder delivered the item, that the item in question was not in the least equal to or equivalent to what was actually sought.

One such story dealt with a state that "let a bid" for "liquid paper" or its equivalent. In this case the state let out a contract on behalf of all state organizations and agencies (schools, colleges, hospitals, prisons, recreational entities) for liquid paper to use to correct mistakes made by typists. Evidently, the specifications stated that the product could be the item called *Liquid Paper* or its equivalent.

The winning vendor submitted the lowest bid, thousands of dollars less than the next lowest bidder, for a product that was supposedly equal to the product with the trade name *Liquid Paper.* However, when the state agencies and organizations ordered and received their equivalent bottle of liquid it was soon discovered that the product was not exactly of the same quality as *Liquid Paper.*

In reality, the substitute "liquid" took almost three minutes to dry whenever it was applied to paper by state employees. This was in contrast to the 10 to 12 seconds it took for the real "liquid paper" to dry when applied.

When one compared the dollar value of the lost time (not to mention the frustration) on the part of all of the state employees over the next two or three years (the supposed length of the bid contract) who had to wait the three or so minutes every time one of them had to use the substitute "liquid," it was clearly evident that the thousands of dollars initially saved by the state by awarding this contract to the lowest bidder was not really any savings at all. On the contrary, over the long haul, the length of the bid contract, the state probably lost a far greater sum in lost time and productivity of state employees.

Writing Specifications

This story highlights the necessity of carefully writing out the specifications of the item or service that one is requesting bids on. One cannot overemphasize the importance of meticulously writing exacting specifications for the product or service one is requesting. Vendors will be submitting bids based on the minimum requirements specified in the bid document.

> **Concept 197:** Write the Specifications for the Item to Be Let to Bid Very, Very, Very Carefully—Then Double- and Triple-Check for Accuracy and Appropriateness.

It is necessary that someone write specifications detailing exactly what type of product is needed. This is perhaps the most important aspect of the bidding process because, if the specifications are not correctly or adequately or stringently written, the result could be obtaining an inferior or unwanted or unacceptable product.

Specifying a Brand Name

In some instances the person seeking bids from vendors on behalf of the organization may wish (and is allowed) to specify a specific brand name as the only type that is acceptable.

In that eventuality, vendors wishing to secure the order for that organization must offer to supply that actual brand.

Concept 198: Specifying a Distinct Brand Name Insures a Minimum Quality Level.

This frequently happens in the interscholastic or intercollegiate sport scene in which a school's conference dictates that only a specific brand of basketball can be used in conference games. Thus, if Spalding basketballs are required by the conference, the athletic director will specify Spalding basketballs as the only brand acceptable in the bidding process. Successful vendors must submit an offer of the exact Spalding basketballs for a specific amount of dollars.

Accepting an "Equivalent" Product

In other situations, it is not permissible to specify a brand name. In that case, the organization seeking an item or service must write exact specifications that describe the minimum qualities that are acceptable in the item or service. Thus, a vendor submitting the lowest bid on an "equivalent basis," providing an item or service that at least matches the minimum requirements of the specifications as written, is given the order.

Definition of a "Quote"

A quote is really nothing more than an informal bid. A quote can be merely a verbal statement of a price by a vendor to a potential purchaser. Typically, organizations utilize a "quote" when the dollar amount for the item or service is less than that which necessitates the more formal structured bidding process. Some states or organizations require an informal quote for any item or service that would cost more than $5,000 but less than $10,000. And, for those items costing $10,000 and above, the formal, written bidding process is required.

To obtain a quote, one would typically call three or four vendors (whatever the policy stipulates in your organization) and request a price quote for a specific type of item, usually referring to a specific brand name (no exceptions or equivalents accepted).

Concept 199: The Bidding Process Is Used Both by Private and Public Organizations.

Bids may be sought by private businesses as well as by state agencies or state entities, including public schools and colleges, hospitals, and prisons. In most states it is mandated that public organizations utilize the bidding process when the amount of money to be spent exceeds a certain dollar amount. For example, the states of New York, Pennsylvania, and Vermont require that expenditures of $10,000 and up on behalf of schools must be via written or "sealed" bids (Bidding at all costs, 1995, p. 47).

Concept 200: The Bid Process Differs among Companies and Organizations, as It Does among States for State Agencies and Organizations.

For public organizations the bidding process can be especially complicated and time-consuming. Even in private entities and organizations the bid process can be cumbersome. Nevertheless, the potential good—reduced costs for quality goods and services—makes the bid process an important one in terms of fiscal responsibility and sound monetary management.

Purchasing from Local Vendors versus Distant Vendors

A common challenge facing many sport organizations is whether to purchase from local companies or to utilize firms that may be a great distance away. In some instances, mail-order firms may well be able to provide items at less cost. But there may be other factors to consider when making purchases other than price. Many organizations subscribe to the belief that they will buy locally if the quality of the item is comparable and the time of delivery is similar.

Concept 201: Generally Speaking, It Is Wise to Purchase from Local Vendors over Mail-Order Vendors unless the Cost Is Greater than 10% over the Mail-Order Company.

There are some definite advantages to consider in making purchasers closer to home. One benefit is that it is frequently easier to select the item(s) to be ordered when the vendor is local, because the merchandise can be physically seen and handled because the company selling the item is nearby. It is also often easier to secure service on what is purchased, especially in situations in which an item must be returned or exchanged. Another factor to consider is being a good neighbor by helping to contribute to local vendors. This is important as long as the sport entity is not ripped off by paying exorbitant prices for the vendor's goods and/or services. Support for local businesses can only go so far.

Example of an Intercollegiate Athletic Budget

Table 7.1 on page 168 illustrates the first page of a college athletic department's budget from the State University of New York–Brockport. This budget illustrates many of the fundamental principles in budgeting and in presenting a budget to staff, high level administrators, and board members. Note that the budget contains a summary of anticipated income as well as expenses and anticipated reserve, all on the cover page (Stier, 1989). Also, note that personnel costs in the form of salaries for professional and support staff (coaches and athletic administrators) are not represented in this budget.

Concept 202: It Is Sometimes Difficult to Compare Budgets between Two Similar Sport Organizations because Some Entities Do Not Include All Expenditures within the Sport Budget; Some Items Are Included under the Entity's General Budget Expenses.

Personnel costs are covered by the college's general instructional budget. Thus, although this athletic budget provides a fairly representative example of general income and expenses for a college athletic department (NCAA, division III), it does not reflect the total expenditures made on behalf of the athletic program because no coaching or administrative personnel costs are included. That is why it is so difficult to compare athletic budgets, even between two similar institutions or programs, because some organizations include some expenses within the sport budget while others do not.

Use of the Contingency or Miscellaneous Account

Concept 203: A Contingency Line-Item Account Should Be Carefully Utilized, Never Abused.

Under *Anticipated Expenses* in Table 7.1 there is a line-item titled Contingency/ Miscellaneous. It is important that this type of category be carefully utilized and not abused. The contingency line item is not a slush fund. Rather, the contingency line item refers to emergencies or special situations that the budget planners cannot foresee but nevertheless wish to prepare for by setting aside a particular amount of dollars in the eventuality that such an emergency should occur. In this example of an actual budget, the contingency amounted to $10,000 out of a total budget of $276,935 (exclusive of salaries), which represents less than 4 percent of the total budget (exclusive of salaries).

Maintaining a Historical Perspective: Reviewing a Past Year's Fiscal Budget Categories

It is important to note that the budget sheet for the fiscal year 1990–1991 in Table 7.1 on page 168 also includes reference to the three fiscal years prior to 1990–1991. This enables the planners (as well as others working with and/or approving the budget document) to have access to a historical perspective of the income and expense status of the entity, in this case, an athletic program.

Being able to look at previous years' budgets, line item by line item, can be helpful in a number of ways. First, one is able to see if there is a pattern or trend in the income or expenses for the program. Second, one can compare the actual increases or decreases (if any) as well as percentages of such increases or decreases in individual line-item accounts for income and/or expenses. However, one must be careful not to assign a specific percentage of increase (or decrease) to a budget (the entire athletic budget, for example) or to subareas within the budget (all sports, for example).

Use of Explanatory Footnotes

Adjacent and to the right of some of the 1990–1991 budget figures (income and expenses) are a series of small cap letters. Each letter refers to a footnote contained in the reference section of the budget. This reference section is located at the end of the budget document, and explains or further clarifies the figures on the budget sheet for those individuals who must review and understand it. Because it is imperative that the budget document be fully understood by those who review or read it, it is important that any unusual or potentially confusing figures be clarified and explained in detail in the footnotes (at the end of the document). In this way there should be no major questions as to what the figures relate to or why or how the specific figures were arrived at.

The goal is to present a concise and clear picture of the financial situation of the sport organization, department, or program, not to confuse, befuddle, or mystify those who would attempt to read and understand the document. Many times those who must read, understand, and eventually make a recommendation regarding the acceptance, rejection, or modification of the budget document are not certified public accountants or even very knowledgeable in terms of financial matters. Thus, it behooves the sport administrator to make the budget document as clear as possible to lessen any difficulty that might arise from misunderstanding the document or misinterpreting its content.

Individual Team Budget Allocations

The second page of SUNY–Brockport's 1990–1991 athletic budget includes the proposed (anticipated) expenses for each of the athletic teams and is shown in Table 7.2 on page 169. Again, just as on the first page of the budget document (illustrating general income, expenses, and reserves), the reader is able to gain a multiyear perspective of the total amount of expenses for each of the individual athletic teams.

Detailed Breakdown of Administrative and Selected Team Expenses

The third page of SUNY Brockport's athletic department's budget consists of a further breakdown of expenses, that is, administrative and team expenses, shown in Table 7.3. This page provides still further detail in terms of the types of expenses and the actual dollar cost of specific items required of the athletic department.

Note that these expenses were further broken down into *State Funds* and *Soft Funds*. State funds are those monies given directly by the state to the institution (athletic department). In this particular situation there were specific expenditures that had to be made (either by institutional rules or state mandates) with state allocated monies (*state funds*). Other expenditures could be made with what is referred to as *soft funds,* that is, monies generated by the athletic department independent of the state of New York. These soft funds (money) represented income from such sources as student government fees, concessions, tickets, and so forth.

As stated above, the individual athletic budget was broken down into the amounts (Table 7.2) to be spent for each of the individual teams sponsored by the college's athletic department. However, as informative as Table 7.2 is, the data provided only show the gross expenditures for each team. Nothing on this sheet provides any insight into how these gross figures for each team were arrived at, that is, how the money allocated to each team is to be spent in detail.

Detailed Breakdown of Individual Team Expenses

There is a need for a further breakdown of the anticipated data for each team in terms of (1) meals and lodging, (2) fees, (3) transportation, (4) equipment and supplies, (5) officials, and (6) other (miscellaneous). These data are provided in Table 7.4. These detailed and informative figures show exactly how each individual team's budget is to be expended. And, there is an eight-year history of prior expenditures for each of the teams that have existed for that length of time.

General Sources of Income for Sport Organizations

What are the actual categories of income for a sport organization? While there are some similarities, there are also different types of income for some sport entities, depending on whether one is talking about fitness clubs, health clubs, professional sports teams, recreation departments, college or high school athletic teams, or corporate fitness sites.

For health and fitness clubs catering to the general public, a significant percentage of income will be derived from membership fees. Additional income can be realized from the sale of apparel and equipment/supplies as well as food and drink. The corporate fitness site might not have membership fees at all because the employees are automatically members by virtue of their working for the organization. In this eventuality, the greatest income might be a specific allotment of monies directly from the company itself to subsidize the operation of the corporate fitness or wellness center.

Concept 204: One Key Element to a Balanced Budget Is to Be Able to Successfully Anticipate the Amount of Income which Will Be Forthcoming in the Foreseeable Future.

In the case of recreation programs sponsored by municipal entities, the major source of income might also be in the form of an allocation from the city or county governmental agency to cover the cost of operating the recreation program for the various constituencies or publics. On the other hand, the professional sports team as well as the school-based athletic program might well enjoy a wide range of income sources.

For example, income at collegiate and professional sport programs typically is derived from various types of profit centers. Profit centers are income-producing activities or operations that, although related to the sporting event, activity, or organization, stand alone in its ability to generate income. Examples of typical profit centers include ticket sales, concessions, program sales, merchandise or product sales (souvenir and apparel items), parking fees, user fees for facilities, vending machines, luxury box seating and

TABLE 7.4 Multisport Budget Summary, Year by Year, Athletics

	82–83	83–84	84–85	85–86	86–87	87–88	88–89	89–90	90–91
Baseball		3,585.32*	2,968.47	2,888.87	5,005.50	4,300.00	6,400.00	5,800.00	6,800.00
Meal & Lodging		460.00	600.00	690.00	690.00	1,234.59	3,273.88	1,260.00	1,430.00
Fee		25.00	25.00	25.00	25.00	25.00	—0—	—0—	50.00
Trans.		445.97	803.47	483.87	860.00	915.41	1,913.88	2,128.00	960.00
Equip.		2,054.35	640.00	640.00	1,765.50	900.00	1,255.32	906.60	1,500.00
Official		600.00	900.00	850.00	1,290.00	850.00	1,020.00	900.00	1,320.00
Other				200.00	375.00	375.00	875.00	375.00	1,550.00
M. Basketball	5,727.47	5,130.20	5,552.71	5,080.14	5,578.60	6,500.00	9,450.00	9,550.00	9,200.00
Meal & Lodging	1,185.00	682.50	1,797.50	1,037.00	1,419.50	1,561.13	2,830.50	3,442.50	2,440.50
Fee	525.00	225.00	275.00	275.00	375.00	275.00	—0—	450.00	450.00
Trans.	952.74	1,031.65	1,974.21	989.14	1,329.10	1,645.87	2,891.03	3,280.73	1,944.15
Equip.	579.00	856.05	670.00	551.00	500.00	600.00	1,043.00	301.77	781.00
Official	2,486.00	1,764.00	750.00	1,512.00	1,740.00	2,160.00	1,845.00	1,740.00	2,737.00
Other		571.00	86.00	716.00	215.00	258.00	836.50	315.00	830.00
JV Basketball		1,181.16	1,571.12	1,465.62	1,713.85	1,800.00	1,450.00	1,850.00	1,990.00
Meal & Lodging		140.00	495.00	495.00	450.00	513.78	405.00	472.50	472.50
Fee		—0—	100.00	—0—	—0—	—0—	—0—	—0—	—0—
Trans.		2,411.90	392.62	392.62	365.85	722.22	534.36	514.50	668.00
Equip.		295.25	5.50	0.00	—0—	—0—	—0—	—0—	—0—
Official		420.00	480.00	480.00	800.00	480.00	400.00	700.00	700.00
Other		84.00	98.00	98.00	98.00	84.00	107.50	150.50	150.50
W. Basketball	5,796.84	5,246.54	4,821.87	4,035.74	5,763.50	6,000.00	8,000.00	8,300.00	9,880.00
Meal & Lodging	1,792.00	2,201.50	994.76	652.50	1,562.50	1,405.63	2,647.50	2,856.00	2,677.50
Fee	270.00	150.00	175.00	175.00	50.00	50.00	—0—	250.00	250.00
Trans.	1,391.55	1,114.44	1,295.11	578.24	1,508.95	1,720.37	2,762.38	3,064.83	2,219.75
Equip.	469.29	199.60	430.00	150.00	1,141.55	150.00	438.42	182.95	1,779.00
Official	1,874.00	1,080.00	1,560.00	1,890.00	1,110.00	2,080.00	1,430.00	1,716.00	2,463.50
Other	—0—	501.00	367.00	590.00	400.50	594.00	736.50	193.50	500.00

(continued)

TABLE 7.4 Continued

	82–83	83–84	84–85	85–86	86–87	87–88	88–89	89–90	90–91
Cross Country	2,303.22	3,000.00	2,870.08	1,908.36	2,689.75	2,500.00	2,100.00	2,150.00	3,600.00
Meal & Lodging	801.00	1,011.00	1,424.00	696.50	1,192.50	158.85	1,314.00	1,044.00	1,463.40
Fee	180.00	325.00	170.00	270.00	203.00	200.00	151.00	100.00	205.00
Trans.	515.61	993.31	1,176.08	841.86	1,064.25	1,591.15	462.04	832.10	1,360.00
Equip.	—0—	670.69	—0—	100.00	—0—	550.00	100.00	155.00	472.40
Official	15.00	—0—	—0—	—0—	80.00	—0—	—0—	—0—	—0—
Other	—0—	—0—	100.00	150.00	—0—	—0—	—0—	—0—	100.00
Football	13,448.35	15,950.00	11,311.77	16,258.21	22,281.55	23,000.00	23,400.00	19,050.00	27,600.00
Meal & Lodging	2,575.00	2,725.00	1,344.00	2,684.50	3,348.00	4,956.00	5,292.00	2,268.00	6,210.00
Fee	200.00	200.00	300.00	350.00	377.50	400.00	375.00	400.00	405.00
Trans.	1,008.45	2,179.24	992.77	1,626.21	1,822.50	4,910.90	4,628.20	2,861.90	6,974.80
Equip.	7,179.90	7,995.76	6,000.00	6,000.00	13,558.55	9,053.10	9,007.35	9,000.00	10,000.00
Official	2,485.00	2,100.00	1,875.00	2,250.00	2,050.00	2,640.00	2,010.00	3,212.50	2,650.00
Other	—0—	750.00	800.00	3,347.50	1,125.00	1,040.00	2,000.00	1,500.00	1,300.00
B. Football		1,451.75	1,740.00	1,621.00	1,560.50	1,600.00	1,800.00	2,500.00	2,300.00
Meal & Lodging		180.00	480.00	540.00	300.00	540.00	480.00	660.00	780.00
Fee		—0—	—0—	—0—	—0—	—0—	—0—	—0—	—0—
Trans.		55.00	440.00	261.00	80.50	782.89	581.30	1,340.00	903.75
Equip.		916.50	—0—	—0—	—0—	—0—	—0—	—0—	—0—
Official		280.00	750.00	750.00	1,075.00	450.00	750.00	500.00	600.00
Other		20.25	70.00	70.00	105.00	—0—	—0—	—0—	—0—
Gymnastics	2,820.56	3,157.00	2,943.95	2,806.78	4,070.50	3,300.00	4,500.00	4,500.00	5,830.00
Meal & Lodging	1,290.00	1,402.50	1,552.50	1,185.00	562.50	607.50	1,147.50	821.70	1,314.00
Fee	190.00	200.00	180.00	180.00	25.00	25.00	225.00	40.00	100.00
Trans.	1,002.36	792.50	603.45	1,263.78	414.00	462.61	1,222.00	1,399.35	1,712.70
Equip.	290.20	442.00	240.00	50.00	2,457.00	1,357.11	1,125.00	1,315.00	1,895.00
Official	48.00	320.00	360.00	120.00	580.00	730.00	1,125.00	840.00	520.00
Other	—0—	—0—	8.00	8.00	32.00	32.00	225.00	75.00	290.00

Field Hockey	4,016.41	5,315.92	3,877.02	3,784.23	5,852.75	5,000.00	5,100.00	7,900.00	9,150.00
Meal & Lodging	1,407.00	1,554.50	2,079.00	1,596.00	2,520.00	1,376.52	840.00	2,205.00	2,299.50
Fee	185.00	212.00	212.00	87.00	325.00	300.00	—0—	—0—	165.00
Trans.	868.63	945.58	956.02	891.23	1,316.75	1,478.52	1,089.72	2,775.00	4,372.50
Equip.	1,072.78	2,064.84	—0—	300.00	631.00	1,250.00	1,740.00	1,543.43	900.00
Official	483.00	539.00	600.00	810.00	910.00	450.00	1,200.00	1,200.00	1,080.00
Other	—0—	—0—	—0—	100.00	150.00	—0—	200.00	150.00	350.00
Ice Hockey	14,075.42	13,717.19	15,052.50	16,255.25	15,298.00	23,000.00	23,850.00	23,100.00	26,850.00
Meal & Lodging	2,593.50	1,291.00	1,942.50	1,858.50	2,047.50	3,874.00	4,011.00	3,403.50	3,864.00
Fee	300.00	275.00	400.00	450.00	75.00	375.00	—0—	350.00	375.00
Trans.	2,414.95	1,321.59	1,860.00	2,072.75	1,260.25	7,212.15	7,047.55	7,327.60	8,722.50
Equip.	6,078.91	7,744.10	6,329.00	6,300.00	10,325.25	10,400.00	9,395.45	9,000.00	10,000.00
Official	2,688.00	2,464.00	2,450.00	2,275.00	1,450.00	2,520.00	2,450.00	2,660.00	3,246.00
Other	—0—	621.00	2,071.00	3,299.00	140.00	474.00	946.00	332.00	650.00
M. Soccer	5,019.93	5,857.22	4,466.23	4,434.52	4,490.50	6,500.00	6,550.00	6,500.00	9,680.00
Meal & Lodging	1,911.00	1,533.00	867.00	726.00	792.00	1,412.00	2,178.00	1,518.00	2,772.00
Fee	125.00	125.00	125.00	125.00	25.00	25.00	—0—	75.00	75.00
Trans.	1,499.17	1,372.46	1,099.23	683.52	1,041.50	1,313.93	2,928.53	1,920.00	3,235.70
Equip.	508.76	1,341.76	500.00	500.00	500.00	1,277.07	144.00	840.00	1.096.00
Official	976.00	1,250.00	1,525.00	2,035.00	1,812.00	1,422.00	1,485.00	1,850.00	2,050.00
Other	—0—	235.00	350.00	365.00	320.00	350.00	725.00	215.00	450.00
JV Soccer		693.00	1,183.41	1,464.20	1,520.00	—0—	—0—	—0—	—0—
Meal & Lodging	n/a	175.00	330.00	450.00	360.00	—0—	—0—	—0—	—0—
Fee	n/a	—0—	—0—	—0—	—0—	—0—	—0—	—0—	—0—
Trans.	n/a	200.00	253.41	394.20	280.00	—0—	—0—	—0—	—0—
Equip.	n/a	—0—	—0—	—0—	—0—	—0—	—0—	—0—	—0—
Official	n/a	318.00	600.00	560.00	820.00	—0—	—0—	—0—	—0—
Other	n/a	—0—	—0—	60.00	60.00	—0—	—0—	—0—	—0—

(continued)

TABLE 7.4 Continued

	82–83	83–84	84–85	85–86	86–87	87–88	88–89	89–90	90–91
W. Soccer		6,419.35	3,232.02	4,680.10	6,370.50	7,000.00	6,600.00	6,150.00	5,550.00
Meal & Lodging		1,312.50	1,152.00	1,128.00	2,556.00	2,088.00	1,752.00	1,903.00	1,419.99
Fee		30.00	100.00	150.00	175.00	175.00	—0—	75.00	75.00
Trans.		661.38	640.02	787.10	1,425.50	2,522.74	972.02	2,339.00	976.90
Equip.		3,568.48	600.00	500.00	500.00	1,199.26	1,280.00	180.00	843.50
Official		742.00	680.00	1,850.00	1,319.00	910.00	1,760.00	1,330.00	1,915.00
Other		105.00	60.00	265.00	395.00	105.00	780.00	235.00	310.00
Softball	3,501.63	3,561.14	2,536.09	3,332.47	4,937.50	5,000.00	6,500.00	8,800.00	7,100.00
Meal & Lodging	1,350.00	1,552.00	1,210.00	1,120.00	1,330.00	1,980.00	3,210.00	3,510.00	2,580.00
Fee	135.00	275.00	25.00	25.00	175.00	175.00	125.00	125.00	165.50
Trans.	932.98	798.08	551.09	977.47	802.50	1,212.85	1,663.34	2,132.00	1,607.00
Equip.	633.65	386.06	200.00	640.00	990.00	967.85	385.00	2,090.00	695.00
Official	450.00	550.00	550.00	570.00	1,540.00	600.00	600.00	910.00	780.00
Other	—0—	—0—	—0—	—0—	100.00	—0—	500.00	50.00	1,250.00
Tennis			1,000.52	1,936.52	2,317.45	2,100.00	1,300.00	2,100.00	2,250.00
Meal & Lodging			470.00	525.00	1,080.00	615.00	420.00	840.00	930.00
Fee			160.00	310.00	265.00	165.00	—0—	—0—	—0—
Trans.			250.52	651.52	376.25	538.57	353.81	733.00	636.45
Equip.			120.00	350.00	316.20	451.43	326.88	396.00	300.00
Official				—0—	—0—	—0—	—0—	—0—	—0—
Other				100.00	280.00	330.00	170.00	140.00	380.00
Men Swimming		1,782.90	2,083.94	3,421.31	3,380.00	4,700.00	2,550.00	6,200.00	5,800.00
Meal & Lodging		600.70	1,496.00	816.00	1,657.50	1,989.00	1,300.50	2,735.50	2,190.00
Fee	55.00	85.00	250.00	90.00	90.00	—0—	—0—	—0—	—0—
Trans.		203.20	312.94	885.31	410.75	1,851.76	413.47	1,933.40	793.40
Equip.		789.00		350.00	501.75	469.24	300.00	1,113.00	1,690.00
Official	126.00	190.00	520.00	570.00	300.00	560.00	—0—	420.00	945.00
Other		9.00	—0—	600.00	150.00	—0—	—0—	—0—	200.00

Women Swim	3,485.58	4,507.10	4,197.50	3,831.27	3,414.55	4,800.00	2,550.00	6,400.00	5,800.00	
Meal & Lodging	1,440.00	1,950.00	2,633.00	1,989.00	1,683.00	1,989.00	1,196.60	2,645.50	2,130.00	
Fee	160.00	185.00	240.00	260.00	190.00	90.00	—0—	—0—	—0—	
Trans.	607.08	937.13	324.50	1,117.20	334.80	1,851.76	323.14	1,853.90	602.60	
Equip.	558.50	804.97	730.00* M&W	350.00	486.75	639.24	700.00	1,486.60	2,211.40	
Official	720.00	630.00	270.00	115.00	570.00	230.00	560.00	420.00	630.00	
Other		—0—	—0—	—0—	150.00	—0—	—0—	—0—	200.00	
Track (combined)	5,003.95	5,947.00	7,481.53	8,095.47	7,696.65	11,900.00	11,800.00	14,600.00	15,535.00	
INDOOR TOTAL						6,200.00	6,300.00	8,050.00	8,400.00	
i Meal & Lodging	2,777.50	1,220.00	2,458.50	2,232.00	2,400.00	4,110.00	3,255.00	4,845.00	4,882.50	
n Fee	501.00	425.00	850.00	810.00	468.00	450.00	125.00	250.00	200.00	
d Trans.	1,204.14	546.61	989.91	1,060.43	845.25	1,640.00	2,942.04	2,950.80	3,233.25	
o Equip.	371.31	840.88	—0—	240.00	584.00	—0—	—0—	—0—	—0—	
o Official	150.00	—0—	—0—	—0—	—0—	—0—	—0—	—0—	—0—	
r Other	—0—	—0—	—0—	—0—	395.15	—0—	—0—	—0—	100.00	
Track—Outdoor										
o Meal & Lodging						5,700.00	5,500.00	6,550.00	7,135.00	
u Fee		2,050.00	1,504.00	2,338.00	1,440.00	3,030.00	1,725.00	3,180.00	4,087.50	
t Trans.		—0—	—0—	—0—	234.00	334.00	—0—	300.00	272.00	
d Equip.		664.51	1,399.12	1,295.04	920.25	1,936.00	1,804.55	2,831.80	1,475.75	
o Official		200.00	200.00	120.00	260.00	400.00	—0—	100.00	200.00	
o Other		—0—	80.00	—0—	150.00	—0—	—0—	—0—	100.00	
r		—0—	—0—	—0—	—0—	—0—	1,949.00	150.00	1,000.00	
Volleyball	4,002.38	5,220.09	5,010.86	6,330.66	5,909.45	6,600.00	7,550.00	6,600.00	8,580.00	(8,580.00)
Meal & Lodging	1,841.00	1,176.50	2,254.00	2,525.00	2,037.00	2,029.00	3,360.00	3,060.00	3,465.00	
Fee	425.00	310.00	585.00	660.00	380.00	630.00	650.00	450.00	550.00	
Trans.	820.43	539.50	1,066.86	1,335.66	1,338.75	1,795.00	1,394.78	1,191.95	1,629.30	
Equip.	105.95	1,519.09	300.00	300.00	767.70	300.00	715.00	345.00	536.45	
Official	810.00	1,600.00	680.00	1,360.00	1,236.00	1,696.00	1,320.00	1,440.00	2,100.00	
Other	—0—	175.00	125.00	150.00	150.00	150.00	85.00	50.00	300.00	

(continued)

TABLE 7.4 Continued

	82–83	83–84	84–85	85–86	86–87	87–88	88–89	89–90	90–91
Wrestling	4,012.22	4,344.60	5,875.52	5,105.84	8,117.85	7,000.00	7,550.00	10,400.00	10,700.00
Meal & Lodge	1,989.00	2,133.00	3,460.50	2,754.50	2,667.00	2,977.50	3,654.00	3,891.00	4,767.00
Fee	255.00	285.00	415.00	385.00	310.00	340.00	175.00	350.00	375.00
Trans.	670.30	539.50	1,175.02	1,206.34	1,885.75	2,004.03	1,925.04	1,995.28	2,293.65
Equip.	692.84	932.10	500.00	500.00	2,255.10	1,378.47	1,436.00	3,651.00	2,393.00
Official	496.00	455.00	325.00	260.00	840.00	240.00	240.00	420.00	300.00
Other	—0—	—0—	—0—	—0—	160.00	60.00	100.00	100.00	600.00
B. Wrestling		466.50	638.37	558.19	1,002.75	800.00	400.00	400.00	700.00
Meal		72.00	162.00	216.00	510.00	332.05	210.00	220.00	189.00
Fee		—0—	—0—	—0—	120.00	120.00	—0—	—0—	169.00
Trans.		69.50	176.37	162.19	312.75	227.55	63.53	60.00	253.45
Equip.		—0—	—0—	—0—	—0—	—0—	—0—	—0—	—0—
Official		325.00	300.00	180.00	60.00	120.00	120.00	120.00	120.00
Other		—0—	—0—	—0—	—0—	—0—	—0—	—0—	—0—
Football Cheerleading						300.00	300.00	400.00	400.00
Meal						150.00	150.00	—0—	
Trans.						150.00	150.00	—0—	
Equip.								400.00	400.00
Basketball Cheerleading						300.00	300.00	400.00	400.00
Meal						150.00	150.00	—0—	
Trans.						150.00	150.00	—0—	
Equip.								400.00	400.00
Equipment Contingency							900.00	1,000.00	1,250.00

Prepared by: Dr. Wm. Stier, Director of Athletics—12/7/89

*These figures do not include postseason.

parking condos (Stier, 1994b, pp. 175, 176). Other sources of income include reserved or special seating, sponsors, direct solicitation of potential donors, radio and television advertising, fence or building advertising, guarantees, gifts and donations, program advertising and sales, as well as other forms of fundraising (Mason and Paul, 1988).

Of course, in the case of big time NCAA Division I sports and professional sports there is the matter of a sizable income via television contracts. Another large source of income for collegiate teams is general student fees, fees assessed on all students and earmarked for the intercollegiate athletic programs.

Sources of Income for Major College Sport Programs

Even big-time division I collegiate athletic powers are continuing to experience severe financial challenges (if not downright crises) in their endeavors to remain financially viable. In 1994 it was reported that the average major college (division I-A) athletic department obtained its income from the following sources: football ($6,226,415 or 42.8%); donations, gifts, and investments ($2,452,830 or 16.2%); men's basketball ($2,207,547 or 15.4%); student fees, state and institutional aid ($1,905,660 or 15.3%); fundraising efforts (such as concessions, program sales, sponsorships, facility rental, and sports camps) $1,396,226 or 9.1%; other men's sports ($132,076 or 0.8%); and women's sports ($56,604 or 0.4%) (Wieberg, 1994).

Concept 205: All Income Must Go through (Be Deposited in) the Organization's Income Account—Never Commingle Funds.

A generally accepted principle of accounting and budgeting is that all income generated for the organization should go directly into an appropriate income account. Never commingle monies that belong to the sport entity with one's own funds. To insure that all income is properly accounted for, it is imperative that all money generated by the organization be deposited in a suitable income account before it is spent.

Only after the income is safely deposited and accounted for can it then be expended through the normal process stipulated in the organization's or department's standard operating procedures. However, to do otherwise, that is, to spend monies generated for or by the sport entity before it is accounted for, is an invitation to disaster. Even the best of intentions will not compensate or protect the transgressor from disastrous consequences ranging from official reprimand to outright dismissal from employment of the organization.

General Expenditures for Sport Entities

Just as there are similarities in income among different types of sport organizations there are differences in the type of expenses incurred by various types of sport entities, whether they be professional teams, fitness clubs, corporate wellness and health organizations, recreation departments, or school-based athletic programs.

Concept 206: The Major Share of Expenditures in Collegiate Athletic Programs Rests in Personnel (Labor) and Related Costs (Benefits).

For most sport organizations a significant portion of expenses falls under personnel (labor). Labor costs include the direct costs of salaries, wages, and benefits, and the indirect cost of staff training. For professional teams this includes players' salaries as well as the salaries for staff, both professional and support personnel. For fitness, health, and wellness organizations, personnel is also a sizable portion of their expenses. Recreation programs as well as athletic departments also are faced with significant expenditures for professional and support staff. "Labor costs constitute nearly 60 percent of the typical short-term operating budget for an athletic department" (Graham, 1994, p. 176).

Big-time NCAA division I athletic programs have other personnel expenses to be concerned about, specifically, scholarships for their elite athletes. And, with the increasing cost of doing business at the division I level of competition, more and more athletic programs are operating in the black. By some estimates NCAA institutions competing at the elite division I level (the nation's major athletic programs) are operating at an annual financial deficit as high as 70 percent (Wieberg, 1994, August 25). Lederman (1993) surmised that, of the biggest college sports programs (Division I) in the NCAA, fewer than 50 are believed to turn a profit, and the latest statistics revealed in 1989 that the average Division I-A profit was a mere $39,000. This is in spite of the millions of dollars in revenue such programs are taking in through big-time football and men's basketball.

Personnel Expenses at the Professional Sports Level

The average salary of professional athletes in the major sports (Major League Baseball [MLB], National Football League [NFL], National Basketball Association [NBA], and the National Hockey League [NHL]) has grown dramatically in recent decades. In professional football, the average player salary during 1960–1961 was $15,000. In 1993 this figure topped $645,000 and the figures continue to rise each and every year. Other professional sports have likewise enjoyed the tremendous growth in individual salaries, with the average player's salary in MLB being $1,076,000, $540,000 in the NHL, and $1,390,000 in the NBA (Salary escalation continues, 1993; The NFL's Television Contract History, 1994).

> Of course, part of the reason why there has been such an escalation in professional athletes' salaries rests in the ever increasing television revenue pouring into the coffers of the teams themselves. In 1960–61 the NFL took in a total of $600,000 in television monies for an average TV income per team of $45,000. Contrast that to the time period 1990–1993 when the TV package involved $3.65 billion dollars for a $32.6 million dollar paycheck to each NFL team (The NFL's Television Contract History, 1994, p. 19).

One wonders what would be the case today without television in the money equation in professional sports.

TABLE 7.5 Greece, New York, School District Interscholastic Athletic Budget, 1996–1997 School Year

Expense Categories	Amount
Athletic Administrator's Salaries	$ 196,086
Coaches' Salaries	375,000
Secretaries' Salaries	52,214
Additional Salaries/Summer Salaries	8,500
Salary Overtime/Substitutes/Part-time	8,500
Fringe Benefits for Personnel	161,356
Equipment Replacement	2,000
Equipment Additional	12,000
Supplies and Materials	66,700
Contracted Services (ice time, etc.)	31,400
Equipment Repair	1,500
Special Fees	3,500
Officials' Fees	56,000
Medical Fees	8,200
Workshops (tournaments)	4,500
Memberships	13,400
Travel District Business	5,100
TOTAL:	$1,005,956

Personnel Athletic Expenses at the Secondary School Level

Table 7.5 illustrates a typical secondary school athletic program in which the vast majority of the expenditures are budgeted for personnel costs. In fact, the Greece, New York Central School District proposed athletic budget for the 1996–1997 school year was just over a million dollars ($1,005,956 to be exact). Of that amount, almost 80 percent was earmarked for personnel costs (coaches, administrators, and secretaries). It should be noted that travel expenses are not included as part of the athletic budget but in the regular school budget.

Other Categories of Sport Expenditure

Other categories of expense that might be appropriate to some sport organizations include, but are not limited to, the following: recruiting costs, travel, insurance, food, nongame equipment and supplies, capital improvements, capital equipment, capital expenses for structures, facilities maintenance, rental of services, game equipment/supplies (including uniforms and laundry), security, police, medical, phone, postage, printing, utilities, programs, souvenirs and premiums, paint, brochures, pocket schedule cards, dues, memberships, guarantees, freight, lease or rental costs, photographs, subscriptions, and general office supplies (Douple, 1990).

The Question of Keeping Expenses in Line with Income

Concept 207: Another Key Element to a Balanced Budget Is to Keep Expenses in Line with Anticipated Income.

Every administrator is faced with the prospect of making sure that all monies spent under that person's watch are appropriate expenditures. That is, that all monies spent are spent wisely and appropriately and that such expenses enable the organization to realize its objectives, goals, and mission(s). An important part of this *wise spending* is being able to keep expenses in line with anticipated income. If sport managers and administrators had all the money and resources they wanted it would be relatively easy to accomplish most objectives and goals. Needless to say, this is not the case in many instances.

Cash Flow

Cash flow refers to one's ability to have sufficient cash on hand to pay current bills (debt). It is this ability to pay current expenses with cash on hand that results in positive cash flow. Unfortunately, some organizations find themselves in a cash flow crisis by having current debt that is greater than available cash, a situation referred to as *negative cash flow.* This situation can result when the company or organization is owed cash from any number of sources but the actual cash is not yet on hand (in the bank) in sufficient amount to pay the bills that are current.

Concept 208: Profit Is Important to Any Sport Organization but Managers Should Not Neglect Positive Cash Flow if the Organization Is to Survive and Prosper.

Foresighted sport managers need to be constantly vigilant in terms of their organization's cash flow situation. Facing a cash flow crisis forces fiscal managers to consider borrowing against receivables or postponing the payment of their own bills. Preventing cash flow problems can be a three-pronged effort. First, one can attempt to accelerate monies owed to one's own organization. Second, efforts can be made to collect late payments or past due accounts as well as bad debts. Third, one may endeavor to postpone entering into debt until sufficient cash is on hand or seek more generous payment schedules from those to whom money is owed.

Cost-Effectiveness and Sound Fiscal Management

Concept 209: The Goal of Financial Managers Is to Keep Costs in Line with Expenses.

In today's business of sport the challenge of most administrators is to be able to work within the budget restrictions and limitations created by a lack of income and the presence of a mul-

Weight training is becoming a major attraction for patrons everywhere.
Read Photography, Cedar Rapids, Iowa.

titude of expenses. Again, the key is to keep the expenses in line with income so that there is a balanced budget at the end of the calendar or fiscal year. Fiscal responsibility is the watchword of the professional sport administrator in the twenty-first Century.

The budget process is a balancing of two factors, income and expenses (Sattler & Mullens, 1993, February). Simultaneously, today's and tomorrow's sports leader must attempt to increase income while also keeping expenditures in line with the income generated. Part of this challenge can be resolved by prudent and frugal use (management) of the financial resources at one's disposal. In the final analysis, one of the cardinal sins of any sport administrator is to misspend or waste valuable resources (monies). To do so exemplifies the inept administrator.

Concept 210: If Sport Managers Had All of the Money and Resources They Needed or Wanted It Would Not Be Difficult to Accomplish Most Objectives and Goals.

Exponential Growth of Big-Time College Athletics

Harris (1994) described the exponential growth of big-time college athletics, which came to an end in the early 1990s when athletic administrators realized that there had to be an end to the continued increasing expenses incurred by athletic departments. The 1980s were a boom/bust financial cycle for most athletic departments. During the 1990s, however, the atmosphere became more grim with the realization that financial restraints would be the order of the day rather than ever-increasing expansion and expenditures. Revenue was not keeping up with expenses and, as any business leader recognizes, when that happens the cure is to reduce expenditures and reduce them significantly and quickly.

Cost-reducing became the catch-phrase of the athletic/sport community in the 1990s in an effort to place the entire athletic programs on an even keel, one which would be close to self-supporting. However, *only a small number of institutions are truly self-supporting*. The vast majority of all athletic programs, even the major Division I institutions, rely on financial contributions from the institution in one form or another (Stier, 1994, April 14).

Concept 211: To Misspend Money or to Otherwise Waste Valuable Resources Is the Epitome of the Incompetent Administrator.

Maintaining a Balanced Budget: Keeping Expenses in Line with Income

One of the ways to keep within a budget (that is, balancing expenses with income) is to reduce costs without sacrificing quality (Sattler & Doniek, 1996). All items of expenditure within a budget should actually be needed. Budgets with "fat" (unnecessary items or expenditures) in them are poorly constructed budgets. The goal is to eliminate such unnecessary expenditures within any budget (Olson, 1986).

Concept 212: When Reducing Costs, the Watchword Is to Do So without Reduction in Quality (Either in Goods or Services).

Today, everyone in the business of sports is experiencing financial pains and restraints. As a result, there is a need for effective and efficient fundraising and income-producing efforts because normal sources of income are insufficient to balance the budget and do what is necessary to be competitive. There is also a great need to cut costs. Ideally, the combination of more income coupled with a reduction in unnecessary costs will produce the desired end result: sufficient funds to operate the sport program and, in the case of for-profit sport entities, greater net income.

Concept 213: Accountability Is the Buzzword in Fiscal Management.

One must be accountable for one's actions and one must hold others accountable. Accountability is important in the purchase of new resources, in the care of resources (supplies, equipment, and facilities, etc.), in the repair of such resources, and in the replacement of items that are of no further use to the sport entity. Competent sport leaders do all they can to be accountable for those resources placed under their responsibility. To do otherwise is not only poor management but, in the final analysis, self-defeating.

Concept 214: Don't Allow Equipment or Supplies to "Walk Away."

With equipment and supplies being so valuable, administrators should do all in their power to insure that such items are not misused, misappropriated, or lost. Every item that must be replaced takes valuable resources away from the organization, dollars that might have been spent for other important purposes. Being able to reduce, if not eliminate, the expenditures for items stolen, lost, or otherwise made unusable, enables the sport manager to put to better use the limited funds available to the sport organization.

Concept 215: Every Dollar Saved Is a Dollar Earned.

Toward this end, it is imperative that a suitable checkout policy be instituted in those instances in which items of supplies and equipment are checked out by participants or club members. One example of a checkout policy is illustrated in Box 7.1. In this instance, those persons checking out items are held accountable for their safe return, in suitable condition.

If items are no longer useful to the sport organization and if a decision is made to dispose of some items, it is important that an appropriate disposal process be determined, with the items then being removed from the active inventory list. Sometimes the items are literally destroyed. Other times the decision is consciously made to give the items away. And, in other situations, some organizations dispose of supply and equipment items that they can no longer use by means of a sale or auction to raise funds. In this fashion, the organization is able to accomplish two objectives simultaneously. Specifically, the items are disposed of, there is income produced, and there is the possibility of generating favorable publicity on behalf of the sport entity.

The Financial Audit

Financial audits are a necessary element of control in that they provide a check on both the financial procedures of an organization as well as measuring how well the sport entity treats both financial expenditures and income, that is, whether the entity is in sound financial condition. Not to be viewed as a negative process, audits should be thought of in a positive vein, as a helpful tool in the process of fiscal management (Jensen, 1992; Sattler & Mullins, 1993b, April). It is normal to double-check the financial management of any organization or business that deals with significant amounts of money, both not-for-profit and for-profit entities.

Concept 216: A Financial Audit Is to Be Viewed as a Helpful Tool to Determine the Acceptability of the Financial Procedures Utilized by the Sport Organization.

BOX 7.1
Checkout and Return Policy Form

Checkout and Return Policies for Intercollegiate Athletics Supplies and Equipment

1. Persons who check out items from the equipment room are required to sign for those items and to provide their social security numbers and other pertinent information.
2. All items checked out *become the responsibility of the borrower* and must be returned in person to the equipment room. Borrowers will be issued a receipt by the equipment manager upon return of all items.
3. Items must be returned in good condition. Ordinary wear and tear is anticipated.
4. All items must be returned by the deadline (two weeks following the last scheduled intercollegiate contest in the sport for which the items were issued).
5. Borrowers may elect to purchase items they have checked out by paying current replacement cost, as determined by the Department of Intercollegiate Athletics. Payment must be made to the Department by the deadline date.
6. After the two-week deadline date, the Department will proceed to replace unreturned items. Therefore, no items can be accepted for return after the deadline date.
7. After the two-week deadline date, if items have been neither returned nor purchased by the borrower, the Bursar's Office will bill the borrower for all unreturned items. (**NOTE:** *Students may not preregister or register for subsequent semesters nor can they obtain grades or transcripts until outstanding bills are paid.*)

I have read the above checkout and return policies and agree to return all items listed below (or to pay the current replacement costs associated with each item) within the two-week time period, or upon request by a designee of the Athletic Director.

Items of equipment/supplies borrowed: ______________________________

____

____

Items listed above must be returned by: ______________________________

Signature: ______________________________ Date: ________________

Name (print): ______________________________ SS #:________________

School Address: ______________________________ Phone: ________________

Home Address: ______________________________ Phone: ________________

____

City/Town State Zip Code

Generally Accepted Accounting Procedures/Practices (GAAPP)

An audit can point out discrepancies, deviations, or irregularities in the management and handling of money within an organization. The management and accounting of monies in businesses and organizations must follow what is referred to in the accounting profession as *generally accepted accounting procedures and practices* (GAAPP).

Internal Audits

There are two types of audits, internal and external. An *internal audit* is conducted by employees of the organization itself to insure that the organization's own policies, practices, and procedures are being followed and implemented in accordance with the organization's own standard operating procedures (SOPs) insofar as the overall fiscal management within the entity is concerned. An internal audit can help prevent fiscal mismanagement. Such an audit can also aid in the increased security of resources and assets of the organization.

Protecting the Resources and Assets of the Organization

> **Concept 217:** The Key to Dealing with Financial Audits Is to Keep Detailed Written Records (Paper Trail) and to Follow both Generally Accepted Accounting Procedures and Practices As Well As the Organization's Own Standard Operating Procedures, Practices, and Policies.

In terms of security, sport administrators are constantly on the alert to protect the financial integrity of the organization. This involves three different aspects. First, the security of the resources and assets (supplies, equipment, and facilities) of the sport organization must be preserved. Second, there is the matter of the integrity of the organization's own personnel, paid and volunteer. Efforts must be made to reduce absenteeism as well as the misuse or abuse of the organization's supplies, equipment, and facilities. And third, there is a matter of protecting the financial well-being of the organization from patrons and/or customers.

External Audits

An *external* (at arm's length) *financial audit,* conducted by an outside, unbiased, expert accountant (auditor), seeks to determine whether the accounting procedures and transactions for that specific entity are in line with generally accepted accounting procedure and practices (GAAPP) for that specific type of business or organization.

> **Concept 218:** Conduct Periodic Value Audits or Analysis of What You Do, How You Do It, and the Costs Incurred in Doing It—Is It Cost-Effective?

An Audit of the Organization's Value: A Different Type of Audit or Self-Examination

A value audit looks at everything an organization does and asks the following questions (Horine, 1995; Sattler & Mullins, 1993b).

1. What is it that we do?
2. What do we do well?
3. Why do we do it?
4. Does it need to be done this way?
5. Is it essential to our prime mission?
6. Is the cost appropriate to the benefit generated?
7. Is there anything that we do that is unnecessary?
8. Is the cost of what we do necessary?
9. Can we do it more effectively or efficiently?
10. How can we eliminate some of what we do without diminishing the results of our efforts?
11. How can we do what we do for less cost without sacrificing quality?

Effective Tactics in Budgeting

Use of a "Wish List" in Budget Planning

Some sport administers have found the use of a "wish list" to be very helpful. This list contains purchase requests for big ticket items (in terms of expense). However, these items are not included within the upcoming budget, but are requested for a future budget cycle, one within the next three to seven years. The "wish list" is typically submitted by coaches and/or program coordinators along with their regular budget requests for the next year's budget to the department or area administrator.

Following the review of all items from the individual "wish lists," those who had submitted individual big ticket items are told whether specific items have been tentatively approved and when (in what budget year) the items may most likely be placed in the regular budget proposal for that particular sport, program, department, or area. For example, an expensive equipment item, such as an exercise machine, might be placed on such a list for possible delivery three years hence. However, the organization, through its financial decision-makers, might respond with an indication that this exercise machine might be approved not three years in the future but rather five years.

Concept 219: The Use of the "Wish List" Can Facilitate Planning As Well As Serve as a Motivating Factor for Employees.

The major advantages of the formal use of such a "wish list" are twofold. First, when such "wish lists" are used throughout the sport organization the immediate and long-term planning process, at all levels of the organization, is greatly facilitated, because the list provides those administrators who must eventually make financial recommendations and decisions with greater insight into specific future needs *and* the accompanying financial commitment to meet them. Second, the presence of a "wish list" within a specific sport or program can serve as a motivating factor for the employees who make and support the recommendation, because those who support an item on the "wish list" are at least told if the request itself has merit. They are also made aware when (in what year) it might be possible to include the item formally as part of the regular budgetary process and, barring some unforeseen difficulty, expect to have the request approved.

Be Open Regarding the Budgetary Process and the Actual Budget

The budget should be open for all to see. In some instances, the state public access laws dictate that financial records, including the budget, of a state entity will be open for inspection to the general public. Nevertheless, it is a good idea to keep both the budgetary process and the budget itself open for all to see. The rationale is simple. If there is nothing to hide, then why keep the budget or the budgetary process under a veil of secrecy? Be open in everything that pertains to the budget and the budgetary process.

Concept 220: Keep No Secrets when It Comes to the Budgetary Process or the Budget Itself.

When the author arrived at the State University of New York (Brockport) as the new Director of Athletics, the student government was demanding to have access to the athletic department's budget because student fees constituted a major portion of the income to the sports program.

When the budget for that year (as well as subsequent years) was indeed made available to *everyone* on and off campus (students, coaches, faculty, community members, etc.), it did not take too many years before the student government leaders indicated that they no longer wanted to take the time to review the athletic budget in such great detail. They reasoned that if the athletic administration had anything to hide, the budget would not have been made so accessible to "everyone under the sun." When the data was truly made available many people lost interest in scrutinizing the document. However, if the budget (or the process) was shrouded in secrecy there would undoubtedly be demands for more and more people to review the budget and the supporting documents.

Keeping Employees Abreast of the Financial Status of the Organization

An Ernst & Young survey of large companies (Jones, 1995) revealed that 86 percent of employees/workers would be motivated to help their companies succeed if they were privy to financial data typically seen only by senior managers, such as balance sheets and cash-flow statements. Also, such information may make it possible for employees to make decisions or devise strategies that will help improve the efficiency of the organization and/or enable the company to save money or find better use of a variety of resources. Some college and university athletic directors subscribe to this principle even to the extent of allowing all coaches on staff to be privy to the team budgets of all the teams at that institution.

> **Concept 221:** Employees Tend to Be More Motivated to Support and Help the Organization when Kept Abreast of Its Financial Health.

"Open Book Management"

This openness mentality would reinforce the trend in management referred to as "open-book management," which encourages employees to assume a greater role for the end-product or service of the organization. No, not everything should be shared with everyone. There are such things as trade secrets which, by their very nature, should be kept within the purview of a small number of individuals who need to know. For example, there is a very good and valid reason why the recipe for Coca-Cola should not become knowledge among the employees of the company or the general public. Those items that should remain a trade secret should do so.

Conclusions

There is perhaps no more important area for a sport manager to be concerned with than the fiscal dimension of the sport business or organization. Whether it pertains to the budgetary planning process, the implementation of the budget, or any of the many related activities and processes associated with the budget or monetary elements of the organization, it is essential that sport managers operate from a position of knowledge. In short, competent sport managers must be familiar with the fiscal dimensions of the sport business in which they find themselves. Failure to be fiscally responsible, at any level within any type of sport organization, is not only professionally inexcusable but is a frequently a professional "death warrant" for the sport manager. Even nonprofit sport entities must be concerned with the fiscal well-being of the organization. Success for every sport, recreation, and fitness business or organization is determined, to a great extent, on adequate planning and sound fiscal management.

REFERENCES

Apostolou, N. G. and Crumbley, D. L. (1988). *Handbook of governmental accounting and finance.* New York: John Wiley and Sons.

Bidding at all costs. (1995, August). *Athletic Business, 19*(8), 45–48, 50–51.

Butcher, C. A. and Krotee, M. L. (1993). *Management of physical education and sport.* St. Louis, MO: Mosby Year Book.

Carter, J. (1977, January). Jimmy Carter tells why he will use zero-base budgeting. *Nation's Business, 65,* 26.

Dirmith, W. W. and Jablonsky, S. F. (1979, October). Zero-base budgeting as a management technique and political strategy. *Academy of Management Review, 4*(4), 555–565.

Douple, T. (1990, January). Building a budget. *College Athletic Magazine, 11*(1), 54–58.
Graham, P. J. (Ed.). (1994). *Sport business—Operational and theoretical aspects.* Madison, WI: Wm. C. Brown & Benchmark.
Haggerty, T. R. and Patton, G. A. (1984). *Financial management of sport-related organizations.* Champaign, IL: Stripes Publishing.
Harris, C. (1994, April/May). Back on budget. *Athletic Management, VI*(3), 10–11, 13–17.
Horine, L. (1995). *Administration of physical education and sport programs.* Madison, WI: Wm. C. Brown & Benchmark.
Jensen, C. R. (1992). *Administrative management of physical education and athletic programs* (3rd ed.). Philadelphia: Lea & Febiger.
Jones, D. (1995, December 12). Open-book policy can motivate employees. *USA Today,* p. 1-B.
Lederman, D. (1993, July 21). Draft report by business officers' group says colleges must rein in sports budgets. *The Chronicle of Higher Education, XXXIV*(46), A-27, A-28.
Mason, J. G. and Paul, J. (1988). *Modern sports administration.* Englewood Cliffs, NJ: Prentice-Hall.
Olson, J. R. (1986, April). Athletic budgeting without headaches. *Athletic Business, 10*(4), 94–96, 98.
Parkhouse, B. L. (Ed.). (1996). *The management of sport—Its foundation and application* (2nd ed.). St. Louis, MO: Mosby Year Book.
Railey, J. H. and Tschauner, P. R. (1993). *Managing physical education, fitness, and sports programs* (2nd ed.). Mountain View, CA: Mayfield.
Salary escalation continues. (1993, December 27). *USA Today,* p. 2-C.
Sattler, T. P. and Doniek, C. A. (1996, April). Trim the extra fat from your facility. *Fitness Management, 12*(5), 38–40.
Sattler, T. P. and Mullens, J. E. (1993a, February). How to budget simply, effectively. *Fitness Management, 9*(2), 25.
Sattler, T. P. and Mullins, J. E. (1993b, April). How to limit the aggravation of audits. *Fitness Management, 9*(5), 12.
Stier, W. F., Jr., (1989, December 7). *SUNY–Brockport intercollegiate athletic budget.* Brockport, NY: State University of New York Press.
Stier, W. F., Jr., (1994a, April 14). *Fundraising for the 90s.* Presentation made at the national convention of the American Alliance for Health, Physical Education, Recreation and Dance (AAHPERD), Denver, Colorado.
Stier, W. F., Jr., (1994b). *Successful sport fund-raising.* Dubuque, IA: Wm. C. Brown & Benchmark.
The NFL's television contract history. (1994, January 3). *Sports Illustrated, 79*(26), 19.
Wieberg, S. (1994, August 25). Sport feels effects of the financial crisis. *USA Today,* p. 9-C.

DISCUSSION AND REVIEW QUESTIONS

1. Explain the importance of sound fiscal planning in the successful operation of a sport, recreation, or fitness organization.
2. Describe the fundamental elements in the budgetary planning and preparation process.
3. What are the advantages and disadvantages of line-item budgeting, incremental budgeting, and zero-base budgeting for a sport organization.
4. Differentiate between requests for submission of bids and quotes and cite some precautions that sport managers should take to help insure that submissions of bids or quotes are appropriate and realistic in terms of the sport entity.
5. Select a hypothetical sport organization and indicate various categories of both income and expenditures that you feel would be appropriate for that entity.
6. Indicate specific ways (strategies and tactics) that a sport manager might attempt to reduce costs and demonstrate fiscal responsibility within the hypothetical entity selected in question 5.

7. Outline the advantages and disadvantages of using the "wish list" in terms of fiscal (budgetary) planning for a sport organization.

8. Cite reasons why you as a sport manager might be willing to share budgetary knowledge with others, under what circumstances and conditions you would feel comfortable as a manager in disclosing fiscal information and data to others (specify the type of information and the people with whom you would share the data).

CHAPTER 8 Facility Management and Maintenance

Big time sports require big time facilities.

CHAPTER OBJECTIVES

After reading this chapter you will be able to:

- Appreciate the importance of proper management and maintenance of both indoor and outdoor sport, recreation, and fitness facilities;
- Locate and research professional literature pertaining to management and maintenance of facilities;
- Understand the essence and reason for periodic audits of facilities;
- Cite the essentials of good facilities for sport, recreation, and fitness programs;
- Ask appropriate questions in terms of planning for and evaluating a potential facility for use by sport, recreation, or fitness organizations;
- Enunciate the potential sources of problems commonly faced by facility planners and sport managers in designing indoor and/or outdoor facilities;

- Be aware of the many problems associated with the management of various types of facilities;
- Acknowledge the importance of Standard Operating Procedures (SOPs) in managing and maintaining facilities;
- Be familiar with costs associated with replacement and annual maintenance of buildings and structures;
- Explain the maintenance of the major components that are utilized by sport, recreation, and fitness organizations;
- Demonstrate a beginning knowledge of the proper care of outdoor facilities, i.e., grounds and grasses.

One of the major challenges that faces sport managers is the care and managing of indoor and/or outdoor facilities, as well as the equipment and supplies associated with various types of facilities. It has been conservatively estimated that $75 million per year is being spent to build and renovate sport facilities in this country (Pate, Moffitt, & Fugett, 1993).

Almost every sport organization, by its very nature, is associated with some type of facilities. And, almost every sport manager, leader, or supervisor is involved, in some way or another, with facilities and/or equipment within facilities. The status or state of facilities directly reflects on the manager(s) in charge and will have a significant impact on the success or failure of the sport organization, its programs, and its activities.

Management and Maintenance of Facilities

The management of facilities refers to the use, scheduling, and operation of the buildings *and* the grounds (turf, fields, and acreage) owned or utilized by the sport organization. Maintenance deals with the upkeep, care, and support of these same buildings and grounds. In this sense the grounds associated with the sport entities can be thought of as outdoor facilities while buildings are indoor facilities. Further, indoor facilities can be thought of as possessing both interior and exterior building systems.

Concept 222: Sport Managers Need to Hire Knowledgeable, Skilled, and Experienced Professionals to Plan, Construct, Manage, and Maintain Indoor and Outdoor Facilities.

In today's sophisticated world of sports it is highly advisable, at almost every level, for management to secure the services of knowledgeable, skilled, and experienced professionals to help plan, design, construct, manage, and maintain indoor and outdoor facilities. Things have gotten too complicated for "amateurs" to be entrusted with the responsibility for these tasks. Even the everyday tasks of managing and/or caring (housekeeping and maintenance) for facilities has gotten so sophisticated that more and more sport organizations are assigning personnel dedicated to these specific tasks.

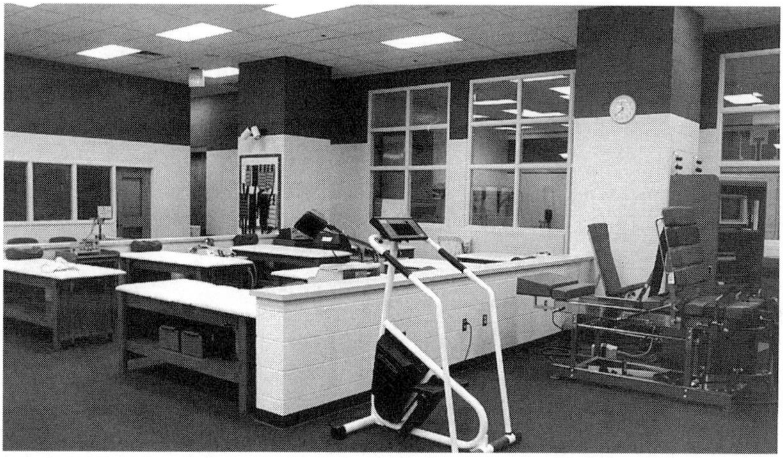

Being able to quickly and adequately treat injuries is imperative.

The Importance of Proper Management and Maintenance of Facilities

To put it simply, there is often too much at stake—for the sport organization, for the sport program, for those involved with the organization, including the sport administrators themselves—for anyone other than knowledgeable people to have responsibility for the facilities used by the sport organization. As a consequence, sport employees within the managerial and administrative ranks have a responsibility to develop and maintain a minimum level of knowledge and competency in these areas.

> **Concept 223:** There Is Too Much at Stake to Assign to Amateurs the Responsibility for the Management and Maintenance of Sport Facilities.

A Variety of Sport Facilities (and Accompanying Equipment and Supplies)

Depending on the type of sport organization in which the manager or supervisor is working, there are a variety of different types of facilities, both indoor and outdoor, to become familiar with if one is to be successful in the day-to-day operation of the business. Table 8.1 provides a partial list of indoor and outdoor sport facilities that the supervisor or administrator might have overall responsibility for within a sport organization. Some of these facilities might comprise only a single room (a wrestling room, for example) while others might involve a much larger space, one that contains a great deal of internal components or elements that must also be carefully monitored and manipulated (for example, an ice hockey arena).

TABLE 8.1 Partial List of Indoor and Outdoor Sport Facilities

Indoor Facilities	Outdoor Facilities
Badminton Courts	Baseball Fields
Basketball Courts	Field Hockey
Combative Rooms (Wrestling, Judo, etc.)	Football Fields
Equipment Rooms	Golf Courses
Fencing Rooms	Lacrosse Fields
Gymnastics Rooms	Rugby Fields
Hockey (Ice and Floor)	Soccer Fields
Hot Tubs	Softball Fields
Locker Rooms	Storage Buildings
Racquetball and Handball Courts	Swimming Pools and Diving Wells
Saunas	Team Handball Fields
Squash Courts	Tennis Courts
Swimming Pools and Diving Wells	Track and Field Sites
Tennis Courts	
Track and Field	
Volleyball Courts	
Weight Rooms	

The sport manager might be required to be somewhat knowledgeable (or become knowledgeable) in terms of any one or more of these facilities. This chapter will provide an introductory glimpse into these facilities. It is the responsibility of the readers to expand on the foundational information and knowledge presented herein in light of the employment situation that one finds oneself following preservice formal education.

Being an Expert versus Being Knowledgeable in Facility Management and Maintenance

Generally speaking, sport managers need not be experts in each and every type of indoor and outdoor facility that is used by the organization or program. That is why experts are secured in the areas of facility management, facility maintenance, and facility construction. Nevertheless, it is necessary for the typical sport manager or supervisor to be generally knowledgeable in the areas of facility management, maintenance, and construction *in order to be able to converse intelligently with such experts in these fields and make appropriate decisions.*

Concept 224: Sport Administrators Need to Be Knowledgeable Enough and to Have Sufficient Experience in Terms of Facilities to Be Able to Intelligently Work and Consult with Experts in the Area.

Such knowledge and information will put administrators in a good position because they will be operating and making decisions from a position of strength, from a position of knowledge. "You can teach the concepts of athletic purchasing, but if you don't understand what you're purchasing, you're just dealing with budgets" (Equipment for success, 1993,

p. 30). Competent managers need to know the "why" of things. They need to know why certain things have to be done, why they have to be done at a specific time, why items have to be purchased, why decisions have to be made, and why certain decisions are the most appropriate in light of existing circumstances.

There are numerous opportunities for sport managers and supervisors to make decisions affecting or relating to facilities and such decisions require some degree of knowledge in order to be effective and efficient. For example, the athletic director or an assistant director of a large NCAA division I university doesn't have to be "the expert" in the care of turf grasses. The "director of grounds" is undoubtedly the expert in this area. Nevertheless, the AD or the assistant AD does need to be somewhat knowledgeable in this area so as to be able to interact successfully with the "expert(s)" and to be able to arrive at an appropriate, timely, and effective decision based on facts.

Availability of Data Pertaining to Facility Construction, Rehabilitation, Maintenance, and Management

There is a wealth of written material available to the sport employee in the area of construction, rehabilitation, maintenance, and management. It is important for the professional sport administrator to know where to go to secure up-to-date information and data when it comes to these areas of responsibility. For example, there are numerous books and journal articles that address these areas in the world of sport. The following is a sample list of periodicals that cover indoor and/or outdoor facilities and are recommended reading by the potential as well as current sport manager or supervisor.

1. *Buildings*—P. O. Box 1888, Cedar Rapids, IA 52406–1888. (319) 364-6167.

2. *Athletic Business*—1846 Hoffman St., Madison, WI 53704. (800) 722-8764 or (608) 249-0186.

3. *Building Operating Management*—2100 West Florist Ave, Milwaukee, WI 53209–3799. (414) 228-7701.

4. *Club Industry*—Sportscape, Inc., Framingham Corporate Center, 492 Old Connecticut Path, 3rd Floor, Framingham, MA 02170. (508) 872-2021 [IRSA members receive this publication].

5. *Club Business International*—253 Summer St., Boston 02222. (617) 951-0055.

6. *Building Operating Management*—P. O. Box 694, Milwaukee, WI 53201–0694.

7. *National Fitness Trade Journal*—P. O. Box 2378, Corona, CA 92718–2378. (714) 371-0606 or 12596 West Bayaud Avenue, 1st Floor, Denver, CO. (303) 753-6422 or (716) 467-4653 [the official publication of the National Health Club Association].

8. *Turf* (Magazine)—P. O. Box 391, 50 Bay Street, St. Johnsbury, Vermont, 05819. (802) 748-8908.

9. *School Planning & Management*—P. O. Box 49699, Dayton, Ohio 45449–0699. (937) 847-5910.

10. *Facilities Manager*—1643 Prince Street, Alexandria, VA 22314–2818. (703) 684-1446 [a publication of the Association of Higher Education Facilities Officers].

> **Concept 225:** One Doesn't Have to Have All the Answers at One's Fingertips—but One Does Have to Know Where to Get the Answers (Information, Data, and Facts).

Part of being able to get such information has to do with having the ability to keep up in the area of professional reading, attending professional meetings and conferences, and being able to conduct meaningful, productive, and fruitful research of the current literature in the field in question. It also involves tapping individuals (experts), organizations, and associations in an effort to secure such information, knowledge, and advice. It is difficult, if not impossible, even for managers within the sport industry to remain at the cutting edge in everything within their respective fields or areas of responsibility.

Thus, sport managers must rely on a variety of sources to retrieve specific data, information, and knowledge. A partial listing of professional organizations that are particularly important in terms of being sources of information about facility design and/or specifications of various sport facilities or structures and their components is included in Appendix B.

> **Concept 226:** Sport Administrators Need Not Be Embarrassed to Admit that They Don't Know All the Answers as long as They Are Successful in Securing the Necessary Information in a Timely Fashion.

The modern sport administrator should be familiar with general standards as they apply to indoor and outdoor facilities as well as with specification (and maintenance) guides for sporting facilities published by the various sport governing bodies. Additional information relating to the construction, rehabilitation, and maintenance of specific sport facilities is provided by various experts in the field as well as published by different organizations, associations, and governing bodies, as well as various manufacturers of products and materials.

It is not the purpose of this book to go into specific details of facility construction or rehabilitation. Rather, this chapter will delve into the general area of *management and maintenance of sport facilities,* indoor and outdoor, as well as providing general concepts or principles relative to the planning, designing, and constructing of suitable sport facilities. For more detailed reading and investigation into the areas of planning, construction, and rehabilitation of facilities the reader is directed to the "Further Readings: Facilities" section at the end of this chapter.

Periodic Audit of Facilities: An Essential Part of the Planning Process

It is a wise practice to conduct an audit of one's facilities periodically both in terms of maintenance and managing (West, 1998). This systematic examination of the facilities themselves and the managerial policies, practices, and procedures affecting the facilities will provide a baseline of data for wise decision-making on behalf of management (Hunsaker, 1992). Without current information, without accurate data, without something to base one's decisions on (other than mere anecdotal opinions) management is effectively "flying blind" and resulting decisions will usually be wanting if not actual impediments to progress.

Concept 227: Facility Audits Should Be Conducted Periodically to Assess the Effectiveness and Efficiency of the Sport Organization.

Facility audits, called "reality checks" by some, can serve many purposes and may take several different forms. First, some facility audits are conducted to determine whether special maintenance (other than routine repair and upkeep) is necessary. Second, audits are initiated in order to determine whether the organization or business is in compliance with specific regulations, rules, or codes (ADA provisions [see Chapter 11], zoning, etc.). Third, audits are instituted to see if the facilities themselves and/or use of same conform with federal, state, or local laws (Title IX, health and safety factors, etc.). Fourth, facility audits are established to determine whether the facilities themselves as well as the policies relating to the facilities are safe from legal liability (risk management) standpoint (see Chapter 12). Finally, some facility audits are set up to determine if new or refurbished facilities might be warranted.

Concept 228: Facilities Should Be Periodically Evaluated (Audited) in Terms of Safety Prior to Use.

Construction of a new big-league baseball facility—always an exciting time.

Management must be constantly vigilant in terms of the safety factor associated with facilities and associated equipment and supplies. The periodic risk management audit is essential in terms of determining the state of the facility (and contents) as well as policies and procedures of the sport organization as they affect the health and welfare of individuals using the facilities (and equipment and supplies).

Concept 229: Preventative Maintenance Is the Mark of an Effective and Efficient Manager.

The cliché "an ounce of prevention is worth a pound of cure" is certainly appropriate in the world of sport facilities. Preventative maintenance of facilities is a must. Don't be "penny wise and pound foolish" when it comes to the care and upkeep of sport facilities or equipment/supplies. This is why the periodic audit of buildings and grounds is so critical in the management of facilities. Prudent and timely decisions relative to maintenance will save

A beautiful and functional facility—one of the keys to a successful sport program.
Bob Beverly, Photographer.

time, effort, and, most importantly, money in the long run. The opposite is also true; failure to spend money in the upkeep of facilities will cost a sport entity dearly in the long run.

Graffiti: A Vulgar Expression or an Art Form?

Another example of the need to be proactive with facility management is in the area of graffiti. Seemingly a never-ending problem with both indoor and outdoor facilities, graffiti "grows onto itself." Once vandalism (and that is what graffiti really is) occurs, it is imperative that quick and decisive action be taken by the appropriate authorities.

> **Concept 230:** To Combat Graffiti It Is Important to Attack the Problem Immediately lest It Become Worse.

First of all, it is necessary that the graffiti be immediately removed. Left unattended, graffiti seemingly replicates itself and can quickly expand to fill the space that is available. Second, close scrutiny and observation of the offending (or attractive) site is often necessary if repeated instances are to be prevented. This is especially important if the graffiti is especially offensive or vulgar. Third, education can also play a part in the prevention (or reduction) of graffiti attacks.

The Essentials of Good Facilities

Quality facilities are those that meet the present and changing needs of the organization and patrons. Quality facilities include those that are cost-effective to run, those that have relatively low maintenance while maintaining their structural integrity for years. Form meets functionality in the world of architecture. The purpose of the facility dictates what form, shape, arrangement, or configuration the structure will take. In short, the ideal facility is one that is patron- or fan-friendly, one that is viewed as being adequate, accessible, clean, safe, convenient, comfortable, visually pleasing, and enjoyable by those who are patrons, fans, spectators, and sports persons.

Facility Planning and Design

When considering the design of a future facility, there are numerous options and variations possible depending on the available budget, its intended use, and the creativity of the design team (Shalley & Barzdukas, 1997), which should consist of experts who are experienced in the area of sport architecture, members of the management team of the sport entity, and representatives of the various constituencies for which the structure is being built (Krenson, 1997).

Advantages of Multipurpose Facilities

One of the recent changes in the planning and design of sport facilities has been to design multipurpose facilities. An integral part of a multipurpose facility is incorporating a plan in which one space opens to another rather than having compartmentalized areas set aside for individual and formal groups. The important concept for the future is *flexibility* in planning a building or facility that is expected to last 40, 50, or more years. The ability to design "a major capital project like a field house is better justified when the design includes plans for adapting to future changes" (Krenson, 1997, p. 76). Again, flexibility within the facility is a key concept for the present as well as the future.

Important Considerations in the Planning and Design Phase of a Building

In the design and planning stage of any building there is always a juggling act between available money, space needs, and design considerations. Consequently, many planners and architects look to combine those sports and/or activities that have common functional and operational needs in a common space (Johnson, 1991, p. 33).

> **Concept 231:** The Use and Purpose of Facilities Will Depend on the Mission(s) of the Sport Organization.

Regardless of the type of facility planned, there are numerous questions that should be asked or areas that should be closely examined by members of the design team, including:

1. Where should the building be erected; that is, where is the site of the proposed structure?
2. When does the facility have to be in place?
3. What about access to and from the structure?
4. What type of parking is required for this building?
5. What should be the layout and actual design of the structure?
6. Should the facility be multipurpose in nature or a single-purpose building?
7. Who will be using the facility? Will there be outside groups using the site?
8. What type of utilities will be involved? Any special needs in this regard?
9. What are the electrical and mechanical requirements?
10. What role does the weather play in the construction and use of the facility?
11. What type of landscaping should be incorporated?
12. What type of maintenance will be required for the structure itself as well as the components of the building, including the mechanicals?

There are several steps to be taken during the initial discussion and planning process for any facility (Fawcett, 1997). These include: (1) identification of the real needs of the organization, (2) determination of how much money might be available to spend for the facility, (3) solicitation of input and suggestions from potential user groups, various constituencies, and staff, (4) consultations with appropriate governmental and regulatory agencies (fire marshal, building inspectors, etc.) to secure information relative to requirements, stipulations, or limitations affecting the proposed facility, (5) anticipation of how various parts of the facility might interact or interfere with one another, and (6) searching for a suitable architect.

Problems Associated with Facilities

There can be a multitude of problems and challenges facing sport managers relating to indoor and/or outdoor facilities. The causes of these difficulties can be many and varied. Some of the more common sources of problems associated with sport facilities include:

1. There was poor upfront planning for the facility in the first place (a lack of anticipation of the future, of future needs);

2. There was a lack of oversight on someone's part during the planning or construction phase (someone failed to double-check to insure that some things actually got done);

3. There was an attempt to cut corners, to cut costs (the resulting compromise failed to meet the need);

4. The planners lacked experience in designing a sport facility (the architect[s] and/or consultant[s] failed to have a broad or extensive knowledge of sport architecture or needs of sport programs);

5. There was failure to recognize the importance of storage space for the facility;

6. The planning and building schedule was unduly accelerated (frequently, in the world of professional sports the time between the awarding of a franchise and the need for a finished structure is short, too short, with the result being a "rush job");

7. The building has a new client with different needs (the building was planned, designed, and constructed in a way that does not lend itself to easy modification or adaptation for new or different needs);

8. Legal or code mandated modifications that are not reasonable in light of the purpose of the building or room(s) (the state of Louisiana required sprinkler heads (fire code) to be installed in the ceilings of a club's racquetball courts; 1500 gallons of water spilled onto the wooden floor when a racquetball struck and broke a sprinkler head);

9. Too much compromising during the planning phase (different and often conflicting needs of various groups necessitate granting concessions, with the result that important elements of the building might be altered or left out with negative consequences) (Gimple, 1992; Stier, 1993; Cohen, 1995).

Refurbishing or Replacing a Facility

Management is constantly faced with the question of whether it is more prudent to repair (rehab, retool, or refit) a facility or to actually replace it. Of course, the answer to this

Ice hockey—a sport enjoying tremendous growth in terms of participation and fan support.
James Dusen, Photographer.

all-important question depends on a host of variables. Consequently, there can be no simple answer. Nevertheless, this question is one that more and more members of management will face as the sport facilities built 20, 30, 40, and more years ago continue to age and pose ever greater challenges to those sport organizations that continue to use them. In fact, in professional baseball, around 60 new baseball parks have opened up in professional baseball since 1985 (Cohen, 1994, p. 35).

Concept 232: To Repair or to Replace, the $64,000 Question.

In some cases the answer to this perplexing question is provided for the sport enterprise. For example, in professional baseball there is *Rule 40, Facility Standards and Compliance Inspection Procedures*. This rule was included in the 1990 Professional Baseball Agreement, the seven-year working contract that was adopted by the major and minor leagues. The rule's 13 sections cover (as recommendations or minimum requirements) almost everything relating to baseball facilities. For example, the rule affects such things as recommended seating grades, distribution and spacing of seating, minimum seating capacity of parks, size of parking lots, as well as specifications for rest rooms, concession areas, beer gardens, ticket windows, first-aid stations, sound systems, scoreboards, press facilities, and administrative areas (Cohen, 1995).

As a result of this rule, plus the acknowledgment of its importance by leaders in the sport, there have been a significant number of upgraded facilities and not a few totally new ballparks among minor league baseball franchises. For example, until recently, the oldest

Demolition of the 66-year-old Silver Stadium, Rochester, New York.

minor league park within triple AAA was the 66-year-old Silver Stadium (built in 1928), located in Rochester, New York. Home of the International League's Rochester Red Wings, an affiliate of the Baltimore Oriole organization, the aging facility did not meet the new standards stipulated by *Rule 40* and was replaced by a brand new ballpark, Frontier Field, located in downtown Rochester. On opening day, April 11, 1996, the hometown fans were treated to a truly beautiful facility, one that included picnic areas, volleyball courts, and extensive grassy areas.

New Frontier Field, home of AAA Rochester Red Wings, Rochester, New York.

Importance of Appropriate Facilities

In today's marketplace sport facilities play a major role in enabling management to provide the amenities expected by the public. Such amenities can serve to entertain the patrons and fans as well as facilitate the marketing of the sport entity itself among the public and various constituencies. One should not overlook the importance and impact of an appropriately well-kept and properly maintained facility in terms of public relations and the publicity surrounding the sport organization and its personnel (see Chapter 10).

The Importance of Image and Professionalism

Appearances are very, very important. Frequently, it is the little things that count for so much, especially in terms of image and perceptions. Perceptions count for a great deal, both with the public and with members of one's own organization. It is amazing what a fresh coat of paint, clean bleachers, seat padding, colorful banners, an improved sound system and acoustical panels, as well as dressed up scorer's tables, can do for a facility (Cohen, 1995). Proper appearances can help motivate people and facilitate the development of pride and self-esteem, a not insignificant consequence (Garner, 1997).

Making Effective (Best) Use of a Facility

The facility must meet the needs of the various constituencies, groups, and individuals who might utilize the building or outside site. One way to see if a facility actually is meeting the needs of the constituencies as well as those of the general public is to examine its usage rate. Is the building being used on a consistent basis? Is the facility occupied a high percentage of time? And, in some instances, are there significant monies being generated from the usage of the facility or site? Many organizations today are looking toward multipurpose sport facilities so as to help insure that the site will be utilized to its maximum (Johnston, 1991).

Use of the Mezzanine Concept in Facility Conversions

More and more sport organizations, especially fitness clubs and recreation type entities, are attempting to make better use of every square foot of their facilities. Towards this end a unique tactic has emerged in respect to getting more out of one's facility, namely, converting an existing structure by constructing a mezzanine level above the existing floor space. Such a move can almost double the organization's existing usable space. The advantage is obvious, being able to double the working square footage without expanding the structure's "footprint" is very cost-effective. This strategy is referred to as "creating more space by looking up" (Jastrow, 1997).

Concept 233: Scheduling Facility Usage Is a Major Challenge—It Is Difficult to Please Everyone All the Time.

Adequate physical conditioning is the foundation for competitive sport.
Photo of Jervey Center Weight Room by Bob Waldrop.

The impact of computers and computer technology (software and hardware) in our society is evident everywhere, and the area of sport is no exception. Perhaps nothing has aided the facility manager more in the day-to-day aspects of the job than the advent of the computer and applicable software packages that facilitate the booking and scheduling of facilities. Indeed, the task of facility scheduling and keeping track of scheduled bookings can be daunting, to say the least. If the booking and scheduling system is not computerized then the manager is left with the old-fashioned method of pen or pencil and the trusty calendar. Needless to say, the manual method of keeping track of a multi-purpose facility is neither time-efficient nor is it effective (Ross & Wolter, 1997).

The question is not so much whether to utilize the computer and a software package but which software application to choose. Management would do well to consider the following factors before rushing out to purchase one of the many software applications that might be suitable in booking facilities as well as scheduling overall maintenance of the buildings and grounds:

1. The *policies* and *priorities* governing facility usage;
2. The *processes* used in scheduling use of the facility;
3. The *cost-effectiveness* of both hardware and software;
4. The specific *hardware requirements* for commercially prepared software programs;
5. The *technical difficulty* in terms of mastery of the software package;
6. The *capability, willingness, and eagerness* of the staff to use computer-assisted technology;
7. The available *technical support and documentation* (in-house or second party);

8. The *cost* of technical support, documentation, and maintenance (Ross & Wolter, 1997; Stier, 1997).

Ross & Wolter (1997) provided seven software companies that produce software that might be suitable for some sport organizations in terms of facility management and scheduling. These companies, along with their phone numbers, are:

1. A. E. Klawitter & Associates (847) 392–6880
2. CEO Software Inc. (800) 441–2581
3. Escom Software Services (800) 661–1196
4. THE-Programmed For Success (800) 488-PFSI
5. Overtime Software (800) 467–0493
6. R. I. C. Corporation (219) 432–0799
7. Vermont Systems, Inc. (802) 879–6993

Managing the Site for Maximum Potential Net Income

Concept 234: In Many Sport Organizations, the More Usage a Facility Receives the Better.

If the facility is to be used by outside groups the first question that comes to mind is whether or not such groups will be charged for their usage. If the answer is "yes," then policies and procedures need to be established governing such outside groups. For example, outside groups might be required to post a bond for damages. Additionally, such groups might be required to pay a sum, in advance, covering all costs (security, preparation, cleanup, etc.) associated with such usage plus a sum that will be the net profit for the owners of the facility.

Concept 235: When Allowing Outside Groups to Use Facilities Be Sure to Take a Proactive Approach in Terms of Potential Damage(s).

It is highly recommended that a representative of the facility and the outside group tour the facility before and after its use by the group. This is done so that detailed, written records can be maintained in terms of the condition of the facility and its contents. These records (including photographs, if appropriate) can go a long way to prove the condition of the facility before and after the outside event. This proactive approach to damage control is most important. It does not take much to cause significant or permanent damage to sport facilities by uncaring or unthinking individuals. Whether damage is intentional or accidental is not really the ultimate question. Damage is damage. Repairs have to be made. And, in most cases, the facility cannot be tied up for long for needed repairs because other groups have been scheduled to use it.

Security Factors in Allowing Outside Groups to Use the Sport Facility

Even though security costs are paid for by the outside group, in many instances it is recommended that the owners of the site hire (provide) the security personnel. This insures that adequately trained security officers are on hand for the outside event or program and that they represent the owners and not the outside group or association.

One last word regarding security, or the lack of it, due to problems with keys, specifically missing, stolen, or misplaced keys. The cost to replace a single key that has been lost is not the issue. What quickly becomes an issue, and an expensive one at that, is when a missing key jeopardizes the security of an entire facility and a decision must be made relative to the feasibility of rekeying the entire building. This type of situation is exacerbated when there is widespread use of the master key. Losing or misplacing a master key is a very, very serious matter. That is why management typically restricts the number of people possessing master keys to the bare minimum.

Concept 236: Restrict the Use of Master Keys to the Minimum Number of Personnel.

The issue of unauthorized use of keys can quickly become the bane of facility managers. Not only is security compromised but there is always danger of injuries to individuals who have gained unauthorized access to buildings or grounds when keys are floating around. With the loss of security many facilities have to be rekeyed, a process that is time-consuming and costly. In many instances managers suggest that buildings simply be rekeyed every five years as a matter of policy because of the concern about lost or missing keys (Ryder, 1994).

Others suggest a more frequent rekeying schedule, as frequently as every year or two, and others believe that the changing of the locks is going about the seemingly perpetual problem from the wrong direction. These proponents suggest that stricter policies regarding the issuing and handling of keys to buildings, *coupled* with persistent educational efforts for those personnel who have been issued keys, are more effective in winning the battle against stolen, lost, or misplaced keys.

The cost of changing the locks or "rekeying" an entire facility can be thousands of dollars, yet security of buildings and grounds is a critical issue for management. Preventative (proactive) measures, if effective, can be worth their weight in gold. Reactive measures, such as rekeying an entire building, will usually cost their weight in gold, not to speak of the adverse publicity spilling over the administrator in charge of the facility.

Managerial Strategies and Tactics for Facilities

One of the keys to wise and prudent management of facilities is to establish "standard operating procedures" (SOPs) for the operation of all facilities and the equipment and supplies within or associated with these facilities. These SOPs should be included in what is commonly referred to as a "standard operation procedures/policies handbook." Included in such a handbook will be policies, procedures, and practices pertaining to the operation and management of the sport facility under a wide range of circumstances. Such a handbook facilitates decision-making in terms of the operation and maintenance of facilities and their contents.

Concept 237: The Standard Operating Procedures Handbook Serves as a Guide for Decision-Making.

The format or structure of the handbook itself can vary. Some administrators utilize a three-ring booklet with loose-leaf sheets containing various procedures and policies for ease of inserting and removing. Others utilize a more formal bound volume containing pages of policies and procedures permanently inserted.

Concept 238: Establishing Appropriate Policies for Use of Facilities Will Help Insure Facilities Are Available for Safe Usage and Will Last Longer.

These procedures, policies, and practices should be thought out well in advance of the time they are needed. In point of fact, managers don't have time to think up policies and procedures "on the fly." Rather, experienced and successful members of management rely on time-tested and well-thought-out policies and procedures to deal with the innumerable challenges and decisions that face them day in and day out. This is especially important when it comes to unexpected emergencies or problems that arise periodically. It is far more effective to think about and consider various alternatives for handling emergencies when one is not harried, when one is calm, cool, and collected.

Concept 239: Establish an Emergency Set of Procedures to Deal with Unexpected Problems or Difficulties Associated with Use of Facilities.

Examples of typical topics in a facility standard operating procedures handbook include statements as to which group or individuals have priority in terms of usage of parts of the facility (i.e., booking and scheduling priorities), costs of using the facility by outside groups, restrictions on the use of the facility itself, hours of operation, setup and breakdown procedures, availability of security personnel, emergency procedures, scheduled care relative to housekeeping and maintenance of various segments of the facility, recommended actions to take in case of emergencies, advertising and marketing efforts, signage, ticket, and box office operations, concession operations, garbage removal, insurance, issuance of keys, snowplowing (in northern climates), availability of medical personnel, utility usage during events, restrictions on people's behavior (smoking, drugs, use of food/drink, parking, etc.), charges for usage of the facility, and staffing of the facility. Of course the actual contents and organization of material within such a SOP handbook will depend on the sport organization and its mission(s), as well as the situation and circumstances in which management finds itself.

Decisions Maximizing Financial Savings

Well-thought-out and prudent facility policies can save the sport organization, in terms of money, personnel, public relations, and effective and efficient use of the facilities. Prudent practices and procedures in the area of energy costs can result in significant savings for the sport entity. "Energy cost avoidance has always been and will always be one of our key money issues" (Leach, 1997, p. 15).

Keeping doors closed during the day, turning off lights in unoccupied areas within a building, minimizing the use of exhaust fans, keeping both inlet and outlet air passages clean and free of obstacles, and removing on-site access to thermostats are just some of the steps that management might consider to maximize financial savings associated with facilities. Being energy-efficient should be a goal of every member of management.

Concept 240: Appropriate Facility Policies and Practices Can Reduce Energy Costs and Save Money.

Decisions Maximizing Staff Effectiveness

Having established appropriate policies and procedures relating to the facility, management is now in a position of following these same policies and procedures with a minimum of oversight and allocation of staff. It is not that facilities do not warrant consistent attention. It is just that, with advance planning (SOP handbooks), much of the challenge of dealing with and utilizing facilities can be significantly reduced. It should be remembered that sport facilities are tools, instruments that are used to fulfill an organization's mission(s). *As such, facilities should not consume an inordinate amount of time, effort, attention, and money.* To be otherwise would indicate either a poor choice of priorities or poor management of facilities.

The Use of Multiple SOP Handbooks for Individual Sporting Events

Within a broadly based school-based athletic program involving a large number of different sports and facilities, the concept of such a SOP handbook might actually involve a number of different handbooks, one for each varsity sport team. Thus, there might be a SOP handbook for the football games that deals with the use of and setup of the facilities used during the football games. Similarly, for the softball team there would be a separate SOP handbook that would detail how the softball field and related facilities would be set up and utilized before, during, and after the actual softball game.

Adaptations of Others' Ideas

In developing a method of operating within one's facilities and in establishing policies for the use and maintenance of them, it is not necessary or even advisable to reinvent the wheel. Rather, borrow, beg, and steal ideas from others and adjust them to fit your particular situation and circumstances (Glazier, 1997). Talk with other professionals involved in facility management or supervision. Solicit their information and advice. Observe and learn. Borrow those ideas that fit your circumstances and adapt or adjust strategies and tactics of others to accommodate your own situation.

Concept 241: Borrow, Beg, and Steal Ideas and Strategies from Others—Adapt, Adjust, and Tailor What Has Worked Elsewhere to One's Own Situation.

Indoor Facilities

When one considers indoor facilities the first thought that most often comes to mind is a building, a structure with four outside walls, windows, interior structural elements, interior walls/supports, a roof, and a floor. Once that picture is firmly entrenched in one's mind there comes the additional realization that there is more to a building than its outer shell or the structural component, much more. In addition to a building's overall outer structure (the shell) there are three additional elements that most facilities or buildings possess: electrical components (lights, motors, pumps, etc.), mechanical elements (heating, air conditioning, ventilation, etc.), and a plumbing system (sewage, water, etc.).

Costs Associated with Replacement and Annual Maintenance/Upkeep of a Building

Replacement Costs

Typically, buildings are constructed to last 50 years. Ideally, management should be placing 2 percent of the replacement value of the facility aside each year so that, eventually, when they have to replace the structure there are funds available either to replace or rehab the facility. Of course, timely and appropriate repairs and rehab efforts on most buildings can extend their usefulness beyond the normal 50-year life span.

Annual Maintenance and Upkeep Costs for the Operation of a Building

Today most managers estimate the "cost for operation" of a typical building to be in the neighborhood of around 4 percent or 5 percent of the replacement value of the structure. One can obtain a rough estimate of the replacement value of an average building by assuming that each square foot is worth between $100 to $125. The "cost of operation" includes those expenses incurred to operate the average building each year just for normal expenditures in the areas of repair and general maintenance.

Concept 242: It Is Easier and Less Expensive to Perform Periodic Maintenance than to Make Alterations to a Facility.

Wise managers insure that proper and timely maintenance and upkeep are done to facilities. This is one area in which procrastination or hesitation will cost big dollars in the future. Routine maintenance, upkeep, and preservation are absolutely essential if the facility is to remain capable of fulfilling its mission and meeting the needs of the sport organization and programs. In short, postponing or skimping in these areas is being "penny wise and pound foolish."

General Comments Regarding Maintenance and Upkeep of Facilities

The following are some general observations that can be helpful to the sport administrator in terms of facilities and their components or essential elements.

Asbestos

Any building over 25 years old has asbestos within the structure. If required, removal is costly. However, under certain conditions it is not necessary to remove all the asbestos from a building. For example, in years past some ceiling and floor tiles were made with asbestos. If such tiles are currently in buildings they can remain unless the asbestos is disturbed and exposed to the air. For example, if individuals puncture the tiles or scratch the tiles so that the asbestos particles are exposed to the air then these tiles are a health hazard and must be removed.

Placement of Drinking Fountains

Do not have water (drinking) fountains situated in exercise areas where there are wooden floors. It doesn't take much to have water overflow onto the floor with the potential for real (and expensive) damage to the floor.

Painting

Establish a painting schedule for different facilities or buildings. Many facility managers choose to paint on a 7- to 10-year cycle. Additionally, because labor costs account for the majority of costs associated with painting, it is recommended that quality paints be used so that painting can be done less frequently.

The Source of Monies to Pay for Routine Maintenance

When management first considers constructing a facility or building, there should be a plan whereby sufficient money can be set aside so that the interest from it will be sufficient to cover the costs of yearly maintenance and upkeep for the future.

Maintenance and Upkeep Efforts Are Sometimes Dictated by Outside Sources

Management must abide by and adhere to the rules, regulations, policies, and standards of various associations and governing bodies when it comes to the proper maintenance and condition of facilities. For example, in the sport of swimming there are maximum and minimum water temperature ranges established by the NCAA in order for competitive swimming events to be sanctioned in a given pool.

Selected Indoor Facilities or Components Necessitating Special Care

There are some areas within an indoor facility that require special mention. Generally speaking these facilities or elements of facilities require special care in terms of maintenance as well as in their management for their intended use.

Floors

Interior floors, especially those surfaces that participants play or run on, must be a matter of concern of the first magnitude for management. Wooden floors (such as basketball courts) are especially susceptible to abuse, misuse, and significant damage. Wooden floors can be easily marred, scuffed, and scratched. Both temperature and humidity can also affect them.

> **Concept 243:** "The Worst Crime against Wood Floors Is Neglect, since Even the Smallest Amount of Care Can Prolong Their Life" (Cohen, 1992, p. 56).

The Maple Flooring Manufacturers Association (MFMA, [847] 480–9138) has a booklet describing techniques and strategies for the general care and repair of hardwood sport floors. Prudent managers should familiarize themselves with the contents of this publication. A question that frequently arises is whether in-house custodial staff should attempt periodic maintenance and repairs or whether such tasks should be farmed out to professionals specializing in such work. "Most sport floor or sport floor finish manufacturers will help train novices with seminars or demonstrations of different products" (Cohen, 1992, p. 54).

Of course there are other floor surfaces besides wood. Today, more and more sport organizations are finding that alternate surfaces work every bit as well as, if not better than, the traditional wood. For example, practice and competitive surfaces can include interlocking plastic tile (volleyball), various types of textured surfaces (jogging tracks), synthetic surfaces (basketball), as well as combinations of surfaces (weight room and fitness facilities).

Floor Coverings

To protect wood floors from abusive foot traffic (street shoes, etc.) it is necessary to utilize appropriate floor coverings. This is part of preventative maintenance. Most floor covers are made of vinyl-coated or laminated polyester, vinyl, or vinyl nylon and all must be fire-retardant. These covers must be cared for and cleaned just as carefully as one would clean the floors.

Viklund (1995, p. 46) suggests that several steps be taken before selecting a particular surface for a floor in one's facility in an effort to become an informed and educated buyer.

1. Select the room or space to be considered;
2. Prioritize the sports/activities that will occur within the space;
3. Decide whether the preferred floor should be *area elastic* (more resilient) or *point elastic* (low absorption levels);
4. Review the performance criteria for the selected floor type;
5. Test flooring options by reviewing samples and comparing costs;
6. Compare life-cycle costs for flooring options; initial costs plus maintenance costs should be compared over 10- and 20-year periods to get a full value picture;
7. Play on different surfaces;
8. Check the manufacturers' referenced projects;
9. Make the final decision.

Movable Dividers or Barriers within a Facility

Dividers are typically utilized in large open spaces such as gymnasiums, field houses, and indoor tennis courts for the purpose of quickly and efficiently separating a large open space into one or more smaller areas. Dividers have added advantages in that they can often reduce the noise factor emanating from other sources within the overall facility. Additionally, use of dividers can help significantly reduce distractions from interfering with what is taking place within the newly defined space. Finally, dividing a large space into smaller areas can reduce the likelihood of physical injuries occurring to participants from other individuals running into their "space."

> **Concept 244:** Movable Dividers (Electric, Motor-Driven) Can Be Very, Very Expensive to Repair.

There are four main types of dividers in use today within gymnasiums. First, there is the traditional type with *accordion-type doors* that are moved across an open space by electric motors. The biggest challenge with these types of dividers is that they are expensive to purchase and expensive to repair. The remaining three styles of dividers are typically constructed of vinyl-coated materials heat-sealed together. The dividers themselves may be constructed entirely from either solid vinyl or mesh, or a combination of both. If a combination of both is used the solid vinyl will comprise the bottom 15 feet while the mesh (net) is used for the top, thus providing increased air circulation and resulting in improved ventilation (Catalano, 1995, p. 49).

The second type of vinyl-coated divider is a sliding curtain that is usually *pulled by hand across* a space on a tracking system located along the ceiling. When not in use the curtain hangs from the ceiling along an end wall. The third type of divider is a *roll-up* type with the curtain rolled up to the ceiling or lowered (rolled) to the floor by means of an electric motor. The fourth type of divider has a *folding* type curtain similar to a venetian blind. An electric motor is used to fold the curtain completely up to the ceiling and to unfold the it from the ceiling to the floor (Catalano, 1995). Both the roll-up type and the folding style of curtain divider can be expected to last around 15 to 18 years, depending on usage.

Weight Rooms and Fitness Centers (Strength and Conditioning)

The modern weight room is a far cry from what it was only a few years ago. In the past, the typical weight room was a gloomy, dingy, smelly, fluorescent-lit, and unglamorous space where males, almost exclusively, grunted and intimidated their way through workout sessions. No more.

Concept 245: Weight Rooms Must Be Kept Spotless and Physically Attractive.

Today, the strength and conditioning facility is spacious and well-illuminated, with a combination of indirect and uplighting, adequate ventilation, and good acoustics that produce a visually pleasing area that is attractive *for both males and females*. Frequently floors are covered in a combination of carpets, synthetic covering, and/or rubber tiles. Wood platforms are provided for free weights lest weights that are dropped permanently damage the base flooring of the facility. Suitable music is perpetually piped in. Hardwood floors are provided for aerobic exercises.

Concept 246: Check the Weight Room(s) Daily for Broken or Abused Items of Equipment.

Specific strategies for maintaining a superior strength and conditioning facility include:

1. Insuring that the ventilation system distributes clean air throughout the facility; an increase in the number of air changes within the area is necessary in response to the potential for excessive odor buildup;
2. Keeping equipment in immaculate condition in terms of cleanliness and appearance, including free weights, exercise machines, padded upholstery, and so forth.
3. Keeping locker rooms, showers, and collateral items of equipment, such as hot tubs and saunas, in perfect condition;
4. Having mirrors prominently displayed throughout the exercise areas;

5. Decorating the facility to attract and retain both male and female clients and patrons;
6. Establishing a nonintimidating atmosphere through policies and practice;
7. Seeking input from customers or patrons (through surveys and questionnaires) about how to upgrade the facilities and equipment and how to improve the service;
8. Establishing suitable hours to meet the needs of the clientele (Sherman, 1997; Glazier, 1997).

Locker and Dressing Rooms and Shower Facilities

Just as weight room facilities have undergone a significant makeover in recent years, so too has the locker room or changing room or dressing room. Today, image is everything (Strock, 1991), and this is certainly true in the area of locker and dressing facilities. Today's locker room patron tends to stay longer in the dressing facility and to view it as more than just a place to change into a different set of clothes. As a result, management is attempting to make this area more pleasant and pleasing (Dillon, 1996). Consequently, dressing facilities (locker rooms) are functional, airy, brightly lit, freshly painted, appropriately decorated, clean, and spacious.

Concept 247: Locker Rooms and Dressing Areas Need to Be Functional, Safe, and Secure for the Client.

Spaciousness of locker and dressing rooms provides easy movement and access between elements such as locker areas, showers, drying areas, the toilet room, and, perhaps, the steam room or sauna (Viklund & Coons, 1997). Rough surfaces on the floor of the dressing area as well as slip-resistant flooring in the showers insure safe use of the facility. Additionally, it should be designed so that vandalism can be held to a minimum while cleaning and maintenance efforts are made easy (Heugli, Richards, Graffis, Kroll, & Epley, 1991).

Lockers

An integral part of the locker/dressing facility are the lockers themselves. There is a need for durable, secure, well-ventilated, and visually pleasing lockers. The type of lockers to add to the dressing facility will depend on the type of use the site will have as well as the type of clientele. Permanent metal lockers might be most suitable in a school setting, designed with an open face or a closed face with air louvers.

In other settings, solid plastic, solid phenolic, wooden, wood-laminate or plastic-laminate, welded metal, or knock-down metal lockers might be more suitable. Welded lockers are welded together in groups of three or six at the factory and shipped that way to the facility where they are installed. Knock-down lockers arrive on site as separate pieces and must be assembled with nuts and bolts (Browser, 1997). Some lockers are constructed so as to be freestanding while others are to be built in. Permanently installed benches might be used or movable benches can be selected (The right lockers, 1996).

Swimming Pools, Whirlpools, Spas, and Hot Tubs

The National Spa and Pool Institute (NSPI), in cooperation with the American National Standards Institute (ANSI), has established and distributed revised guidelines, American

National Standard for Public Spas (ANSI/NSPI-2 1992), for the design, installation and use of public spas and hot tubs (Staying, 1993).

Concept 248: Proper Pool Maintenance and Management Is a Matter of Public Health.

Pools are often the focal point in many sport facilities. Yet, taking care of pools (of all types) can be one of the more challenging tasks facing facility and sport managers. One of the reasons for this is that the public's health is at stake should anything go awry (Schmid, 1997b). In an effort to combat the challenge of mastering maintenance of public pools, the state of New York instituted a requirement that every organization that has a pool open to members of the public must designate at least one staff member as the expert pool manager. This certification process places the burden of responsibility directly on the organization or business operating the pool to see that a properly trained and experienced individual is in charge of the day-to-day operation of the pool. This individual is required by state law to attend specific courses and classes in an effort to master the intricacies of pool management and maintenance.

Concept 249: Commercial Pools Are Different from Home Pools in Terms of Maintenance and Care.

Managers of large commercial pool operations (schools, health clubs, recreation departments, etc.) should be very cautious in accepting "expert" counsel from the neighborhood pool supply clerk. The reason for this is that the "single greatest variant in the safe and efficient operation of any pool lies in the number of swimmers the pool has on a given day. The number is the central determinant for the amount of contaminants in the pool, which in turn affects the chemical consumption and the amount of debris to be filtered out by the system" (Schmid, 1997b, p. 52). The greater the number of swimmers or bathers the greater the strain on the chemicals and the harder the pool's filtration system has to work. Therefore, pool managers need to be careful to solicit advice and counsel from appropriate sources, individuals, and organizations familiar with the type of pool operation that the sport manager has responsibility for.

Sanitation: The Essence of All Pool Management

One of the critical factors when dealing with pools of all kinds and types is sanitation. "Sanitation management is really an euphemism for disease prevention" (Vest, 1995, p. 42). One cannot be too careful when dealing with health matters, from both the perspective of what is right and proper and the legal obligations and potential for being successfully sued. In this light it is always better to play it safe, to be cautious, and to establish rigorous guidelines governing the supervision, testing, and maintenance of water facilities such as swimming pools, whirlpools, spas, and hot tubs. When dealing with the sanitation of such facilities there are three elements that must be dealt with: water, air, and surface areas (Vest, 1995, p. 39). Thus, standard operating procedures (SOPs) in terms of facility maintenance and management must include these three elements.

Cleaning Up a Fecal or Vomit Accident

It is frequently difficult enough to keep a pool safe and sanitary for one's clients under normal circumstances. However, there is always the challenge of addressing additional challenges brought about either by accidents on the part of youngsters or deliberate acts by those who should know better.

> **Concept 250:** The Health of the Patron Must Take Precedence over the Convenient Use of Facilities.

When such an accident occurs, such as a child eliminating in the pool or someone vomiting in the water, immediate and decisive action must be taken. In fact, two actions by management are required *immediately*. First, everyone must be removed from the water. Second, the fecal matter or vomit must be removed. The pool should be closed down for a minimum of 24 hours. In a typical commercial swimming pool this allows for four six-hour cycles of water.

Additionally, Vest (1995) recommends that management must (1) shock the area where the incident occurred with chlorine to a level 20 to 30 parts per million, (2) superchlorinate the pool, (3) backwash and clean the filters with a chlorine-based solution, (4) subsequently the pool chlorine should be neutralized with sodium thiosulfate (down to 5 parts per million), and then (5) backwash and clean the filter a second time before the pool is reopened. Even after the pool is opened for public use there must be biological testing repeated for several days to insure it is safe.

Common Myths of Pool Maintenance

There are many myths in the area of pool maintenance. Many of these myths have been perpetuated by ignorance and lack of formal training on the part of those individuals who have been given the responsibility for overseeing and managing pools of all types. Some of these myths are harmless, while others are not only costly or inefficient to the sponsoring organization but also have the potential to be dangerous to those individuals utilizing the pools. Schmid (1997b, pp. 48–54) lists 13 myths of pool operation and maintenance.

1. Pools with high-rate sand filters need to have the filters running 24 hours a day.

2. The best way to maintain clear water and save operational expenses is daily or scheduled backwashing of pool and spa sand filters.

3. An indoor pool doesn't need a cover (on the contrary, commercial operators can save $30,000 in natural gas costs and conserve one-third of a million gallons of water on an annual basis).

4. If total dissolved solids (TDS) accumulate to levels over 2,000 parts per million (or 1,500 parts per million above the water supply value), it becomes necessary to empty and then refill the pool, and chlorine can lose up to half of its effectiveness.

5. Use of bleach (sodium hypochlorite) to sanitize pools necessitates large amounts of acid to maintain an acceptable pH level.

6. Total dissolved solids (TDS) affect the water clarity or give it color.

7. One can superchlorinate a pool with the cover on.

8. Cyanuric acid improves chlorine by making it better, stronger, and more effective.

9. High cyanuric acid levels have no significant effect on chlorine's efficacy.

10. Chlorine does not kill cryptosporidium.

11. New algicides are regularly developed for pool use.

12. It is O.K. to store liquid chlorine out in the sun as it does not degrade.

13. If a pool has an underdrain system, it won't hurt the pool to drain it.

Outdoor Facilities: Fields, Lawns, and Athletic Turf

The goals of management insofar as fields, lawns, and athletic turf are concerned center around three major elements: insuring that there is healthy turf growing; making certain that there is a full ground cover (no bare spots where grass is suppose to be) over the appropriate areas, thus providing for safe usage; satisfying the participants who play or compete on the grass surface and those patrons or spectators who view the activity.

Turf, Grass, and Athletic Field Management: Problem Areas

There are a number of sources of potential problems facing administrators in their efforts to maintain healthy turf and grass fields. The number one problem is soil compaction brought about by constant use, overuse, or abuse. A second problem involves the time that it takes to establish new turf or the time it takes for grass to grow back so that it can be utilized in a sport setting.

Concept 251: The #1 Challenge with Athletic Turf Is Soil Compaction.

The weather can be another source of problems in terms of soil and grass condition, either by creating saturated soil conditions or droughtlike conditions. Whenever there is inclement weather one must be concerned about the general field conditions, the safety conditions of the field itself, and the safety of the participants and spectators.

Two factors related to the weather that can create havoc with the condition of fields, turf, and grasses are poor crowning (raised area extending throughout the middle of a field and slopping to the edges) and/or insufficient or inefficient drainage (Watson, 1998). And, of course, drainage capabilities and the compaction rate and growth rate of grasses is directly related to the type of soil (hard clay, for example) that exists. Finally, the presence of pests, specifically, fungi (the cause of most lawn diseases), insects, and weeds can prove to be significant challenges for the management (Dernoeden, 1997).

Types of Grasses

It is the responsibility of management to establish a routine turf and field management and maintenance program and then to follow it (Schmid, 1992). An essential part of any management or maintenance program is being knowledgeable about various types of grasses, soils, and seeds as well as methods and techniques of enhancing the growth and development of athletic fields and lawns. Generally speaking, seed selection is determined on the basis of the desired color, the density of the grass, its disease resistance, fertility requirements, moisture needs, mowability, and germination time.

Concept 252: Weather and Soil Type Will Determine the Type of Grass Utilized for Athletic Fields.

Warm Season Grasses

There are a variety of grasses that may be appropriate for different athletic, competitive, and recreational fields depending on the sport or activity planned for the site, the type of soil, and the general weather pattern. Grasses can be classified as *warm season grasses* and *cold season grasses*. With some 14 different warm weather grasses, the two that are best suited for athletic fields because of their growth habit are Bermuda grass and Zoysia. The majority of football and soccer fields are Bermuda grass. Other warm weather grasses include St. Augustine or Bahia grass (Rogers & Stier, 1995).

Cold Season Grasses

There are three general types of cold season grasses, Kentucky bluegrass, perennial grass, and tall fescue. The more common cool season grass species include bluegrass, a tall fescue/bluegrass mixture, and a perennial ryegrass/bluegrass mixture. Because Kentucky bluegrass is a slow-growing grass and difficult (time wise) to repair, it is not recommended for football or soccer competition due to the high volume of physical activity. Although perennial grass germinates rapidly it fails to recuperate from heavy traffic and it does not easily spread to fill in open or bare spots. Tall fescue is very tolerant to heavy traffic due to its wide and course blade. It is a very good cold season grass for football, as long as there is not a time factor in terms of establishing the grass on the field, because this grass requires a good deal of time to firmly establish itself.

Roots

For adequate plant growth one of the essential elements is to have sufficient roots, both in terms of quality and quantity. Without strong and vibrant roots, the grass blades simply cannot grow and prosper. Roots serve as the anchoring points for plants and grasses, and facilitate the absorption of nutrients and water. The root systems in some warm season grasses (Bermuda grass, St. Augustine, Bahia grass) can be as deep as five to seven feet because their peak time for growing is during the summer months. On the other hand, cool season grasses grow more in the spring (and somewhat in the fall) and have more abbreviated root systems, usually between 18 and 24 inches deep (Howell, 1997, pp. 56, 59).

Root Replacement

Some grasses retain their roots over a number of different growing seasons and as such are referred to as *perennial rooting grasses*. An example of such a grass is Kentucky bluegrass. On the other hand, there are grasses that must replace almost all of their roots each and every growing season. These grasses are called annual rooting grasses. Bentgrass, perennial ryegrasses, and rough bluegrass are examples of the annual rooting grasses.

Root Growth

Successful root growth is dependent on a number of different factors. Weather, geographical location, type and looseness of the soil, sufficient nutrients, adequate drainage, appropriate mowing, and sufficient moisture are all essentials for adequate root growth. Roots must be sufficiently deep to be able to serve as a foundation for the grass blades above the ground and to enable the plant to withstand stress, especially during times of drought. Similarly, without strong root growth grasses cannot survive under the almost constant bombardment of foot traffic and activity usually associated with sports and vigorous physical activity. To be better able to assess the current status of a root system, it is recommended that soil core samples be periodically taken (Schmid, 1992; Indyk, 1997).

Proactive Strategies and Tactics to Combat Field and Grass Problems

In order to insure that athletic fields and grassy areas are adequately cared for and provide for appropriate and safe competition or participation, it is important that a turf or field management program be in place, one that is based on sound agronomic practices and involves regularly scheduled, proactive maintenance activities. Figure 8.1 shows 10 elements of grass and lawn management for sport management fields. Depending on the individual situation, any of these elements might be critical in the proper management of fields, lawns, and grassy areas used for competitive or recreational activities.

Seeding and Overseeding

Seeding refers to distributing seed, usually by a mechanical spreader, over the (bare) area for the purpose of growing grass in the near future. This is done while the ground area is not being used for physical activity, that is, while the ground is not being compacted by foot traffic. Germination time for various types of grasses will vary depending on the type of seed being used as well as general weather conditions. Overseeding involves the application

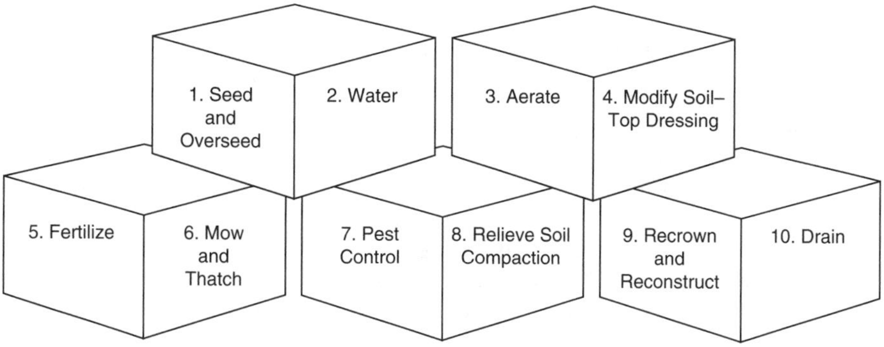

FIGURE 8.1 Elements of Grass and Lawn Management

of additional seed distributed over grassy areas in an attempt to encourage additional growth while the field or grassy area is being used for competitive or recreational purposes.

Watering

The challenge when dealing with the use of water on fields of grass is being careful to apply the correct amount, that is, not too much and not too little. A guiding principle in water application is that irrigation should be scheduled when needed and supplemental to rainfall.

> **Concept 253:** Supplemental Irrigation Efforts Should Be Planned around Natural Rainfall.

Grass requires sufficient water in order to grow. However, too much water and the ground becomes saturated and growth is stunted, if not thwarted altogether. And, if insufficient moisture gets to the roots the grass can be deprived of essential nutrients and the end result will be the same, insufficient growth. Experienced turf managers irrigate when there are signs of initial moisture stress. Such irrigation is usually done to a depth of six inches. On medium type soils irrigation is typically one inch per week during the peak growing season.

Naturally, one would not want to water just before the field or grassy area is to be used because the foot traffic would tend to destroy or injure the wet grass. Finally, if when watering the field water runs off it is recommended that one stop watering and allow the moisture to soak into the ground. Overwatering to the extent that water merely drains off the surface of the ground without penetrating into the layers of the soil beneath the grass blades is wasteful and can result in oversaturation of the ground itself.

Aerating

As stated earlier, compaction can be a major problem for turf and field management. Compaction is when the ground becomes so hard, so compacted from foot traffic (and weather conditions) that moisture and nutrients cannot penetrate beneath the ground to reach the roots. Ground compaction can cause real root damage and result in the eventual death of the turf.

Concept 254: Ground Compaction Can Result in Root Damage and Eventual Root Destruction.

Aerating (also called *coring*) helps break soil compaction up by pulling plugs of earth (3" or 4" cores) from the ground (depositing them on the ground) thereby leaving holes in the earth. Aerating should be completed before one fertilizes so that nutrients can get to the root zone. Typically, coring is completed twice a year, once before fertilization and again during midsummer. When aerating a field it is recommended that two passes at a minimum (in a crisscross or interlocking pattern) be made over the ground area. Aeration should take place when the ground is moist, but not wet and not when very dry.

There are a variety of aerators on the market today (Aerators, 1997). Essentially, they all perform the same task; that is, they accomplish the same results: reducing compaction, improving drainage, improving water, air, and fertilizer absorption, as well as providing for better conditions for seed development or germination. The end result is improvement in the root development of the turf or grass. The plugs or cores pulled from the earth may be left on the ground. It is also possible to drag the field, thereby breaking up the plugs/cores and spreading the soil over the ground.

Top Dressing: The Introduction of Soil Modification Materials

The condition of grasses and turf may be improved by the addition of a soil amendment to the earth. There are various soil modification materials that consist of commercially prepared chemicals as well as sand. These materials may be added straight to the soil, usually not more than an one-eigth of an inch in depth. These modification materials can be especially effective when administered to a field that has recently been aerated as the materials can be deposited beneath the surface of the ground. Top dressing can be completed after coring in an effort to level and smooth areas of the field that have been damaged due to heavy use.

Fertilizing

The spreading of fertilizer on a field can pay big dividends if applied at the proper time of the year and in the correct amounts. Most fertilizers are absorbed by the roots. Relatively few fertilizers are actually absorbed by the leafs of the grass. On the individual container of fertilizer is a three-number sequence indicating the proportion of three essential chemicals: nitrogen, phosphorous, and potassium. The three-number combination might read 10–6–4, indicating that the three chemicals are in the fertilizer in that combination: 10 parts nitrogen, 6 parts phosphorous, and 4 parts potassium.

Exactly what do these chemicals do? Nitrogen helps make the grass green. Phosphorous aids in the photosynthesis process. It also facilitates root growth and is the least important of the three ingredients. Potassium is the key chemical because it helps roots grow.

Mowing and Thatching

Proper mowing is essential if the grasses on the sport or recreation field are to reach their potential. Two important factors relate to mowing grass. The first factor is the quality of the cut, that is, the sharpness of the blade doing the cutting. The cutting effectiveness can be affected by sharpness of the blade(s), so the blade(s) must be kept sharp or there will be damage to the grass. Other factors that can have an effect on the quality of the mowing effort include the speed of blade(s), the cutting unit suspension, wheelbase size, grass discharge, and dispersion characteristics as they relate to terrain and grass conditions (Trotter, 1996, p. 61).

The second factor involves the cutting height. The health of the grass is directly determined by the height of the grass. As a result, one must remember the one-third rule, that is, no more than one-third of the leaf or blade should be removed at a single cutting. The greater the percentage of the blade or leaf removed from the grass the less extensive the root system may be. And too shallow a root system is a potential source of trouble for all grasses.

Concept 255: To Create Striping or Cutting Designs on Playing Fields Utilize Reel Mowers and Cut in Opposite Directions.

There are two types of mowers with two distinct types of different cutting actions, *impact* and *sheer*. The impact cutting action is what is normally seen from gas-powered mowers with the blades moving in a rotary motion (rotary and flail mowers). On the other hand, sheer-cutting is the result of using reel mowers that cut with a scissors-type action. This is the type of mowing machine that can be used to create a striping or creative pattern on the field. Such striping patterns can be seen on professional baseball and professional football fields on game days. The reel mower pushes the blades of the grass down in one direction. When the mower is moved in the opposite direction on the return cut, again pushing the blades in the opposite direction, an appearance of both dark and light shaded grass on the field is created (Trotter, 1996, pp. 62–63).

Concept 256: A Little Bit of Thatch Is Desirable—Too Much Thatch Can Inhibit Growth of Roots and Grass.

Similar to watering efforts, cutting of grasses should not be done on a regular schedule but rather only as needed. In fact, excessive mowing can result in an accumulation of too much thatch. What is thatch? Well, it is nothing more than a layer of organic material that is decomposing while sitting between the dirt or soil and the living turf or grass. A little bit of thatch is fine; in fact, it is highly desirable because it serves as a cushion for the ground should participants hit the dirt.

However, too much thatch can be negative. Too much thatch can choke the grass by inhibiting or altogether preventing water, fertilizer, and other nutrients from penetrating the too thick organic substance and reaching the all-important root system. An overabundance of thatch can also prove hazardous to athletes with cleats on their shoes as the cleats can get caught in the thatch, resulting in ankle and knee injuries. Thus, systematic removal (thatching) of this potential impediment, twice a year and more frequently if needed, is suggested to prevent this buildup of a barrier that can prove cataclysmic to the root system. One-eighth of an inch of thatch is no problem in most cases, but thicker patches might prove to be a potential problem.

Pest Control: Weeds, Fungi, and Insects

Any comprehensive and effective program of field and grass management must include pest control. Pests include weeds, fungi, and insects. Weed management is influenced by three factors: (1) the species of grasses and weeds, (2) the type of usage of the field (light, moderate, or heavy), and (3) the season of use (Lewis, 1994). The objective is to be able to create a turf or ground cover that is vigorous, strong, and competitive with weeds. Weeds not only look bad but they compete for water and fertilizer with grass. Strong grass (leafs) will choke out weeds if the grass is allowed to get a competitive head start. Weeds overtake the ground when grass is in a weakened condition and is unable to stave off the emergence of the weeds. Strong, vibrant, and vigorous grass is one of the best determinants in reducing weed problems.

Concept 257: Healthy Grasses and Turf Help Keep Weeds in Check.

Insects and diseases can ravage turf. Don't hesitate to seek help from area universities or county extension offices to detect potential problems and identify insects and diseases that are threatening your fields. There are a variety of pest control products that can be safely used to combat potential disasters. The key is to get to the root (no pun intended) of the problem early and to address the challenge aggressively. Hesitation and procrastination are not qualities of successful outdoor facility managers.

Delivery of Distribution Systems. Pest control products (such as preemergence and postemergence herbicides) may be spread on the soil when rain is anticipated because most such products need to have moisture to be effective. However, this is not the case with fungicides. When distributing fungicides it is best to have them land on soil that is dry. A variety of distribution techniques can be used to broadcast the numerous pest control materials such as a spreader, sprayer, aerator, or mower. One caution: Be sure and have the individual who is involved in using pest control products wear protective clothing while spraying or spreading and that this person has the necessary applicator's license applicable in your locale.

Providing Relief for Beleaguered Fields through a Rotation System

Perhaps one of the easiest solutions to giving fields and grassy areas a breather from the heavy usage and activity of recreational or competitive physical activity is to simply take that specific field or area out of circulation for a period of time. That is, utilize other fields for the activity and allow the heavily worn facility to have a rest, a breather. This period of rest will enable the roots and grass to make a much needed comeback on the worn field.

Concept 258: Don't Destroy Your Own Field or Playing Area by Overuse or Misuse.

Of course this sounds easier than it is in actual practice. For those sports organizations that do not have extra fields they can use to rotate activities, this option is not available. Nevertheless, supervisors should attempt to explore all possible avenues in which additional fields may be used so as to provide a period of downtime for the much worn or damaged field to make a comeback.

One should not destroy one's own field through use, misuse, or abuse. During the downtime major repairs and renovations can be initiated to enable the soil, root system, and grasses to recuperate from the wear and tear of heavy use. In many instances, time is a great healer with nature providing much assistance to rejuvenate a tired field.

Reconstructing and Recrowning

Reconstruction of a field involves heavy-duty repairs as well as sizable sums of money. Some examples of reconstruction include digging up the ground under and around a football field to install new subsurface drainage pipes or tiles or removing the top surface of a baseball field and replacing the soil with an upgraded version. Recrowning involves improving drainage by digging up the surface of a field and creating an elevated portion of ground in its middle running from one end to the other, with the land gradually slopping to the sides. The result is that water runoff can easily move from the center of the field to the sides where the subsurface drainage system can take the excess water to the storm drains.

Draining Water (Drainage)

Lack of proper drainage is the bane of most facility managers and coaches of outdoor sports. There are three kinds of permanent drainage systems used to combat the problem of surface water on fields. First is the passive system, or surface drainage, in which the slope of the field (crowning) allows the water to drain or run off the field. The second system is referred to as the subsurface system. This involves moving water through the porous level of soil and sand at the top of the ground to the subsurface where the water is collected at various points and then guided along an underground perforated tile system to various drainpipes and into the storm sewer or other suitable outlet. The third system of drainage is a combination of the two methods. Additionally, there is yet a fourth technique utilized to remove surface water, especially in an emergency. This involves sucking the water via mechanical means, by electric or gas pumps, and moving it to an area where it can drain away from the affected field.

By some estimates, 80 percent to 90 percent of all athletic fields are native soil-fields with heavy clay content that does little for proper drainage. Drainage can be maximized by having turf that relies on a root-zone mixture that is heavy on sand, light on clay, with a sufficient amount of peat to provide nutrients for the grass. The presence of sand enables excess water to drain naturally under the surface (Berg, 1993).

Artificial Turf versus Natural Turf

There is no definitive evidence that artificial turf is safer than natural grass (Forbes, 1993; Patterozzi, 1997, p. 41). Artificial turf has been around for a generation. Today, the newest innovation is what is referred to as *hybrid fields,* that use an integrated package of natural and synthetic elements. For example, Schmid (1997a, p. 42) described how the Baltimore Ravens designed and constructed their new hybrid turf field at Memorial Stadium around a combination of natural and synthetic elements, including a sophisticated drainage system and a system that heats the field during inclement weather. Because of the multitude of different systems that are available today, there is no consensus as to which type is superior. That is a decision that must be made by management (Patterozzi, 1997).

Lighting

There are two factors that are used to determine quality lighting for athletic and recreational activities. The first is the brightness of the light as measured in *footcandles.* Average sunshine is considered to be 8,000 footcandles during the summer months. Moonlight is a mere .01 footcandles. The second is the *uniformity ratio.* This is the smoothness or evenness of light throughout the area over which the light is dispersed. Uniformity is commonly conceptualized as a comparison between the darkest location and the brightest location of the total area being lit.

Concept 259: Proper Lighting Facilitates Safe and Appropriate Physical Activities.

Outdoor Security Lighting

In selecting the most appropriate outdoor lighting for security purposes one should consider the effectiveness of the lights and their efficiency (cost, etc.). Additionally, management should take into consideration the quality of light given off and how people as well as colors look under various lights. In terms of getting the most for your money, high-intensity discharge (HID) bulbs give off the most light for the least amount of electricity. While these bulbs are more expensive to purchase, they last up to 20 times as long (20,000 hours compared to 700–1,000 hours) as a standard light bulb (Dulley, 1997).

The three popular types of HID security bulbs are: (1) high-pressure sodium, (2) metal halide, and (3) mercury vapor. High-pressure sodium lights provide a warm golden glow while enhancing natural colors. Metal halide is a cool white light that is used to emphasize blues and greens. Mercury vapor lights, like metal halide lights, enhance plant and focal points among grounds and gardens. Mercury vapor lights also provide excellent moonlight effects outdoors (Dulley, 1997, p. 3-E).

Artificial lights are also calibrated or categorized according to the specific color-rendering index (CRI). This is defined as the ability of the light source to accurately reproduce the color of the object under the artificial light in comparison with sunlight. The resulting value is given as a percent where sunlight is 100 percent. For example, an incandescent lamp has a CRI of 95 percent and projects a warm feeling. On the other hand, the high-pressure sodium lamp has a much hotter feel and a CRI of only 22 percent. And, metal halide lamps, with a cool feeling, have a CRI of 70 percent. Metal halide lamps are the lights of choice for most outdoor playing fields due to their high CRI, lamp life, lumens per watt, and the high color temperature (Thieken & Love, 1995).

Comparisons of Lighting Requirements at Different Events

Lighting for sporting events has been around for a long time. The first baseball night game took place in Lynn, Massachusettes in 1924. This was some 11 years before the Major League's first official night game at Cincinnati's Crosley Field in 1935. Today major league baseball games usually have 300-footcandles in the infield and 200 in the outfield. The new requirements for AAA and AA teams are 100 footcandles for the infield and 70 in the outfield with a 1.2 to 1 uniformity ratio. Recreational baseball and softball competition typically requires 30 footcandles in the infield and 20 footcandles in the outfield, as does Little League baseball (Lindstrom, 1993, pp. 47, 50). On the other hand, high school stadiums with fewer than 2000 seats require 30 footcandles, those with more than 2000 seats 50 footcandles. College and university stadiums (NCAA) will have 50 footcandles while professional teams' stadiums will have lighting at 150 footcandles (Rogers, 1994).

Pool Lighting

Swimming pool facilities need a high intensity discharge lamp such as the metal halide type. High pressure sodium lamps are also appropriate. These tend to be more efficient than the metal halide variety. Their drawback, however, is that they lack the sharpness or crispness as well as the spectrum of color that metal halide seems to project. They also don't last as long (Johnston, 1996).

Parking Lot Lights

Low-pressure sodium lights, as well as mercury lights, can be used for parking lots as well as for weight rooms. However, low-pressure sodium lights, while being very efficient, have poor color quality (monochromatic yellow) and they are slow to start up (Dulley, 1997). However, neither would be appropriate for areas that require reading or quiet concentration because they cast a blue light and are slightly noisy.

The Importance for Sport Managers to be Knowledgeable about Facilities

The world of sport management has many challenges. One area in which there are challenges in abundance is facilities. Not only are the management and maintenance of facilities very important but the process of dealing with facilities can be very complicated and time-consuming. There is so much to learn about facilities and the various components associated with facilities that the typical sport manager or administrator (other than one who is officially designated as "facility manager") is hard pressed to keep up with the latest trends and innovations.

Nevertheless, it is very important in today's world of sport and business to at least be generally knowledgeable and aware of the basics associated with the management and maintenance of selected indoor and outdoor facilities. The extent of one's knowledge will be dependent on the exact job responsibilities one holds within the organization. Nevertheless, sport administrators in the twenty-first century will find it hard to operate within a sport business environment without coming into contact with some aspect of the facility side of the organization. To that extent, it behooves every future member of management to strive to develop and maintain a minimal level of competency and knowledge in the expansive world of sport facilities.

Conclusions

For many sport organizations the management and maintenance of facilities comprise a major responsibility for the entity. Thus, sport managers who find themselves involved with such businesses or organizations must be familiar with the basic fundamentals and foundational knowledge relating to indoor and/or outdoor facility management and maintenance. Of course, not all sport managers will necessarily have direct oversight responsibility for the day-to-day management and/or maintenance of either indoor or outdoor facilities. Nevertheless, it is important that sport managers be sufficiently knowledgeable that they can adequately interact with, supervise, and successfully delegate to others who do have such day-to-day oversight responsibility.

FURTHER READINGS: FACILITIES

A baseball facility: Its construction and care. The United States Baseball Federation. (609) 586–2381.

Farmer, P. J., Mulrooney, A. L., and Ammon, R. (1997). *Sport facility planning and management.* Morgantown, WV: Fitness Information Technology.

Flynn, R. B. (1993). *Facility planning for physical education, recreation and athletics* (2nd ed.). Reston, VA: American Alliance for Health, Physical Education, Recreation and Dance.

Martens, R. (1995). *Event management for sport directors.* Champaign, IL: Human Kinetics.

Pate, D. W., Moffit, E., and Fugett, D. (1997). Current trends in use, design/construction, and funding of sport facilities. *Sport Marketing Quarterly, 2*(4), 9–14.

Perry, F. (1994). *Pictorial guide to quality groundskeeping: Covering all the bases.* Orlando, FL 32809: Holland communications, Suite 423; (800) 809–3952.

Perry, F. (1995). Groundskeeping—Floyd Perry's pictorial guide to quality groundskeeping II, "There ain't no rules." Grounds Maintenance Services, Orlando, FL 32809: Holland communications, Suite 423; (800) 809–3952.

Planning facilities for athletics, physical education, and recreation. (1974). Washington, DC: American Alliance for Health, Physical Education, and Recreation; Chicago, IL: Athletic Institute.

Polk, R. (1983). *Baseball playbook.* Mississippi State, Mississippi 39762: P. O. Drawer 5327 (called the Baseball Bible by many).

USTC & TBA track construction manual, 3rd ed. The United States Tennis Court and Track Builders Association, 3525 Ellicott Mills Drive, Suite N., Ellicott City, MD 21043, (410) 418–4875.

REFERENCES

Aerators. (1997, November). *Turf,* p. C-3.

Berg, R. (1993, May). High tech turf. *Athletic Business, 17*(5), 47–50.

Browser, J. E., III. (1997, November). Move over, metal. *Athletic Business, 21*(11), 16.

Catalano, J. (1995, Feb.–Mar). A gym divided. *Athletic Management, VII*(2), 49–53.

Cohen, A. (1992, March). Easy does it. *Athletic Business, 16*(3), 53–57.

Cohen, A. (1995, August). Rains of error. *Athletic Business, 19*(8), 28–34.

Dernoeden, P. (1997, March). 6 turf diseases and their cures. *Lawn & Landscape, 18*(3), 39, 42, 44–45, 48, 50, 52, 54.

Dillon, J. (1996, August/September). Changes in the changing room. *Athletic Management, VIII*(5), 45–49.

Dulley, J. (1997). Outdoor security lighting best deterrent to vandals. *Democrat and Chronicle,* p. 3-E.

Equipment for success. (1993, August). *Athletic Business, 17*(8) 27–30.

Fawcett, P. (1997, May). Deep trouble. *Athletic Business, 21*(5), 43–44, 49.

Forbes, G. (1993, November 18). The jury's still out on Astro Turf. *USA Today,* p. 5-c.

Garner, S. (1997, August/September). Fresh coat of paint. *Athletic Management, IX*(5), 47–50.

Gimple, J. (1992, September). Laying the foundation. *Athletic Management, IV*(5), 32, 35, 37–39.

Glazier, J. (1997, June/July). From weight room to fitness center. *Athletic Management, IX*(4), 42–46.

Heugli, R., Richards, T., Graffis, K., Kroll, B., & Epley, B. (1991, May). Weights & Measures. *AD,* pp. 18–21.

Howell, C. N. (1997, March). Better root growth. *Lawn & Landscape, 18*(3), 56, 59, 62, 64–65.

Hunsaker, D. J. (1992, December). Under the surface. *Athletic Business, 16*(12), 67–68, 70–72.

Indyk, H. W. (1997, June). The basics of soil management. *Turf,* pp. A6-A11, A15, A16, A18-A19.

Jastrow, S. (1997, February). Facility planning. *Club Industry, 13*(2), p. 37.

Johnston, R. (1996, December). Inside-out pools. *Athletic Business, 20*(12), 81–84, 86–88.

Johnston, R. J. (1991, May). All in one. *College Athletic Magazine, III*(3), 28–33.

Krenson, F. (1997, April). Making it multipurpose. *Athletic Business, 21*(4), 67–68, 70, 72, 74, 76.

Leach, K. (1997, March). An energy audit in action. *School Planning & Management, 36*(3), 14–17.

Lewis, W. (1994, April/May). Weeding out unwanted growth. *Athletic Management, VI*(3), 28–30, 32, 37, 40.

Lindstrom, C. (1993, September). Light up the night. *Athletic Business, 17*(9), 47–48, 50–51.

Pate, D. W., Moffit, E., and Fugett, D. (1993). Current trends in use, design/construction, and funding of sport facilities. *Sport Marketing Quarterly, II*(4), 9–14.

Patterozzi, V. (1997, September). Turf tech. *Athletic Business, 21*(9), 41–43, 46–48.

Rogers, J. (1994, December). Bright prospects. *Athletic Business, 18*(12), 52–56, 54.

Rogers, J. N. & Stier, J. C. (1995, May). Sowing Seeds. *Athletic Business, 19*(5), 49–56.

Ross, C. & Wolter, S. (1997, April). On-time facilities. *Athletic Business, 21*(4), 55–61.

Ryder, C. (1994, Summer). Unauthorized keys: A risk management headache. *Sport Supplement,* p. 3.

Schmid, S. (1992, May). Grass—roots maintenance. *Athletic Business, 16*(5), 51–55.

Schmid, S (1997a, September). Year-round turf. *Athletic Business, 21*(9), 42.

Schmid, S. (1997b, October). Pool maintenance. *Athletic Business, 21*(10), 47–48, 50, 52, 54, 56.

Shalley, W. and Barzdukas, A. (1997, March). Dive right. *Athletic Business, 21*(3), 41–42, 43, 44, 46, 48, 50, 51.

Sherman, R. M. (1997, October). Strengthening weight rooms. *Athletic Business, 21*(10), 23, 74, 76, 78, 80.

Staying out of hot water, part 2. (1993, January). *Athletic Business, 17*(1), 17.

Stier, W. F., Jr. (1991, Fall). A winning combination—Physical education. *American School & University—Facilities, Purchasing and Business Administration, 63*(6), 52f-52h.

Stier, W. F., Jr. (1993, June). The ins and outs of evaluating coaches. *Athletic Management, V*(3), 34–37, 39.

Stier, W. F., Jr. (1997, June 3). *Physical education and the use of technological strategies and tactics.* Presentation at the Sixth Annual FACT Conference on Instructional Technologies (CIT), Learning with Technologies, Brockport, New York.

Strock, R. E. (1991, April). A dozen locker room dilemmas—solved. *Club Business International, 12*(4), 31–37.

The right lockers. (1996, November). *Athletic Business, 20*(11), 52–58.

Thieken, H. and Love, G. (1995, April/May). Let there be light. *Athletic Management, 7*(3), 26, 28–30.

Trotter, B. (1996, January). The cutting edge. *Athletic Business, 20*(1), 61–64.

Vest, S. E. (1995, March). Sound sanitation. *Athletic Business, 14*(3), 39–44.

Viklund, R. (1995, July). High-performance floors. *Athletic Business, 19*(7), 41–42, 44–47.

Viklund, R. and Coons, J. (1997, September). Locker rooms. *Athletic Business, 21*(9), 63–66, 68–71.

Watson, J. R. (1998, January). Waterworks. *Athletic Business, 22*(1), 59–61, 64.

West, B. (1998, January). It's time for an audit. *Lawn & Landscape, 19*(1), 66, 68, 70, 72.

DISCUSSION AND REVIEW QUESTIONS

1. Explain the importance of having appropriate management and maintenance of indoor and outdoor facilities.

2. Discuss the following statement: *It is not always necessary for the top-level sport manager to be an expert in facility management and maintenance.* Justify your position.

3. Specify ways in which management can be engaged in preventative activities.

4. Select a specific indoor or outdoor facility commonly utilized by a sport, recreation, or fitness organization and outline potential problems that astute managers should be aware of in terms of management and maintenance of the facility.

5. Cite some of the contents in a hypothetical Standard Operating Procedures Handbook for a specific sport organization and explain how this information can play an important role in the maintenance and management of a facility.

6. Arbitrarily select five elements (components) of an indoor sport facility and explain factors relating to the maintenance and upkeep of such components.

7. Indicate some critical maintenance factors when dealing with a swimming pool, both in terms of management and maintenance.

8. Explain some general concepts relative to the maintenance of outdoor fields for recreation and/or competitive use.

CHAPTER

9 Personnel Management

Competition—the foundation of university sports.
James Dusen, Photographer.

CHAPTER OBJECTIVES

After reading this chapter you will be able to:

- Recognize how important personnel are to the success of any sport organization;
- List five types of personnel within an organization;
- Explain the advantages and disadvantages of outsourcing;
- Understand the importance of personality and attitude in selecting personnel;
- Appreciate the potential value of diversity among the personnel of a sport entity;
- Comprehend the process of attracting, selecting, hiring, and keeping quality personnel;

- Indicate potential sources of personnel for various sport, recreation, and fitness organizations and programs;
- Acknowledge the importance of networking in the personnel process;
- Explain the relevance of various federal laws pertaining to the hiring process;
- List various electronic home pages where job announcements can be found;
- Differentiate between various qualification parameters of potential employees;
- Cite the purposes of evaluating personnel and various techniques of such evaluation;
- Outline and explain the six components of the personnel process;
- Describe the advantages of using a departmental or organizational personnel handbook.

A Glimpse into the Heart of any Organization: Personnel Management

At the heart of every sport entity or program, regardless of whether it is a for profit or a not-for-profit organization, are the people who work with and for the organization. Adlai Stevenson is credited with saying, "There are only three rules of sound management: pick good people, tell them not to cut corners, and back them to the limits. *But remember, picking good people is the most important*" (Sattler & Mullen, 1994, p. 40; emphasis added).

It is indeed the people who work for the organization, the personnel, who make the organization what it is. It is the people who work within the organization who make it the success or failure that it is or will become. This is true whether they are top level administrators, middle managers, supervisors, or entry-level staff.

Concept 260: When Defining the Terms *Staff* or *Personnel* One Should Include Both Paid Employees As Well As Volunteer Helpers.

It is imperative that managers and administrators view the terms *staff* or *personnel* in the broadest sense to include those who are paid and those who volunteer. Today, many sport administrators find themselves frequently working (sometimes on a daily basis) with a variety of volunteers. It would be a severe mistake not to consider these volunteers as anything other than members of one's staff. Granted that there are differences, in light of special circumstances and varying situations, in how volunteers are treated when compared with salaried staff. Nevertheless, both categories of people, paid and volunteer, should be viewed as personnel.

Concept 261: The Ultimate Success of Every Organization Is Dependent on the People Who Make Up That Organization.

Experienced and successful sport managers recognize that the eventual success or failure of their individual organization is dependent on the quality of the people comprising the staff, both paid staff and volunteer staff (Stier, 1997a). Similarly, the success of individual programs or activities is also dependent on the individuals who have responsibility for implementing the programs and carrying out the activities associated with such programs. Harvey Mackay, president of Mackay Envelope and author of *Swim with the Sharks without Being Eaten Alive* and *Beware the Naked Man Who Offers You His Shirt,* states that success in business is not simply a matter of "how and what to buy cheap and sell high," but rather "a better understanding of people" (Success, 1988, p. 32).

Personnel Management: A Major Responsibility of Sport Managers

The skill level and scope of competencies possessed and demonstrated by personnel, at all levels, are keys to having an effective and efficient organization, one that achieves its various objectives, goals, and ultimate mission(s). A major responsibility of today's administrator is to be on top of what is referred to as "personnel management," that is, *being capable and willing to attract, train, and retain qualified staff and to work successfully with various personnel within the organization.* That is what this chapter is all about: working with individuals who make up, in one way or another, the organization's "team."

> **Concept 262:** Competent Sport Managers Surround Themselves with Superior Staff.

It is vital that administrators and managers surround themselves with bright, articulate, motivated, competent, and dedicated personnel. The reason for this is obvious. No person in the business world of sport, in today's society, can be successful unless that individual is willing to work with others *and* to delegate appropriate responsibility and commensurate authority to other personnel and staff.

Sport managers and administrators can look brilliant if they have capable and skilled personnel working for and with them. On the other hand, these same managers and administrators can look truly incompetent or woefully inadequate if their personnel or staff members fail to perform as expected; the resultant failure reflects negatively on the administrators in charge.

> **Concept 263:** Teamwork and Teambuilding Are Two Essential Components of Personnel Management.

Competent managers must have abilities, must possess competencies. This goes without saying. However, a significant aspect of this competency is the ability to recognize abilities and competencies in other people. Additionally, managers need to demonstrate confidence in their personnel, give them the tools they need to do their jobs, provide adequate support, and adequate supervision and training. This, of course, implies teamwork and teambuilding, two vital elements of any successful business or organization (Barlow, 1993).

Teamwork is so important because "8 out of 10 US workers are involved in some kind of workplace teamwork " (Balog, 1995, p. 2-B). Teamwork among personnel implies skill in interpersonal relationships, a skill that is highly prized in the sport business world.

In fact, it is estimated that as high as 85 percent of employees who fail at their jobs do so because of a lack of interpersonal skills or what business leaders call "personality."

Five Types of Personnel or Staff

Generally speaking, there are five types of staff members or personnel working for, with, or on behalf of any sport entity: (1) those individuals who are employed on a full-time basis, (2) those who are employed on a part-time basis, (3) those individuals who are volunteers, and (4) those who serve as paid consultants. The fifth and last category includes (5) those individuals who are hired by the sport business on a contracting out basis.

Working with Paid Staff, Volunteers, Consultants, and Contract Companies

> **Concept 264:** There Are Different Advantages to Working with Paid Staff, Volunteers, Consultants, and Outsourcing Companies.

Depending on the situation, there are varying advantages for the sport entity to utilize different categories of personnel or staff. It is up to the administration to assess the situation and the varying circumstances in which the organization finds itself before committing the resources of the organization to the use of paid (full-time or part-time), volunteer, consultant or outsourcing staff or personnel (Stier, 1989). There are advantages as well liabilities to using each type of staffing for sport programs. It is up to those individuals who have the power and authority to make such decisions to come up with a rationale for moving in one direction or another in terms of the type of staffing that will be pursued for any given task, activity, or program.

Working with Full-Time Paid Staff

Full-time paid staff include those individuals, as the term implies, who work full-time for the sport entity and receive a decent, living wage and, typically, full benefits. These are the persons whose livelihood depends on the sport entity that hires them. As a result, these employees owe their total allegiance and professional time commitment to their employers. Securing full-time employees is a major commitment on behalf of the organization and involves a significant financial stake as well. And, when dealing with full-time employees, the employing business is faced with rather strict legal interpretations relative to how these full-time employees are to be treated in respect to terms of employment, expectations, evaluations, benefits, and termination.

> **Concept 265:** Many Sport Jobs Involve Both Salary and a Commission Arrangement, Especially at the Entry Level or with Sales Positions.

It should be noted that in many instances the concept of a full-time paid position may involve a specified salary plus additional income in the form of a commission based on some previously agreed-on formula. This is frequently found in professional sports, where the employee is significantly involved in sales. For example, in the health, fitness, and wellness industry it is common for salespeople in the area of memberships to be paid a salary plus commission based on the number of new members or renewals secured. In some sport businesses, salaries for some personnel might be totally based on commissions. In professional sports, commission plus a base salary is common in some specific jobs involving selling and marketing tickets to events.

Working with Part-Time Paid Staff

Part-timers are those employees who have limited rights as employees (in comparison to full-time employees) and, usually, no significant benefits in terms of life, health, dental insurance, or vacations. Also, part-time employees, as the term implies, are rarely paid sufficient money to earn a living wage. Rather, these individuals typically earn minimum sums from the businesses for their part-time work. Unless these individuals have other sources of income, such as retirement benefits from a prior place of employment (or are independently wealthy), they frequently must supplement the part-time salary from the sport business with income from other employment.

Thus, the loyalty and the time commitment of the typical part-time employee are frequently also limited or "part-time." Yet, for many tasks, securing part-time help or assistance is indeed the best way to proceed. The use of part-time employees is usually necessitated when the job is very specific and involves tasks that do not require people working on-task for 40 hours a week. Also, part-time help is frequently necessary when the rate of pay is going to be very low.

Concept 266: Administrators Should Treat Full- and Part-Time Personnel Similarly and Yet Differently.

Whether the salaried personnel are full-time or part-time, there are times when they should be treated in a similar, if not an identical, manner, because employers and supervisors need to build a cohesive team consisting of all of the paid staff. From this perspective, both part-time and full-time staff need to be dealt with similarly as both groups of personnel frequently need to work together to accomplish tasks and to reach objectives and goals.

On the other hand, these two groups of personnel need to be treated differently because of the very nature of their employment. For example, part-time employees may not be involved in some of the high-level decision-making meetings because they are not full-time staff. On the other hand, in some instances these part-timers might be included in some discussions and meetings.

Then there is the matter of confidentiality. In many situations part-time employees have no need for some facts or knowledge nor do they need to be privy to information about future plans. There is no all-encompassing rule or regulation that states when or to what degree part-timers are to be involved in such activities or to be provided with information or knowledge. This is an individual judgment by the management and individual supervisors, depending on the situation and any extenuating circumstances.

The point that supervisors and administrators need to remember is that just because a person is a part-time employee does not mean that that individual can't make real contributions (in terms of ideas, suggestions, questions, etc.) just like any full-time employee. Nevertheless, there are times when the part-timer needs to be treated differently than a full-timer because of the nature of their employment.

Working with Volunteers

Whenever volunteers are involved it is imperative that supervisors and administrators recognize that they occupy a rather unique position in comparison to the other personnel associated with the sport organization or business: These people can up and quit at any time if they are not satisfied, if they feel that they are not appreciated, if they feel that their efforts have no positive impact, or if they are unhappy in any way. Paid employees can't do this as readily. Even part-time employees find themselves in need of the extra cash that their part-time positions provide. Not receiving monetary payment for one's services places the volunteer in a slightly different situation than the paid staff member.

Administrators certainly need to recognize the subtle and not so subtle distinctions between their paid and volunteer personnel. However, both categories (paid and volunteer) should be thought of as the organization's personnel, for both represent the sport entity to the general public as well as to the organization's constituencies. If these people, paid or volunteer, represent the organization, or are perceived to represent the organization, then it behooves the administrators and supervisors to see to it that volunteers act and behave in as professional a manner as the paid staff.

Concept 267: Expect Volunteers to Demonstrate the Same Professionalism, Dedication, and Image as Paid Personnel.

Volunteers represent the sport entity just as much as paid staff does. Often the general public is unable to distinguish between volunteer and paid staff. To the public staff members are staff members, workers are workers. One of the fundamental tenets of effective personnel management is recognizing the importance of seeing that all personnel, whether paid or volunteer, bring credit and distinction to the organization in everything that they do.

Toward this end it is advisable to employ various strategies that will impart to and impress on the volunteers the importance of assuming the role or persona of a regular staff member in terms of the quality of their image and work on behalf of the sport entity. This act of including the part-timers is imperative (in terms of expectations) if successful teamwork and team building is to take place. And teamwork and team building are essential for true success in the business world of sport.

Just as with part-time paid employees, there is the important matter of confidentiality that must be addressed when dealing with volunteers. Because these individuals are volunteers and not paid staff, there are some things that should remain confidential. There are reasons for volunteers not to have access to some information, some data, and some plans, because of the nature of their association with the sport entity. Keeping some information confidential in no way diminishes the importance of the volunteers or of the work that they do for the organization.

Working with Consultants

The use of outside (paid) consultants enables the sport organization to secure the temporary use of experts, with specialized skills, to address specific needs. Typically, the use of consultants is necessitated or warranted when one of three situations exists: The sport organization does not possess personnel or staff with the necessary skills, competencies, or experiences to address a specific task or solve a particular problem, all within a specified period of time; the organization cannot spare qualified staff or doesn't want to redirect the efforts of their regular personnel to address a specific issue, problem, or situation; there is a need for a fresh perspective, a different vantage point, or an outside expert's opinion(s) (expertise) concerning a particular issue, problem, or situation.

Concept 268: The Use of Paid Consultants Can Provide a New Perspective Concerning a Particular Problem, Issue, or Situation.

Consultants are often referred to as "hired guns" as they come to an organization from the outside with specific skills, competencies, and experiences (and a fresh perspective) to deal with a specific situation. This is not a negative conceptualization. Their major responsibility is to provide, within a temporary time frame, information, data, and advice as well as to make assessments, carry out evaluations, and to provide specific recommendations for the organization to consider.

It is not normally the job of consultants to carry out or implement the recommendations. Their job is to provide insight, assessment, input, suggestions, and recommendations. It is up to those in authority within the sport entity to weigh the data, the information, the input, and the recommendations, and then to decide whether to implement the suggestions fully, partially, or not at all. Sport administrators need not abdicate their responsibilities when employing outside consultants. Rather, consultants are used as another tool or source of information or data. The final decisions must still be made by those administrators and managers who have the power, authority, and responsibility to do so.

Concept 269: Sport Administrators Must Not Abdicate Their Administrative and Managerial Responsibilities when Working with Outside Consultants.

There are numerous types of consultant situations that only require an individual consultant. Other situations might call for a corporation or group of consultants and involve any number of different individuals, all performing various tasks, on behalf of the sport organization. Regardless of the actual form that the consultancy takes, the essential elements include: (1) The consultant(s) is (are) hired from outside the sport organization; (2) the consultants are paid for a specific task assigned by the sport organization; (3) the consultancy is for a designated period of time; (4) the consultants are responsible for how they address the task, problem, or assignment; (5) payment is for the specific task(s) identified; (6) financial payment is made by the sport entity directly to the consultant (or the consulting firm) for the job(s) or task(s) agreed to; and (7) the consultants are responsible for making their recommendations or providing their services to the sport administrators in the form that the consultants deem most fitting or suitable.

As with regular paid staff and volunteers, consultants can also be viewed as "personnel" of the sport entity and as such can affect how the public and various constituencies view the organization. Thus, it is imperative that the behavior and actions of such consultants be exemplary in every sense of the word. How the public views consultants working on behalf of the sport entity reflects directly on the sport organization, its programs and activities, its personnel, and everything that the organization represents. It is important that sport managers pay strict attention to the actions and image of their paid consultants.

Working with Contract Companies

Contracting out jobs is a common method by which a sport business is able to secure, on a regular and consistent basis, professional assistance in performing a job or assuming a specific responsibility. Unlike consulting, contracting is a longer-term prospect and calls for the outside company and its personnel actually to perform (not just advise but execute or implement) a specific job or series of jobs on behalf of the sport business for a long period of time. Examples abound and include, but are not limited to, contracting out security for home events, securing secretarial assistance (from temporary service firms), contracting out for services such as accounting, food and/or concession operations, cleaning and/or maintenance of facilities, and travel arrangements.

There are numerous advantages of contracting out for services and jobs: (1) not having to devote the time, regular staff, or energies to these jobs or tasks, (2) taking advantage of the highly technical expertise and extensive experience of firms and their employees who specialize in these types of responsibilities and activities, (3) not having to spend time training staff to perform special or technical jobs, and (4) passing on the legal responsibility and (in many cases) the risk to the firm or individuals(s) accepting the contract to perform the job(s) or task(s).

Outsourcing: A Form of Contracting Out. One type of contracting out is called *outsourcing,* which refers to the management of the sport business or company taking jobs that are currently being filled by regular full- or part-time employees and outsourcing these jobs to firms whose staff will, in the future, do these jobs and perform these tasks. Thus, there will be employees of an outside firm being paid by that firm and performing jobs or tasks on behalf of the sport organization. One possible result of this type of arrangement is that the sport entity's regular staff, who had previously performed these jobs or tasks, find themselves with no justification for being employed and seeking employment elsewhere.

Contracting out makes a lot of sense for sport businesses in respect to those areas of responsibility that are rather specialized or require very special training, such as travel, security, food operations, and so on. The more specialized and complicated the tasks are, the more likely they will be looked at as possible candidates for contracting out. Similarly, the more distant the tasks are from the primary operation of the sport entity the more likely they are to be contracted out.

Concept 270: Contracting Out Can (Sometimes) Save Money while Improving Service or Performance.

In reality, contracting out and outsourcing are done for one or two basic reasons: to save money (and/or time and headaches) on behalf of the sport firm, and to assure a high quality service that might not have been possible otherwise without a great deal of effort, time, and money. It frequently comes down to the bottom line: How can things be accomplished with the least financial exposure or risk?

Risks Associated with Contracting Out. What are the risks of contracting out in all of its different forms or variations? On the downside, there is one fear that every sport manager has in terms of contracting out or outsourcing jobs: The jobs (that are contracted out) might not be done properly or with as much professionalism as desired or expected. There is always the danger that the management of the sport entity will lose a certain degree of oversight or power over the jobs that are contracted out or outsourced, because the company to whom the job was contracted out has direct, day-to-day supervisory responsibility and control over its personnel assigned to these tasks. *Nevertheless, it is still the sport business that will be held responsible, sometimes in the eyes of the law and always in the eyes of the public, if the employees of the firm contracted to do a job for the sport organization fail to do the job satisfactorily.* The employees of an outside firm that has been contracted to do one or more specific jobs are seen by others (public and various constituencies) as the "personnel" or "staff" of the sport business. This has significant implications for the management of the sport business.

Right-handed starter Steve Schrenk instructing youths during a pre-game clinic at Frontier Field (Rochester Red Wings, New York).
Bernie Liberatore, Photographer.

Expectations of Staff and Personnel

As stated earlier in this chapter, personnel working for and with the sport organization are all important. The sport manager who understands how to work with the staff and manage the overall personnel process will be much more successful than the would-be manager who does not. Sport businesses rely on teamwork and cooperation as much as, if not more so than, the traditional sports team that so many sport businesses are involved with today. The key words are *cooperation* and *teamwork*. It cannot be overemphasized how important these attributes are for the eventual success or failure of the organization and its programs.

Concept 271: Staff and Personnel Who Demonstrate an Innate Ability and Willingness to Learn and Improve Are Worth Their Weight in Gold.

Desirable Characteristics of Staff

What do managers want from staff? They need and want people who are competent. People who are skilled (capable) in the tasks assigned to them. Individuals who possess cutting-edge proficiencies in areas critical to the organization's success. Individuals who are, for the most part, self-starters and who are self-motivated.

Managers need leaders. They also need followers (one can't be a leader all the time), people who are loyal to their organization, the program, and the management. They need honest, dedicated, and committed personnel, people with the proper attitude and personality; and, perhaps above all, individuals who have the ability and willingness to learn, to improve, to expand their horizons, and who don't think they know it all (Stier, 1990, p. 35).

Personality and Attitude: Twin Pillars, Essential Traits for Potential Personnel

Before a sport business or organization begins the process of adding new members to its personnel ranks it is imperative that management decide well in advance exactly what type of individual(s) would be most desirable, in terms of specific qualifications, experiences, skills, capabilities, competencies, personality, attitude, and potential for professional growth. Only then should the search process be initiated. Without such clarity the search process can be an exercise in futility.

Two characteristics that are receiving special attention by today's sport managers are personality and attitude. Although many skills can be learned on the job, some more easily than others, personality and attitude are two attributes that cannot. Both personality and attitude are the result of life's experiences, in addition to formal education and interactions with other people (McDermott, 1993). Yet both personality and attitude are very important for the professional engaged in the business of sport, at every level (Stier, 1994).

An individual who works in the people-oriented world of sport and possesses an appropriate personality and a positive attitude has a tremendous advantage over the person who lacks these attributes. Kurt Einstein, a professor and behavioral scientist at the Einstein Institute in North Carolina, delivered a speech several years ago in which he indicated that capability only leads to performance while personality leads to behavior. He also indicated that most failures in organizations are the result of people with the wrong personality attempting to perform the wrong job. "Personality must suit the work and vice versa, so 90 percent of what I teach is how to evaluate personality" (Balog, 1995, p. B-2).

The Value of Diversity within a Sport Organization

Finally, there is the need for diversity within the organization in terms of personnel, in terms of their life's experiences as well as professional experiences, of skills and skill level, of culture, of gender, of race, of education, and of perspective.

Such diversity brings an important element to any organization, and that is, different perspectives and different ways to address tasks, challenges, and problems. Diversity among the personnel can also bring about new options, new ideas, and new approaches. In short, diversity can be good for the organization because such diversity among individuals fosters creativity, ingenuity, and productiveness, all desirable consequences for any business or organization.

The Challenge of Hiring and Keeping Quality Personnel

It is obvious that a quality organization, a quality program, and quality activities are dependent on quality personnel. Although good personnel cannot guarantee a successful program, successful activities or a successful organization, it is almost impossible to have a successful sport organization or program without good personnel/staff. Just as "location, location, and location" is a mantra within the world of real estate, "personnel, personnel, and personnel" is an equally significant mantra within the world of successful sport business.

> **Concept 272:** Desirable Personnel Are Those Individuals Who Exhibit Superior Skills, Competencies, Attitude, Personality, and the Potential for Professional Growth.

One of the recent trends in terms of selecting and hiring personnel is the "raising of the bar." This refers to sport companies raising standards and expectations of its personnel (across the board). Even in tight job markets, in terms of companies and firms, many managers are taking the posture of going that extra step to insure that their new personnel are of the highest quality in terms of skills, competencies, attitude, personality, and potential for professional growth (Jones, 1997).

Dealing with "People Problems" Outside of the Sport Organization

Because of the nature of most sport entities, whether they are professional or amateur sport teams, health and fitness organizations, recreation-related programs, profit or nonprofit organizations, public or private firms, most of their problems or challenges will be because of people. It is as simple as that.

Concept 273: The Majority of Problems Faced by a Sport Organization Can Be Traced to People Problems.

Anytime any organization deals with people, with human beings, and most sport-related organizations deal with a great many people, both internally and externally, it will be people who create the most challenges, difficulties, and problems. It is sometimes a formidable task indeed dealing with various constituencies, the general public, (and in some cases) athletes, customers or patrons, fans, and the press to boot.

Dealing with "People Problems" Inside the Sport Organization

Just as a majority of the problems facing most managers–administrators in the world of sport are generated from people, most of the internal difficulties within a sport organization itself can be traced to staff and personnel problems. Thus, it is very important, in fact it is critical, for modern management to be extremely successful in securing the services of highly qualified, dedicated, and professional personnel. Doing so will reduce, although not entirely eliminate, many of the problems that seem to plague many sport businesses in this country.

Concept 274: The Majority of Internal Problems within a Sport Organization Can Be Traced to Staff/Personnel Problems.

Having the support of the "right" personnel is the first step to being a successful sport organization. Locating, attracting, securing, retaining, and working with competent staff is one of the fundamental challenges facing management today. Mastery of all the phases in the personnel process are important for the health and well-being of the sport entity, its personnel, and its programs or activities.

The Personnel Process

What exactly is meant by the phrase "personnel process"? Although these words can mean different things to different people in different organizations, generally speaking the phrase refers to activities, treatments, procedures, policies, and practices affecting personnel throughout the time when these individuals are an integral part of the sport organization or being considered as potential personnel.

The personnel process involves steps or procedures to follow when dealing with staff (paid and volunteer) at every conceivable point along a continuum from the beginning of employment or association to the end or termination of said employment or association. This includes activities and decisions associated with or related to the search for new personnel, the interview process, hiring or selecting new personnel, treatment of personnel within the workplace, as well as those activities associated with termination, resignation, or retirement.

Concept 275: Members of Management Must Be Fully Aware of All Aspects of the Personnel Process.

In reality, the personnel process can be viewed as six distinct yet related stages, activities, or actions: the attempt to identify potential personnel or staff members who might be a suitable match for the organization; the activity of officially seeking out and recruiting qualified candidates for a position; the interviewing stage of potential personnel or staff; once someone is hired, the personnel process goes into a proactive stage in which management attempts to insure that the new staff member will experience success; consistent, fair, and continual evaluation and assessment of personnel; and actions that management takes in light of (as a consequence of) the perceived performance level of the personnel.

Identification of Potential Personnel or Staff Members for the Organization

Almost every sport organization, at one time or another, becomes involved in the process of adding new personnel. One secret to the process of securing quality staff is for members of management to always be in a "search" or "watch mode." This simply means that one is always seeking to identify outstanding professionals. Once one becomes aware of highly skilled and competent professionals the business is in a better posture, if and when an opening becomes available, to seek out these persons as potential candidates for a vacancy.

This is sometimes referred to as "networking in reverse" and it refers to keeping an eye out for potential employees so that when one's own organization has an opening there already is a list of quality professionals whom management might wish to consider as new additions to their own organization or business. The best time to identify potential personnel is when the company doesn't presently need to hire anyone. Rather, developing a list, a database, of highly desirable individuals who might be suitable as additional personnel in the future is similar to planning for a rainy day and can pay big dividends when a vacancy does occur.

Concept 276: Maintain an Active Database of Highly Qualified Individuals Who Might Be Candidates for Potential Positions before There Is an Actual Need to Fill Such Vacancies.

Some sport administrators have said that they would prefer not to hire anyone for an opening within their sport entity who applied only as a result of an advertisement. These members of management take the position that they want to pursue the very best candidates for vacancies within their sport organizations or businesses by inviting outstanding individuals to apply for their position(s), the rationale being that high quality personnel might not apply on their own. Thus, it becomes the responsibility of the management where the vacancy exists to take a proactive approach to seeking out highly qualified individuals, identifying possible candidates, and then pursuing them in an effort to entice them to become interested in the position.

Consequences of Imprudent Hiring

The consequences or risk of ending up with the wrong candidate for a position within a sport organization is too great to treat the selection process in a cavalier fashion. Great care must be spent in terms of identifying the right candidate(s) for the position. This takes work, it takes effort, it takes commitment, and it takes time. But, the ultimate consequence, a competent professional (paid or volunteer) being a part of the personnel team, can have far-reaching positive consequences.

> **Concept 277:** Poor Hiring Efforts Usually Result in Poor Hires and Future Problems for the Organization As Well As for the Employee(s).

A cardinal sin of the hiring process is for managers to rely on their overall or "gut level" impression of candidates. This informal "seat of the pants" approach by administrators is nothing more than relying on the process of intuitive judgment, a process that is suspect at best. Such efforts lack sophistication and substance. It is important that management be capable of correctly evaluating the actual skills and abilities of potential personnel if there is to be appropriate employee selection and eventual success on the job (Hopp & Swedburg, 1996, p. 58). Such decision-making should be based on facts rather than hunches or "gut" feelings. Poor or inadequate selection of personnel can have devastating consequences for the climate of the organization itself as well as other staff. The risks are too great for management to take unnecessary chances. Thus, the search and selection process of appropriate personnel should take top priority in today's sport business arena.

Consequences of Prudent Hiring

Selecting the right person for the right position or job has obvious benefits for the organization, management, and other personnel as well as the new staff member. First of all, the job for which the new person was selected will be accomplished and the objectives and/or goals realized. Second, the interpersonal relationships between individuals working within the organization will be facilitated.

> **Concept 278:** Selecting Quality People to Work for the Sport Entity Prevents Many Problems in the Future.

Third, less difficulties and fewer problems will result from the latest addition to the personnel "team." Fourth, prudent and timely selection of personnel may significantly reduce costs associated with employee turnover (e.g., hiring, screening, training, evaluating, etc.) (Miller, Pitts, & Fielding, 1993, p. 47). Sport business success in the real world is difficult enough even with all appropriate and necessary resources. Without a resource as vital as skilled personnel such success can easily be out of reach regardless of the effort expended and the time spent working at it.

Putting Together a Winning Combination of Personnel

Sport managers at all levels shouldn't hesitate to seek personnel who may be more experienced or more highly skilled than they are. Administrators should not be intimidated by their own personnel just because these individuals possess unique skills or highly advanced skills (Roberts, 1993). On the other hand, there is a very real danger of hiring overqualified individuals for specific positions. This is especially true in the health and fitness industry (Pessin, 1997, p. 32).

> **Concept 279:** Managers Should Not Feel Intimidated if They Are Surrounded by Highly Skilled, Motivated, and Talented Personnel.

Overqualified individuals may feel that they are underutilized and become dissatisfied in their current positions, therefore being less productive than expected or even disruptive within the organization. Then, of course, there is always the possibility, the probability, that this overqualified and dissatisfied staff member will end up leaving for another position as soon as a more suitable one becomes available. When that happens the entire search and hire process for the company begins all over again.

Surrounding oneself with highly skilled and motivated people is one way to insure that the total team possesses sufficient experiences and adequate skills to get the job done. Managers have certain strengths and weaknesses. Wise and confident managers seek to surround themselves with individuals whose own skills, competencies, and experiences complement and add to the skills of the manager. In this instance, the whole is indeed greater than the sum of its parts. In this regard, synergism is an important element in the personnel process (Roberts, 1993).

Sources of Personnel

Where are potential employees found? What are the various sources of personnel for the increasing number of sport organizations and businesses in the United States? Specifically, where does management go to obtain the skilled workers necessary in the modern-day sport business? What options are open in terms of soliciting appropriate personnel in sport? The sources of potential employees are many as are the methods of finding out about potential employee candidates. Some of these techniques, tactics, and strategies are presented below.

Retired or Older Workers

One source of ready-made staff is the retired or older individual who may be looking for an association or part-time or full-time employment with a sport organization or business. Research as well as anecdotal information leads one to believe that there may be significant advantages to having the typical older and/or retired worker as a member of one's organization (Plummer, 1997). Some of these advantages include, but are not limited to, the following:

1. Anticipation of patrons' or customers' needs;
2. Punctuality;

3. Low absenteeism;
4. Positive role model for younger staff;
5. Variety of life experiences;
6. Maturity facilitates wiser decisions and positive interactions with people;
7. A wide range of skills, competencies, and capabilities;
8. A track record of performance as an employee or worker in the real world;
9. Infrequent turnover.

Concept 280: Not Only Is It Illegal to Discriminate against Potential Employees on the Basis of Age, It Is Also Bad Business Practice.

"Growing" One's Own Personnel

"Growing" one's own personnel refers to looking internally to select individuals for vacancies that occur. Such a practice has the advantage of positive motivation, as hiring one's own people encourages others within the organization to hope for and look toward similar happenings for them. On the other hand, hiring one's own people can be likened to inbreeding, because there may be fewer opportunities for new ideas as well as less creativity and less ingenuity. Nevertheless, use of the "feeder system" in filling vacancies has merits.

Interns from Collegiate Professional Preparation Programs

A variation of the "homegrown" method of selecting personnel is the use of sport management interns. These college students serve an internship (typically a semester or, less frequently, a calendar year) within a sport organization. Management is able to take advantage of these interns in two ways: First, to put them to real work doing real jobs in the real world of sport business. In reality, many sport organizations could not run their actual business operations without the use of sport management interns. These interns, usually college seniors and graduate students, can provide significant assistance in the day-to-day operation of many sport businesses and organizations.

Concept 281: Sport Managers Should Carefully Select and Evaluate Their Interns as Potential Future Employees.

Second, management can size these interns up, under pressure and in real-life situations, in an effort to determine whether these students have what it takes to be a professional in this exciting business. As a result, those interns who have distinguished themselves in the internship setting frequently find themselves being selected as employees by the organization where they interned, or at another organization as a result of the positive recommendations received from their internship site.

"Stealing" or Attracting Staff Directly from Other Organizations, Sport and Nonsport Entities

Outstanding employees are seemingly fair game insofar as being coveted and sought by other employers. Today, many organizations attempt to steal or appropriate other organizations' outstanding and talented employees. In fact, this raiding of highly qualified and competent personnel is quite frequent in some aspects of the sport business world, especially in the health, fitness, and wellness industry. Part of the reason for this is that sufficient numbers of quality personnel are frequently difficult to find (for the wages paid) and harder yet to keep. One way to prevent having highly qualified, talented, and valuable personnel from being "stolen" is for management to provide a healthy work environment, consistent training, adequate professional support, and a decent wage (Plummer, 1997, p. 36).

Concept 282: Management Must Treat Their Personnel Well lest Highly Qualified and Desirable Staff Jump Ship and Go to Work for Another Organization.

Networking within the Business Community

Just as prospective employees are encouraged to network in order to find out about possible jobs, employers are getting into the act in an effort to find out about talented and desirable personnel. Networking in this instance involves a process of communicating, keeping in touch, with other individuals in an attempt to keep abreast of current developments within the personnel arena. In particular, such communication efforts, both formal and informal, can be initiated with managers and nonmanagers at businesses of all types, descriptions, and sizes.

In fact, professional and productive networking is possible with a wide variety of individuals within the community who might have knowledge of and experience with talented personnel. Potential personnel for sport organizations do not necessarily have to have prior experience in the world of sport or sport business. They could come from any type of business or work experience, because, in many instances, specific skills and competencies can be learned on the job. This is especially true when the individual already possesses a propensity for learning and important attributes like a positive attitude, an appropriate personality, drive, and the ability to be a self-starter.

Concept 283: There Is a Difference between Professional Networking and the Improprieties Associated with the "Good Old Boys Network."

One should not confuse proper networking for employee candidates with the unprofessional "Good Old Boys Network" or the "Good Old Girls Network." In the former instance there is no discrimination or exclusion involved at all. Rather, members of management and search committee members seek to find out about possible prospective candidates without reservation or limitation as to who the individuals are or whether they are male or female, or whether they are African American, Caucasian, blue, or purple. The problem with the traditional interpretation of the "Good Old Boys/Old Girls Networks" is that they excluded people from consideration on the basis of factors that (legally and morally) should not enter into the employment equation (see below).

Planning for and Initiating an Official Search for an Actual Vacancy within the Organization

It is very important when initiating an official search for a position to follow both the letter and intent of the laws of the land as they affect the hiring process (see Chapter 11, The Legal Aspects of Spot Management). This is important for two reasons. First, it is the right thing to do to from a professional and ethical standpoint. Second, it is a matter of law, and violations of law can result in severe punishments and embarrassments for the individuals involved as well as for the sport entity itself.

Concept 284: Good Hiring Practices Are a Matter of Law As Well As Ethics.

Two very important acts or laws that affect the personnel process are the Civil Rights Act of 1964 and the Age Discrimination in Employment Act of 1967. The importance of the Civil Rights Act of 1964 is that this piece of legislation sought to stop unfair employment practices. It essentially prohibits and forbids discrimination on the basis of race, color, sex, religion, or national origin in areas of employer–employee relationships, including advertising for employees, discrimination against current employees, termination, or retirement practices.

The ADEA, Age Discrimination in Employment Act of 1967 (as amended), forbids discrimination against employees *or* job applicants because of age. Specifically, when applicants or employees are *age 40 or greater,* the provisions of ADEA are applicable (Hiring, 1993). The opportunity to select or invite one or more individuals to join one's organization as staff is so important that the process and activities associated with the selection process must be flawless.

Writing the Job Description

Preparation is the key in the search process. One of the first steps to take when a vacancy becomes available is to be sure that management has a clear concept of what the person is to do and what skills and attributes the person should possess.

Concept 285: Advance Planning Is Absolutely Essential in the Hiring Process.

In order to identify the character traits necessary for any position, management should answer such questions as what needs to be done in this particular job? What responsibilities would be assumed by the new hire? What skills and attributes are needed to do these tasks effectively and efficiently? What qualifications would be necessary for a person to be able to successfully complete these tasks and do the job required (Sattler & Mullen, 1994)? Only after one has such information can the search process really begin. Developing a clear job description is one of the first steps in the hiring process (McCutcheon & Robinson, 1997).

An important element of the job description is a list of qualifications. Many employers choose to utilize two categories of qualifications, required and preferred. Similarly, it must be decided what potential candidates must submit as part of their application for the position. Typical requirements include:

1. Letter of application addressing specific requirements of the position;
2. Résumé or vita;
3. Either a list of references (with addresses, phone numbers, e-mail addresses) or actual recommendations from references sent to the search committee.

Advertising and Recruiting Efforts

The ultimate goal of management is to find the best candidate for the vacancy that exists within the sport organization. However, potential candidates need to be made aware of it. Usually this involves publicly announcing the vacancy (or anticipated vacancy) through the media as well as mass mailings and individual contacts with others via the mail, phone, Internet, or in person. Networking is very important to insure a sufficiently large applicant pool.

Concept 286: Utilize All Available Means of Communication when Announcing Job Vacancies.

Examples of communication and announcing job vacancies include, but are not limited to, the following:

1. Sending out printed announcements of the vacancy to:
   a. College placement offices;
   b. Other sport organizations;
   c. Specific college/university departments of sport management;
   d. Selected individuals working in the field.

2. Submitting advertisements for the vacancy in national, regional, and statewide publications, such as *The Chronicle of Higher Education, The New York Times, JOPERD, UPDATE,* and so on.

3. Submitting the announcement to various electronic home pages or checking out World Wide Web sites for candidates, including:
   a. http://www.careermosaic.com
   b. http://www.monster.com
   c. http://www.fentonnet.com/jobs.html
   d. http://www.tiac.net/users/jobs
   e. http://www.recruiting-links.com
   f. http://www.ipa.com
   g. http://www.washingtonpost.com/parachute

- **h.** http://www.careersite.com/
- **i.** http://www.cweb.com
- **j.** http://www.careerpath.com/
- **k.** http://www.espan.com
- **l.** http://www.napehe.org

4. Searching the World Wide Web for potential candidates who have created and posted their own home page;

5. Attending national, regional, and state conventions and conferences (such as winter meetings in the sport of baseball) and posting notices of the vacancy.

Establishing Qualification Parameters

In evaluating potential employees selection committees and management typically look at a number of different factors, depending on the type of vacancy being filled and the organization itself. Some of the factors used to differentiate between various candidates and to identify those individuals who are most likely to experience long-term success within the organization include:

1. Formal education of applicants;
2. Formal and informal training;
3. Type of certification(s) held (if applicable), such as:
   - **a.** American College of Sports Medicine,
   - **b.** Various aerobics certifications,
   - **c.** American Council on Exercise (ACE);
4. Professional and personal experiences;
5. Specific skills and capabilities;
6. Personalities;
7. Attitudes.

A recent national study, sponsored by the Education Department, of some 3000 managers indicated that there were four very important factors or criteria to take into consideration in the hiring of new personnel. These factors and their respective ranking on a five-point scale were attitude (4.6), communication skill (4.2), work experience (4.0), and previous employers' recommendations. Interestingly enough, the respondents indicated that grades earned in college were deemed to be the least important factor in terms of whether an individual is hired or not (Henry, 1995).

Reviewing, Screening, and Assessing Applicants' Applications

Once applications have been received by the search committee or by management it is necessary to screen and assess the contents of each application package. At this point it is recommended that management double-check to insure that the pool of applicants is sufficiently large to warrant further action by the search committee. If the advertisement and distribution of the vacancy notices were adequate, the pool of aspirants should be fairly large. If the search process up to this point has failed to produce an adequate pool of candidates, a decision must be made whether to continue with the hiring process or to abort it and try again.

Concept 287: There Must Be a Sufficient Number of Applicants to Warrant Continuation of the Search Process.

Assuming that the pool of candidates is sufficient in terms of numbers and diversity, the next step is to evaluate the application packets or materials submitted by those interested in the position. In many searches the range of applicants in terms of their qualifications can vary greatly. In some searches there are large numbers of people who apply who do not even meet minimum qualifications. However, with an effective search and advertisement (notification) effort there should be a sufficient number of minimally qualified aspirants for the position.

The process of wading through numerous application folders can be daunting to say the least. To facilitate this process and to be objective in this initial evaluation stage, it is highly advisable to have a written list of criteria or factors with which to evaluate applicants. The list should also include the preferred and minimum (required) qualifications included in the advertisement for the position. With this list management and the search committee can begin to assess and evaluate each of the applicants.

To bring order to the screening process, it is suggested that candidates initially be placed in one of three categories. For example, category or group "C" would be for those applicants who failed to meet the minimum advertised requirements for the post. Group "B" would include those individuals who met the minimum requirements but were thought not sufficiently strong to warrant a personal interview. Those candidates who meet the minimum requirements, score high in terms of the preferred qualifications, and are possible candidates who might be invited for an interview are placed in the third group, the "A" group.

Contacting References: Another Phase of the Screening Process

At this point, it is highly advisable to begin to check the references and backgrounds of each of the candidates in group "A," in an effort to further cull the number of candidates in this category to a select few, perhaps two, three, or five. Many search committees do not limit their communications with those references whose names were supplied by the candidates but seek to cast a wider net. They do this by contacting individuals who might know of the individual candidates and who were not identified as references by the candidate.

Concept 288: Double-Check the Veracity of Résumés and Vitas.

In addition to checking references, conscientious committee members should also verify the information supplied by candidates. For example, such items as employment history, certifications, degrees, skill level, and professional accomplishments and honors.

Conducting such checks thoroughly may save management from making a very costly mistake in terms of money, image, and staff morale.

There is a need to be very careful and cautious in believing everything that one reads on a person's résumé or vita. Not every résumé or vita is 100 percent accurate (Stull, 1990). In fact, the increasing creep of inadequacies, exaggerations, fluff, and outright falsehoods found on many of today's résumés and vitas places even greater pressure on search committees and management. Double-checking, certainly in the case of the finalists, should be automatic.

Inviting Candidates for an Interview

Inviting one or more candidates to an interview with the search committee and selected administrators is a critical stage in the hiring process. Great care must be taken to identify—from the written application dossier and the follow-up phone calls and personal inquiries of references and others—a small number of highly qualified individuals who might be a good match for the position. When these individuals have been identified from those applications in group "A," the next step is to extend an invitation for a personal interview to them.

Interviewing Prospective Candidates

There is a science and an art to interviewing candidates successfully for sport management positions. There are fundamental things to do such as attempting to make the applicant at ease and asking the "right" questions. There are also things that should not be done, such as not asking questions that would be discriminatory, offensive, or no one's business other than the candidate's, for example. Everyone who is in management or who serves on search committees should be made aware of all of these issues or standard operating procedures, as they relate to the interview process, in a minimum amount of time.

During the interview inquiries are made of each candidate in an effort to secure answers to such questions as:

1. Does the candidate meet all of the job requirements?
2. Does the person have the mental and physical capabilities necessary to perform the tasks associated with the job?
3. Does the person have the knowledge, skills, and understanding essential for achieving outstanding performance?
4. Is the individual motivated?
5. Does the person's personality or attitude match the demands of the position and the employment climate of the organization?
6. Will the person meet the organization's expectations? (Is there evidence or some indication that would support this assumption?)
7. What are the long-range career plans of the candidate?
8. Does the aspirant possess a basic understanding of the organization, its personnel and its mission(s)?

9. Does the person have the potential for further growth within the profession and within the organization?
10. What type of contributions might this individual make to the sport entity? (Fritz, 1992).

Concept 289: Interviews Should Delve into the Very Essence of the Person Who Is Seeking the Position to Determine if There Is a Suitable Match.

However, the art of interviewing is not so easily taught or learned. This aspect of the interviewing process involves getting into the heart and the soul of the applicant to determine what resides inside the individual. Interviews should serve more of a purpose than merely to confirm what the individual's application had provided. The real essence of an interview experience, from the perspective of the employer, is being able to get inside the human being to find out what makes Johnny or Jeannie really tick, what makes Johnny or Jeannie "run"? What is the true essence of the individual who wants to join the organization and be part of the team? Will this person be a good partner in terms of the sport organization and in respect to other personnel? Will the person be a good fit or a good match in all aspects of the organization, its programs, its activities, and its "people"?

Thus, the kind of atmosphere or climate that is created for each of the candidates during all phases of their interview experience is of paramount importance. This is true both for the formal interview session(s) as well as subsequent informal meetings, gatherings, and discussions held with the candidates. The type of environment that evolves is frequently dependent on the personality and attitude of the candidates themselves as well as members of the search committee.

In reality the interview is a two-way, give-and-take experience in which both the interviewer(s) and the candidate are able to project an image and to learn about the other. It should be a time of mutual evaluation and information-sharing. Toward this end it is strongly advised to have a set of questions that have previously been agreed to by members of the search committee and management that speak directly to the individual candidates' ability to fill the position. These questions should be based on what information is desired. The questions should focus on integral job-related issues. And the same questions should be asked of each candidate interviewed to insure fairness and consistency (Carpenter, 1997).

Concept 290: Never Hire Just to Fill a Slot—Better to Abort the Search and Start Again than to Take "Second Best" or Worse.

Not all searches end on a positive note. Sometimes, for whatever reason, the search fails to produce the right individual for the position. Or the perfect candidate is offered the position but turns it down. What does the organization do if, at the end of the search process, there is not an acceptable match between the sport organization and an individual?

Should management offer the permanent, full-time position to someone who is not really a good match for the job or for the business? The answer is simple, **NO!** Instead, start the search process again. Don't hire just to be hiring. Generally speaking, it is better to abort the search and start again to locate an acceptable candidate than to be saddled with an inferior or unacceptable staffing choice. An offer of a full-time, permanent position is a big decision and commitment on behalf of the organization. Accepting such an offer can be even more of a decision for the candidate. Of course, if the search process has been carried out with due diligence then the likelihood of finding one or more suitable matches among the finalists is greatly enhanced.

The Proactive Stage of the Personnel Process: Helping Personnel Experience Success

Management has an obligation to help each and every individual working for the organization. After all, it was the organization that hired the personnel working for the business. It is important that managers, administrators, supervisors, and other employees take this responsibility, this obligation, seriously. In fact, these same managers, administrators, supervisors, and peers should be shocked if someone fails to experience success as a member of the organization's team. If an individual is not successful, as an employee, then not only has this person failed but so too has management, as well as the entire organization. In reality, either the selection/hiring process was flawed or the support process that should have been provided to the individual as an employee was lacking. Perhaps both were deficient.

> **Concept 291:** Failure of an Employee Is an Indictment against Management and the Organization.

Use of Mentors

Management's responsibility for personnel continues after the individual is hired. In fact, it intensifies. Now that the person is a member of the personnel team it behooves the organization, management, and other personnel to see to it that the person experiences success in the job. Part of this process rests in the day-to-day support given to the staff member. In some organizations a formal mentor system is employed in which an experienced staffer is paired with a new person to watch over the new hire and to advise, guide, and otherwise help the person adapt to the new surroundings and the new environment or job climate.

> **Concept 292:** Management Should Provide In-Service Education Opportunities for Personnel in order for Them to Remain at the Cutting Edge.

Another important aspect of helping staff members is education and training. Providing opportunity for personnel to engage in formal and informal (in-service) educational programs or training sessions is vital for the health of the individuals involved and for the business (Stier, 1987). Examples of such educational experiences include formal classes (on or off site), workshops, clinics, training sessions, peer tutoring or counseling, travel, access to telecommunication classes, correspondence courses, and the like. Supporting in-service education for personnel involves recognizing that learning never stops among an organization's staff.

Of course both neophyte and experienced personnel within the sport organization should be given appropriate educational opportunities. Generally speaking, the lower the level of employee the more training and supervision that individual may require (Plummer, 1997). Such educational options help to insure that one's staff remains at the cutting edge or at least close to it. And in sport management this is very, very important for the health and longevity of the organization.

Hiring Personnel and Letting Them Have the Freedom to Do Their Jobs

An important element of managing personnel is allowing them to do the job(s) for which they were selected in the first place. Far too often managers and supervisors interfere and meddle in the affairs of their subordinates to the extent that they actually interfere with or impede the progress of their staff. Being able to delegate responsibilities and then to stand back while subordinates go about their business of doing their job is sometimes difficult for supervisors, but it is an important part of the managing process. Members of management must resist the temptation to micromanage (Stier, 1997b, October 6).

Concept 293: Managers Must Resist the Temptation to Micromanage.

Fringe Benefit Packages (or Lack Thereof)

Employees today are as concerned about fringe benefits, such as health insurance, dental insurance, and retirement programs, as they are about their regular salary, if not more so. This is especially true in some segments of the sport industry because many employees, both those working full-time and part-time, are not recipients of significant fringe benefit packages. In fact, many employees within the sport industry have no benefits to speak of at all.

In today's marketplace insurance and health packages have become more and more important in terms of attracting and keeping quality employees. For those personnel working for sport organizations who receive the low wages with few, if any, health insurance or retirement benefits, there is little incentive to remain with the sport firm. Rather, these minimally paid personnel are often marking time in their current place of employment while constantly looking for a better employment environment, one in which they are better compensated for their efforts. This type of situation does little to establish stability and longevity among the personnel. With constant turnover come low morale and poor performance.

Evaluation and Assessment of Staff

There are eight questions that sport managers should answer before engaging in personnel appraisal or job performance evaluation. First, what is the purpose of the appraisal? Second, what exactly should be evaluated or assessed? Third, what specific criteria will be

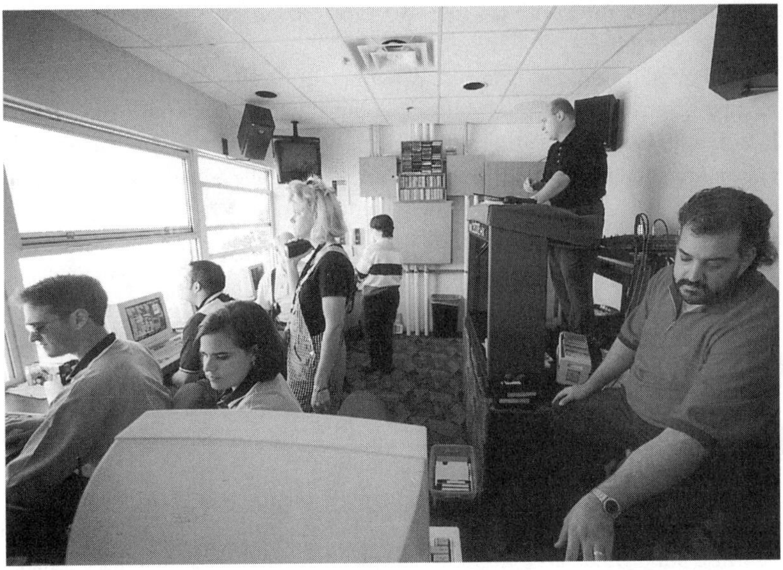

Behind the scenes—work that few people see or appreciate yet is vital for the overall success of the franchise.
James D. Lathrop, Photographer.

used to assess performance? Fourth, who should conduct the assessment? Fifth, when should it take place? Sixth, where should it take place? Seventh, what specific techniques or "instruments" should be used? Lastly, how will the results be used?

Concept 294: Evaluation Is a Necessary Element of Personnel Management.

The evaluation and assessment process of personnel is an essential component of the personnel process. Staff evaluation is conducted for numerous reasons (Stier, 1993; Haney, 1995):

1. To let employees know how they are doing;
2. To motivate employees;
3. To help the individual in terms of efficiency, productivity, and competency;
4. To enhance communication and employee feedback;
5. To improve employee weaknesses in job performance;
6. To encourage ownership, accountability, and employee involvement;
7. To justify specific personnel actions by management, such as:
   a. Promotion,
   b. Reassignment,
   c. Salary increase, decrease, or no increase,
   d. Increase or decrease in autonomy,

e. Increase or decrease in authority and responsibility,
f. Granting a sabbatical for study,
g. Provision of additional educational (training) opportunities,
h. Giving a letter of reprimand or letter of warning,
i. Demotion,
j. Firing or termination.

The most important justification (purpose) for evaluating one's personnel (both paid and volunteer) is to help them become better employees and to assist them in developing greater skills. In this sense, assessment is done to evaluate, critique, and improve the performance of personnel. Thus, management must always remain in the "help" mode when considering the evaluation process.

> **Concept 295:** Remain in the Help Mode when Evaluating Personnel.

The Importance of Constructive Feedback

When dealing with employees who are performing at an unacceptable level, supervisors should concentrate on providing constructive feedback rather than negative criticism. Supervisors need to be sensitive. *Correction or criticism should never be made personal.* Critical remarks should be made in private and praise should be given in public. Similarly, if correction is warranted, cite the work or the mistakes that are the subject of the correction, not the individual staff member.

In other words, deal with the problem itself, deal with specifics rather than generalities, and keep the criticism focused on the problem and not the person. Of course if the problem is with a person's behavior or attitude then obviously the subject of the correction will be the offending individual (Wakin, 1991). When providing feedback concerning errors or mistakes, supervisors should always point out ways that these problems could be corrected. Also share a willingness to assist the employee, thus remaining in the help mode.

> **Concept 296:** Consistent Feedback Is an Essential Component for Good Performance Appraisal.

Many employees view personnel appraisals in a negative manner because of the possibility for negative personnel decisions such as dismissals, demotions, or other forms of punishment. Thus, they see staff evaluation as punitive, threatening, intimidating, and menacing. Some even see something sinister about the entire process. Nothing should be further from the truth. This is why it is sometimes recommended that the personnel be involved at the onset, when performance appraisals are first being considered within the sport organization (Koch, 1994). If such appraisals are already in place, management should endeavor to educate the staff as to the positive purposes for which the process is implemented. In this way management remains in the help mode.

Essentials of a Performance Appraisal/Review System or Program

Any method of evaluating or assessing an individual must be good enough to distinguish between top, average, and poor performers. Such a system (as well as any instrument or procedure) must also be, and be viewed as, fair, just, objective, consistent, and actually capable of measuring what is to be measured.

Stier (1993, p. 39) provides 10 commandments of evaluating personnel in sport organizations:

1. Follow the kiss concept, keep it simple and short;
2. Make sure that expectations are reasonable, clear and understood, and in writing;
3. Seek input from many individuals, use subjective and objective criteria;
4. Inform the staff of deficiencies as soon as they are detected and don't hesitate to compliment when warranted;
5. Provide opportunities for the staff member to improve; remain in the help mode;
6. Have high standards and expectations; mediocrity breeds mediocrity;
7. Take the evaluation process seriously and your staff will, too;
8. Be honest, fair, and consistent in implementing the system and be sensitive to the needs and concerns of each person;
9. Don't let personality clashes distort or cloud the evaluation process;
10. Don't make mountains out of molehills; concentrate on those areas that can affect the quality of the clients' experiences.

Objective and Subjective Criteria in Performance Appraisals

Employees may be evaluated using both objective and subjective criteria. The important point is that employees must know what is expected of them in advance as well as how they are going to be evaluated so that they can plan and act accordingly. Evaluation of staff is really an ongoing process, although formal evaluations of personnel are more common at regular intervals such as every 6 or 12 months. The important thing is that if there is to be performance appraisal then it should be done periodically (Fardelmann, 1994).

One of the challenges of personnel appraisal with both paid and volunteer staff is that supervisors often have a difficult time actually implementing the evaluation process. Research reveals that supervisors tend to give higher ratings when they know the subordinates will see it, yet it is imperative that this is allowed. Otherwise, how will the employee know what to try to improve?

Also, most supervisors find it much easier to recognize and discern superior performers as well as incompetent performers. It gets more difficult with average performers.

Finally, there is often a lack of consistency among members of management and supervisors as they evaluate different employees. Some are very lenient in their assessment of subordinates while others hold their subordinates to a much higher standard. This lack of consistency threatens the very essence of the appraisal system.

Performance Appraisal Instruments

There are numerous pen and paper instruments currently in use by all types of sport businesses to assess the competency and performance of their personnel. The common elements of the forms include statements that reflect the subordinate's job responsibilities and the person's ability to perform at an acceptable level. Next to each statement are spaces for the evaluator to check off indicating at what level the person is currently performing. For example, for each area of performance or job responsibility there might be spaces marked excellent, above average, average, below average, and unsatisfactory. In addition, some instruments provide space for the supervisor to provide narrative remarks clarifying the numerical ranking.

Concept 297: Employees Should Have a Right to See and React to Their Job Performance Appraisal.

Many such forms also provide a place at the bottom of the appraisal instrument for the employees to sign and add their own comments if they wish. In reality, the employee's signature really only attests that the individual has at least read the document. For example, at the bottom of a typical appraisal form might be a statement: The signature of the staff member below does not necessarily indicate agreement with the above performance appraisal statements but merely indicates that the staff member has read it. The staff member may attach a memo explaining any factor concerning this evaluation form or explaining the staff member's disagreement or agreement with any part or phase of the assessment.

Personnel Actions Resulting from Performance Appraisals

What are the options open to management if an employee's performance is such that it is unsatisfactory? What are the possibilities if the assessment reveals that the person is performing at a satisfactory or superior level? In either instance, employees need to be informed of how management views their work. In the case of the exceptional or satisfactory worker, it is important that the individual receive positive feedback to know how much management appreciates productive work.

Naturally, even with personnel performing at an acceptable level (or higher), there will always be areas in that improvement can be made or areas or tasks that might necessitate special effort or attention in the future. However, with those personnel who are adequately performing their tasks and fulfilling their responsibilities, it is a matter of showing genuine appreciation, continuing to challenge and motivate them, adequately rewarding them, and seeing to it that they remain at or even improve on their current level of competency.

Options Open to Management when Employees Fail

In respect to those individuals who do not fare well as a result of an employee appraisal, the possibilities boil down to three scenarios. First, the person could be retained as an employee and life could go on within the organization with little if anything happening to or with the employee. Second, the person could be dismissed, either fired or not rehired. Third, the person is retained (at least for a time), but is put on notice that performance is subpar.

In the third scenario, management may alter the person's job responsibilities and duties (reassignment) or restrict areas of responsibilities (demotion). Additionally, management may provide specific assistance (help mode) to aid the employee in overcoming deficiencies and increasing skills and competencies in the hope that performance will be enhanced in the future. Such assistance may require that the employee participate in some kind of training, clinics, workshops, tutoring, and formal class work.

Concept 298: It Is "Easy" to Fire Someone; It Is Far More Difficult to Help the Individual to Improve Performance and Become Competent and More Skilled.

The Cost of Terminating an Employee

Management should not be so eager to merely discharge or terminate an employee. In many instances firing someone is just too easy a way out, a "cop-out," for the employer or sport organization. The employing entity usually has a great deal of time, effort, and money invested in each of its employees. To remove or get rid of a seemingly unproductive person is an admission that management has failed, failed in fostering professional competency among its employees, failed in the selection/hiring process, failed in the teaching or training efforts, and/or failed in spotting earlier potential performance deficiencies among its personnel.

It is also very expensive and time intensive to go through a complete search process to replace a discharged staff member. If the sport entity had hired the right person for the right job, and then had supported that person appropriately and provided the person with suitable resources, the likelihood of that employee being successful would have been greatly increased.

It is very important that management provide to an employee the resources (time, money, assistants/staff, training, equipment, supplies, etc.) necessary for that individual to experience success as a member of the sport organization's team. Because it costs additional money and time to secure the services of a replacement for a fired staffer, management should ask itself if discharging or firing an employee is appropriate or necessary.

Frequently, in the world of sport business, if the former employee had received the support (financial and otherwise) that the new employee will inevitably be given perhaps there might not have been a need to discharge the previous employee. And, in many cases, the new employee replacing a fired individual will certainly be given "all of the resources requested" because management would not want to see a second failure on their hands.

Concept 299: Firing an Employee Should Be the Last Resort.

Employees typically do not become incompetent overnight. In the case of a nonperforming or underperforming employee there surely must have been early warning signs (cues) along the way pointing to the performance slippage of the person in question. If management and peers failed to pick up on these cues then they too must bear the burden and share the responsibility for the failure by the underperforming or nonperforming employee. *Firing someone is the avenue of last resort, it is an act of desperation, and it is an acknowledgment of failure on behalf of management.*

Concept 300: Firing an Employee Is an Admission of Failure by the Employing Organization.

Questions to Ask Oneself when an Employee Underperforms

Supervisors and managers need to ask themselves some searching questions whenever a subordinate fails to perform as expected. There could be many reasons why a person is acting a certain way or performing in a specific manner. The task of the supervisor is to find out why, and then to take corrective action, if possible.

For example, does the employee understand what the job is and the responsibilities are? Does the person understand specifically what tasks are to be accomplished and the time restraints? Does the person know what and how to give superiors what they want? Does the person want to do the job? Has the person been given adequate resources to do the job? Does the person know how to do the job? Are the job expectations and time restraints reasonable? Members of management need to remember that even a "superhero" cannot create miracles nor meet unreasonable expectations (Pitts, 1996). There is a shared responsibility between management and the employee for the employee's success.

"Rewarding" the Incompetent and "Punishing" the Competent

There is always the danger that management will fall into the trap of "rewarding" the incompetent and "punishing" the competent when it comes to assigning tasks to various personnel. What this means is that when personnel fail to perform satisfactorily, having been assigned important tasks to complete, they are less frequently to be trusted with significant responsibility in the future. This is especially true when there are other personnel who have demonstrated by past accomplishments that they are willing and capable of successfully completing important tasks within specified time restraints.

Supervisors tend to delegate major tasks and significant responsibilities to those individuals in whom they have the greatest confidence. Thus, the competent employees seemingly are "punished" by being given more and more tasks to do and greater and greater responsibilities to assume, and the less competent personnel are not given (rewarded) tough assignments for fear that they will fail to produce or perform up to expectations. If this scenario plays out to its natural conclusion, the consequences are obvious. The workplace climate suffers, the job performance and overall production can suffer, and internal dissension can result.

Management must be careful and not allow personnel to escape responsibilities by performing at an unacceptable level. In fact, supervisors must be constantly on the alert to detect, at the earliest possible time, any significant deficiency among staff members in terms of their job performance. Supervisors must also not engage in "punishing" the competent and "rewarding" the incompetent as in the examples above. Rather, they must insist that all personnel assume their fair share of the total job responsibilities and perform at an acceptable level of competency on behalf of the sport business.

Termination of Employees

Inevitably there will be times when it will be necessary to terminate an employee, as regrettable as that prospect might be, both from the perspective of the sport organization and from the viewpoint of the employee. Management must consider a variety of legal issues and consult with appropriate legal counsel prior to initiating termination proceedings. The whole termination process can be likened to a minefield. Maneuvering through this minefield requires careful thinking and cautious planning.

> **Concept 301:** Beware of Wrongful Termination Suits; Follow the Letter of the Law, Be Just, and Keep Exacting Records.

The exact nature of the termination process depends to some extent on the type of employment contract, if any, the employee has and the type of organization employing the person. Nevertheless, there are some general principles that are applicable in almost every personnel situation. For example, it is essential that supervisors keep excellent written records. Similarly, regular reviews and performance appraisals should be conducted. There are certain expectations of performance reviews that must be present if companies are to avoid successful wrongful termination suits brought by disgruntled current or former employees. There are certain obligations that the sport organization has in respect to employees. Members of management should:

1. Provide clear, specific, and consistent expectations of performance;
2. Include regular reviews and evaluations that should be given to the employee and maintained in personnel records of the sport organization;
3. Tell the employee of deficiencies as soon as they are detected;
4. Cite the employee's strengths as well as weaknesses;
5. Provide tips and suggestions on how to improve performance;
6. Take specific steps to help the employee improve performance and keep records of such actions;
7. Encourage and give opportunities for the person to improve;
8. Document everything in writing and keep detailed records;
9. Officially inform the employee that if improvement does not take place dismissal will occur;

10. Include a witness when meeting with an employee to discuss serious breaches of job responsibilities and non-performance of tasks.

Some managers suggest that employees be asked to sign new job contracts that outline their specific duties and exact responsibilities within the organization, at least once a year, even if their jobs have not changed. This provides a paper trail relating to job assignments and performance expectations.

Wong (1997) indicates that when an employer has utilized objective criteria as part of an appropriate personnel evaluation system, has provided verbal and written notice to the individual of inadequate performance, has expressed reasonable expectations of the individual for the future, there is an obligation on the part of the employee to meet these expectations in order for employment to be continued.

Finally, if the overall evaluation process and the specific performance appraisal were proper and effective, the affected employee would have been forewarned. As a result, the individual certainly should not be totally surprised that one's performance has been viewed as unsatisfactory and that the employment is being terminated, for cause.

Working with Personnel within a Union Setting

Sport managers need to be cognizant that in some instances there is yet another wild card to be played in terms of personnel management. That wild card is the union shop. Many sport businesses have employees who are unionized, and many sport organizations work with firms whose employees are represented by unions. There are many advantages involving the presence of unions just as there are many challenges when unionized employees are part of the organization's personnel.

One of the major challenges facing administrators and supervisors when dealing with employees represented by a union is that there are specific (and detailed) expectations and obligations placed on both management and employee, especially in terms of performance expectations, benefits, and working conditions, among others. In this regard sport administrators need to be cognizant of the contents of their own personnel handbook, the union contract, and the applicable laws governing employment practices when dealing with personnel matters.

The Personnel Handbook

A helpful tool in the area of personnel management is the personnel handbook, which contains all the pertinent and relevant policies, practices, and procedures concerning personnel (paid and volunteer) for a particular sport business or organization. With such a document to guide future actions, management is aided in its efforts to make wise, timely, and appropriate decisions. The personnel handbook provides guidance in terms of which actions and decisions are appropriate and which are not, as well as spelling out specifically, and in some instances exactly, what steps should be taken in numerous situations dealing with and affecting personnel within the organization.

Concept 302: Personnel Handbooks Provide a Blueprint for Future Actions and Decisions Relating to People Working within the Organization.

Such a handbook also serves as an important informational tool for all people within the sport organization, including those in management, because everyone needs to be fully aware of what is expected of both personnel and management and to be able to plan and act accordingly. Finally, such a handbook means that, with the establishment of appropriate and timely policies, procedures, and practices, there is no need to reinvent the wheel when it comes to making decisions or implementing various procedures, policies, or actions that affect people within the business.

It is always better and more effective to establish procedures, policies, and practices relating to staff well in advance of when they are needed. Waiting until a "situation" exists (especially a controversial one) and then attempting to create or establish such procedures and policies, as well as make major or significant decisions in "the heat of battle," is not only foolish but also self-defeating in the long run.

The Importance of Quality Personnel

The key to the success of most businesses rests in the personnel of the organization. It is personnel who work with the public. It is personnel who deal with issues, problems, and challenges, both internally and externally. The sport leader who is skilled and experienced in dealing with personnel (paid/unpaid) and knowledgeable about all aspects of personnel management is in an excellent position to be a successful manager. It takes a person who is aware of the general principles of personnel management and possesses excellent interpersonal skills to serve successfully as a leader and manager within a sport business in today's society. And it will only become more difficult in the future. The challenge is sometimes daunting, but the rewards and satisfaction can be significant, both on a personal and professional level.

Conclusions

The heart of any sport, recreation, or fitness organization is the people who work within the entity. Sport managers need to be highly skilled and adept in working with personnel, paid and volunteer. It is especially important that one is competent with the process of attracting, selecting, hiring, evaluating, training, rewarding, and retaining qualified and competent personnel. With adequate, talented, and motivated personnel the sport manager will have the necessary resources with which to meet the myriad of challenges successfully that surely will be present in most profit as well as not-for-profit organizations.

REFERENCES

Balog, K. (1995, May 17). Coaches find fans in management. *USA Today,* p. 1-B, 2-B.

Barlow, S. (1993, April). Words of wisdom: Harvey Mackay tells how to outswim the sharks. *Entrepreneur, 21*(4), 75–79.

Carpenter, L. J. (1997). Interview questions. *Strategies, 10*(4), 11–12.
Fardelmann, M. A. (1994, June). Up-to-date ideas in evaluations. *Athletic Management, VI*(6), 41–44.
Fritz, R. (1992, June). The competitive edge—Managing your entrepreneurial company. *Entrepreneur, 20*(6), 58, 60–61.
Haney, M. W. (1995, December). Employee evaluations. *Fitness Management, 11*(12), 38–40.
Henry, T. (1995, February 21). On a five-point scale. *USA Today,* p. D-1
Hiring—No longer a piece of cake. (1993, Fall). *NASPE NEWS,* #5, p. 5.
Hopp, B. and Swedburg, R. (1996). Hiring the wrong candidate. *Journal of Physical Education, Recreation and Dance, 67*(3), 58–59.
Jones, D. (1997, December 11). Employers going for quality hires, not quantity. *USA Today,* p. B-1.
Koch, W. B. (1994). Common evaluation goals with unique faculty roles in higher education. *The Chronicle of Physical Education in Higher Education, 6*(1), 1, 11.
McCutcheon, B. and Robinson, M. J. (1997, September). New coach on the block. *Athletic Management, IX*(4), 23–24, 26–29.
McDermott, M. (1993, March). High-stakes headhunting: 15 tips on hiring the best employees. *Club Industry, 9*(8), 24–31.
Miller, L. K., Pitts, B. G., and Fielding, L. W. (1993). Legal concerns in writing job recommendations. *The Physical Educator, 50*(1), 47–51.
Pessin, F. (1997, March). Hiring by degree. *Fitness Management, 13*(4), 31–33.
Pitts, E. H. (1996, March), Getting the desired job performance. *Fitness Management, 12*(4), p. 6.
Plummer, T. (1997, October). Staffing for success. *Fitness Management, 13*(10), 31, 33–36, 39–40.
Roberts, W. (1993). *Victory secrets of Attila the Hun.* New York: Doubleday.
Sattler, T. P. and Mullen, J. E. (1994, December). Hiring for success. *Fitness Management, 10*(13), 40, 42, 44.
Stier, W. F., Jr. (1987). Competencies of athletic administrators. *The Bulletin of the Connecticut Association for Health and Physical Education, Recreation and Dance Journal, 33*(2), 8; reprinted in *The Athletic Director,* (1988, January). American Alliance for Health, Physical Education, Recreation and Dance, p. 3.
Stier, W. F., Jr. (1989, March). Doing their part—Employment of part-time employees in sports. *College Athletic Management, 1*(3), 38–39.
Stier, W. F., Jr. (1990) Wanted: Renaissance athletic directors. *Athletic Director, 7*(3), 34, 35, 42.
Stier, W. F., Jr. (1993, May). The ins and outs of evaluating coaches. *Athletic Management, V*(3), 34–37, 39.
Stier, W. F., Jr. (1994, April 15). Job marketability and career planning within HPERD & A. Paper presented at the National Conference of the American Alliance for Health, Physical Education, Recreation and Dance (AAHPERD), Denver, Colorado.
Stier, W. F., Jr. (1997a, March 23). How to secure a professional position in the 21st century. Paper presented at the National Conference of the American Alliance for Health, Physical Education, Recreation and Dance (AAHPERD), St. Louis, Missouri.
Stier, W. F., Jr. (1997b, October 6). The essentials of corporate sponsorship (partnership) in physical education, sport and recreation in the Americas. Paper presented at the International Conference, Alianza Estratégica Para La Educación Física, El Deporte Y La Recreación (Strategic Alliance for Physical Education, Sport and Recreation). México City, México.
Stull, G. A. (1990). The effective vita: Veracity, integrity, truthfulness, accuracy. *Journal of Physical Education, Recreation and Dance, 61*(1), 28–29.
Success is the same in business or sports. (1988, September). *Athletic Business, 12*(9), 30–32, 34, 36.
Wakin, E. (1991, August). Give employees feedback, not criticism. *Today's Office, 26*(3), 22, 23.
Wong, G. M. (1997, May). The official story. *Athletic Business, 21*(5), 20, 22.

DISCUSSION AND REVIEW QUESTIONS

1. Explain the advantages and disadvantages of working with the five different types of personnel or staff within a sport, recreation, or fitness organization.

2. Identify a specific sport, recreation, or fitness entity and relate how outsourcing might be most appropriate in terms of use of personnel.

3. Arbitrarily select a hypothetical sport business and identify a specific task(s) facing the entity, then enumerate the specific qualities of personnel whom you would want to be involved with addressing the task(s).
4. Differentiate between various sources of personnel for any typical sport, recreation, or fitness organization. Specify the advantages and disadvantages of each source.
5. Write a specific job description for a new employee whose main responsibility will be to market and sell season tickets for a triple-A minor league baseball team located in a metropolitan area with a 500,000 population.
6. Write a specific job advertisement suitable for national distribution for the imaginary job mentioned in 5 above.
7. Search the WWW and secure 20 listings of openings for positions related to the sport, recreation, and fitness industries.
8. Establish appropriate questions to ask of potential interviewees in the imaginary job mentioned in 5 and 6 above.
9. Establish ways and means of evaluating and assessing one's own personnel within a hypothetical work situation in the world of sport, recreation, or fitness.

CHAPTER

10 The World of Sport Fundraising, Promotions, and Marketing

Fans start at an early age.
Bob Waldrop, Photographer.

CHAPTER OBJECTIVES

After reading this chapter you will be able to:

- Differentiate between marketing, fundraising, and promotional activities;
- Understand the importance of generating additional resources for sport entities;
- Appreciate the need for sport managers to be competent in generating additional resources for their organizations;
- Cite three types of resources or tools commonly sought by sport organizations;
- Understand that fundraising is a means to an end, not an end in itself;
- List three common methods of generating additional financial resources;
- Outline the components of fundraising;
- Conceptualize the essential elements of a successful corporate sponsorship or partnership agreement;
- Illustrate the differences between hard and soft data;

- Define the role of marketing within a sport organization;
- Explain the components (5Ps) of the marketing mix;
- Provide examples relating to the 11 fundamental standards of fundraising.

The Problem Today: The Lack of Adequate Financial Support

At no other time have American sports—at all levels—undergone as much change as they have in recent years and are, in fact, currently experiencing (Fox, 1990). Accompanying these changes are myriad problems, as well as challenges and opportunities unprecedented in our history. Many of these problems and challenges revolve around money, or, more aptly put, the absence of sufficient monies to adequately fund a variety of sport programs at all levels from youth and recreational sports to the professional level (Stier, 1998).

As a result, successful modern sport managers are those individuals who are able to secure sufficient funding for their programs. In the past, this has usually meant being able to secure funding through the normal budgetary process of the organization. Today, and in the foreseeable future, this also involves the securing of resources through outside fundraising and promotions. The purpose of this chapter is to provide a glimpse into an exciting and demanding area of sport in which there have been significant changes in recent years, seeking outside financial support and funding through fundraising, marketing, and promotions.

The Challenge Today: Adapting to the Changes in the Sport Scene

One of the major tasks currently facing managers at all levels of sport is to remain current and up-to-date and to continue to learn and to be able to adapt to the changes and innovations that occur in all areas and levels of sport. One area that has seen a great deal of change in recent years is the need for additional financial and moral support for most sport programs. Both school and nonschool sports programs are seemingly always in need of more financial resources. Failing to obtain outside support has required some sport organizations and some schools to curtail segments of their activities or eliminate entire programs (Stier, 1987a).

> **Concept 303:** Sport Mangers Need to Be Up-To-Date and Abreast of Changes in the Profession, and Be Able to Meet Current Demands and Needs.

Because financial resources are becoming more difficult to obtain through the traditional budgetary request process made within the sponsoring organization, the frugal management of available funds and the securing of additional (outside) financial resources remains a formidable challenge. This remains true whether one is at the youth sport level or in recreation programs, a school-based athletic organization, or involved in professional sports. The modern sport professional is expected to be highly skilled in a variety of fundraising strategies as well as educated in the allied activities of promotions, marketing, and public relations (Stier, 1993b).

The Need to Generate Additional Resources

Concept 304: Fundraising and Promoting Have Become Essential Responsibilities for Many Sport Organizations Today, at All Levels.

The reason that the need to generate additional resources for sport programs has never been greater can be traced principally to two factors. First, the increasing cost of supporting quality sport programs requires it. This increase in cost is due to both inflation and the desire or the perceived need to do more and more within individual sports programs. Second, money that is being allocated to sports programs through the normal budgetary process is often insufficient to get the job done (Stier, 1992).

Inflation affects all areas of sport. Salaries, insurance, equipment and supplies, and rent, as well as transportation are just a few of the areas that are hard hit by annual inflation. Almost everything costs more today than yesterday and there is no end in sight. Almost every category of expenditure in the area of sport will continue to increase the cost of doing business in the future. Even the cost of raising additional resources will continue to rise (Palmisano, 1984).

The result is that youth sport groups, recreational departments, and athletic programs in schools and colleges, as well as professional sport organizations, are more and more frequently experiencing increasing pressure to obtain additional monies if sizable deficits are to be avoided (Wieberg & Witosky, 1991b; Stier, 1994b). Today, the budget allocation of many sport organizations meets less of the programmatic needs of their constituencies, because money via the regular budget is not inexhaustible. Even attempting to increase the efficiency and effectiveness of the day-to-day fiscal operations with an eye to saving money through the wise management of existing resources will free up only a finite amount of funds, which is frequently insufficient.

As a result of these frequent budget shortfalls, coupled with the increased cost of doing business, those involved in the management of sport are forced to increasingly look to outside sources to obtain additional assets (money, goods, and services). Frequently, the only alternative left, in schools as well as outside of the school-based sport programs, lies in fundraising and promotional activities (Wieberg & Witosky, 1991a). As a result, sport leaders need to possess an accurate and comprehensive understanding of the total fundraising process and all that that entails. Only by having such an understanding will individual sport organizations be able to meet the financial challenges facing them now and in the years to come.

Concept 305: Many Financial Challenges Are Not Solvable Merely by the Frugal Management of Available Funds.

Even frugal money management and parsimonious spending may not be enough to provide a quality athletic experience in the twenty-first century. Sports people need to face reality and contemplate the possibility of engaging in some type of internal and/or external fundraising activity, in addition to their efforts to secure money through the regular budgetary process and by frugal money management (see Figure 10.1).

Ticket sales form the foundation of professional sports.

The problem, however, is that most sport managers in the past have had no formal training or education in fundraising, promotions, and marketing. Rather, many have learned the ins and outs of fundraising and promotions through the school of hard knocks, that is, experientially. This has to change if sport administrators are to remain in the forefront of managerial professionals.

Types of Resources and Tools

What resources should the sport administrator or fundraiser seek? What types of resources are there? When one thinks of fundraising one naturally conjures up efforts to raise dollars—

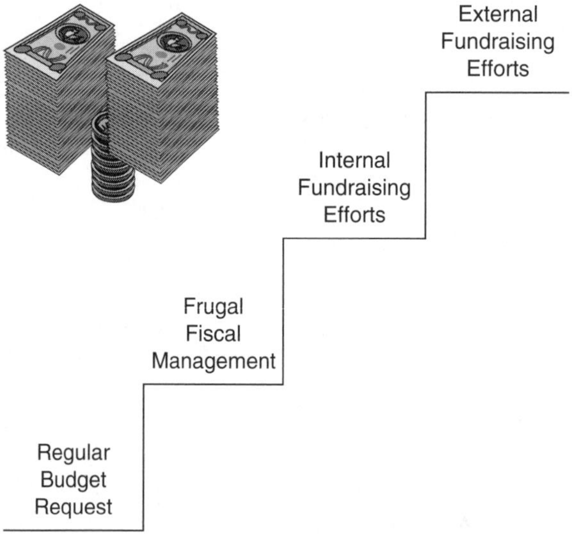

FIGURE 10.1 The Funding Model of Sports: Climbing the Steps to Fiscal Solvency

cold, hard cash. This is entirely understandable. However, fundraising efforts should not be limited to mere *cash solicitation* but can include attempts to garner needed *services* as well as tangible *goods* and *products*.

Concept 306: Fundraisers Are Involved with the Solicitation of Various Types of Resources, Tools, and Assets.

Fundraisers need to think in terms of cash, of course. However, they should not neglect the solicitation of any resource when seeking contributions. In point of fact, anything that can be used for the benefit of the sport organization becomes a legitimate objective of any fundraising effort. Services can include accounting services, graphic arts assistance, secretarial help, legal advice, reconditioning of equipment, laundry services, and so forth. Goods and products encompass a whole range of physical objects donated such as food, specific sport equipment and supplies, actual vehicles, facilities, and office supplies and equipment, among others.

Concept 307: Fundraising Is Merely a Means to an End, Not an End in Itself.

Resources (money, services, and goods) should typically be viewed as means to an end and not as an end in themselves. Money raised enables administrators to purchase needed services and/or goods for the benefit of the sport program (Wieberg, 1991). The donation of resources, such as goods, products, or services, frees up money that may have been earmarked for the purchase of such goods or services.

For example, an owner of a print shop who agrees to provide the paper and printing free of charge for an athletic department's football brochure might save the school some $4,000 to $6,000 in production and material costs. The money saved can then be spent to satisfy other needs. Similarly, when an accounting firm agrees that there will be no charge (a donation of services) for conducting this year's annual audit, the money thus saved may be appropriated for other purposes. The donation of services and goods should be viewed in the same way as the receipt of cash, because such donations free up cash to be used elsewhere within the sport program.

Financial resources form the foundation on which most successful sport programs rest. Resources are the tools that enable the program to realize its objectives. Without adequate resources the sport administrator sits behind the proverbial eight ball and is left without a full arsenal with which to sustain the sport operation. Thus, the generation of sufficient resources and their effective and efficient management are essential responsibilities of the modern competent sport administrator (Stier, 1990b).

Modern-Day Fundraising

Modern fundraising efforts are those activities designed to generate, from other than the traditional budgetary process, additional financial resources. These resources can take the form of monies and goods as well as services.

Concept 308: All Fundraising Projects Involve Promotional Activities.

By definition, all fundraising projects are associated with promotional activities. One cannot have a fundraising project without also involving promotional strategies, tactics, and activities. Planning a fundraising project means having some type of activity or activities, which helps promote the sponsoring organization.

Components of Fundraising

Figure 10.2 illustrates a conceptualization of the fundraising process. At the core of the process is the specific fundraising project or activity itself. The process is dependent on successful relationships among various individuals, both one's own staff (paid and volunteers) and with the various constituencies or segments of the public toward whom the fundraising effort is to be geared or targeted. Additionally, the process may be enhanced through the prudent use of specific marketing, promotions, and public relations tactics that facilitate the successful implementation of the actual fundraising project.

Permeating the entire process of fundraising and fundamental to its success is the planning of all details within a specified time frame. Planning is also an active component in the strategic marketing or "positioning" of an idea, a service, or a product, in the selection of *effective promotional techniques,* and in the establishment of an *efficient public*

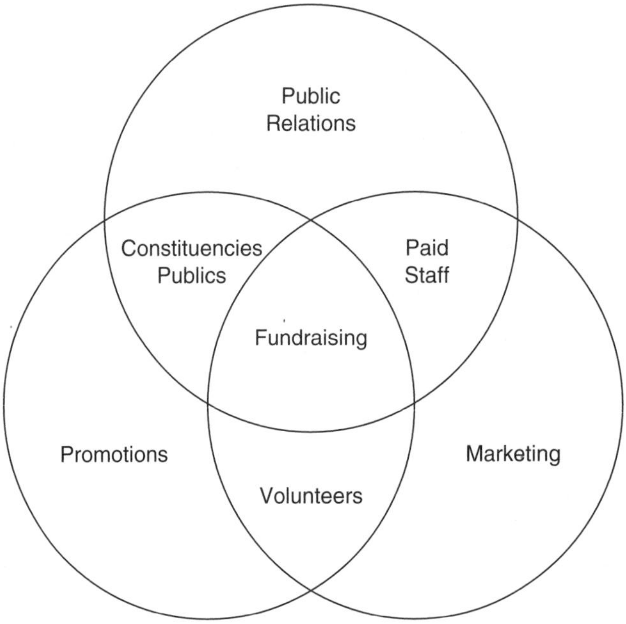

FIGURE 10.2 Conceptualization of the Fundraising Process

relations effort. A successful fundraising experience is contingent on the existence of all of these components (Stier, 1990a).

Because the planning process is the very essence of any fundraising, promotion, and marketing strategy, those professionals involved in the management of sports and sport-related entities should be familiar with the planning process as well as with the fundamental principles or concepts involved in developing and implementing effective and efficient fundraising projects, promotional tactics, and marketing strategies (Stier, 1995).

Developing a Fundraising and Promotional Plan

A fundraising or promotional plan should be established through a meaningful, realistic, and accurate assessment or evaluation process that identifies the needs and the limitations or parameters as well as the attributes or resources of the athletic entity and the public(s) that are to be targeted. The goal of such a plan is the creation of a road map to guide the staff's actions toward the ultimate objective, the creation of a more visible entity, a more positive public image, a more viable and attractive athletic, sport, or recreational program, solvent both in terms of financial resources and in terms of human resources (Stier, 1996).

Although there are innumerable fundraising projects available to the modern sport administrator or manager, it is helpful to think of individual projects in terms of what is needed to make each individual effort truly successful. This involves the creation of a plan or a strategy that serves as a blueprint for those responsible for carrying out the fundraising project. Stier (1994a) has created a template containing essential categories for *planning* that are applicable for each and every type of fundraising and promotional project one might implement, (see Table 10.1). Filling in the appropriate information, in sufficient detail, will greatly aid the potential fundraiser and promoter in planning, organizing, and

TABLE 10.1 Components of a Fundraising Plan

1. Detailed description of the fundraising plan or scheme
2. Desired objectives
   - **A.** Resources sought (money, goods, and/or services)
   - **B.** Desired image
3. Level of difficulty of the project
4. Written summary of the details of the project
5. Support and backing required
   - **A.** The facilities needed
   - **B.** The equipment and supplies necessary
   - **C.** The publicity, promotional and public relations efforts that are required
   - **D.** The time frame—in terms of planning as well as the actual length of the fundraising effort itself
   - **E.** The case needed
   - **F.** The people and/or organizations necessary (special skills or competencies needed)
6. The initial risks, perils, or hazards to be anticipated
7. Permissions and approvals that are necessary
8. Other information that might be helpful to explain the project

understanding all aspects of the project, and will further aid in the implementation and subsequent evaluation of the total effort.

Identifying Specific Markets

Concept 309: The Identification of Specific Markets Is Essential in Fundraising, Promotions, and Public Relations.

One essential element in the strategic market planning process is to identify specific target market(s) (McCarthy, 1960; Parkhouse, 1996, p. 257). Potential fundraisers, promoters, and marketers need to identify those individuals and groups who will most likely respond in a positive manner to the fundraising project or promotional effort. Qualifying prospects by identifying those most likely to contribute (on the basis of a variety of criteria) to the request for financial assistance and then narrowing one's efforts on these high priority "targets" saves time and effort in the long run and thereby increases the overall effectiveness and efficiency of the fundraising effort (Stotlar, 1989).

Generating Resources for the Sport Program

Concept 310: Administrators Must Be Adept at Solving the Fundraising Puzzle, in Addition to Their Other Duties and Responsibilities.

Because there is a recognized increase in the need for sport fundraising, it is essential that sport managers develop a sound knowledge base as well as practical skills and experience in the area of fundraising. How does one go about raising resources? Essentially, there are four generally accepted categories of generating additional resources, whether such resources are actual money, goods, or services. Within each of these broad categories are literally thousands of individual fundraising ideas, techniques, strategies, methods, projects, and activities.

Concept 311: There Are 1001+ Different Fundraising Projects.

Those who would be successful fundraisers need to examine the numerous possibilities that exist within each of the four categories listed below for potential ideas that may be helpful in their own future fundraising programs. The key is to be able to utilize basic fundraising principles, guidelines, or commandments outlined in this chapter while borrowing and adapting ideas from others so that one can create an individualized, personalized fundraising project or activity that will be successful in light of one's own situation or circumstances.

Four General Methods of Generating Resources

The first method of raising resources is to simply ask (solicitation) people and organizations for contributions and donations (of money, time, services, goods). This strategy includes both single-person cultivation and appeals to groups and organizations. Examples include solicitation via phone, the mail as well as person-to-person contacts. The second method may be generated through securing special projects or fundraising tactics such as bingo nights, cow chip bingo, antique car shows, auctions, and raffles. The third method involves establishing various profit centers (concessions, ticket sales, merchandise sales, parking, etc.) within the sport area. Fourth, money as well as other resources may be generated through sponsorships or partnerships with businesses, organizations, and corporations (Stier, 1994b; Stier 1995).

Corporate Sponsorships and Partnerships

Today, a major avenue of securing big money for sport programs is based on financial arrangements with businesses and organizations. These have become known as corporate sponsorships and partnerships (Irwin, 1996). What exactly are corporate sponsorships or partnerships? Today, they are not usually considered philanthropy. "With the price of sponsorship escalating, traditional corporate rationale may no longer suffice. Return on investment has replaced the philanthropic philosophy of the past" (Lough, 1996, p. 11).

It is a mutually beneficial business arrangement entered into for very specific purposes from the perspective of the corporation as well as for the sport entity (White and Irwin, 1996). From the corporate side, the objectives include the potential enhancement of the corporate image, the increase of the company's visibility and its awareness among various publics, the reaching of new market segments, the securing of a greater market share, the development of new distribution channels, and the increase in sales (Gray, 1996, p. 33).

Concept 312: In Sport Sponsorship Agreements, One Hand Does Indeed Wash the Other.

Of course, the ultimate objective of the business or corporation is to improve the financial bottom line and to enhance its image. But there has to be significant benefits accruing to the sport entity as well. From the perspective of the sport organization, business partnerships and corporate sponsorships are desirable because of an infusion of additional financial resources, coupled with a sharing of the positive image of the business partner or sponsor. The bottom line for the sport organization is money, much needed additional resources.

"Perhaps at no time in history has there been more competition among sport properties for corporate sponsorship funding" (Morris & Irwin, 1996, p. 7). Where once such sports-related sponsorships or partnerships were thought to be the exclusive domain of the professional sports setting, this is not the case today. In fact, such sponsorships and partnering efforts have not only grown at the collegiate levels but have permeated secondary school sports as well as the recreation area.

Women's sports have been especially successful in securing significant corporate sponsorships, especially in professional golf and tennis and at the NCAA division I level. "The projected future growth rate in sponsorships from sport industry leaders has been estimated at 20% per year" (Lough, 1996, p. 11, citing Schlossberg, 1990). Stotlar (1993) estimated that the combined dollars spent for sport marketing and sport sponsorships in the United States totaled $2.4 billion in 1990. Only a year later (1991) this spending figure had increased over 50 percent to some $3.5 billion. And, not only has the spending increased but the number of businesses and corporations becoming sponsors has similarly risen (Stotlar, 1993).

Concept 313: Hard Data Is Needed by Businesses in Order to Evaluate the Effectiveness of Any Corporate Sponsorship.

In order for any sponsorship agreement to be truly successful there must be an appropriate match between the sport entity and the business partner, with the likelihood of benefits being realized by both parties. In order for any business organization to make an accurate assessment of a proposed sponsorship, and the possible benefits resulting from such an agreement, hard data must be provided to show the likelihood of meaningful benefits accruing to the potential sponsor.

Likewise, there must be accurate records kept in terms of the actual results of any sponsorship or partnership so as to prove to the business entity that such an arrangement is indeed worthwhile. Without such documentation about the impact such an agreement has had on the company's image enhancement, increased visibility, greater awareness among groups or constituencies, new market segments, greater market share, new distribution channels, and/or increase in sales, there might be little optimism for a repeat agreement with the same corporation or business.

In conducting marketing research, Stotlar (1989, p. 47) cites two different ways to conduct marketing research, utilizing primary or secondary sources. Primary research sources are those conducted directly with customers—for example, the use of mail surveys and phone and personal interviews. Secondary research efforts are conducted from other sources, such as an analysis of data that already exists. For example, the examination of the organization's past activities, tickets sold and to whom, gross sales from concessions operations or from the apparel store staffed by sport staff. Other examples of using secondary sources would be searching for information (hard data) from the public library, Chamber of Commerce, and/or subscribing to any number of professionally constructed or researched databases or statistical data.

Some examples of such organizations include *Team Marketing Report, IEG Sponsorship Report,* and the *Sports Report.* Using hard data from any of these sources enhances the sport manager's ability to make (and justify) informed, current, and appropriate decisions. Possession of such information also helps inform others and helps to justify courses of action (Stotlar, 1996).

Marketing

Marketing is often referred to as the essential component in identifying the needs of others. Marketing activities can be used to motivate people to want your product, service, program, or to accept your ideas and positions. It means satisfying an individual's real or perceived needs. Marketing encompasses all of the efforts used in moving goods and services (and ideas) from the sport administrator (producer) to the general public (consumer) and can involve the acts of selling, promoting, advertising, and packaging (Guarlnik, 1970; Buell, 1984: Cutlip, Center, & Broom, 1985; Railey & Railey, 1988).

Concept 314: Consistency Is an Important Concept in Marketing and Promoting—No One Wants to Be Considered a "Flash in the Pan".

Anything, both tangible goods as well as intangible concepts and ideas, may be marketed to individuals or groups. Buell (1984) indicated that marketing not only identifies needs and wants of constituencies but also helps marshal the organization's resources to produce the desired products or services.

> Marketing is the key to securing and satisfying customers. In a free market economy consumers have a variety of choices as to how they will satisfy their needs. Therefore, those institutions that survive are the ones that are most efficient at identifying the needs and wants of consumers (Buell, 1984, p. 616).

Marketing can also help create needs in individuals where such needs either did not previously exist or the potential customer was not aware of such needs (Stier, 1987b). Effective marketing can even help persuade potential consumers to partake of products or services because of a perception that its offerings will satisfy a real or perceived need. The 4Ps of marketing (the marketing mix), coined by E. Jerome McCarthy, refers to the four basic components of marketing (that is, how any product, service, or idea might be acquired or procured by individuals and/or groups) that includes *product, price, place,* and *promotion* (Mullin, 1983; Railey & Railey, 1988; Stotlar, 1993, p. 24; Horine, 1996).

Today, the marketing mix might properly be thought of as the 5Ps with the addition of the category, *publics* (Stier, 1990a). Thus, the marketing mix can be viewed as:

1. The **Product,** service, or idea that is to be accessible;
2. The **Place** or niche in which the product, service, or idea will be most readily acceptable, distributed, or shared;
3. The appropriate and acceptable **Price** that the market will bear;
4. The **Promotional** activity or strategy associated with the product, service, or idea;
5. The **Public**(s) or constituencies that will be identified as potential customers, consumers, or recipients.

In marketing as well as in fundraising, one needs to be concerned with the product (service or idea) that is to be marketed to the intended consumer. Additionally, the price or cost of that which is marketed needs to be established as well as the place or site where the marketing will take place. In addition, one must be concerned with the promotional aspects of those specific techniques designed to garner increased sales and/or acceptance by the targeted population. Finally, those individuals and/or groups (publics) to whom the marketing will be targeted should be identified.

A Strategic Fundraising, Promotion, and Marketing Plan

It is essential that a global athletic strategic fundraising, promotion, and marketing plan, one compatible with the sport program's multiple missions, be identified, developed, and implemented. Such a plan or strategy needs to be established by means of a realistic and accurate identification and evaluation of the needs, the limitations or parameters, as well as the attributes or resources of the athletic entity.

Thus, the strategic marketing plan serves as a road map to guide staff members' actions toward the ultimate objective, i.e., a sound program, both in terms of financial and human resources. Such a program results in greater visibility, a more positive public image, and ultimately a more viable and attractive athletic program (Buell, 1984).

Promotional Activities

Sport promotion is associated with the selling of ideas (images, attitudes, and opinions), services, and products to the general public. The goal is to motivate others to accept specific ideas or concepts and/or to purchase or accept specific services and/or products as a result of identifiable promotional and communication efforts (Stier, 1994b). Promotion involves specific activities or techniques used to further or advance the organization by increasing the sales of ideas, services, and/or products to others (Horine, 1996, p. 67). Promotion is thought of as part of the marketing process. Promotional efforts may be implemented to establish, reinforce, or even change opinions and attitudes regarding the sport program. "The promotional tools consist of personal selling, publicity, advertising and sale promotion" (Graham, 1994, p. 9).

Concept 315: Not All Promotional Activities Are Associated with Fundraising Efforts.

The key to promotion is innovation, uniqueness, appropriateness, and attractiveness as viewed by the public or the targeted population. Such activities may motivate specific changes in behavior concerning not only the sports program itself but also those individuals associated with the program. Promotional activities can also be used to increase or create a demand for a product or service or the acceptance of an idea. Promotional activities do not necessarily have to be related to or associated with fundraising efforts.

Concept 316: You Have to Have Something of Worth, of Interest to Promote, to Emphasize, to Highlight.

A sport program that offers (promotes) a special family night experience to the community, complete with special activities for all family members, is attempting to sell the concept that the sport event itself can be a family affair and enjoyed by youngsters and

Excitement is the name of the game.

adults alike. Other reasons for conducting such a specific promotion might be to generate additional paying fans in the future as well as to help create a positive image and wholesome reputation on behalf of the sporting event and the sponsoring organization itself. However, the promotion is more effective if members of the general public find the activity to be of value or of interest. There has to be a motivating factor (a hot button) that entices individuals to action, to take part, to become involved.

Public Relations and Publicity

Public relations can involve everything associated or connected with the sport organization. Everything, literally, having to do with the sport program becomes part of or is a component of public relations. Public relations are the aggregate product of all activities and things existing under the umbrella of the sport entity (Stier, 1986). The objective of public relations is to secure support or a positive acceptance from others (Bucher, 1987).

The manner in which any home athletic event is organized and carried out in terms of concessions, treatment of officials, conditions of the bleachers, lighting in the facility, cleanliness of the restrooms, availability of suitable and safe parking, and the actions of coaches and athletes can affect the public relations efforts of the host organization either positively or negatively.

Concept 317: Public Relations Involve Everything That Is Associated or Connected with the Sport Entity.

When considering fundraising promotional activities, it is important to recognize that there is a significant difference between the isolated, fragmented promotional or fundraising type effort and a planned, coordinated system or strategy of athletic promotional activities designed to achieve objectives on a large scale (Ensor, 1988). How many sports-minded people become caught up in the rat race of conducting and promoting multiple, isolated, and fragmented fundraising efforts without the benefit of an overall strategic marketing plan? In all probability, too many.

Publicity is a sub-set of public relations, but its goals and purposes are more immediate (Mason & Paul, 1988). Its message is more short-term and is meant to inform or establish a general (positive) awareness of something, some program, or someone among those to whom the publicity is directed. It is also meant to inform, that is, to provide very specific information to others. Publicity may be thought of as targeted or general in nature. As targeted publicity, the message is geared toward a specific targeted population. General publicity is more of a shotgun approach aimed at the general public.

Coordinating Promotional Activities, Fundraising Tactics, Marketing Strategies, and Image-Enhancing Efforts

When a sport program's promotional activities, fundraising tactics, marketing strategies, and image-enhancing efforts are concerned, it is absolutely essential that these activities be part of an overall, coordinated, approved institutional or organizational plan. No, this is not suggesting that every single activity (associated with promotions, fundraising, publicity, public relations, etc.) of the sport entity must be scrutinized and approved by others outside of the sport arena or by higher-ups within the sport organization.

What is indicated, however, is that there is a need for all individuals involved in sport management, in the planning and the implementation of sport promotional activities, to cease acting and competing like the "Long Ranger" and to begin to act as members of the sport organization's team, a team that views areas of publicity, image enhancement, public relations, fundraising, and promotional activities from a larger perspective of the total institution or organization. Only through close cooperation with other entities within the organization can the sports program survive unscathed, both internally and externally, in its efforts to achieve objectives that can be facilitated by promotional activities.

Fundraising Viewed as a Cure-All

Fundraising itself is not a guaranteed solution to the financial crunch or other challenges that currently plague so many of our sports programs and organizations, at all levels. Nor is fundraising as easy as it looks or as simplistic as many would have us believe. There is usually more to fundraising than merely gathering a bunch of youngsters together and having a car wash at the local convenience store to raise $300 on a Sunday afternoon.

Concept 318: Fundraising Is Not a Cure-All.

Fundraising should not be merely selling candy bars in the school or around the neighborhood whenever the fancy strikes us. Unfortunately, fundraising is all too frequently viewed as nothing more than nickel-and-dime car washes or the nonchalant selling of candy bars. And, all too often, the results are ill-conceived projects, resulting in wasted or failed efforts, and bruised or negative feelings generated among the general public as well as among supporters of the sport or athletic programs.

Characteristics of Fundraisers and Promoters

Successful fundraising requires specific knowledge, skills, and experiences. Those involved in fundraising need to understand the concepts and the principles that are applicable to all fundraising efforts and projects. Not everyone can be a successful sport fundraiser. It takes effort and work and an understanding of general fundraising concepts and principles.

Concept 319: Successful Fundraisers and Promoters Are Producers, Not Mere Talkers.

An adage in fundraising circles is that "talk is cheap." It is far more challenging to be truly successful (effective and efficient) in fundraising and promotion. There are many wannabes and would-be promoters and fundraisers in the sport world today. However, there are also fewer producers in terms of meaningful, sustained promotions, fundraising, marketing, and public relations.

Concept 320: Fundraisers Are Risk-Takers and Quick Learners.

Of course, no self-respecting fundraiser or promoter could exist for long without being capable of taking *calculated risks* tempered with good *judgment* based on *facts* and *data* (as well as just a smidgen of intuition). Successful sport managers are no strangers to risk-taking. This trait serves them well in the area of fundraising, promotions, and marketing. Another positive attribute of successful fundraisers is the willingness to learn from their experiences and the experiences (both successful and unsuccessful) of others. This characteristic, the ability to learn from past experiences, involves both the willingness to borrow ideas and the skill to adapt them to suit one's own peculiar circumstances, needs, resources, and objectives.

Another factor that can help an individual become more proficient in fundraising and promotions is further education. One must remain at the cutting edge of fundraising, promotion, marketing, and public relations if one is to be competitive. Toward this end, it is recommended that would-be practitioners of the art and science of fundraising, marketing, and promotions attend clinics, workshops, conventions, and forums as well as be avid readers of the professional literature. Only by doing so can one remain at the cutting edge of a very, very competitive field. There are thousands and thousands of variations of fundraising activities and more adaptations are being developed every day. One must keep up with the latest innovations.

Questions to Ask Prior to Initiating Any Fundraiser

There are many different factors that must be considered and questions that must be answered when making informed decisions regarding the implementation of any specific fundraising project. Ten such questions are listed below to aid the would-be fundraiser–promoter in arriving at an informed decision about whether to implement a fundraising and promotional project (Stier, 1996).

Guiding Questions for Potential Fundraisers and Promoters

1. Is there a bonafide, legitimate need for the fundraising effort?
2. What special conditions or unique circumstances exist that might affect the fundraising project?
3. What special skills, competencies, or experiences are needed by the individuals involved in this project to make it a success?
4. What are the realistic timetable and priorities for the project?
5. Are there any organizational restrictions or philosophical differences that might interfere with or restrict the effort?
6. Will outside staff be utilized in addition to one's own personnel?
7. Will only one project be initiated or will there be multiple fundraising activities?
8. How will the activities be evaluated? What criteria will be used?
9. What can reasonably be expected in terms of net profit (goods, services, and cash)?
10. What are the reasonable and obtainable objectives of the organization insofar as public relations and promotion activities associated with this fundraising project are concerned?

Eleven Fundamental Standards of Fundraising

There are numerous general principles of fundraising and promotions. In fact, Stier (1994b) provided 127 such principles. Listed below are an additional 11 fundraising guidelines that are applicable for all types of fundraising projects and promotional activities sponsored by a high school, a college, a recreation department, or a professional sports team. These guidelines originally appeared in the journal *Athletic Management* (Stier, 1993a) published by College Athletic Administrator, Inc., Ithaca, New York. Permission to include portions of this article is gratefully acknowledged.

1. *Develop an overall plan for fundraising and promotion within your organization not only for the immediate present but for the future as well.*

Those involved in fundraising must be organized and have thought both the process and the potential challenges through. Each project or event must be carefully thought through from beginning to end. Organizers should undertake a "needs" and a "wants" assessment. The organizers must have a clear idea of why they are going to raise funds and how the money will be put to use.

Concept 321: Have Clear Reason and Rationale for One's Fundraising Efforts—Don't Raise Funds Just for the Heck of It.

It is important to remember, when fundraising plans are being made, that decisions must be based on facts rather than emotions, hunches, or merely anecdotal information. Planning well in advance also prevents the sport fundraiser from interfering with the organization's overall development and fundraising efforts. This is especially important in schools and colleges where the central administration might well be involved in more general fundraising efforts.

The kiss of death for athletic fundraisers in schools is to fail to obtain prior permission to initiate a specific project from high-level administrators within the school or college. This is where a supportive central administration is invaluable. Don't be surprised, however, if specific individuals or organizations are declared "off limits" to athletic fundraisers by the central administration.

2. *Evaluate your fundraising efforts continuously; keep meticulous records to facilitate repeat projects.*

Good record keeping is an absolute must. It facilitates the conduct of repeat fundraising projects. Some projects lend themselves to being annual events. Others may not be annual projects but can be repeated at some time in the future. Always look to see how your event or project can be improved if and when you implement it again. The time to evaluate is while you are engaged in the event and immediately afterward, while the ideas and memories are still fresh in your mind. Even projects that are one-time fundraising events should be critically evaluated because the organizers and promoters can learn things from such an event that might be applicable to a completely different type of fundraising project.

Concept 322: Plan Repeatable Fundraising Projects—They Are Easier to Implement the Second and Third Time Around.

There are three types of fundraising projects when one considers the factor of time. First, there is the one-time fundraising event. This activity will only be conducted one time. It will not be repeated. Perhaps the sports building or turf is being replaced. Parts of the old facility might be packaged and sold to the general public and fans. However, once the building is torn down or the turf is pulled up and sold, there will be no similar fundraising project the next year.

Second, fundraisers can become an annual event, much like the annual spring golf outing that patrons eagerly look forward to every year. Third, there are fundraising projects that are thought of as repeatable events. These are activities that can be repeated but are usually not for any number of reasons. Instead, this event might be conducted every two or three or four years, but it is not of such substance that it is considered worthy of being an annual event. This category of fundraising project falls between the one-time event and the annual fundraiser.

There are two reasons why it is much easier to run fundraising projects that have been implemented successfully in the past. First, the organizers can learn through their experiences and thereby improve their skills and competencies. The workers are able, in later years, to bring off the project with less worry and work because they have done it before. Second, those participating in the fundraising event (athletes, boosters, community people, etc.) also become familiar with the project because they enjoyed attending the activity and being a part of it. In fact, they anticipate the next time that it will take place, and they eagerly agree to participate in the fundraiser when it is implemented once again.

3. *Keep things simple—both in terms of the number of fundraising activities and in their implementation.*

Keep the actual fundraising event simple in its concept and its implementation. Don't overcomplicate matters. Complex projects are prone to becoming bogged down due to myriad details. Also, keep the actual number of fundraising events to a minimum. Generally speaking, planning for three to five projects a year should be all that is necessary for school-based athletic programs. This is especially true if the projects are well planned and are big producers in generating a great deal of money, goods, and/or services (not to mention positive public relations).

Concept 323: Don't Plan 1001 Different Fundraising Projects in a Single Year—Do Fewer Projects but Do Them Well.

It is important to be a strong advocate of keeping fundraising events simple in their structure and few in number, but, in initiating fewer projects, it is essential that they are quality projects and that they are well executed. However, fundraising events should be highly visible and they must generate significant revenue, otherwise effort and time is wasted. It is important not to waste time and effort on nickel-and-dime fundraising projects. It is better to have two fundraising projects generating some $20,000 in net profit than 15 smaller projects raising a mere $10,000. Fewer projects that are quality events can generate significant resources for the sports program.

4. *Anticipate and plan for the worst possible consequences so that the prospect of failure is minimized.*

You can't prevent problems if you don't anticipate them. And you can't anticipate problems or roadblocks if you don't plan. It is important to be able to anticipate pitfalls and problems through realistic fundraising planning while at the same time remaining flexible. Unsuccessful promoters find themselves operating in a crisis management mode much of the time. Successful fundraisers are known for their foresightedness and anticipatory skills.

Concept 324: All Fundraising Projects Will Have Problems—That Is Just the Nature of the Beast—Anticipate Them so You Can Prevent Most of Them.

One can sometimes avoid failure or negative consequences by copying or adapting other people's and other organizations' successes. There are few things that are really new or truly unique in the world of fundraising. Usually events and tactics are variations and adaptations of what has been done previously, somewhere else. For example, the *athletes' walk,* an event during which pledges are solicited on behalf of those taking part in a walk over a predetermined distance, has been successfully utilized by a number of schools.

The women's athletic department at the University of Nebraska at Omaha has successfully conducted such an event for some years. The concept has also been implemented at Northern Kentucky University and is called the *NKU Women's Walk*. The event has also been used at Cal State Bakersfield as well as Boise State, where it generated some $28,000 in its first year and over $65,000 four years later. Similarly, the Fabulous Reverse Raffle that is held annually on the evening of the NCAA national basketball championship game (which allows participants to watch the big game on various large screen TVs strategically placed around the room) has been successfully used as a fundraiser for years at Ohio Northern University as well as the State University of New York–Brockport.

5. *Practice preventative measures in terms of risk management and legal liability.*

Reduce legal liability by conducting a risk management study and taking appropriate precautionary action. This is an area in which advance planning and anticipation can pay big dividends. No one wants anyone injured as a result of his or her involvement in the sport organization's fundraising project. Not only would such an occurrence result in poor public relations and negative publicity, but there is always the distinct possibility of a successful lawsuit being brought against the organizers of the fundraising project as well as against the sponsoring organization itself.

Concept 325: It Is Far Better to Prevent Legal Exposure than to Defend against the Charge of Negligence.

Organizers need to be especially conscious of potentially hazardous situations. The goal is to provide a safe environment for all of the organizers, workers, and participants. Thus, great care must be taken in the training of workers (both paid and volunteer), the provision of appropriate supplies, equipment, and facilities, as well as the actual fundraising activities themselves.

6. *Adhere to all state, county, and local laws, regulations, and rules.*

Concept 326: Sport Fundraisers Must Be Knowledgeable about Applicable State, County, and Local Laws, Rules, and Regulations.

Fundraising organizers must be aware of all the legal implications surrounding the fundraising event. It is imperative that all state, county, and local rules and regulations are complied with to the fullest extent. Such rules might involve special permits and licenses that authorize the sponsoring group to conduct a specific activity. Additionally, there may be restrictions against a specific type of activity without special permission being granted, for example, peddling items on a door-to-door basis without a peddler's or hawker's permit.

Concept 327: When Dealing with the Law, It Is Always Best to Secure Advance Permission than to Seek Forgiveness after the Fact.

Adhering to appropriate laws and regulations is especially important for those fundraisers who are involved with gambling activities and those who provide or sell liquor as part of a fundraising project. Even food events have the potential for difficulty in terms of meeting specific health standards before being able to secure appropriate licensing and permits.

It is important to secure permission before embarking on a specific course of action rather than having to seek forgiveness if one gets caught in the act of violating a law or regulation. If there are permits that should be secured or licenses that must be obtained, do so. Don't assume that just because you are associated with a sporting organization or that your group is a nonprofit entity that you are exempt from meeting the standards set out in various governmental laws and statues or community rules and regulations. One must never run afoul of the law. The negative consequences, both in terms of actual penalties and embarrassment, can be significant for the sponsoring organization as well as for the individuals involved.

7. *Keep the fundraising process in its proper perspective—fundraising is a mechanism to reach an objective or goal.*

Those involved in fundraising should never forget that the purpose of their efforts is to garner additional and much needed resources (money, goods, and services) so that these resources can then be utilized to meet other, larger objectives and goals. *Fundraising is merely a vehicle.* It is not the end or the ultimate objective in and of itself. Obtaining these additional resources enables administrators to use these resources to satisfy other wants and needs.

Concept 328: Don't Lose Sight of the Ultimate Objective—Better Support for the Athletes, the Team, the Program.

Publicizing how the money generated from a fundraising event will benefit athletes or the overall sports program also helps make the event successful. Always promote and publicize how each fundraising project or activity will result in a better sports program. Emphasizing how the amateur athletes will benefit from the additional resources can be a key motivating tactic or strategy in soliciting donations for the program.

Promotional contests before games are always fun.

8. *Fundraising must be cost-effective, in terms of money, personnel, and time.*

One must never waste resources. One should not spend a dollar to make a dollar, much less to raise only a quarter. Yet, all too frequently this is exactly what happens in some instances when all factors are considered. In some instances, the time, money, and effort spent to generate additional resources turns out not to be worth more than what is actually raised in new or additional resources.

Concept 329: To Be Truly Successful Every Fundraising Project Must Be Cost- and Time-Effective.

Two of the criteria used to judge the success of any fundraising activity are the *cost* or *time effectiveness* of the effort. This involves the weighing of expenditures in terms of personnel, money, time, and other resources against the actual net results gained. If the fundraising effort is neither time- nor cost-effective in terms of net advantage(s) accruing to the sponsoring organization, the fundraising project is a failure. The mark of a truly successful fundraising effort is one which is cost- and time-effective in terms of generating needed resources for the sport organization while establishing or reinforcing positive rapport with various outside constituencies and with the paid and volunteer staff.

9. *Fundraising projects should be appropriate for the sponsoring organization and for the community.*

Concept 330: Before Initiating a Fundraising Project Check to See What Would Be Appropriate and Acceptable within Your Community.

Sport organizers must be sensitive to the mores and the expectations of the community. Don't risk offending the community with inappropriate or unacceptable fundraising projects. Skilled and experienced fundraisers should know or find out what can be accomplished in a given community and what the community will find acceptable in the way of a fundraising project.

In some communities dancing might be frowned on. In others, card playing or other forms of gambling, including bingo, might be taboo, while in others, alcohol may be disapproved. Every community has the potential for being different in terms of what might be appropriate and suitable as a fundraising project. Similarly, it is also imperative that the fundraising project doesn't become a burden or nuisance to either your volunteers, boosters, or to the people or businesses in the community who will be asked to donate or otherwise participate in your fundraising effort. In other words, don't wear out your welcome in the community either by too many events or by inappropriate projects.

10. *Work closely with volunteers—educate and motivate them.*

Sport administrators and coaches usually do not do all of the fundraising work themselves. In fact, just the opposite. Volunteers, students, parents, booster club members, community people, and alumni comprise the bulk of the fundraising team led by the sport manager or administrator appointed by the organization.

In school-based sports programs, a booster club or athletic support group (ASG) can be of immense help if the club is properly structured, organized, and supervised. Such booster organizations provide much needed elbow grease, support, and numbers that are so necessary for major fundraising projects (Stier, 1987c).

Concept 331: One Must Treat Volunteers Differently from Paid Staff—Volunteers Can Walk if Their Needs Are Not Met.

Volunteers form the hub of any such booster or support group. It is important that fundraising organizers and leaders take time to orient, train, and motivate the helpers, the boosters who have been recruited or who have volunteered. No one needs well-meaning volunteers standing around, getting in the way, and becoming discouraged. Rather, organizers must work closely with boosters and volunteers to see that they are given meaningful tasks that they can successfully complete. This usually requires some formal training or orientation.

11. *Never fail to express your appreciation and thanks to donors, supporters, and helpers—both within the organization and in the community.*

Not only is it polite to say "thank you" to those who have contributed to your program by donating money, time, effort, and/or services as well as general support, but it is also simply good business. Most fundraising organizers will return to the same constituencies and publics to solicit resources and assistance once again. Having paid the proper respect in the past helps pave the way for subsequent successful fundraising projects.

Concept 332: Always, Always Express Publicly Your Gratitude to Those Who Help You—You May Need Their Assistance Again in the Future.

It is very important that volunteers and donors not be taken for granted. In fact, many success stories in fundraising would not be possible without the support and assistance of highly dedicated, skilled volunteers and boosters. It is important that these individuals not be taken for granted. Quite the contrary. Those who have helped in the past should be made aware of how much they are appreciated and how much their assistance and backing has meant in the overall success of the fundraising process. To accept the help, the assistance, the services, the money from others and then not to respond in a demonstrative and definitive (and public) fashion is foolish indeed.

The Future of Sport Fundraising and Promotional Activities

Sport fundraising and promotional activities are here to stay. In the past sports people sometimes dabbled in fundraising merely because they liked the idea of being involved in such activities. However, the current situation is such that fundraising is all too frequently becoming a necessary venture. The generation of outside resources is necessary if sports programs—in youth sports, in junior and senior high schools, at the collegiate levels, in recreational departments as well as at the professional sport level—are to survive at an acceptable level in terms of both quality and quantity.

Concept 333: Fundraising and Promotional Activities Are a Permanent Fixture in Sport.

It is important for sports personnel to have a realistic understanding of the fundraising process and to be able to make sound decisions with respect to the generation of outside resources. In today's world, keeping fundraising in its proper perspective is essential if the overall goals of the sport organization are to be realized.

As fundraising becomes more of an integral and expected part of the total funding process of sport organizations, it behooves those involved in such programs to develop and refine their understanding and skills in fundraising and promotions. This is especially important if one's peers are likewise engaged in fundraising efforts and are providing competition for the already scarce dollars, goods, and services.

In the end, those who fundraise need to be highly skilled and motivated, unafraid of taking calculated risks, capable of learning from past experiences. It is these experiences, coupled with the ability to adapt general principles involved in fundraising to their present situation, that enable successful fundraisers to make appropriate and timely decisions in the world of fundraising and promotions.

Concept 334: Fundraising Is either a Necessary Evil or a Golden Opportunity for Sports Personnel to Demonstrate Their Competency.

The information provided within the earlier sections of this chapter provides a beginning point for sport personnel and booster organizations to begin to build their own, individualized fundraising plan to generate the much needed resources for their own sports teams. One does not need a crystal ball to foretell that in the future more demand and greater stress will be placed on the financial capabilities of sport programs and organizations than ever before. It is up to sport personnel to be willing and able to meet this challenge through effective and efficient fundraising tactics and methods involving the coordination and management of highly qualified, thoroughly trained, and motivated individuals.

Conclusions

Sport managers must be capable of adapting to the changes that are continually taking place in the world of sport and in our society. Part of this challenge is for sport managers to be capable of securing sufficient resources (money, goods, and services) with which to run their respective programs and promote and market their organization and their various programs. Almost every sport, recreation, or fitness organization is faced, at some time or another, with the necessity and the challenge of becoming actively involved in marketing, promoting, and fundraising. For those sport managers who are prepared to aggressively address this challenge, with both an understanding of and an appreciation for the potential benefits of such involvement, the future is bright. For those who are less prepared, and who do not possess the knowledge and skills relating to fundraising, promotions, and marketing, the future is bleak.

REFERENCES

Bucher, C. (1987). *Management of physical education & athletic programs* (9th ed.). St. Louis, MO: Times Mirror/Mosby College Publishing.

Buell, V. P. (1984). *Marketing management: Strategic planning approach.* New York: McGraw-Hill.

Cutlip, S. M., Center, A. H., and Broom, G. M. (1985). *Effective public relations* (6th ed.). Englewood Cliffs, NJ: Prentice-Hall.

Ensor, R. (1988, September). Writing a strategic sports marketing plan. *Athletic Business, 12*(9), 20–23.

Fox, D. (1990). A time to sow, a time to reap—Marketing and promotions. *Journal of Physical, Education, Recreation and Dance, 61*(3), 65–70.

Graham, P. J. (1994). *Sport business—Operational and theoretical aspects.* Madison, WI: Wm. C. Brown & Benchmark.

Gray, D. P. (1996). Sponsorship on campus. *Sport Marketing Quarterly, V*(2), 29–34.

Horine, L. (1996). *Administration of physical education and sport* (3rd ed.). Madison, WI: Wm. C. Brown & Benchmark.

Irwin, R. L. (1996). The data-driven approach to sponsorship acquisition. *Sport Marketing Quarterly, V*(2), 7–10.

Lough, N. L. (1996). Factors affecting corporate sponsorship of women's sport. *Sport Marketing Quarterly. V*(2), 11–19.

McCarthy, E. J. (1960). *Basic marketing: A managerial approach.* Homewood, IL: R. D. Irwin.

Mason, J. G. and Paul, P. (1988). *Modern sports management.* Englewood Cliffs, NJ: Prentice-Hall.

Morris, D. and Irwin, R. L. (1996). The data-driven approach to sponsorship acquisition. *Sport Marketing Quarterly, V*(2), 7–10.

Mullin, B. J. (1983). *Sports marketing, promotion, and public relations.* Amherst, MA: National Sport Management, cited by Railey, J. J. & Railey, P. A. (1988).

Palmisano, N. J. (1984, May). Fund-raising first rule: Get organized. *Athletic Business, 9*(5), 20–23.

Parkhouse, B. L. (Ed.). (1996). *The management of sport—Its foundation and application* (2nd ed.). St. Louis, MO: Mosby Year Book.

Railey, J. J. and Railey, P. A. (1988). *Managing physical education, fitness, and sports programs.* Mountain View, CA: Mayfield.

Schlossberg, H. (1990, June). Hispanic market strong but often ignored. *Marketing News,* p. 26.

Stier, W. F., Jr. (1986, June 26). Fundraising and promotional activities for the successful athletic department. A paper presented at the National Convention of the High School Athletic Coaches Association, Orlando, Florida.

Stier, W. F., Jr. (1987a). Managing for survival in higher education: Athletics in academe. *The Journal of Applied Research in Coaching and Athletics, 2*(3), 153–167.

Stier, W. F., Jr. (1987b, August 6). Promotional techniques and ideas for a small budget. Paper presented at the National Convention of the National Collegiate Athletic Association (NCAA)—Professional Development Seminar, Washington, D. C.

Stier, W. F., Jr. (1987c, October). The establishment of an effective athletic support group. *JUCO Review (Journal of the National Junior College Athletic Association)*, pp. 4–6.

Stier, W. F., Jr. (1990a, January 3). Fundraising tactics and promotional practices for intercollegiate athletic programs. Paper presented at the National Convention of the National Collegiate Athletic Association (NCAA)—Professional Development Seminar, Dallas, Texas.

Stier, W. F., Jr. (1990b, August). ADs walk fine line on promotion. *Athletic Administration, 25*(4), 18–19, 21.

Stier, W. F., Jr. (1992). Understanding fundraising in sport: The conceptual approach. *Sport Marketing Quarterly, 1*(1), 41–46.

Stier, W. F., Jr. (1993a, July). Project profit. *Athletic Management, V*(4), 44–46.
Stier, W. F., Jr. (1993b, July 9). Meeting the challenges of managing sport through marketing, fundraising and promotions. Paper presented at the International Meeting of the World University Games (and FISU/CESU Conference), Buffalo, New York.
Stier, W. F., Jr. (1994a). *Fundraising for sport and recreation*. Champaign, IL: Human Kinetics.
Stier, W. F., Jr. (1994b). *Successful sport fund-raising*. Dubuque, IA: Wm. C. Brown & Benchmark.
Stier, W. F., Jr. (1995, June 19). The future of fundraising and promotions in international sport competition. Paper presented at the annual convention of the Ontario Hockey Association. London, Ontario, Canada.
Stier, W. F., Jr. (1996, May). An overview of administering competitive sport programs through effective marketing, fundraising and promotion. *Applied Research in Coaching and Athletic Annual, 11*(1), 116–128.
Stier, W. F., Jr. (1998, April 8). Fundraising, promotions, public relations and publicity for the 21st century. A presentation made at the national convention of the American Alliance for Health, Physical Education, Recreation and Dance, Reno, Nevada.
Stotlar, D. K. (1989). *Successful sport marketing and sponsorship plans*. Dubuque, IA: Wm. C. Brown.
Stotlar, D. K. (1993). *Successful sport marketing*. Madison, WI: Wm. C. Brown & Benchmark.
Stotlar, D. K. (1993). Sponsorship and the Olympic winter games. *Sport Marketing Quarterly, II*(1), 35–43.
Stotlar, D. K. (1996). On teaching about sponsorship. *Sport Marketing Quarterly, V*(2), 41–42.
White, A. B. and Irwin, R. L. (1996). Assessing a corporate partner program: A key to success. *Sport Marketing Quarterly, V*(2), 21, 24–28.
Wieberg, S. (1991, October 16). Spiked—Sports cut to trim costs. *USA Today,* p. 5-C.
Wieberg, S. and Witosky, T. (1991a, October 14). Most college sports lose money. *USA Today,* p. 1-C.
Wieberg, S. and Witosky, T. (1991b, October 16). Schools seek solutions to athletic budget woes. *USA Today,* p. 5-C.

DISCUSSION AND REVIEW QUESTIONS

1. Differentiate between fundraising, marketing, promoting, public relations, and publicity in terms of sport entities.
2. Provide examples of the type of resources or tools needed by various sport organizations.
3. Why is it frequently necessary for sport managers to go outside to secure needed resources?
4. Create an outline of a specific fundraising project utilizing the components of a fundraising plan presented in this chapter.
5. Enumerate various target markets for a fictional sport management organization and indicate how a sport manager might seek to reach selected target markets.
6. Outline a potential situation in which a sport organization might solicit a corporate sponsorship or partnership with an outside business and describe how such an arrangement might be mutually beneficial to both parties.
7. Cite sources and examples of both hard and soft data and reveal how both forms of data can be used as tools in sport promotion, marketing, and/or fundraising.
8. Indicate some of the very real risks involved in fundraising, marketing, and promoting activities and how these risks might be avoided or lessened by mangers in sport, recreation, and fitness programs.

CHAPTER

11 The Legal Aspects of Sport Management

Women play a major role in competitive and recreational sports.
James Dusen, Photographer.

CHAPTER OBJECTIVES

After reading this chapter you will be able to:

- Appreciate the importance for sport managers to be knowledgeable in the law insofar as their organizations and programs are concerned;
- Understand the two key elements in successfully meeting the legal challenges of managing sport programs;
- Be familiar with the employment laws relating to sport organizations;
- Differentiate between employees and independent contractors;

- Recognize the importance of affirmative action and various forms of discrimination within the employment scene;
- Describe the four patterns of hiring minorities and women;
- Define and provide examples of sexual harassment in the workplace and how such discrimination might be avoided;
- Explain the history of Title IX and the current challenges relating to gender equity;
- Provide illustrations appropriate for sport, recreation, and fitness programs regarding the importance of American with Disabilities Act of 1990 (ADA) and Section 504 of the Rehabilitation Act of 1973;
- Cite the relevance of the Family and Medical Leave Act for the modern sport manager;
- Illustrate how the Occupational Safety and Health Administration (OSHA) plays a major role in the management of sport and sport-related organizations and businesses;
- Understand the importance of sport licensing laws;
- Be appreciative of and sensitive to the need to be politically correct in the business of sport, recreation, and fitness.

Understanding the Legal Aspects of Managing Sport

Every sport manager, regardless of the type or level of the organization, must pay particular attention to the laws, rules, and regulations that may affect the organization itself as well as the myriad activities associated with it. Because sport management revolves around people, both as individuals and as members of various groups, the ramifications of adherence (or failure to adhere) to legal directives can be significant.

Concept 335: Knowledge of the Law Itself Is Not Sufficient for the Sport Manager—Appropriate and Timely Action Is Also Required.

When dealing with the legal aspects of sport and sport management and making appropriate decisions, it is imperative that managers and administrators be knowledgeable about the laws, rules, and regulations that may affect their organizations, personnel, and programs. However, knowledge in and of itself is not enough. Sport managers must also be capable of anticipating how the laws and regulations might affect their organization and their obligations to others, both individuals and groups.

Concept 336: Anticipation and Prevention Are Two Key Elements in Successfully Meeting the Legal Challenges of Managing Sport Programs.

This understanding of the possible impact of laws, regulations, and rules enables sport professionals to make appropriate decisions and take suitable steps (corrective action), if necessary. The objective is to insure that the organization, the program(s), the activity(ies), and the personnel involved are in full compliance with all applicable legal requirements and directives.

Accurate anticipation of possible consequences relating to applicable legal directives is absolutely essential for the sport manager. Such anticipation aids in the ability to prevent negative consequences. It is imperative that everything be done that can be to prevent negative consequences or problems for the people who are involved in or associated with the organization, either as paid/volunteer personnel or as customers and/or consumers. In short, for the ultimate success of the sport organization all legal obligations must be fully met (see Figure 11.1). To do otherwise is not only foolish but self-defeating and capaciously negligent.

By meeting the legal requirements and being in full compliance with all applicable rules and appropriate regulations, the sport organization takes a giant step toward protecting the organization itself, its personnel as well as the general public, especially those individuals who are involved as spectators or as consumers of the sport entity.

Concept 337: Failure to Adhere to Legal Requirements Can Have Disastrous Results, both in Terms of Finances and Public Relations.

The consequences of failing to adhere to the requirements and rules or of violating laws can be severe, both in terms of monetary damages and irreparable damage to the reputation of the organization and those associated with it. Of course, in many instances, one obeys laws and regulations not just because one is fearful of "breaking the law" or getting into trouble, but because "it is the right thing to do."

Usually, laws and regulations are in effect for good reasons, for the health, welfare, and safety of people. Adherence to such regulations and rules may be considered, in effect, self-serving in that these directives enable the organization to better meet the needs of its customers and personnel. Thus, the task of reaching the objectives and goals of the sport entity are facilitated.

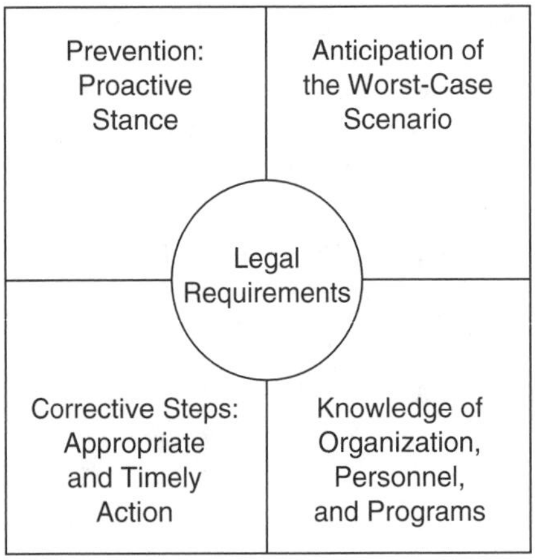

FIGURE 11.1 Dealing with the Legal Challenges of Sport

The television of sport—expanding one's audience.

> **Concept 338:** Naivete Is No Excuse when It Comes to Obeying the Law or Being in Compliance with Legal Requirements and Regulations.

It should be pointed out here that it is the responsibility of the competent sport manager to be knowledgeable about the authoritative restrictions and legal requirements affecting one's organization and programs. One cannot shirk this obligation. Naivete is no excuse.

If the sport manager is ignorant of the law, the responsibility remains with that individual. The appropriate response to such ignorance is that the individual should have known the legal requirements and been aware of the consequences of not adhering to the stipulations of the directive. The responsibility is still that of the sport manager. One cannot avoid or delegate away that responsibility.

The Scope of Laws and Legal Requirements Pertaining to Sport

There are a number of areas in which laws and regulations are especially important for the sport manager in the twenty-first century. Many of these legal decrees are also applicable for any type of business or educational institution. Some of the more important legal directives or categories of laws and regulations that sport managers must be especially attentive to are listed in Figure 11.2.

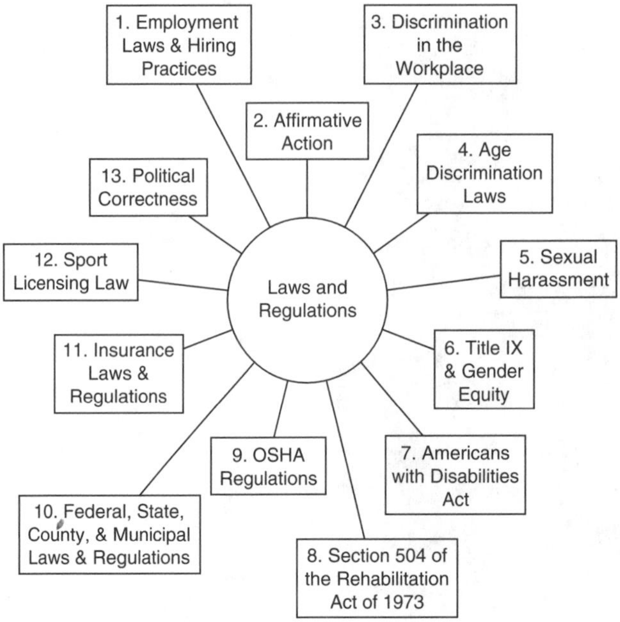

FIGURE 11.2 Applicable Laws for the Sport Manager

Employment Laws and Hiring Practices

Every business organization, whether it be a for-profit or a not-for-profit entity, must adhere to the appropriate local, state, and federal employment laws. Some of these laws relate to affirmative action, discrimination, harassment, and workers' safety. Other applicable laws, rules, and regulations involve the areas of taxation (income, sales, payroll unemployment, etc.), and insurance. Some laws and regulations are applicable at the federal level, others at the state level, and still others at the local or county level.

Differentiating between Employees and Independent Contractors

Some sport entities utilize employees to staff their organizations. Others utilize employees and volunteers while still others utilize independent contractors in addition to employees and/or volunteers. Because the organizations that utilize independent contractors pay only a specified salary and it is up to the individual who is classified as an independent contractor to pay withholding tax, it is essential that the person being classified as an independent contractor be so viewed by the IRS.

Today, what determines whether one is an independent contractor or an employer is often in a "gray area." In fact, in many instances it comes down to a judgment call by a representative of the Internal Revenue Service (IRS), because the criteria by which a person might be classified as an employee or an independent contractor has changed as changes have occurred in our society. For example, in the past anyone who worked from home was considered, almost automatically, as an independent contractor. Today, with the shift of more and more employees to working from their homes, this is no longer the case. Similarly, in the past employees used to wear the uniforms of the employing company. Today, more and more independent contractors are wearing the uniforms of the company for which they are serving as independent contractors (Jones, 1996).

It is very important, in terms of complying with federal tax laws, to understand the legal difference between employees and independent contractors (Wong, 1996), because failing to do so can have severe legal and financial repercussions. Organizations need to have a clear-cut standard for determining whether a person providing services is an independent contractor or an employee. According to the current safe-harbor law, employment taxes that might result from an employment relationship are not the responsibility of the employer if the organization or individual receiving the services had: (1) a "reasonable basis" for treating the individual as an independent contractor, (2) filed the required tax returns at the federal level, and (3) not considered or treated as an employee any other worker doing similar task(s) as the individual being claimed as the independent contractor (Gray, 1995, p. 28).

Some of the other factors (part of the 20-part test utilized by the IRS) that can help prove that the individual was an independent contractor and not an employee include: (1) the person performs duties on a schedule set by the individual and not the organization, (2) the person utilizes his or her own tools, (3) the person consistently seeks employment from other companies or individuals, (4) the person is allowed to hire one's own assistants to do the work, (5) the person works on a schedule established by the individual and not by the organization or company, (6) the person cannot just quit or be fired without there being a breach in the contract, and (7) the company or organization does not determine when, where, or how the work is to be carried out (Jones, 1996).

Affirmative Action

Affirmative action seeks to achieve, at all levels and segments of an organization, prompt and full utilization of women and minorities wherever deficiencies in their representation exists. This is accomplished through a set of very specific guidelines and procedures that guide businesses and organizations in their "good faith" efforts to be fair, just, and lawful. The purpose of affirmative action is to establish criteria and procedures that guide employers to make good faith efforts to provide equal employment opportunity to qualified applicants.

Affirmative action was not designed to be permanent but to address a specific ill in our society. The initial purpose of affirmative action was certainly laudatory; that is, it sought to remove barriers of discrimination and eliminate injustices based on race, gender, religions, and ethnicity. A significant facet of affirmative action is that it is supposed to take a proactive stance against discrimination. As a result, affirmative action policies seek to create a positive environment to insure that individuals are treated fairly and appropriately, now and in the future.

Any employer that has 50 or more employees and has entered into at least one government contract for $50,000 or more in any 12-month period with a federal "executive" agency is considered a "contractor" or "subcontractor" and as such is required to develop a written Affirmative Action Program (AAP). Many other organizations and businesses, while not legally required to have an affirmative action program and policies, nevertheless establish them.

Concept 339: The United States Has Actively Sought to Encourage Adherence to Affirmative Action Practices through Significant Enticements—Including Tax Breaks and Cash Incentives.

Even private organizations, if they receive federal money or have a federal contract, must adhere to affirmative action rules and regulations. In fact, there are entitlement awards, special grants, to organizations that follow affirmative action rules. These include tax breaks (incentives) and actual cash awards. These are very powerful incentives for organizations to adhere to affirmative action rules. Some have called these efforts "social engineering."

Concept 340: An Important Element of Affirmative Action Is the Availability of a Grievance Process—Such a Process Insures the Possibility of Redressing an Injustice.

Affirmative action involves grievance processes to protect one's rights. Grievance can be prevented with good policies and good faith efforts to do away with discrimination and provide a just and fair environment where people are treated equally.

Components of Grievance Procedures and Policies

Grievance procedures usually include the following:

1. An established policy in terms of to whom should the individual go;
2. Stated procedures involving the dates within which to bring a complaint;
3. An honest effort to treat each complaint seriously and with due diligence;
4. Assurance that the relevant facts will be dealt with;
5. A conscious assumption that either party may be right;
6. If more than one form of harassment/discrimination developments, each is treated separately.

Equal Employment Opportunities

Concept 341: One of the Goals of Affirmative Action Is to Prevent Employers from Practicing Overt as well as Covert Discrimination on the Basis of Race, Gender, Ethnicity, or Religion.

The organizational climate is all-important in the workplace in terms of creating an environment for discrimination or nondiscrimination. The work climate must be free of harassment, free of discrimination, and free of intimidation. The work climate within the sport entity must be conducive to enabling those present to do their jobs and to fulfill their respective responsibilities without undue hindrance, obstruction, or interference.

Equal employment opportunities include effective recruitment and retention of minorities, nondiscrimination policies, practices, and procedures, effective and impartial performance appraisals; successfully communicating and disseminating the nondiscrimination policies, practices, and procedures to appropriate constituencies, and educating and training personnel (including supervisory and administrative personnel) in terms of equal employment opportunities.

> **Concept 342:** The Organizational and Work Climate Is One of the Most Important Factors in Terms of Establishing and Maintaining Discrimination or Nondiscrimination within the Workplace.

One of the goals of affirmative action is to provide equal employment opportunities for citizenry, by redressing wrongs, protecting minorities and other protected classes, providing for equal employment and protection in the workplace against discrimination as well as charges of reverse discrimination against males and members of the white race.

> **Concept 343:** Affirmative Action Seeks to Recognize and Remove Barriers That Discriminate against Individuals.

Affirmative action seeks to correct past evils and injustices, prevent current injustices involving discrimination, and prevent future discrimination from taking place. Affirmative action policies and procedures should help those individuals who have been unfairly excluded or held back, who have been denied equal opportunity, who have been passed over unfairly, who have been screened out inappropriately, and who have been underutilized unfairly.

Lack of Women and Minorities Involved in the Business of Sport

Numerous studies (Acosta & Carpenter, 1992b, 1992c; Baize, 1995) have revealed the shortage of women and minorities involved in sport, both as coaches and as administrators and managers. It is imperative that great effort be taken to insure that these individuals are not discriminated against in their efforts to secure appropriate employment commensurate with their education, training, and experience. Roadblocks and hindrances must be removed for women and minorities in order for them to be able and willing to become involved as coaches, leaders, and managers in the world of sport (Acosta & Carpenter, 1992a). Role models are needed as are mentors to potential employees and volunteers in the world of sport.

The move to select women as athletic administrators within the NCAA division I level has been extremely slow, although some progress has been made. As of October 1996 there were only 17 female athletic directors at 305 NCAA Division I schools. Among those

NCAA division I schools (totaling 111 universities) that play big-time (division I-A) football, there were only six women serving as athletic directors. The first woman athletic director at an NCAA division I-A football school was Mary Alice Hill, who served as AD at San Diego State between 1983 and 1985, when she was fired (Blauvelt, 1996, October 2).

Backlash against Affirmative Action by Angry White Males: The California Initiative

Concept 344: Many Critics Claim That Reverse Discrimination Is Frequently a Consequence of Affirmative Action—Critics Believe That "White Males Need Not Apply" (WMNNA) when Affirmative Action Policies Are Strictly Implemented.

In 1995 and 1996 affirmative action came under tremendous criticism as being discriminatory against white males. California led the way in challenging the way affirmative action programs were being implemented (Holland, 1996). The California Civil Rights Initiative (CCRI) involved a statewide ballot question that would forbid the use of ethnicity or gender "as a criterion for either discriminating against, or granting preferential treatment to, any individual or group" by the government (Klein, 1995, February 13, p. 105).

Johnson, in a 1995 article in *USA Today,* revealed how affirmative action, its interpretation, and its implementation have been and are being closely scrutinized by the citizens of this country. In more recent times it has also been examined by the United States Supreme Court, which also will continue to examine the effects and implications that affirmative action continues to have on our society. Critics of affirmative action, such as Northern California Republican state senator Bernie Richter, claim: "Affirmative action has become a vile and corrosive system that threatens to blow us asunder" (Johnson, 1995, p. 2A). Those in favor of affirmative action cite the need to redress and prevent current discrimination. These individuals feel that both minorities and women need, as said by the Reverend Zedar E. Broadous, "time to find themselves on equal footing in the workplace and in the classroom and that time has not come" (Johnson, 1995, p. 2A).

California (1996) Rolls Back the Impact of Affirmative Action with Proposition 209

During 1995 legislation was introduced in 26 states as well as in the United States Congress to repeal or significantly diminish affirmative-action programs. None passed during that year. However, this trend came to an abrupt halt when Proposition 209 passed in the most populous state in the union, California, by a 54 percent to 45 percent majority (Calif. proposition, 1996). In fact, 4,736,189 Californians voted for Proposition 209, which contained the words: "The state shall not discriminate against, or grant preferential treatment to, any individual or group on the basis of race, sex, color, ethnicity or national origin" (Beck, 1997).

Proposition 209 asked the voters: Should the state "not discriminate against, or grant preferential treatment to any person or group in public employment, education or contracting?" With the passage of this first statewide attack against what has become known as affirmative action, the citizens of California authorized the amendment of the constitution to ban race and gender considerations in public hiring, contracting, and college admissions.

One immediate consequence of this was at least three lawsuits designed to block the enforcement of this amendment to the state constitution. On the other hand, gaining encouragement from the victory in California, those individuals leading the anti-affirmative action efforts in other states rallied to submit similar amendments to their state constitutions. Needless to say, the question of affirmative action and its value or worth to the U.S. public remains at the forefront of the nation's consciousness (Prop. 209 still under fire, 1996).

In early April of 1997, the 9th Circuit Court of Appeals decided in favor of California's hotly contested Proposition 209. The ruling (3–0) swept aside an earlier injunction established by United States District Judge, which had prohibited Proposition 209 from being implemented. The ruling indicated that voters can indeed ban affirmative action based on race and gender in government hiring, contracting, and education (Price, 1997).

Concept 345: Quotas Are Illegal within Affirmative Action—but "Everyone Knows that 'Goals and Timetables' Means 'Quotas'" (Leo, 1995, p. 18).

The impact of the Bakke decision (1978), in which Allan Bakke sued Regents of University of California at Davis, was significant and far-reaching. Bakke claimed "reverse discrimination" based on quotas in admissions practices that the university used in their efforts to remedy what they called past discrimination against minorities. The decision struck down a university program that set aside 16 of the 100 open slots to medical school for minorities.

The Supreme Court of this country states that less formal race-conscious efforts might be acceptable while outlawing such blatant quota systems as that used by the University of California. As a result of the Bakke decision, goals and timetables replaced quotas. However, Leo (1995, p. 18) believes that, although quotas were supposedly done away with, in reality, "Everyone knows that 'goals and timetables' means 'quotas' but nobody is suppose to say so out loud."

Although Title VII, Section 703 (j) clearly prohibits preferences by race, gender, ethnicity, and religion in business and government, interpretation has evolved over the past 30 years. The courts and bureaucrats have adopted, adapted, and otherwise converted and explained away the clear statements in Title VII that prohibit preferences based on race, gender, ethnicity, and religion, all in the interest of a greater good, a higher justice. As a result, the interpretation involving a system or proportional representation by race and gender has evolved (Leo, 1995).

Four Patterns of Hiring Minorities and Women

McWhirter, in his book *Your Rights at Work* (2nd edition, 1993), describes several different versions of hiring plans. Some of these efforts are associated with affirmative action employment plans. Some of these practices have been accepted at some levels while at other levels they have been rejected as inappropriate or illegal. Some of the different versions of hiring plans include:

1. Instances in which employers actively encourage minorities and women to apply for positions. In such cases, the companies actively seek out and recruit such underrepresented individuals for vacancies. Although this is not really affirmative action, according to McWhirter, this practice has gained wide acceptance throughout the nation.
2. When two otherwise qualified candidates (one male or nonminority individual and the other a woman and/or minority candidate) are essentially comparable or equal in their qualifications, the company hires the minority or female candidate over the nonminority or male candidate if the applicant is underrepresented within that particular company or entity. The United States Supreme Court has approved this kind of affirmative action plan or policy.
3. Companies hire women or minorities (if they meet the *minimum qualifications for the position*) even though there are clearly more qualified white male candidates. Court decisions differ in accepting this type of affirmative action. Some (typically on the state and local levels) have declared it unacceptable while others (on the federal level) have endorsed the concept and permitted this pattern of hiring to continue.
4. Organizations continue to search for an acceptable woman or minority, regardless of whether or not a qualified male is presently available for employment. McWhirter (1993) indicates that this not only involves a very rigid quota system but is currently illegal. Such a practice is not viewed as part of affirmative action and has not been upheld in the courts.

Recent Actions by the United States Supreme Court Limiting Affirmative Action

The Supreme Court on June 12, 1995 made two decisions that significantly affected affirmative action as well as how affirmative action had been interpreted in this country during the previous 30 years. In fact, the decisions "took a direction far removed from the traditional liberal approach to civil rights" (Mauro, 1995, 1-A).

One case, *Adarand Constructors v. Pena,* involved a situation in which Adarand was the losing bidder as a subcontractor on a federal highway project even though that company had submitted the lowest bid. The winning bid went to a minority-owned company because under the affirmative action program of the Federal government the main contractor received a cash bonus having given the work to the Hispanic-owned company. The other case that had far-reaching consequences had the high court siding with the state of Missouri, which sought to end federal supervision of the Kansas City, Missouri school desegregation efforts.

Both decisions "expressed outright exasperation with civil rights remedies that take race into account, give minorities a boost in government contracts and hiring, and involve the courts in running public schools" (Mauro, 1995, p. 2-A). In essence, the Court has moved in a direction that will significantly diminish the role of the courts at the Federal level as well as Federal agencies in remedying racial and gender bias.

Supreme Court Justice Clarence Thomas made a statement that probably represented best this shift of the high court when he said, "These programs stamp minorities with a badge of inferiority and may cause them to develop dependencies or to adopt an attitude that they are 'entitled' to preferences" (Mauro, 1995, p. 2-A).

The *New York Times* reported on March 8, 1996 that President Bill Clinton effectively put affirmative action programs on hold in early 1996 when he elected to suspend, for at least three years, all federal programs that reserve some contracts exclusively for minority and female-owned firms. Many experts believed that this three-year moratorium on set-aside programs would be very difficult to reintroduce at the end of the three years, effectively making this decision more far-reaching (Clinton to put, 1996; Administration to suspend, 1996).

Examples of Arguments against Affirmative Action

Steele (1994) has provided several reasons why affirmative action should not be followed: (1) People should be selected on the basis of merit alone, (2) our society should be a color-blind society, (3) affirmative action balkanizes the community, (4) causes reverse discrimination, (5) produces feelings of inferiority in women and people of color, (6) creates negative stereotypes about women and people of color, (7) young people of color expect affirmative action to get them jobs and promotions, and (8) minorities stand to lose more from affirmative action than they gain.

Discrimination in the Workplace

There are several laws that purport to protect employees against discrimination in the workplace. Typically, these laws prohibit discrimination on the basis of sex, sexual preference, race, age, religious beliefs, national origin, and physical limitations.

Unlawful Discrimination in the Form of Unequal Pay for Essentially Equal Work

One such law is the Equal Pay Act. This federal law stipulates the same pay for men and women who do substantially equal work, requiring substantially equal skill, effort, and responsibility under similar working conditions in the same establishment (Wong & Barr, 1994). Yet, studies continue to reveal that women, across the board, typically receive less salary than their male counterparts in the business world. The same is true for faculty members at the college and university levels throughout the country, both private and public.

The Family and Medical Leave Act

Yet another law (Act) that has placed additional pressure on employers is *The Family and Medical Leave Act*. Becoming effective on August 5, 1993, this piece of legislation requires employers with 50 or more workers to provide them with up to 12 weeks a year of unpaid leave to care for a new baby or sick family member. This has proven to be expensive for the companies that have to hire and train temporary replacements while still paying the health benefits of those employees on leave.

Age Discrimination Laws

The Age Discrimination Act of 1975, as amended, prohibits discrimination on the basis of age in programs or activities receiving federal financial assistance. This act specifies that it is unlawful for an employer to fail or refuse to hire or to discharge any individual or otherwise discriminate against any individual with respect to compensation, terms, conditions, or privileges of employment, because of an individual's age.

Concept 346: The Equal Employment Opportunity Commission Was Created in 1972 as the Enforcement Agency in Cases of Discrimination on the Basis of Race, Color, Religion, Sex, or National Origin.

The Civil Rights Act of 1964 prohibits and provides relief against discrimination in public accommodations, protects constitutional rights in public facilities and public education, and prevents discrimination in federally assisted programs. The Civil Rights Act was amended (Title VII of the Civil Rights Act of 1964 as amended by the Equal Employment Opportunity Act of 1972) in 1972 to include prohibitions against discrimination in employment on the basis of race, color, religion, sex, or national origin. This act created the Equal Employment Opportunity Commission as the enforcement agency in cases of such discrimination.,

Concept 347: Nondiscrimination Policies Should Be Prominently Displayed in the Workplace.

Nondiscrimination policies and statements are very important in any organization and must be widely disseminated. However, there must be more than merely posting signs. There is also a need to actively train and educate employees and members of management to recognize, react, prevent, and redress discrimination. And, of course, there must be a willingness by management to treat the whole subject of discrimination in a serious vein. This means that the sport leaders and managers must be willing to take positive action to prevent (proaction) any form of discrimination and be prepared to react to such abominable behavior in a decisive manner.

Sexual Harassment

The United States Supreme Court has ruled that sexual harassment is illegal discrimination covered by Title VII of the Civil Rights Act (Discrimination because of sex, 1980; Meyer et al., 1981). This Act recognizes that adverse employment conditions subject workers to stresses that have nothing to do with actual job performance. In addition, sexual harassment is frequently accomplished by threats of adverse job actions or promises of raises or promotions or other rewards (Carpenter, 1989). Sexual harassment is also a violation of many state laws as well. In the state of New York it is a violation of NYS Human Rights Laws (Article 15 of Executive Law, Sections 290–301).

Sexual Harassment Defined

There are several key concepts that define sexual harassment: (1) being unwanted, (2) being intentional, (3) frequently being repeated, (4) resulting in intimidation, (5) involving cohesiveness, (6) being demeaning and insulting, and (7) interfering with one's normal performance (work, school, or play).

Sexual harassment may be thought of as any *repeated* or *unwarranted* verbal or physical sexual conduct or advances, sexually explicit derogatory statements, or sexually discriminatory remarks made by someone in the workplace that are offensive or objectionable to the recipient, or that cause the recipient discomfort or humiliation, or interfere with the recipient's job, work, recreational, or school performance (MacKinnon, 1979; Sandler et al., 1981; Somers, 1982; Dziech and Weiner, 1984).

Sexual Harassment within the Workplace

The Equal Employment Opportunity Commission has defined sexual harassment as: "Unwelcome sexual advances, requests for sexual favors, and other verbal or physical conduct of a sexual nature...when (1) submission to such conduct is made either explicitly or implicitly a term or condition of an individual's employment, (2) submission or rejection of such conduct by an individual is used as the basis for employment decisions affecting such individual, or (3) such conduct has the purpose or effect of substantially interfering with an individual's work performance or creating an intimidating, hostile, or offensive working environment."

Examples of Sexual Harassment Activities

Specific examples of sexual harassment include, but are not limited to, the following:

1. Sexist remarks about a person's clothing, body, or sexual activities;
2. Unnecessary touching, patting, pinching, or cornering;
3. Visual harassment—leering at or ogling of a person's body;
4. Demanding sexual favors accompanied by implied or overt threats concerning one's job, grades, letters of recommendations, and so on;
5. Physical sexual assault;
6. Verbal harassment or abuse—propositions, lewd comments, sexual insults;
7. Subtle pressure for sexual activity;
8. Overt solicitation of sexual favors (in the face of a threat of some type of punishment);
9. Subtle or overt pressure or solicitation of sexual favors in exchange for a promise of a reward ("quid pro quo" harassment).

Employers need to also be aware of and concerned that employees do not practice subtle discrimination through the use of "code words." The 3rd Circuit Court of Appeals ruled in late 1996 that a jury was to decide whether or not a pattern of code words used by white workers and managers at a Maple Shade, New Jersey, furniture rental store constituted discrimination. This decision will have significant repercussions throughout the workplace. One consequence will be that "words spoken at work that aren't literally racist—such as 'you people,' 'poor people,' and 'that one in there'—now can be grounds for employment discrimination lawsuits" (Jones, 1996).

Concept 348: Companies and Organizations Need to Take a Proactive Stance against All Forms of (Blatant and Subtle) Racism and Discrimination, Not Only to Prevent Lawsuits but because It Is the Right Thing to Do.

Sport businesses need to educate their employees and volunteers. They also need to police the actions of these individuals in the entire area of discrimination and racism to insure that improper actions and communication do not take place. The key is to make everyone involved, employees and volunteers, managers and nonmanagers, aware of what is expected in terms of actions and attitude and that improper behavior (overt or covert) will not be tolerated, and that all complaints will be thoroughly and impartially investigated.

Many companies expect a great deal of litigation as a result of the action of the 3rd Circuit Court of Appeals. The response from many companies has been to formally communicate with their employees warning them of the law and the need for a nondiscrimination atmosphere in the workplace. Others have begun to offer sensitivity training for their employees, including supervisors and managers (Jones, 1996).

Concept 349: Women and Men May Be Offenders as well as Victims in Respect to Sexual Harassment—although a Far Greater Number of Offenders Are Men and a Far Greater Number of Women Are Usually the Victims.

Although the vast majority of sexual harassers are men, this is not to say that women are not guilty of such sexual misconduct. Sexual harassment may also involve males harassing males as well as females or females harassing females as well as males.

Concept 350: Sexual Harassment Can Take Place Anywhere, at Anytime.

Sexual harassment can take place at any time. It can take place anywhere: in the workplace, in the school environment, and in recreational settings. Various studies have indicated a very high rate of sexual harassment in the workplace. Some studies indicate that over 50 percent of women in the total workforce have experienced sexual harassment. It is estimated that 20 to 30 percent of female college students experience some form of sexual harassment during their academic careers. A survey released in the early 1980s by the Merit Systems Protection Board (MSPB) indicated that 42 percent of all women working for the federal government indicated that they experienced sexual harassment. This was the same percentage that an earlier study found in 1981.

There is a growing phenomenon in educational institutions involving students suing the school and school personnel for the sexual harassment that they perceive from other students. A mother (Pat Schofield) charged in 1994 that her daughter (Eve Bruneau) was sexually harassed by her sixth-grade class at an elementary school in New York state's South Kirtright Central School district and that the school officials failed to respond in a timely fashion. Specifically, the suit claims that the young girls in the sixth-grade "were often referred to as lesbian, prostitute, retard, scum, bitch (and) whore" (Henry, 1996). The lawsuit claims that the district violated Title IX's prohibition against gender discrimination in schools receiving federal aid. The suit also claims punitive damages in addition to compensatory damages.

The trend is clear. There are increasingly greater numbers of lawsuits as a result of peer sexual harassment in the school setting. Athletic officials and administrators must be extremely careful lest this type of unacceptable behavior take place within the sport environment.

Concept 351: Sexual Harassment Typically Involves "Power" that the Offender Wields over the Victim and Can Happen to Anyone.

Sexual harassment usually involves "power." Such instances typically take place when one person has power over another. The person in authority, the person with the power over another, can utilize this power to intimidate and coerce or reward another individual in a sexual manner by means of such power.

Sexual harassment can happen to anyone. Employers can sexually harass employees. Coaches can sexually harass athletes. Coaches can be sexually harassed by administrators (Lackey, 1990). Bosses can sexually harass their secretaries. Superiors can sexually harass their assistants. Anyone can sexually harass anyone else (Pike, 1994).

Same-Sex Harassment

The United States Supreme Court decided in a unanimous decision in March of 1998 that federal law provides protection against same-sex harassment in the workplace. The court indicated that the "...person's gender or sexual orientation didn't matter. The critical issue under federal civil-rights law, the court said, was whether a person was singled out and discriminated against because of his or her sex" (Same-sex harassment illegal, 1998, p. 1-A). As a result of this court decision, the determination of what is and what is not appropriate behavior in the workplace has become even more complex than before (Nasser, 1998). The court made its decision on the basis of Title VII, which prohibits discrimination (in the workplace) on the basis of race, color, sex, or national origin.

Concept 352: Employers (Individuals and Organizations) Are Responsible and Liable for Actions of their Employees and Nonemployees.

Sport entities must be very careful regarding sexual harassment, not only because such actions are inherently wrong and hurtful to the victims but also because the sport organization (and management) can be held liable for the actions and inactions of its employees. The tort law doctrine of *respondent superior* holds that the employer is liable for all acts of an employee committed within the scope of the employee's employment or job responsibilities (Pike, 1994). In fact, the organization and management can be held liable for the actions (sexual harassment) of nonemployees if such individuals engage in such offensive behavior.

The consequences of a business or organization being found guilty of sexual harassment can be significant. Under current federal law (the Civil Rights Act of 1991) plaintiffs can sue companies with less than 100 employees/workers for up to $50,000 in damages (Workplace, 1992). At larger businesses and organizations successful plaintiffs can collect compensatory and punitive damages of up to $300,000. If related claims, such as assault, battery, or intentional infliction of emotional distress, are involved, there is no limit (Loyle, 1995).

Concept 353: Employers and Managers Need to Create an Environment That Is Free of Sexual Harassment.

Management and/or owners should know of such reprehensible behavior among its employees as well as nonemployees associated with the sport entity, its programs, and its activities. The point to remember is that sexual harassment is not to be tolerated. As a result, concerted steps must be taken to educate individuals in terms of what constitutes sexual harassment, how to deal with such harassment as a victim, and how to prevent such occurrences in the first place (Marchell et al., 1992).

Concept 354: The Existence of Employment Policies Prohibiting Harassment and Discrimination Does Not Guarantee that Such Discrimination, Harassment, or Intimidation Is Not Present or Prevalent.

An integral part of creating a harassment-free work, play, or educational environment consists of appropriate training and education of those individuals associated with the organization or business. A suitable anti-harassment program involving a written policy statement prohibiting sexual harassment is highly recommended. Additionally, a public acknowledgment that the climate within the organization is such that sexual harassment will not be tolerated is also advisable as part of the overall educational and informational efforts on the part of the company or organization. Of course, the essence of any appropriate environment is that there be swift, fair, and just reactions to instances of sexual harassment.

Sexual Harassment within Schools and Colleges: Violation of Title IX

Concept 355: Sexual Harassment Is Now a Violation of Title IX.

Sexual harassment of students is a violation of Title IX of the 1972 Educational Amendments. In August of 1981, the United States Department of Education, Office of Civil Rights (OCR), reaffirmed its jurisdiction over sexual harassment complaints under Title IX. The OCR defines sexual harassment as "[consisting] of verbal or physical conduct of a sexual nature, imposed on the basis of sex, by an employee or agent of a recipient (any educational program or activity receiving federal financial assistance) that denies, limits, provides different, or conditions the provision of, aid, benefits, services or treatment protected under Title IX."

Title IX and Gender Equity

With the enactment of Title IX of the Educational Amendments of 1972 (the Education Amendments to the Civil Rights Act of 1964), which was signed on June 23, 1972, the role of women in competitive sports was changed irrevocably. Specifically, Title IX forbade sex discrimination in educational institutions that received any type of federal funds. The law specifically states: "No person in the United States shall, on the basis of sex, be excluded from participation in, be denied the benefits of, or be subjected to discrimination under any program or activity receiving Federal financial assistance" (Title IX, 44 Fed. Reg. at 71413).

> **Concept 356:** Title IX Affects Every School Sports Program where the School Itself Receives Federal Assistance.

As initially interpreted, this law had a direct effect on the sports program in every junior high, senior high, and college or university in this country that received any type of federal assistance whatsoever. Today, some proponents of gender equity have taken the position that the definitive definition of gender equity is "when either the men's or women's sports program would be pleased to accept as its own the overall program of the other gender" (Herwig, 1993a; Herwig, 1993b).

Competitive Sport Opportunities for Women Prior to Title IX

To better grasp the tremendous impact that Title IX initially had on women's athletics both in high schools and colleges during the past 25+ years, one must understand the status of women's sports prior to the passage of this federal mandate. To put it bluntly, prior to the mid-1970s opportunities for athletic competition for girls on the secondary level were far behind the opportunities available for boys in most schools in this country. At the collegiate level the situation was similarly dismal. Although there were some exceptions, for the most part girls and women were treated as second-class citizens in terms of sport participation opportunities.

Lack of Encouragement Coupled with Outright Discouragement

> **Concept 357:** It Is Hard to Obtain an Increase in Sport Participation when Individuals Are Not Encouraged to Do So or Are Actually Discouraged from Such Participation.

For the most part, girls and women were neither encouraged to participate in competitive sports nor were they financially supported to the degree that the boys and men were at the high school and collegiate levels. Even when sports programs and activities were made available for girls and women, the amount of financial and other types of support provided fell far, far short of what was provided for boys and men in similar situations.

Concept 358: There Were Many Reasons in the Past for the Lack of Competitive Sport Opportunities for Girls and Women.

In many instances girls and women were actually discouraged from seeking additional competitive sports opportunities or from taking advantage of those programs and activities that were available. This was done for several reasons. First, because of the belief that any increase in sport involvement by girls and women might impair or hinder the sports programs for boys and men. The view was that there were only so many sports dollars available and an increase in female sports might mean a corresponding decrease in the financial support of male sports. Second, in some quarters, females participating in competitive sports were viewed as being unfeminine, inappropriate, or even unhealthy. Third, females did not truly have interests in becoming involved in competitive sports. And, fourth, there was no overriding reason, internal or external, to change the status quo.

As a result, opportunities for competitive athletic experience for girls and women were minimal at best, prior to the federal mandate referred to as Title IX. At the collegiate level participation was hampered because of the small number of high school graduates coming to college with prior competitive sport experience. Yes, schools offered intercollegiate sports for women but the number of sports were fewer than those provided for men, and the resources (financial and otherwise) supporting the women's sports were far, far inferior, for the most part, to what was available to men's sports.

In summary, girls in high school and women in college were not given their just due either in terms of opportunities for competitive sports or support, financial or otherwise, for adequate sports programs. The reasons were many and varied but the consequence was the same: Sexual discrimination was pervasive in our schools throughout the country insofar as sports were concerned.

Changes Brought about by Title IX

Title IX, passed in 1972, required that, by 1978, all educational institutions receiving federal aid practice nondiscrimination on the basis of sex (Title IX of the Education Amendments, 1972). One of the largest consequences was the expansion of sport opportunities for women, especially in the area of sport participation (Durrant, 1992). For example, in the state of Indiana the number of female participants involved in interscholastic sports recognized by that state's High School Athletic Association increased from 27,000 in 1972 to over 50,000 in 1992. On the national level, similar gains have been experienced. In 1972 some 300,000 girls participated in organized competitive sports at the secondary level compared to over 1.8 million just 20 years later (Sawyer, 1992). By the 1994–1995 school year the number of girls participating in organized competitive sports at the secondary level was at an all-time high. In fact, 2,240,461 girls were participating during that year (Girls' participation, 1996).

Concept 359: Title IX Has Changed School Athletics in Innumerable Ways.

Similar gains have been realized at the collegiate levels. For example, the average number of women's sports offered by colleges and universities increased from 5.61 per school in 1977 to 7.24 in 1990 (Berg, 1990). During the 1994–1995 academic year there were over 105,532 women participating in organized competitive sports at the collegiate level (Girls' participation, 1996).

However, even the passage of Title IX did not result in total equality, then or today. In fact, the schools of this country were brought kicking and screaming into some resemblance of compliance as a result of Title IX, but certainly not total compliance (Acosta & Carpenter, 1990; Fox, 1992; Acosta & Carpenter, 1992c).

The Challenges of Compliance and Title IX

However, there was still strong resistance to the changes suggested by Title IX. Some of this resistance was subtle. Other instances were not. The attitude held by many athletic administrators is best summarized by the response obtained by a survey of sport departments within small colleges and universities. One of the respondents, in answering a question of whether the respondent's institution was in compliance with all aspects of Title IX, replied: "We are in compliance until someone tells us we are not" (Stier, 1983).

Another challenge associated with Title IX is that an inordinate percentage of athletic administrators in both junior colleges and in smaller 4-year colleges and universities believed that not only were they currently in full compliance but that they had always been in conformity with the mandates of Title IX, even before it was enacted (Stier, 1982–1983; Stier, 1984a; Stier, 1984b). Of course, this was not the case for most schools, regardless of size or level. Nevertheless, some 85 percent of the respondents indicated that for their sports programs, this was indeed the case. Either athletic administrators had faulty memories or they did not understand the full implications and ramifications of the act.

Grove City versus Bell

The teeth were temporarily taken out of Title IX insofar as sports were concerned when the United States Supreme Court ruled on February 28, 1984 that specific programs, not an institution, must receive federal funds in order to fall under the auspices of Title IX. This suit (*Grove City College v. Bell*, 465 U.S. 555, 79 L. Ed. 516, 104 S. Ct. 1211 [1984]) was a result of Grove City College of Pennsylvania challenging the tenets of Title IX. Thus, because practically no athletic department was receiving federal funds directly, the athletic programs were not under the purview of Title IX legislation. Unfortunately, many of the lawsuits that had been filed under Title IX and were in the process of being litigated became moot with the *Grove City versus Bell* ruling.

Concept 360: The Grove City Case Took the "Teeth" out of Title IX.

Closing the Barn Door after the Horse Ran Out

However, this temporary setback to Title IX legislation for equality in sports for girls and women did not curtail the existing opportunities for sport participation for girls and women. It was like attempting to close the barn door after the horse ran out. The tremendous growth experienced by women's sports in the 1970s and early 1980s could not be reversed. In fact, opportunities continued to increase, albeit not at the same rate as prior to the Grove City case.

The Civil Rights Restoration Act

The teeth were put back into Title IX by the Civil Rights Restoration Act of 1987, which was passed by Congress on March 22, 1988 over then-President Reagan's veto. This law restored institution-wide coverage of Title IX, effectively nullifying the Grove City versus Bell ruling. Almost immediately after the passage of this act several law suits were filed or filed again under Title IX. For example, on June 13, 1988, Temple University settled a Title IX lawsuit just three weeks after going to trial. The lawsuit, originally filed in 1980, prior to the Grove City case, charged the school with systematic sex discrimination by its athletic department. As a result of the agreement, Temple University agreed to add two women's sports and to raise its women's athletic participation rate from 34 percent to 43 percent.

> **Concept 361:** The Civil Rights Restoration Act of 1987 Put the "Teeth" Back into Title IX.

Opening the Door to Punitive Damages under Title IX

The Supreme Court made a most important legal decision relating to Title IX on February 26, 1992. The decision (*Franklin v. Gwinnet County Public Schools,* 117 L. Ed. 2d 208 [1992]) resulted from a suit filed by a secondary school student in the state of Georgia who accused a teacher, who was also a coach, of sexual harassment. The Supreme Court ruled in the Gwinnet County case that individuals who file a lawsuit under Title IX are eligible for *monetary damages in addition to having their grievances redressed.* This decision of the court significantly raised the penalty for noncompliance with this law at schools and colleges that receive federal aid by making athletic departments liable for punitive damages if found to be in violation of Title IX (Mauro, 1992).

> **Concept 362:** Now That Monetary Damages May Be Awarded, in Addition to Having Grievances Redressed, It Is Far More Costly to Be Found in Violation of Title IX.

Previously, if schools were found guilt of noncompliance, they were, in effect, slapped on the wrist and told to get in compliance. There was not a great risk in failing to comply with the letter and the intent of the Title IX legislation prior to this latest decision by the Supreme Court (Supreme court rules, 1992). Subsequently, however, there was more motivation for adhering to the Title IX regulations, and that motivation was fear of monetary damages being awarded. The matter of monetary damages also served as a motivating factor on behalf of potential plaintiffs and attorneys. Now, lawyers would be able to secure potentially greater financial awards for their plaintiffs (and for themselves) as a result of favorable Title IX verdicts than in the past.

On February 27, 1992, the United States Office of Civil Rights rendered a decision in which it found that Brooklyn College (a division I NCAA institution) was in violation of 10 of the 13 areas that comprise Title IX compliance. This investigation resulted from a complaint filed some 14 months earlier (December 1990) by athletes and staff at that institution. As a result of this ruling, the school agreed to remedy the discrimination but, shortly after, elected to eliminate all collegiate competitive sports and disbanded the entire athletic department for the next year.

On March 11, 1992, the NCAA released its long-awaited Gender Equity Survey, revealing that after some 20 years of Title IX, college men still receive twice as many athletic scholarships as women at NCAA institutions. Additionally, while women make up 50 percent of the NCAA institutions in terms of full undergraduate population, they receive only 20 percent of athletic budgets and a measly 18 percent of the recruiting budget.

Determining Gender Equity: Three Criteria for Determining Compliance with Title IX

Today, there are three generally accepted criteria by which compliance may be determined in terms of competitive athletics. The three-pronged test emanated from the United States Office for Civil Rights and should be utilized to determine whether gender equity exists in competitive athletics in any given school or institution. Meeting any one of these criteria would be prima facie evidence of compliance with Title IX and meeting the benchmark for gender equity in the competitive sports arena (Frankel, 1992).

These benchmark tests or criteria include: (1) providing opportunities for competitive sport participation for women and for men that are substantially proportionate to their respective rates of enrollment within the school, (2) showing a history and continuing practice of expanding opportunities for the underrepresented sex, (3) actually proving that the organization has truly accommodated (fully and effectively) the interests and abilities of the underrepresented sex (Achieving gender equity, 1994; Lederman, 1995). The proportionality concept is an important one in that "it means that the gender ratio of the student body should be a benchmark for participation opportunities for athletes" (Herwig, 1993a).

> **Concept 363:** Compliance with Title IX Depends on More Than Having the Appropriate Number of Teams for Both Sexes.

There are nine areas or components that should be examined in the athletic arena in terms of determining whether a school or department is in compliance with Title IX: (1) effective accommodation of student interests and abilities, (2) provision of equipment and supplies, (3) scheduling of games and practice times, (4) travel and per diem allowances, (5) opportunity to receive coaching and adequate compensation of coaches, (6) provision of a locker room, practice, and competitive facilities, (7) provision of medical and training facilities and services, (8) publicity, and (9) provision of support services (Paling, 1996).

The Elementary and Secondary Education Act

Title IX gained even more teeth when, on October 5, 1994, Congress passed and President Clinton, on October 20, 1994, signed, the Elementary and Secondary Education Act (more commonly known as "Improving America's Schools Act"). This law included the "Equity in Athletics disclosure" amendment that now required colleges to disclose information on their intercollegiate athletics programs relating to gender equity, starting October 1, 1996.

"Similar to the Student Right-To-Know Act, which requires colleges to release information and publicize graduation rates of their students participating in their intercollegiate athletic programs, the Elementary and Secondary Education Act mandated institutions that take part in the federal student-aid programs and have intercollegiate athletics to provide an annual report containing specifics about opportunities and benefits provided to male and female student-athletes" (Gender equity, 1995, p. 7). The reports are to contain, among other data, the following information:

1. Number of students by sex;
2. Number of participants by sex;
3. Total operating expenses for intercollegiate athletes;
4. Gender of all head and assistant coaches;
5. Amount of money spent on athletically related student aid;
6. Recruiting expenses;
7. Coaches' salaries for all men's and women's teams (varsity and subvarsity).

The result of this 1994 law has been greater scrutiny on the spending for both men's and women's athletic programs at the collegiate level. High school students seeking an appropriate collegiate setting to become involved as a student and as an athlete now have much more data on which to base the important decision as to where they should go to college.

A long, drawn-out court fight over Title IX was waged between April 9, 1992 and April 21, 1997 by Brown University, which contested the charge that it was violating Title IX. The initial suit was brought against Brown University by members of the school's gymnastics and volleyball teams alleging gender discrimination because, in May of 1991, the university had eliminated funding for these two sports in addition to men's water polo and golf. The school cited financial problems and a need to reduce almost a $1.6 million athletic budget deficit as a rationale for the withdrawal of financial support of the four teams.

After a long series of events and legal decisions (injunctions, charges, decisions, appeals, and a partial settlement) the United States Supreme Court was asked by Brown University to hear the case. The result was that on April 21, 1997 the Supreme Court, without comment, let stand the lower court ruling that determined that Brown University (Rhode Island) had indeed discriminated against women in its varsity sports offerings (Mauro, 1997; Brady & Wieberg, 1997).

Brown University was accused of lacking gender parity in light of the fact that only 38 percent of its varsity sport participants were women although women comprised 51 percent of the total student body. It should be noted that the U.S. Supreme Court's action was not a ruling but an act that let a lower court's ruling stand. Similarly, this act affects Brown University and other educational institutions in those states covered by the appeals court in this case, including Maine, Massachusetts, Rhode Island, New Hampshire, and Puerto Rico.

However, every educational and sport leader has been watching this case with great attention because of its potential fallout. Perhaps the real significance of this ruling was expressed by NCAA official Janet Justus who observed, "This is a significant moment in the history of Title IX. With this decision, I think way more schools are going to come in compliance" (Mauro, 1997, p. 1-A).

Violations of Civil Rights: Equal Opportunities in Sport

Equal opportunities in sport continue to be a controversial topic at all levels of competition. In 1994 12 girls who played slow-pitch softball for high schools in the state of Kentucky sued that state's high school athletic association, arguing that the Kentucky High School Athletic Association and the Kentucky State Board of Elementary and Secondary Education denied girls equal athletic opportunities. The sixth U.S. Circuit Court of Appeals ordered a federal judge to reconsider the girls' claim that the state sanctioned fewer sports for girls than boys and improperly refused to sanction girls fast-pitch softball, preventing them from competing for college scholarships (Jurisprudence, 1994).

The 14th Amendment to the United States Constitution: Equal Protection

The 14th Amendment to the United States Constitution provides equal protection to the citizenry. This equal protection in the courts in which individual athletes are concerned has tended to result in the courts finding for females whenever there has been only one team offered by a school and that team has been for males. In these cases, girls and women have generally been allowed to join the boys' or men's teams. However, the opposite has not usually been the case, generally because of what the courts have felt would be unfair advantages which would accrue to the male should this individual be allowed to join an otherwise all female team (Durrant, 1992).

Americans with Disabilities Act of 1990 (ADA) PL 101–336, Title 42, U.S.C. 12101 et seq: U.S. Statues at Large, 104–327–378

Viewed as the most significant civil rights legislation in 25 years, the Americans with Disabilities Act of 1990 (ADA) was signed into law on July 26, 1990, by then-President George Bush. The final rules were published by the Department of Justice, the entity that has the authority and responsibility to interpret the ADA guidelines. Many advocates for the disabled or challenged feel that this statute will have the most impact on companies and organizations in this country since the Civil Rights Act of 1964, which prohibited discrimination based on race, color, gender, religion, or national origin. The ADA, coupled with the Architectural Barriers Act, which required that all facilities built with any percentage of federal monies must be accessible to the challenged, will help insure greater accessibility for the disabled in this country (Block, 1995).

Concept 364: The Americans with Disabilities Act of 1990 Is Viewed as the Most Significant Civil Rights Legislation in the Past 25 Years.

Reiner (1994) indicates that the intent of the Act is not to separate but to include, integrate, and mix those individuals without disabilities and those individuals who are challenged. The ultimate goal is to dispel stereotypes and prevent wholesale discrimination based solely on any person's disability.

Impact of the ADA

In the United States approximately 17 percent of the total population can be classified as having a disability. That means that 1 in 6 of our citizens are disabled. The result of the act is that some 43 million Americans will have adequate access to goods, programs, and services of all types (Nasser, 1993).

This far-reaching statute affects almost all companies (over 4 million) and organizations in this country, including schools (Hall, 1993). The only groups exempted from the ADA guidelines are religious organizations and entities controlled by religious organizations. Nevertheless, many such organizations have voluntarily agreed to abide by the ADA law (Munson & Comodeca, 1993; Block, 1995; Epstein, McGovern, & Moon, 1994).

ADA as an Extension of Section 504 of the Rehabilitation Act of 1973

The ADA was indeed a significant and sweeping piece of civil rights legislation. The act extended Section 504 of the Rehabilitation Act of 1973 to the private sector. This law (Section 504) specifically states: "No otherwise qualified handicapped individual in the United States shall, solely by reason of his handicap, be excluded from the participation in, be denied the benefits of, or be subjected to discrimination *under any program or activity receiving federal financial assistance*" (emphasis added). In essence, discrimination based on physical or mental handicap is prohibited in all programs receiving any type of federal financial assistance.

Section 504 prohibited federal agencies and organizations that received federal funding from discriminating against people with disabilities. The private employer section of the act became law in July 26, of 1992. The ADA became effective in July 1993 requiring companies with at least 25 employees to accommodate workers with disabilities. For employers with 15–24 employees, the act became law in July of 1994. In 1994, the law was extended to employers with at least 15 workers (Lawlor, 1993).

The Scope of the ADA

The ADA prohibits discrimination on the basis of any disability. The impact of the law affects almost every organization in this country and many aspects of life in the United States, including where we work, what facilities we utilize, how we live, how we travel, what programs and activities are available to us both at work and at play. Its impact is significant and its scope is extensive. The ADA strictly prohibited discrimination on the basis of disability in terms of employment, public accommodations, and public services, including public transportation (ADA Compliance Guide 1992; Hall, 1993; Nasser, 1993; Block, 1995).

Concept 365: The ADA Prohibits Discrimination on the Basis of Any Disability.

Definitions

The ADA act uses the broadest meaning of *disability*. Specifically, a person with a disability is any individual with (1) a mental or physical impairment that impedes or hinders one of the major life functions; (2) who is regarded as having a disability or impairment; or (3) who has a history of disability or impairment. A disabled individual is someone with a physical or mental impairment that limits one or more "major life activities," or who has a record of such impairment. One cannot be discriminated against because of past problems or disabilities. The major life activities include walking, seeing, hearing, speaking, breathing, learning, or working. Thus, "the disabled" becomes an all-inclusive term covering a broad range of circumstances, including the wheelchair-bound, hearing impaired, visually impaired, and mentally impaired.

Individuals who are currently involved in drug rehabilitation programs are considered disabled under current ADA guidelines. Those who would not be considered disabled include kleptomaniacs, transsexuals, drug abusers, sex offenders, and those who practice voyeurism.

The Five Sections within the ADA

The ADA has five specific chapters or "titles" in the statute. *Title I* forbids discrimination in employment in the private and public sector against individuals with disabilities (Munson & Comodeca, 1993; Block, 1995). The Equal Employment Opportunity Commission (EEOC) enforces Title I of the ADA.

Hiring, firing, not rehiring, promotion, and all other employment practices fall under the jurisdiction of the ADA. Although companies do not have to hire the disabled, by the same token one cannot discriminate against the disabled candidate. That means one cannot fail to hire a person merely because that individual has a disability covered by the ADA legislation. Medical questions may not be asked of potential employees, nor can one ask about absenteeism, accident claims, or medical problems at previous workplaces.

Employers need to be sure to define the essential functions of any job vacancy so that a disabled person is not eliminated from consideration because of the disability when a reasonable accommodation would enable that person to handle the duties and responsibilities of the position. To determine whether a person is indeed qualified and competent to perform a specific job or assume a certain responsibility, the potential employer must identify, in advance, the "essential" and "nonessential" elements or functions of the job or position. Then there can be an honest and realistic determination as to whether the individual can or cannot perform the job. For those individuals who become disabled while in the employ of a company, that person shall be provided reasonable assistance so as to be able to continue such employment.

Concept 366: Employers Need to Define the Essential Functions of Any Job Vacancy.

There is a need for supervisors, administrators, and staff to update organizations' and companies' policies, procedures, and practices, to provide auxiliary aids, and to improve accessibility unless that would impose an undue (financial or otherwise) hardship on the organization or company. Policies need to be established whereby individuals can notify the organization of the person's disability and special needs. There should be a trained and interested compliance officer appointed, much like the Title IX compliance officer or the Section 504 compliance officer. Additional suggestions pertaining to the hiring process include:

1. There is a need for clear and explicit job description for each position within the organization;
2. All job descriptions should have defined essential and nonessential functions;
3. Be prepared, in advance, to be aware of the type of reasonable accommodations that could be provided for the position;
4. All personnel policies should be reviewed in light of the ADA act;
5. Safety procedures and accident procedures (including first aid, evaluation, transportation, etc.) should be established and/or renewed;
6. All personnel should be trained in the intricacies of the ADA in an effort to keep all staff and administrators up-to-date with local, state, and federal rules and regulations;
7. All legal and pertinent ADA rules and regulations should be prominently posted;
8. There should be an oversight review by an impartial individual(s) of each search process for new vacancies;
9. Search committees and administrators involved with each search for a vacancy should be "charged" with their mission by a trained and competent personnel staffer;
10. Make sure that individuals who are disabled are made aware of the vacancy or vacancies.

Title II became effective January 26, 1992. It applies to all state and local governments, their departments and agencies, and any other special purpose districts of state or local governments. This section prohibits discrimination by public services and on public transportation. In short, this section of the ADA prohibits governmental entities from preventing or discouraging individuals with disabilities from participation in state and local governmental activities, programs, services, or the use of transportation. This also covers public entities such as local governments sponsoring community youth sport programs and interscholastic sport programs (Reiner, 1994).

The reality of the Act necessitates that selected public sites must be accessible to the disabled. "This means that elevators, ramps and wheel-chair-height fare machines are made available" (Hall, 1993, p. 7-A). The consequences are that more and more organizations are going to have disabled individuals attending private and public facilities, programs, and activities because they will have access to transportation as never before.

Title III is that section that deals with the complete, full, and equal use by the disabled individual of goods, services, programs, activities, facilities, privileges, and advantages of any facility or site that is owned, leased, rented, or operated by a private entity and is available to the public. This involves almost every sporting entity in the country, including private entities, such as the YMCA and Little League of America, that are open to the public. *Public accommodation* is an umbrella term that includes stadiums, auditoriums, convention centers, gymnasiums, ballparks, recreation centers, and the like.

Concept 367: The ADA Requires Sport Entities to Allow the Disabled to Participate in Appropriate Athletic and Recreational Programs.

The legislation also requires sport organizations to allow participation by disabled persons in appropriate sport programs. It is unlawful to discriminate against disabled individuals and prohibit them from participation unless their involvement would result in the likelihood of dangers to others, participants and/or spectators. "In order to justify exclusion, the athletic program would have to show that the likelihood of injury is much greater than in the normal course of participating in a program" (Munson & Comodeca, 1993). In recent years there has been little reluctance on behalf of school-aged athletes and their parents to sue for the right to have exceptions to state eligibility requirements because of the young athlete's disability (Cohen, 1995).

In these cases reasonable accommodations must be made for the disabled individual that would not disrupt the program or significantly distort the activity. However, the interpretation of what constitutes "reasonable accommodations" can differ significantly. So too, how one defines what constitutes a significant disruption of the sport activity is open to varying interpretations. The law requires that the disabled must be accommodated in a fair, equal, and appropriate manner. When there are disagreements in terms of what is fair, equal, and appropriate in light of "reasonable accommodations " without "significant disruption" of the actual activity, the disagreement may very well find itself in a court of law. At the federal level, the Justice Department is assigned as the enforcement arm of the government for this particular section.

The ADA and Its Impact on Existing and Renovated Facilities

Concept 368: The Application of ADA Regulations Is Different for New, Existing, and Renovated Structures.

In terms of facilities, all new construction and significant alterations of public accommodations must adhere to current ADA standards and guidelines. The regulations are different for (1) new structures, (2) existing structures, and (3) those which receive major overhauls or are otherwise significantly renovated. "For existing facilities, the law is less clear—but...The rule states that entities must remove all architectural and communication barriers to disabled access that are structural in nature; this applies only where removal is 'readily achievable,' which is defined as removal that is easy to accomplish and can be carried out with little difficulty or expense" (Munson & Comodeca, 1993, p. 16). The bottom line is that barrier removal in existing facilities need not require a great deal of effort or expense. The rule is to use common sense.

Concept 369: "Use Your Common Sense" Is the Rule of Thumb when Renovating Existing Structures (in Light of the ADA Laws/Regulations).

It is interesting to note that not only owners of facilities but also tenants are held responsible for seeing to it that all areas within a facility where public accommodations and public services are provided are accessible for the disabled. There is no justification for failure to adhere to the ADA regulations.

Some of the areas that should be closely examined to see that accessibility is available and meets ADA standards include: parking lots, sidewalks, ramps leading to doors and the entrance to buildings, door sizes, interior mobility within the facility, front desks, restrooms (wider stalls and grab bars), concession areas and vending machines, accessibility to telephones, water fountains, signs, Braille dots, raised letters signage, removal of obstructing furniture and objects, elevators, seating availability, size of aisles, availability of wheelchair spaces, seats with removable aisle-side armrests, elevators, and guest rooms, among others (*The Voice,* 1994).

"If possible, seating should be dispersed throughout the seating area, provide lines of sight, and choices of admission prices comparable to those for members of the general public, adjoin an accessible route of egress in case of emergency, and permit individuals to sit with family and other friends" (Munson and Comodeca, 1993, p. 16). The goal is to enable the disabled to gain access to the building or facility, have mobility within it, and be able to view and/or participate in the programs or to receive the goods and services available there. To accommodate the disabled, organizations may need to remove or alter any obstacles that would prevent the individual from having access to the stadiums, courts, fields, rest rooms, and locker rooms that are accessible to the general public (Munson and Comodeca, 1993).

Concept 370: Changes in Existing Facilities Need Only Be Made if They Are "Readily Achievable."

Title IV deals with telecommunication services. Those with disabilities of hearing and sight are most affected by this section of the Act. It requires telephone relay services for persons who are deaf and telecommunications must be accessible to those who are hearing impaired. A quote from the Act itself states: "(a) A public entity shall take appropriate steps to ensure that communications with applicants, participants, and members of the public with disabilities are as effective as communications with others" (Wentzel, 1994, p. 16-A). Employees who develop a disability may ask for a reasonable accommodation.

The final chapter of *Title V* is a general category or section dealing with housekeeping tasks—for example, the determination of exceptions to the Act, the awarding of attorney fees, and the various responsibilities of Congress and how the Act itself may be amended (Munson & Comodeca, 1993).

Challenges to the ADA Act as Written

One of the perceived problems with the ADA act as it was written was its lack of specificity. ADA is deliberately broadly written. As a result it will be up to the courts to provide specifics of the law and to define the exact boundaries, the essence of the act. The fact that the ADA is subject to various interpretation is a land mine waiting to be stepped on. The courts will be needed to guide both organizations and the disabled to maneuver their way through this minefield.

One of the results of the lack of specificity for sport organizations and schools is the extensive litigation that schools and organizations are being subjected to. Cohen (1995, p. 34) complains that people are out in the communities "fighting because of an inarticulate law, passed by Congress, that wasn't explicit in its intent and coverage, and is costing us a lot of time and money and aggravation." The reality of the situation is that the ADA is couched in vague terms, leaving to the Equal Employment Opportunity Commission (EEOC) and the courts the responsibility of defining them.

This can be seen in the tremendous number of complaints (11,550) implemented since July 26, 1992, the date that ADA became effective for the private employer section of the act and only 12 months later, in July 1993. However, attorney general Janet Reno has gone on record as stating that "knowing its requirements is a key to compliance" (Dillon, 1993). Reno also indicated that one of the more significant results of the act will be to not only remove the physical barriers for our citizens of all ages but also to reduce and remove social barriers.

In an effort to help define specific sections of the Act relating to facilities and accessibility, Reiner (1994) cites the Architectural Transportation Barriers Compliance Board, more recently referred to as the Access Board, which worked on developing a clearer definition of how the ADA applies to public and private recreation facilities. The Access Board may be contacted for an updated ADA publication checklist by calling 800-USA-ABLE.

Reasonable Accommodations Required by the ADA

Facilities and activities must be available and readily accessible. However, in terms of employment, this does not mean that special accommodations are needed to make an unqualified person qualified. However, employers must be able to modify work equipment or to secure such items. They must adjust work schedules and make existing facilities accessible for the disabled. The act requires that reasonable accommodations be made depending on each individual's specific disability. As defined by the Equal Employment Opportunity Commission (EEOC) regulations, a "qualified individual with a disability is someone able to perform the 'essential functions' of a job, with 'reasonable accommodation.'"

Although the act does not specifically address how the facilities or programs are to be made accessible nor define what "reasonable" is, it does mention that there should not be an undue burden on the organization. An undue burden is defined in the law as "an unduly costly, extensive, substantial, disruptive, or, one that will fundamentally alter the nature of the program." Many experts have voiced the opinion that most commercial organizations can make their facilities accessible for less than $500.

Penalties for Violating ADA

There are civil and punitive damages that can be administered for violations of the Act. Fines of not more than $50,000 for an initial violation and $100,000 for subsequent infractions may be levied. In addition, individuals can seek temporary restraining orders or permanent injunctions through the court system. However, only those individuals whose civil rights are being violated can bring suit under the ADA. Others cannot do it on their behalf.

In terms of employment, violation of the ADA allows the injured party to receive back wages and reinstatement to the position the person previously held or had applied for. Then-President Bush signed a new civil rights act in November of 1991 that provides for punitive damages of up to $300,000 on the basis of "pain and suffering." Individuals bringing complaints under the ADA act may sue to insure that their rights are respected under Title II of the Act and are entitled to receive the same relief as provided under Section 504 of the Rehabilitation Act of 1973, including reasonable attorney's fees (Reiner, 1994).

The Attorney General of the United States may initiate, under Title III of the ADA, a civil action if it is determined that there has been a consistent pattern or practice of discrimination in equal employment opportunities or in accessibility to facilities, services, and programs on the basis of a disability.

Additional Information: ADA

Interested professionals and/or those with disabilities may secure additional information or submit a complaint by contacting the Office on the Americans with Disabilities Act, Civil Rights Division, U.S. Department of Justice (Hot Line: (202) 514–0301 or (800) 514-0301) or the Equal Employment Opportunity Commission, (800) 669–4000.

Occupational Safety and Health Administration (OSHA, 29 U.S.C. Sec. 651)

The Occupational Safety and Health Administration (OSHA) was created in 1970. Its purpose is to protect the health and welfare of employees by insuring that safe and appropriate physical environments are provided in the workplace (Fisher, 1996). The goal is to provide a safe and wholesome workplace for individuals of all ages. OSHA is concerned with preventing accidents in the workplace, insuring that safe work environments are provided, that employees are adequately trained in areas of safety, and that appropriate accident and follow-up procedures and policies are in place. Toward this end, OSHA requires covered companies, businesses, and organizations to prepare written programs relating to safety and to establish policies, procedures, and practices regarding safety precautions and plans of action in the event of injury or accident.

Concept 371: Sport Leaders (and Organizations) Are Held Accountable for the Safety and Welfare of Their Employees As Well As Volunteers in the Workplace.

A wide range of areas within various businesses and companies (both profit and non-profit) are covered by the OSHA rules, regulations, and standards, which have been established to cover various types of work sites, including public and private schools (all levels), and the private business sector. Noncompliance can be especially costly to those businesses and organizations that are found guilty, with fines up to $70,000 levied against violators of the law (O'Leary, 1995).

Concept 372: OSHA Affects a Wide Range of Areas within Businesses and Organizations.

In the sport world, OSHA affects a wide range of areas within the organization, from equipment management (the handling of blood-soaked or bloodstained laundry) to operations of facilities, such as pools, spas, whirlpools, and concessions, among others. In terms of dealing with blood-soaked or stained laundry, sports managers need to be aware of and follow the stipulations and standards established by the Public Employees Risk Prevention Act passed by Congress in July of 1994. This law requires employers to establish policies and procedures for their employees who may be exposed to blood or other potentially infectious materials on the job.

Federal, State, County, and Municipal Laws and Regulations

There are numerous laws, ordinances, rules, statutes, and regulations at the federal, state, county, and municipal levels that have both direct and indirect impact on any number of sport organizations and their respective activities. Some of these regulations have to do with securing permissions or permits to be allowed to do something. Some relate to insurance coverage, while others concern health matters. Still others are associated with tax laws.

Concept 373: Sport Programs and Organizations Must Always Be in Compliance with All Applicable Laws, Regulations, Rules, Ordinances, and Statutes; to Be Otherwise Is Like Shooting Oneself in the Foot.

The important thing for sport managers and leaders to remember is that all applicable laws must be adhered to—both in terms of the letter of the law and the intent of the regulation. It is imperative that organizers and administrators not attempt to shirk their responsibility by disregarding the existence of such rules, laws, and regulations. Failure to abide by existing and applicable rules, laws, and regulations can have disastrous results for the sport leaders, the sport organization itself, and for the public or patrons who are involved with the activity or program.

Concept 374: There Is Never an Acceptable Reason for Failure to Be in Compliance with Appropriate Laws, Rules, and Regulations.

There can be no justification for failing to be in compliance with applicable rules and regulations—period. If the sport administrator was not aware of such laws or regulations, the individual should have been aware, period. And, if a sport administrator was aware of such regulations but nevertheless ignored them or failed to take appropriate positive action, that individual acted in a totally irresponsible fashion because of the person's failure to do what is right, what is required, what is necessary.

Federal, State, County, and Municipal Tax Laws and Regulations

The tax codes for U.S. citizens are very complicated. For businesses, including sport businesses, the situation can sometimes be even more complicated and intimidating. There is a wide range of tax laws at the federal, state, county, and municipal levels that sport leaders must be cognizant of.

Additionally, many sport entities are faced with the question of whether or not to apply for official federal not-for-profit or nonprofit status with respect to the Internal Revenue Service (IRS) and their own state tax code. This decision is one that must be answered on an individual case-by-case situation, taking into account a multitude of facts and factors. Nevertheless, the decision must be made whether to apply for tax-exempt status if the sport organization is eligible for such a classification. In this respect, it is well to seek the advice of qualified counsel.

Federal, State, County, and Municipal Alcohol and Gambling Laws

As is the case with tax regulations and laws, there are statutes governing the sale and use of alcohol and gambling (games of chance) activities at various governmental levels. Sport leaders must be sure that the appropriate rules and regulations are strictly adhered to due to the very nature of alcohol and gambling, coupled with the potential for lawsuits arising from incidents related to the misuse of alcohol and inappropriate gambling activities.

Accounting Rules and Regulations

The area of business affairs/financial accounting is one that can involve many complicated issues for some sport entities, while others can be the very model of simplicity itself. The more complicated the sport operation is the greater the likelihood that professional accounting services will be needed. When in doubt always consult with an experienced and knowledgeable accountant or financial adviser.

Behind the "action"—organization is a must.

Health Regulations and Rules

There are numerous health rules, regulations, and laws in addition to ADA and OSHA that can have a significant impact on sport organizations. Some of these regulations pertain to how concession stands are to be staffed and operated. Other rules relate to the physical environment of the various indoor and outdoor facilities in terms of fire and safety (including seating capacity, ingress and egress avenues, placement of fire exits, lighting standards, etc.).

Insurance Laws and Regulations

Every sport business or organization needs to be cognizant of insurance rules and regulations as they pertain to the sport entity. Insurance involves not only liability insurance for the organization and its employees, but may also include health insurance, vehicle insurance, and so on.

Concept 375: Sport Entities Must Be Adequately Insured.

In a complicated society sport leaders and managers need to be knowledgeable and understand the terms of various types of insurance policies relating to their organizations. They must recognize whether or not specific policies actually provide appropriate and suitable protection for the sport entity itself, the employees, the participants, and the patrons (customers and consumers).

Adequate insurance coverage is a must, an absolute must. Insurance, by its very nature, provides protection, financial protection for the organization and individuals as well as peace of mind. Financial protection can take the form of providing reimbursement for financial losses as well as protection against successful lawsuits based on accident, negligence, and oversight.

Concept 376: Modern Sport Leaders Are Knowledgeable about Insurance Coverage for Their Organizations, Programs, and Activities.

Managers and administrators must be constantly on the alert that their sport activities, programs, and facilities are adequately protected against financial damages and possible ruin in the event of negative occurrences dealing with people, things, and activities. In this respect, foresight is an integral part of the administrator's repertoire of skills and competencies.

Sport Licensing Laws

More and more sport organizations, such as colleges and universities as well as recreation departments and even some high schools, have joined the ranks of the professional teams in terms of becoming involved in sport licensing efforts. The major reasons for this are simple: to increase the funding base of each organization and to increase name recognition associated with the sport organization.

Concept 377: Increased Income and an Expansion of Name Recognition Places Greater Importance on Sport Licensing Laws.

It is essential that today's sport organization create an identity, a link, between the general public, the fans and supporters, and the sport entity through the use of team mascots, logos, and colors. The individual logo, mascot, and/or symbol that is representative of the sport entity is an essential element in the overall marketing strategy of any organization.

The importance of such symbols cannot be overemphasized. However, just as the creation and use of such logos, mascots, and symbols are important, so too is the protection of the exclusive right to use them by the sport entity and those other organizations that have been given permission (through licensing agreements) to use them.

Sport Licensing Forms the Foundation of the Sport Organization's Marketing, Promotion, and Public Relations Efforts

Concept 378: More and More Sport Entities Are Registering and Obtaining Trademark Registration (Protection) for Their Unique Logos and/or Mascots.

Sport licensing is defined as authorizing, for a specific fee, another organization or company or individuals to become a licensed producer and/or seller of a wide variety of goods bearing a team's or school's trademark, which may consist of a special, unique logo or mascot. Almost anything can be licensed. The Federal Trademark Act of 1946 (known as the Lanham Act) authorized the licensing of characters, sayings, slogans, names, and symbols, as well as athletic logos and mascots. The Trademark Law Revision Act that was passed and signed into law in 1989 updated the Lanham Act.

Concept 379: An Increasing Number of Sport Entities Are Licensing Their Registered Trademarks for Use on a Variety of Goods to Be Sold by Various Vendors and Businesses.

Sport licensing "enables the holder of the trademark to retain quality control of the merchandise bearing the trademark, to enjoy expanded market opportunities, and to realize significant potential royalties from the sale of merchandise bearing the protected trademark" (Stier, 1994, p. 187). *Indicia* refer to those trademarks, names, designs, and symbols that are associated with the holder (the sport organization, the company, or the school) of the trademark.

Concept 380: The Demand to Purchase Sport and Sport-Related Products (Identified with Specific Teams and/or Individuals) by the General Public Has Never Been Greater than Today.

"As the sports industry has grown, so has consumer demand for sports-related items, and so has trademark litigation...Under the Federal Trademark Act of 1946, the sale of goods involving trademarks is prohibited without a licensing agreement if the sale is 'likely to cause confusion in the mind of the consumer about who is sponsoring or producing the goods'" (Wong & Barr, 1991, page 18).

Abandonment of Sports Trademark

Securing the protection of the federal registered trademark protects the school or sports organization from unauthorized use (referred to as a trademark infringement) of the registered trademark, whether it is a logo, mascot, saying, character, symbol, or name.

Concept 381: Holders of Trademarks Must Vigorously Defend Their Right to Use Such Trademarks lest They Be Judged to Have Abandoned Same.

It is imperative that organizations protect their trademarks and not abandon them in the eyes of the law. "Abandonment is one means by which an entity can relinquish rights to a trademark. In the past, courts have decided that abandonment has occurred when a trademark has lost all significance as an indication of its origin" (Wong & Barr, 1991, p. 18). Additionally, abandonment can also result when the organization that holds the trademark fails to defend its right to hold the trademark aggressively against those who might infringe on that right. Failure to defend may lead to abandonment.

Problems with Logos, Mascots, and Trademarks

It has become increasingly important for sport entities to be politically correct. Nowhere is this more important than in terms of the use of nicknames, logos, and mascots. Some traditionally acceptable nicknames, logos, and mascots have now become not only questionable but also offensive.

> **Concept 382:** Some Sport Logos, Nicknames, and Mascots That Have Been in Use for Many Years are Nevertheless Offensive to Some Individuals and Groups within Our Society.

Beginning with the 1970 American Indian Movement, the sports world was made keenly aware of the politically sensitive situation surrounding the use of Indian names as mascots. As a result, several colleges and universities actually changed their logos and/or the names of their mascots. In the 1990s there has been great concern about the use of inappropriate and/or insensitive team names and mascots in the secondary, collegiate, and professional ranks. Today, any decision whether to utilize certain names, mascots, and logos needs to be made not only from a politically correct (public relations) perspective but also from a business and legal position (Cohen, 1993).

> **Concept 383:** Insensitive and Inappropriate Use of Team Logos, Mascots, Nicknames, and Trademarks That Are Offensive, Inconsiderate, and Insulting to Those Individuals and Groups Should Be Discontinued.

Professional teams are also subject to criticism in terms of their logos as well as other actions associated with their teams' names. Witness the Atlanta Braves and the Tomahawk Chop, which became famous (or infamous) during their World Series appearances in 1992 and 1993. Similarly, the Cleveland Indians (with their Chief Wahoo logo) as well as the Washington Redskins have also come under severe criticism for their registered trademark of a Native American.

There continues to be a concerted effort, initially started in the early 1970s, to have all sports teams stop the use of sports nicknames, logos, and mascots that would be offensive to any recognized racial or ethnic group within our society. This is especially so with the Native American population due to the fact that there are so many teams with Indian nicknames, mascots, and logos.

The issue of politically correct nicknames of athletic teams extends to those names that have the word *Lady* associated with the mascot itself. For example, as early as 1987 college women's basketball teams began to remove the word *Lady* from their nicknames. This was part of the gender equity movement that was sweeping the country (Politically correct nicknames, 1996). Some reasoned that because athletic programs did not identify male athletic teams as Gentlemen Eagles or Gentlemen Bears there were no reasons for women's teams to have nicknames such as Lady Eagles or Lady Bears.

Concept 384: Whether the Term *Lady* Is Retained in Women's College Athletic Nicknames Depends on the Circumstances and Situation Associated with Each Institution.

However, not all women's collegiate teams have rushed to remove all such references from their nicknames. In fact, of the 16 teams in the NCAA final Sweet 16 during the 1996 season, one-half still used *Lady* with their institution's nicknames. Supporters of retaining *Lady* in the school nicknames claim that the term provides their women players with an identity. These schools include Tennessee (Lady Vols), Louisiana Tech (Lady Techsters), Texas Tech (Lady Raiders), Penn State (Lady Lions), Stephen F. Austin (Ladyjacks), Georgia (Lady Bulldogs), San Francisco (Lady Dons), and Old Dominion (Lady Monarchs). In fact, one institution, Texas Tech, actually went against the trend in political correctness by changing their nickname from Red Raiders to Lady Raiders in 1990 (Politically correct nicknames, 1996).

The implications of having politically correct nicknames, mascots, or logos for women's teams necessitates that the choice of the sports team nickname, and the process of actually choosing such names, be viewed as appropriate for the team and the sponsoring organization. Similarly, the nickname must accurately and adequately reflect the nature of the team and the institution, and not be offensive to the athletes, the community as a whole, or any specific group of individuals within that community.

Concept 385: Sometimes What May Be Appropriate or Politically Correct for One Sport Organization May Not Be Appropriate or Suitable for a Different Sport Organization—It Depends on the Circumstances Surrounding Each.

The author served as athletic director at the NCAA division III institution, Ohio Northern University, in 1982. There women decided to retain the term *Lady* and to be referred to as the Lady Polar Bears. This reflected the desires of the athletes, the coaches, the alumni, the fans, and the local community. However, when the author moved to the State University of New York–Brockport, the opposite action was taken. At SUNY–Brockport, the women's teams were officially designated as the Golden Eagles and the word *Lady* was officially removed when referring to the women's teams. Again, the reason for this action was in response to the wishes of the athletes, the coaches, the alumni, the fans, and the community.

Sport managers must remain constantly vigilant of any action (conscious or unconscious, deliberate or accidental) that would offend any individual or group of individuals. The concern for managers in sport is threefold. First, there is always the possibility of negative consequences resulting from decisions in a court of law. Second, there can be severe financial consequences as a result of a loss of patronage at specific sporting events. Third, sport administrators must be concerned with doing or not doing things because "it is the right thing to do or the right thing not to do."

Political Correctness in Other Areas of Sport

> **Concept 386:** It Is Imperative to Be Politically Correct in Our Society—Not Just Because Failure to Do So Can Have Severe Consequences, but because It Is the Right Thing to Do.

The words and terms we use as well as the actions we take or fail to take as members and citizens of our society are evidence of and reflective of the attitudes that we possess towards ourselves, others, and our communities. It is imperative that members of any profession, including the sport field, be aware of acceptable and unacceptable behavior.

Today, this encompasses the area of political correctness, a phrase that refers to the actions that are deemed socially acceptable in our society. There are a wide range of actions and spoken words and phrases that in the past might have been acceptable in polite society, but today, with increased knowledge, understanding, and perception of human needs, these same actions and words are deemed inappropriate and, in many cases, actually offensive.

> **Concept 387:** Political Correctness Involves an Attitude As Well As Use of Words and Actions (or Inactions).

It is important for sport professionals to be cognizant of what actions and words are unacceptable in our society because of their offensive nature to some individuals, groups, or to the society as a whole. Failing to use common sense when speaking or in carrying out one's duties and responsibilities can have grave consequences. For example, Jimmy the Greek's insensitive response to a reporter's question as to why African American athletes excelled in sports cost him his lucrative television announcing–commentary contract. Management at the network could not survive the subsequent negative fallout as a result of television replays of his comments.

> **Concept 388:** Misuse or Abuse of Language Can Have Severe Consequences, Personally As Well As Careerwise.

Another example is Marge Schott, the principal owner of the Cincinnati Reds. She was fined and then eventually suspended from day-to-day operations by major league baseball because of her insensitive remarks regarding Hitler and his infamous actions during World War II. Such situations can play havoc with public relations and the marketability of an organization.

Neither ignorance nor forgetfulness are excuses readily accepted by the community at large when it comes to outrageous and insensitive and hurtful remarks and/or actions. This has become increasingly so in recent years with the growing sensitivity on the part of more and more of our citizens regarding politically correct actions and communications.

Concept 389: The Choice of Words Can Indeed Hurt and Harm.

Communication is very important in our society, as well as in the world of sport management. Choosing one's words with care, with foresight, and with an understanding of how these words will affect others is essential.

Nonsexist Use of Language

It is very important that professional organizations, such as sport entities, utilize nonsexist language in all of their written publications as well as over the airways. "Because language plays a central role in the way human beings think and behave, we still need to promote language that opens rather than closes possibilities for women and men" (National Council, 1985, p. 1). The central issue is one of fairness and equality for both men and women.

Concept 390: Nonsexist Language Is Expected of Professionals—Both Verbally and in Written Form.

The goal in the adoption of nonsexist language is to attempt to offer alternatives to traditional usage of words, terms, and phrases that, today, are considered to be sexist and/or detrimental to women in our society. The use of such alternatives is strongly encouraged, in both written and verbal communication.

Problems with the English language include the use of the psuedo-generic *man* as well as sex-role stereotyping. Common problems with the traditional use of *man* are identifying men and women in different ways. Instead, men and women should be identified in the same way; that is, diminutive or special forms to name women are usually unnecessary. Rather, use generic terms such as doctor or actor to include both males and females. Also, such terms as *stewardess, authoress, waitress, coed, lady lawyer,* and *male nurse* should be avoided and in their stead the following should be used: *author, food server, student, lawyer...she, nurse...he* (National Council, 1985, p. 2).

Concept 391: Language That Patronizes or Trivializes Women Is Totally Unacceptable.

It is also important that language not patronize or trivialize women. Nor should language that reinforces stereotype images of either men or women be used. For example, instead of using the statement that "team X has scheduled too many weak sisters," the following should be used: "team X has scheduled too many weak opponents." Another example is the use of "the president of the company hired a gal Friday." This should be changed to "the president of the company hired an assistant" (National Council, 1985, p. 3; Miller & Swift, 1980).

Negative Connotations of Some Words and Terms That Refer to Individuals with Disabilities

The objective is for sport leaders, managers, and administers to create and promote environments that are positive for individuals with disabilities. The environments at work and at play must be conducive to enabling individuals to take advantage of the purposes for which the environment was created or provided in the first place. Frequently, such a positive environment can be greatly facilitated by the usage of correct or appropriate language. "Person first" language is the recommended method of speaking, which means that the individual is emphasized first while the disability (what it happens to be) is second. Thus, an individual who does not have a disability should be referred to as *nondisabled* rather than *normal* or *able-bodied*. Also, the term *handicapped* should not be used when referring to an individual, but it is appropriate when talking about a condition or a physical barrier. For example, the steps are a handicap for John, or Mary is handicapped by the lack of a suitable desk (Person first, 1992).

When dealing with individuals with disabilities, the word *handicapped* is no longer acceptable. In fact, the term *handicapped* originated in Great Britain shortly after the Crimean War, when veterans returned to England with severe injuries. The English Parliament made it legal for these injured veterans to beg on the streets. Hence, the word *handicapped* implies that people with disabilities are being made into beggars (Douglas, 1992).

> **Concept 392:** Although "Sticks and Stones" (Words) May Not Break Anyone's Bones—Carefully Choose Words and the Context in Which They Are Used lest Individuals and Groups Be Injured and/or Offended.

Frequently, political correctness simply means using different words and phrases; affirming rather than negative terms and phrases are the order of the day. When describing individuals with disabilities, it is important that the individual's worth and abilities, not the disabling condition, be the emphasis, be the focus of the words or terms. Examples of affirmative and negative phrases are provided in Table 11.1 (Douglas, 1992).

Problems with Political Correctness

Not all actions on behalf of political correctness are without controversy. Take the Spartanburg (South Carolina) Methodist's diversity plan in regard to the college's efforts to achieve what its leaders refer to as adequate diversity. The school, "claiming its athletic teams should reflect the racial composition of its 1,000-member student body, wants more white players on what has been an all-black men's basketball team" (White, 1996, p. 6-C). With a population of 73 percent white students, 24 percent African American, and 3 percent Hispanic and Asian, the school is committed to diversifying its athletic teams. As a result, the diversity policy regarding the athletic teams went into effect in January of 1996 and one of the consequences was the termination of the head men's basketball coach, Scott Rigot, when he refused to comply. The same thing happened to the women's tennis and soccer coach, Jim Rinker (White, 1996).

TABLE 11.1 Examples of Affirmative and Negative Phrases

Affirmative Phrases	Negative Phrases
person who is blind	the blind
person who is deaf	suffers a hearing loss
person who has multiple sclerosis	afflicted by MS
person affected by cerebral palsy	CP victim
person who has muscular dystrophy	stricken by MD
person with mental retardation	retarded; mentally defective
person with epilepsy	epileptic
person who uses a wheelchair	confined or restricted to a wheelchair
person without disabilities	normal person
physically disabled	dumb; moot
seizure	fit
successful, productive	courageous (implies the person is a hero or martyr)

Concept 393: Not All Efforts to Be Politically Correct Are without Controversy.

The issue raised by this action by this small, two-year college in South Carolina is whether the recent Supreme Court decision outlawing preference according to race is being violated. When asked to comment on this specific controversy, Alex Johnson, a University of Virginia law professor, indicated that he is troubled by the situation. He was quoted in a *USA Today* article (White, 1996, p. 6-A) as saying: "Politically and legally, I think it would be difficult to defend a concept where you hold slots open for people of a certain race...It would be similar to a school setting aside a number of scholarships for blacks." Although the college is a private college, there are very few such institutions that receive absolutely no state or federal support money. And, if Spartanburg Methodist does receive such financial assistance, it runs the risk of violating established law should they actually establish quotas.

Being Cognizant of the Intent and the Letter of the Laws and Regulations Affecting Sport Programs and Sport Organizations

Concept 394: It Is Imperative that Sport Administrators and Managers Be Conscientious in Following All Applicable Laws and Regulations; Both the Intent and the Letter of Such Laws Must Be Adequately Addressed.

Leaders in sport organizations have a very real responsibility when it comes to being knowledgeable of and following the letter and the intent of various laws and regulations.

These leaders also share the responsibility of insuring that their staffs, both paid and volunteer, are also aware of and obey or adhere to such regulations, rules, and laws.

Concept 395: Sport Managers and Administrators Remain Keenly Aware of All Laws and Moral Expectations if They Are to Be Truly Effective and Efficient.

There can be no excuse for not being aware of legal requirements or restrictions. Ignorance is no excuse. One of the major responsibilities of sport managers and administrators, those individuals entrusted with leadership roles within sport entities, is to insure that all aspects of the sport operation be conducted in appropriate ways, that is, in compliance with all requirements imposed by society and by the communities in which the sport entity operates.

Concept 396: Sport Leaders Should Do What Is Right, What Is Just—Not because It Is Required but because It Is Right, It Is Just.

This responsibility extends to areas in which there may not be specific laws or regulations governing some actions or inactions. For example, there may be occasions or situations in which something is legally permissible but morally (sensibly) one clearly understands that something should be done or that something should not be done. Sport administrators, sport leaders, should not hide behind the law, should not use the law (or the absence of a law or regulation) as a shield or an excuse for inappropriate behavior. The key concept is for the sport leaders and sport followers to do what is right, to do what is just—not because it is legally required but because it is right and it is just, period.

Conclusions

It is not only important for modern sport managers to be cognizant of the legal aspects of their organizations and their programs, but it is imperative that actions taken on behalf of the sport entities be in complete compliance with all applicable laws and regulations. Failure to operate within the legal restraints can have disastrous consequences for the sport organization, its programs, and its personnel. Not only can there be severe legal consequences but there can be tremendous negative public relations fallout as well when laws and regulations are not scrupulously adhered to by representatives of the sport entity. In terms of the legal aspects of sport management, it is best to be on the safe or conservative side rather than risk the dangers of being guilty of or being perceived to be acting contrary to the legal requirements.

REFERENCES

Achieving gender equity, a basic guide to Title IX for colleges and universities. (1994). Overland Park, KS: NCAA, pp. 61.

Acosta, R. V. and Carpenter, L. J. (1990). *Women in intercollegiate sport: A longitudinal study—Thirteen-year update.* Unpublished manuscript, Brooklyn College.

Acosta, R. V. and Carpenter, L. J. (1992a). As the years go by—Coaching opportunities in the 1990s. *Journal of Physical Education, Recreation and Dance, 63*(3), 36–41.

Acosta, R. V. and Carpenter, L. J. (1992b). *Women in intercollegiate sport—A longitudinal study—Fifteen year update 1977–1992.* Unpublished manuscript, Brooklyn College.

Acosta, R. V. and Carpenter, L. J. (1992c). *Job status: Reflections of immobility and resistance to job change among senior women athletic personnel.* Unpublished manuscript, Brooklyn College.

ADA compliance guide. (1992). Washington, DC: Thompson Publishing Group.

Administration to suspend 'set-asides,' report says. (1996, March 8). *USA Today,* pp. 1-A, 4-A.

Baize, S. (1995, October/November). Hiring for diversity. *Athletic Management, 7*(5), 40–43.

Beck, J. (1997, April 15). Affirmative action: End, don't mend it. *Democrat and Chronicle,* p. 8-A.

Berg, R. (Ed.). (1990, October). Women in sports—Reluctant role model. *Athletic Business, 14*(10), 15.

Blauvelt, H. (1996, October 2). Women slowly crack athletic director ranks. *USA Today,* pp. 1-C, 2-C.

Block, M. E. (1995). Americans with disabilities act: Its impact on youth sports. *Journal of Physical Education, Recreation and Dance, 66*(1), 28–32.

Brady E. and Wieberg, S. (1997, April 22). Ex-Brown player hails Title IX court move. *USA Today,* p. 3-C.

Calif. proposition motivates foes of anti-bias plans. (1996, November 10). *Democrat and Chronicle.* p. 4-A.

Carpenter, L. (1989). Legal issues: Sexual harassment. *Journal of Physical Education, Recreation and Dance, 60*(4), 18–20.

Clinton to put affirmative action programs on hold. (1996, March 8). *USA Today,* p. 1-A.

Cohen, A. (1993, October). Chief injustice. *Athletic Business, 17*(10), 16, 18.

Cohen, A. (1995, March). Running risks. *Athletic Business, 19*(3), 16, 18.

Dillon, T. (1993, July 26). Reno: Disability law will be enforced. *USA Today,* p. 9-A.

Discrimination because of sex under Title VII of the Civil Rights Act of 1964, as amended; Adoption of final interpretive guidelines. Federal Register, November 10, 1980, 74676–74677.

Douglas, Rick. (1992, October). Speech presented to senior executive service (by the executive director of the President's committee on employment of people with disabilities) and reprinted in Faculty Connection (Fall 1996), pp. 2, 3. State University of New York, Office of Student Affairs.

Durrant, S. M. (1992). Title IX—Its power and its limitations. *Journal of Physical Education, Recreation and Dance, 63*(3), 60–64.

Dziech, B. and Weiner, L. (1984). *The lecherous professor—Sexual harassment on campus.* Boston: Beacon Press.

Epstein, R. S., McGovern, J. N., and Moon, M. S. (1994). The impact of federal legislation on recreation programs. In M. S. Moon (Ed.), *Making school and community recreation fun for everyone: Places and ways to integrate* (pp. 87–96). Baltimore: Paul H. Brookes.

Fisher, K. (1996, November). Slip up. *Athletic Business, 20*(11), 26.

Fox, C. (1992) Title IX at twenty. *Journal of Physical Education, Recreation and Dance, 63*(3), 33, 34.

Frankel, E. (1992, November). Charging ahead. *Athletic Management, IV*(6), 14–19.

Gender equity disclosure act signed into law. (1995, December/January). *Athletic Management, VII*(1), 7.

Girls' participation in sports at an all time high. (1996, Summer). *GWS News, 23*(4), 6.

Gray, R. T. (1995, December) Shaky declarations of independence. *Nation's Business,* pp. 26–28.

Hall, M. (1993, July 22). More access due under landmark law. *USA Today,* p. 7-A.

Henry, T. (1996, October 1). More kids sue school over peer sex harassment. *USA Today,* D-1.

Herwig, C. (1993a, May 19). True equity, gender ratio top report. *USA Today,* p. 1-C.

Herwig, C. (1993b, May 19). Gender task force has more work to do. *USA Today,* p. 8-C

Holland, G. (1996, October 24). Calif. seems poised to vote out affirmative action. *USA Today,* p. 4-A.

Johnson, K. (1995, January 11). Affirmative action next target in California. *USA Today,* pp. 1-A, 2-A.

Jones, D. (1996, October 1). 'Code words' cloud issue of discrimination at work. *USA Today,* pp. 1-B, 2-B.

Jurisprudence. (1994, December 23). *USA Today,* p. 11-C.

Klein, J. (February 13, 1995). Time to pull the plug on affirmative action, *Readers Digest,* pp. 105–107.

Lackey, Donald. (1990). Sexual harassment in sports. *Physical Educator, 42*(2) 22–26.

Lawlor, J. (1993, May 10). Business owners feel weight of laws. *USA Today,* p. 2-E.

Lederman, D. (1995, November 3). Murky clarification. *Chronicle of Higher Education, XLII*(10), A-51, A-52.

Leo, J. (1995, March 13). Endgame for affirmative action. *U.S. News & World Report,* p. 18.

Loyle, D. (1995, January). Sexual harassment: The employer minefield. *Club Industry,* pp. 18–20, 22, 23–25.

MacKinnon, C. (1979). *Sexual harassment of working women.* London: Yale University Press.

Marchell, T., Hofher, J., Parrot, A., and Cummings, N. (1992, November). Prevention by education. *Athletic Management, IV*(6), 44–48.

Mauro, T. (1992, February 27). Sex bias law applied to schools. *USA Today,* p. 1-A.

Mauro, T. (1995, June 13). Court signals 'end for era' in civil rights. *USA Today,* pp. 1-A, 2-A.

Mauro, T. (1997, April 22). Sex equity in sports backed—Court supports Title IX. *USA Today,* p. 1-A.

McWhirter, D. A. (1993). *Your rights at work* (2nd ed.). New York: John Wiley & Sons, Inc.

Meyer, M., Berchtold, I., Oestreich, J., Collins, F., and Chaddock, P. (1981). *Sexual harassment.* New York: Petrocelli Books.

Miller, C. and Swift, K. (1980). *The handbook of nonsexist writing: For writers, editors and speakers.* New York: Harper and Row.

Moon, M. S. (Ed.). (1994). *Making school and community recreation fun for everyone: Places and ways to integrate.* Baltimore: Paul H. Brookes.

Munson, A. L. and Comodeca, J. A. (1993, July). The act of inclusion. *Athletic Management, V*(14), 16–19.

Nasser. H. E. (1993, December 29). Calif. firm sued under disabled rights act. *USA Today,* p. 3-A.

Nasser, H. E. (1998, March 5). Ruling puts workplace behavior under a harsher spotlight. *USA Today,* p. 11-A,

National Council of Teachers of English. (1985). *Guidelines for nonsexist use of language in NCTE publications* (Revised). Urbana, IL: Author.

O'Leary. (1995, February–March). Evading exposure. *Athletic Management, VII*(2), 55–57.

Paling, D. (1996, June–July). High school's Title IX story. *Athletic Management, VIII*(4), 22–24, 27.

Person first: A lexicon affirming those with disabilities. (1992, November). *Brockport Statements.* Brockport, NY: SUNY–Brockport, p. 2.

Pike, L. (1994, August). Harassed: Sexual harassment could prove costly to athletic departments. *Athletic Business, 18*(8), 12–13.

Politically correct nicknames. (1996, March 22). *USA Today,* p. 4-C.

Price, R. (1997, April 9). Preference ban upheld in California. *USA Today,* p. 1-A.

Prop. 209 still under fire. (November 9, 1996). *Democrat and Chronicle,* p. 11.

Reiner, L. (1994, August). The ADA challenge. *Athletic Business, 18*(8), 27–30, 32, 34.

Same-sex harassment illegal. (1998, March 5). *Democrat and Chronicle,* pp. 1-A, 7-A.

Sandler, B. and Associates. (1981). Sexual harassment: A hidden problem. *Educational Record, 20,* 52–57.

Sawyer, T. H. (1992). Title IX: Some positive changes have occurred. *Journal of Physical Education, Recreation and Dance, 63*(3), 14.

Somers, A. (1982). Sexual harassment in academe: Legal issues and definitions. *Journal of Social Issues, 38*(4), 23–32.

Steele, S. (1994). *The content of our character.* Unpublished manuscript.

Stier, W. F., Jr. (1982–1983). Physical education faculty and programs in small colleges and universities. *Physical Educator, 39*(4), 23.

Stier, W. F., Jr. (1983). Athletic policies, procedures, and practices in small colleges and universities. *Athletic Administration. 17*(4), 14.

Stier, W. F., Jr. (1984a, Spring). Physical education and athletic programs on the junior/community college campuses in the United States. *Research Consortium—Research Papers-Abstracts.* American Alliance for Health, Physical Education, Recreation and Dance.

Stier, W. F., Jr. (1984b, December). Survey determines present status of junior colleges. *Athletic Administration, 14*(2), 14.

Stier, W. F., Jr. (1994). *Successful sport fund-raising.* Dubuque, IA: Wm. C. Brown & Benchmark.

Supreme court rules that victims of intentional sex bias can sue colleges for punitive damages under Title IX. (1992, March 4). *Chronicle of Higher Education, XXXVIII*(26), A39.

The Voice. (1994, May). State University of New York, p. 2.

Wentzel, M. (1994, April 3). Getting ready for the ADA. *Democrat and Chronicle,* p. 16-A.

White, C. (1996, July 22). Spartanburg Methodist's diversity plan raises concern. *USA Today,* p. 6-C.

Wong, G. M. (Ed.). (1996, October). Contract law. *Athletic Business, 20*(10), 10, 14.

Wong, G. M. and Barr, C. A. (1991, June). Sports licensing gets a boost from Carolina case. *Athletic Business, 15*(6), 18, 21.
Wong, G. M. and Barr, C. A. (1994, October). Pay attention. *Athletic Business, 18*(10), 10, 14.
Workplace: The cost of sexual harassment. (1992, May). *Inc.*, p. 145.

DISCUSSION AND REVIEW QUESTIONS

1. List possible consequences for sport management personnel in situations where laws and regulations are not adequately followed.
2. Provide examples of sport businesses engaging both employees and independent contractors to perform tasks.
3. Define the essence of grievance procedures and policies within the sport entity for its personnel.
4. Outline the history of affirmative action in this country up to the present time, including the California Initiative (Proposition 209).
5. Cite examples of offensive behavior that might be considered to be sexual harassment of another person.
6. Trace the history of Title IX and indicate what administrators in schools can do to see that their athletic programs are in compliance.
7. Indicate how, with specific examples, the ADA can affect most sport, recreation, and fitness programs.
8. How can OSHA affect the planning, management, and maintenance of sport programs? Provide a specific example in an area of sport, recreation, or fitness and wellness.
9. Why is it important for the sport organization to be concerned with political correctness in terms of decisions and the behavior of its employees and representatives?

CHAPTER

12 Risk Management and Legal Liability

One of the newest and finest basketball facilities in the nation, Gund Arena, Cleveland.

CHAPTER OBJECTIVES

After reading this chapter you will be able to:

- Be cognizant of the potential of litigation for activities sponsored or carried out by sport personnel;
- Understand tort liability insofar as sport organizations are concerned;
- Explain how sport, recreation, and fitness programs should be active in terms of risk management activities and risk management audits;
- Know the role that CAPS play in the area of legal liability and risk management;
- Define the term *negligence* and cite its implications for sport entities and their personnel;

- Differentiate between civil law, criminal law, and contract law;
- List the essentials for proving slander, libel, and defamation of character;
- Illustrate the differences between contributory and comparative negligence;
- Cite common areas of concern for negligence in sport, recreation, and fitness programs;
- Explain the advantages and importance of using a risk statement document and release forms;
- Comprehend the concept of product liability.

Concept 397: Sport Managers Must Be Constantly Aware of the Potential for Litigation as a Result of the Activities They Sponsor or Provide.

It is imperative that the activities and programs of sport businesses be conducted in a safe and secure manner. This is especially true in what has become a truly litigious society. Today, liability is a very real concern for professionals at all levels who are involved in sports, recreation, and fitness programs. "Litigation has become the nation's secular religion and it is practiced regularly against public and private park, recreation, sports, and leisure enterprises" (Kaiser, 1986, p. 1.).

Appenzeller (1993) traces the tremendous increase of sports-related injury litigation, in part, to a 1964 case, *Miller v. Cloidt,* one of the earliest lawsuits that sought damages because of the failure of a physical education teacher to supervise a student properly who was subsequently injured. The fact that the lawsuit resulted in the astronomical and unprecedented sum (at that time) of $1.2 million dollars in damages opened the flood gates for future litigation in the area of sports injuries.

It should be pointed out, however, that the *Miller v. Cloidt* decision was certainly not the first case of lack of supervision of a youngster involved in a physical activity. As early as 1937, a lawsuit was initiated when a youngster in a physical education class received injuries while being supervised by a school janitor (Berg, 1993).

Tort Liability

Tort liability has been the basis for most of the litigation that has been brought before the American courts by injured parties who have been hurt as a result of their involvement in and association with sport, recreation, and fitness activities. "A tort is a private or civil wrong or injury, other than a breach of contract, suffered as a result of another person's conduct" (Wong, 1989, p. 16).

The fundamental objectives of sport managers involved in conducting and supervising various sport, recreation, and fitness programs should be threefold. First, there is the matter of attempting to provide a safe and secure environment, so that few, if any, personal injury accidents occur. It is imperative that the individual sport organization and its agents be able to prevent injuries and harm to individuals associated with the sport entity (Berg, 1996).

Concept 398: Securing Adequate Insurance Protection Is a Key Element in the World of Risk Management.

The second fundamental objective is to protect the sport organization itself and its employees as well as volunteers from the potential threat and consequences of legal action brought about because of a charge of negligence (Cotten, 1993). The third objective is to provide financial protection for itself and its agents (employees as well as volunteers) against findings of negligence in a court of law through adequate liability protection. This third objective can typically be met by securing adequate insurance coverage or protection (Lubell, 1987; Conn & Tompkins, 1994).

Consequences of an Unsafe Environment

The negative consequences of failing to create a safe and secure environment for sport organizations are many. First of all, there is the matter of the actual injury(ies) to the person(s) who sustained the damage as the result of the incident. Second, there is the not inconsequential matter of financial exposure in the event of a successful and substantial lawsuit. And in the climate we live in, this financial risk is often significant. Third, there is the matter of negative public relations and adverse publicity that frequently accompanies an accident and injury.

Concept 399: The Negative Fallout from Serious Accidents and Harmful Injuries Can Be Significant and Varied.

Fourth, there can be an important loss of prestige and tarnishing of the image of the sport organization as a whole as well as for specific personnel, distinct programs, or activities sponsored by the organization. Finally, there can be very real negative consequences resulting from any negative publicity surrounding an accident and injury. For example, fallout from an accident can include reduced patrons and support (funding) by the general public, fans, and constituencies.

All in all, the consequences of accidents and injuries associated with the sport operation can be significant for the organization, for its programs and activities, and for its personnel. The risks are great indeed if care is not taken to prevent those accidents and injuries that are preventable. Providing a safe environment for all associated with the sport entity is one of the top priorities of the sport leader and manager (Hart & Ritson, 1993; van der Smissen, 1990).

Providing a Safe and Healthy Environment

Concept 400: Athletes, Sport Patrons, Employees, and Volunteers Deserve to Have a Safe and Secure Environment and Experience in Their Involvement with the Sport Organization or Business.

No one wants to be responsible for an injury to another human being. Nor would anyone want to be sued for negligence. To prevent such events it is essential that risk management be the concern of every sport manager. Obviously, sport fans, patrons, employees, and volunteers deserve a safe and protected environment and a secure experience in their association and involvement with the sport entity. It is the responsibility of the sport manager to see that such an environment is created and maintained as part of the overall sport experience.

Risk Management

Concept 401: Risk Management Implies Looking at the Worst-Case Scenario.

Sport managers must be constantly vigilant in the area of risk management. Today, risk management is a frequent phrase in both management and legal circles. Risk management implies the evaluation of risks associated with any activity or event and planning for the worst-case scenario. Risk management involves the concept of planning, planning well in advance, in an effort to prevent situations in which accidents will occur and injuries result. It involves the management of acceptable risks with the goal of preventing those accidents and injuries that are preventable. It is always better to prevent accidents than to have to deal with their occurrences and the potential injuries that often result, both from the perspective of financial exposure and from the standpoint of negative public relations.

Concept 402: Risk Management Involves Managing Acceptable Risks with an Eye toward Preventing Those Accidents and Injuries That Are Preventable.

An important element in risk management is education. A national organization called the Coalition of Americans to Protect Sports (CAPS) was established in December of 1987. Originally it was incorporated as Product Liability—Sports but changed its name in 1988. A year later CAPS was authorized to transact business in the state of Florida (on May 3, 1989). CAPS is a not-for-profit service organization and program of the Sporting Goods Manufacturers Association (SGMA). CAPS exists in order to educate the American sports and recreation community about the dangers created by liability and litigation problems facing such programs (Lincoln, 1992).

Today, an important role of CAPS is to conduct risk management education programs (clinics, workshops, and seminars) for a wide range of sport and recreation professionals. The objective of such educational efforts is to make these various sports providers not only aware of possible risk management techniques that might reduce the risk of injury to sports participants, but enable them to take proactive measures to prevent or minimize the number and type of situations that might result in injuries and subsequent lawsuits. The ultimate goal is to encourage healthy and safe sport and recreation activities, thereby reducing "the threat of litigation while maximizing the health of both the athletes and the sports programs" (Dropkin, 1996). The organization provides manuals and videos as well as a variety of brochures that are used by volunteer instructors in the educational programs that are provided throughout the country.

Cotten (1993, p. 58) has identified four specific components of risk management: (1) identifying or revealing real and potential risks, (2) evaluating these risks, (3) determining the acceptable and appropriate approaches in handling the dangerous situation(s), and, (4) attempting to prevent the risky situation(s) from either continuing or coming into existence by implementing and taking timely and effective action that will minimize the possibility of accidents and injuries.

A well-thought-out risk management plan can be an excellent means of protecting a sport, fitness, or recreation entity from litigation and from being found negligent. No plan, regardless of how well-thought-out it may be, can eliminate all risks or injuries or lawsuits. Nevertheless, this fact does not diminish the wisdom and the necessity for creating and implementing a sound risk management plan. The phrase "risk management plan" describes a proactive rather than a reactive posture on the part of the sport leader or manager (Siegenthaler, 1996; Peterson & Hronek, 1992).

Concept 403: Sport Managers and Others in Authority Are Held Responsible for the Actions and Inactions of Their Agents, Employees, and Volunteers.

Within any organization, those individuals having responsibility and authority over different areas have responsibility for those individuals working (either as paid employees or as volunteers) for them within the organization. This assumes that the employees and/or volunteers are performing their official responsibilities as assigned by the higher administration.

Thus, it is imperative that managers and supervisors carefully supervise those individuals who are delegated specific responsibilities and assigned defined duties, because the ultimate responsibility rests with the managerial staff that delegates tasks, duties, and responsibilities to others. Needless to say, the sport organization itself is responsible for the actions of all of its personnel, both paid and unpaid.

Concept 404: Accidents Happen and Injuries Occur—Sometimes They Are Preventable, Other Times They Are Not.

Accidents will happen and injuries will take place, sometimes in spite of all of the care taken and the planning accomplished by highly qualified and dedicated sport managers and sport leaders (Cohen, 1996). On the other hand, preventable accidents and predictable injuries will also take place, unfortunately. There are two major responsibilities facing sport managers in the area of risk management. The first is to attempt to avert the preventable accidents and injuries, and, second, to react in an appropriate and timely fashion to those accidents and injuries that do occur, for whatever reason.

Concept 405: Risk Management Involves Planning to Prevent Accidents As Well As Planning How to React and Handle Accidents Should They Occur.

Smaller markets don't necessarily mean a lack of fan support.
James B. Rombough, Photographer.

Risk management involves the establishment of written plans dealing with the prevention of situations that might lead to injuries and harm to individuals. It involves an assessment of those areas (physical facilities and programmatic domains) in which hazards exist and accidents are more likely to occur, it involves plans for preventing such calamities from occurring, and, should catastrophes actually take place, how to effectively and efficiently deal with such emergencies.

Concept 406: All Employees and Volunteers of the Sport Organization Should Be Actively Involved with Risk Management.

Every person involved in the sport organization, whether employee or volunteer, should be cognizant of the safety issues and factors related to their own areas of responsibility. No one within a sport business or organization is exempt from being actively assertive in the area of risk management. It is everyone's concern. It is everyone's duty and obligation, commensurate with their assigned responsibilities, to play a role in preventing dangerous situations from happening.

Negligence

Within the realm of legal liability, the term *negligence* refers to the failure to act or perform one's duties and responsibilities at the standard (of care) that is expected of a prudent professional in similar circumstances. Standards of care or standards of performance to which sport professionals are held accountable in terms of legal liability or negligence center on what is generally accepted practice and behavior within the profession by one's peers (Gray, 1995).

Concept 407: The Determination of Negligence Is Made in Light of What Is Normally Expected of Professionals (Peers) in Similar Situations and under Similar Circumstances.

"Negligence is the failure to act as a reasonable and prudent professional would have acted in a similar situation, assuming the person possessed similar educational credentials, practical experiences, training and expertise" (Stier, 1994, p. 126). In reality, the question asked is: "What action or behavior would a similarly trained, educated, and experienced professional have taken in a similar situation and under comparable circumstances?"

Civil Law, Criminal Law, and Contract Law

Civil law involves an individual bringing charges against another person or entity, based on a violation of law, seeking to make the injured or damaged party or person "whole" again, to correct the injustice. Compensation can take the form of actual or compensatory damages as well as punitive damages. Compensatory damages seek to make whole, to correct, to compensate for damage, pain, suffering, and loss. The objective of punitive damages is to punish the defendant rather than to merely compensate the injured person. Punitive damages are awarded when the defendant is found to have acted maliciously, fraudulently, or with a wanton or reckless disregard of the rights and feelings of the plaintiff.

A plaintiff who successfully sues may be entitled to be awarded past, current, and future medical expenses. Additionally, loss of earnings may also be awarded the successful plaintiff as well as compensation for loss or impairment of the individual's future earnings. Judgments in favor of plaintiffs may be based on past, current, and future physical and mental pain and suffering. Even injuries or disabilities based on emotional distress can result in sizable monetary awards to the injured (wronged) party.

Preponderance of Evidence in a Civil Lawsuit

Concept 408: To Prevail in a Civil Lawsuit Requires a Different Degree of Evidence than in a Criminal Case.

To prevail in a civil lawsuit it is necessary that there be a preponderance of evidence. This means that the evidence is very convincing and most satisfying in light of the facts revealed. The proof necessary to sustain charges brought by the plaintiff against the defendant is far less in a civil case than is required under criminal law.

Criminal law involves a situation in which the "state" or an individual brings charges against the defendant for violation of the criminal code. The defendant is arrested on the basis of the charges, and must answer the charges in a court of law. To be found guilty of violating criminal law it must be shown beyond a shadow of doubt (beyond a reasonable doubt) that the person was guilty as charged. Sanctions against a convicted defendant can include incarceration. In U.S. justice, the burden of proof is on the prosecutor as the defendant is presumed innocent until proven guilty.

Contract law refers to violations relating to agreements between two parties, individuals as well as organizations. As such, employment contracts, gender equity, and Title IX all fall within contract law. Lawsuits can be brought against sport entities, employers, and employees for alleged violations of laws applying to each of these areas. Thus, it is very important that sport managers fully comprehend the intent and letter of the laws as they pertain to contract provisions in the area of civil rights, such as gender equity and Title IX (Clement, 1993).

Governmental Immunity

The doctrine of governmental immunity is based on the English legal principle that "the king (government) can do no wrong." Thus, some elements of governmental organizations, in some instances, are immune from lawsuits (Berg, 1995a). "Governmental immunity means, generally speaking, that school districts, school boards, or authorities in charge of public schools are immune from tort liability in the absence of legislative enactment or judicial abrogation of the doctrine of governmental immunity" (Baley & Matthews, 1989, p. 40). However, it is important to remember that immunity refers to the corporate entity and does not necessarily provide any protection for employees or volunteers associated with the organization, whether they are managers, supervisors, or lower level personnel.

Determining Negligence for the Sport Professional

How does one become legally responsible or liable for being negligent in the performance of a job? Generally speaking, there are five criteria that must exist for an individual to be held legally liable in the area of negligence. First, the sport organization or professional (employee or volunteer) must owe a *duty* or *obligation* to provide a safe environment for the individual who becomes injured (Carpenter, 1994). Second, this duty or obligation must be breached. That is, there must have been a failure to perform the duty, either by omission or commission. For example, an employee or volunteer must have done something or must not have done something that breached this duty to another person.

Third, what did or did not take place must have been the actual or proximate cause of the damage to the person who was actually injured. Fourth, the injury must have been avoidable, and the injured party must not have been responsible for his or her own injury or predicament. Lastly, there must actually have been some type of injury or damage (physical, emotional, or psychological) to someone (Stier, 1995, p. 416).

Other Forms of Negligence: Slander, Libel, and Defamation of Character

Negligence, an intentional tort or wrong against another person or entity, can also take the form of slander or libel. Slander involves verbal communication while libel occurs in the written word. Defamation law protects against defamation of character. It also guards against an individual's reputation being impinged by untrue, damaging statements, within the public forum (Wong & Covel, 1995b, p. 20). The defense against a charge of libel, slander, or defamation of character is the truth. If a person writes the truth or speaks the truth (and it can be shown to be true) charges of liable, slander, and defamation of character will not be sustained. The key to protecting and defending oneself against such charges is to document everything, to keep detailed records, and to speak and write honestly and truthfully.

Concept 409: Ignorance Is Usually No Defense in Determining Responsibility or Negligence.

Within the realm of legal liability the claim of ignorance is usually no defense against a charge of negligence if one has responsibility for a given situation, because the sport professional, by the mere fact that the person has accepted a particular job or a specific responsibility, should not be ignorant of the commensurate obligations and responsibilities. In short, the person with the responsibility or job should possess the knowledge, wisdom, judgment, and skill to do that job. Ignorance is no excuse.

Concept 410: Negligence Can Result from Acts of Commission As Well As Acts of Omission.

Accidents and injuries (involving negligence) can result from acts of commission as well as acts of omission. An act of commission is when an individual does something that should not have been done and the consequence is that an unsafe situation resulted and an accident took place. The ultimate consequence is that a person is injured. For example, if a concession operation sold meat that was contaminated and the result was that customers became violently ill, the person(s) in charge of the concession might well be determined to have been negligent. Similarly, if defective merchandise is sold or premiums given away at an athletic contest with the result being that several youngsters who played with the items became injured, negligence might well be determined in a court of law.

On the other hand, the failure to do something (omission) can also result in a charge of negligence being determined in a court of law. For example, a liquid was accidentally spilled by a fan or patron on a concrete surface near a concession stand located at a sporting event. The end result is a slippery surface. If this slippery service is not cleaned up in a reasonable time (very, very quickly) and if someone slipped, fell, and injured him- or herself as a result of the liquid, negligence might very well be present.

Another example of omission involves the failure to check, on a timely basis, the structural integrity of the stadium seats. If there is subsequently a structural failure and fans are injured when the bleachers collapse, there might well be negligence through omission.

Defenses against Negligence

In defending oneself or one's organization against a charge of negligence in a court of law, it is necessary to show that one or more of the five essential elements of negligence (listed above) did not exist in that particular situation or case. For example, proving that there was no duty or obligation for the injured person, or, if such a duty did exist, that the duty was not breached; that the act or failure to act did not cause the injury; that the injury was unavoidable, not foreseeable, and not preventable; and/or, that the plaintiff did not receive any real or actual injury.

Concept 411: There Are Numerous Factors That May Negate or Mitigate Charges or Negligence in a Court of Law.

An Act of God

Sometimes accidents just happen. They are truly just accidents, just dumb, freak, chance happenings. They cannot be prevented. They are called *Acts of God*. This is true even when the consequence of the accident is horrific. The determining factor is that the incident or accident is unavoidable because of the forces of nature that could not normally have been anticipated, foreseen, or prevented. These are true accidents, chance happenings, Acts of God.

Assumption of Risk

There are a number of other factors that might negate or mitigate the responsibility and exposure to a finding of negligence. One such factor is referred to as *assumption of risk* (Sharp, 1996). Assumption of risk comes into play when an injured party assumes certain risks when that person willingly becomes involved with or participates in a specific event, or when the person freely enters a designated area or facility (Wolohan, 1995).

There are always some risks that one must assume when involved in specific activities. These are the normal and expected risks that one would normally expect when being involved in specific activities. There are common, customary, and normal risks that come with the territory and individuals voluntarily expose themselves to such risks. However, it is important for sport personnel to remain cognizant that the concept of assumption of risk does not exempt them from liability resulting from actual negligent supervision. Berg (1995a) pointed out that this concept was reinforced in two court cases, specifically the 3rd District Court of Appeal's ruling in the case involving *Zalkin v. American Learning Systems,* 1994, and the 4th District Court of Appeal's ruling in the 1993 case *Nova University v. Katz.*

Contributory Negligence

Contributory negligence is an applicable defense when it can be shown that the person contributed to or was at fault in causing one's own injury. Contributory negligence is more difficult to use as a defense in those cases in which the injured party is very young. If the injured youngster is younger than 8 years of age, there is almost no chance of proving contributory negligence. Even if the injured youngster is between 9 and 13 years of age, it is extremely difficult to use contributory negligence as a defense or mitigating factor because the burden of proof is usually placed on the defendant. However, if the individual is 14 or older, contributory negligence can be more easily shown, especially if the person injured is legally considered an adult.

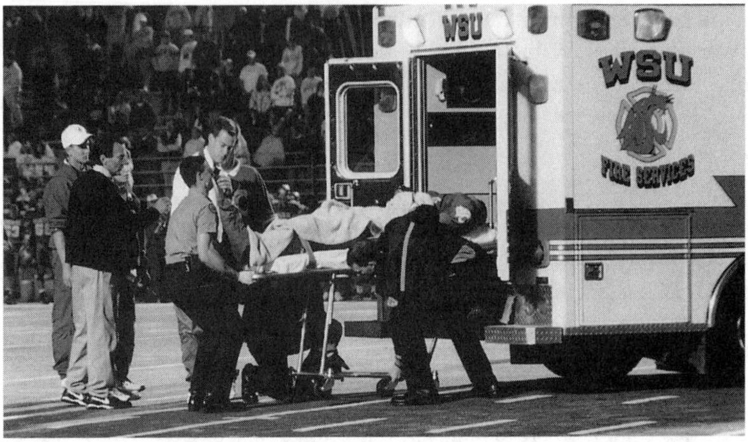

Sport administrators must plan for all eventualities.

Comparative Negligence

Comparative negligence is a term increasingly recognized in more and more states. When used, comparative negligence completely replaces the concept of contributory negligence explained above. The concept of comparative negligence is based on a determination (or comparison) of negligence between the plaintiff and the defendant. A percentage of blame (responsibility) is assigned to both. Thus, the injured party may be found to be only partly responsible for an injury to another party (and assigned a percentage of guilt or responsibility). Similarly, the defendant is also held partly responsible (and assigned an appropriate percentage of guilt or responsibility). In this situation, there is an apportionment of guilt or fault (expressed in percentages) made between the plaintiff and the defendant. Again, the age of the plaintiff plays a significant role in whether the apportionment favors the defendant or the plaintiff.

The Matter of Foreseeability

> **Concept 412:** Foreseeability Is the Key to Preventing Catastrophes in Terms of Accidents and Legal Liability.

Foreseeability is the key to preventing accidents and injuries that might result in lawsuits and determination of negligence (Neal, 1995). Being able to anticipate possible negative consequences is a very important skill for sport managers. So too is the willingness and ability to do all that is humanly possible to prevent accidents (or diminish the consequences) from taking place. Several groups and individuals have suggested common areas of concern for negligence in sport (Promote safer sports for youth, 1993; National Youth Sports, 1993; Stier, 1995), which include:

1. Failure to warn others of possible perils and dangers associated with the activity, equipment, supplies, and facilities (Turner, 1994);

2. Slow, insufficient, or inadequate medical attention (Gray, 1993; Wong & Barr, 1993; Berg, 1994);

3. Inappropriate or unsafe reactions to accidents or injuries (Pike & Rello, 1994; Berg, 1995c);

4. Unsuitable, faulty, or dangerous facilities (Maloy, 1995, 1993; American College of Sports Medicine, 1992);

5. Improper instruction or coaching (Wong & Barr, 1993);

6. Lack of proper supervision of participants (Rauschenbach, 1994; Borkowski, 1996);

7. Improper, defective, or inappropriate equipment (Blauvelt, 1993; Brown, 1993; Wong & Covell, 1995a);

8. Use of defective supplies (*Eye protection recommendations,* National Society, 1981; Kroll, 1990);

9. Lack of safety equipment and warning signs (Turner, 1994);

10. Use of poorly or ill-fitted uniforms and/or protective items such as helmets (Borkowski, 1993a);

11. Lack of staff training and/or coaching education (Sharp, 1993);

12. Having an individual perform an activity that is not appropriate and/or safe for that particular person (for any number of reasons) (Lehr, 1993);

13. Grouping teams by age instead of size in youth sports (Borkowski, 1993b; Lehr, 1993);

14. Inadequate preparticipation physical exams (Edwards, 1993);

15. Presence of attractive nuisances, that is, circumstances or situations that could be hazardous to certain individuals but are very inviting and attractive to them (Berg, 1995b);

16. Inadequate physical conditioning programs and training errors (Gaskin, 1993; Sharp, 1993);

17. Failure to do warm-ups, stretching, and cool-down exercises (Merriman, 1993);

18. Hazardous or unhealthy practice or playing conditions associated with grounds, playing fields, or buildings and other facilities (Herbert, 1995);

19. Improper selection of activities (Adams, 1993);

20. Inappropriate or improper instruction or directions to individuals, including athletes (Gray, 1995);

21. Inappropriate or insufficient teaching, instruction, or coaching decisions (Pine, 1991);

22. Lack of crowd control and protection for spectators, fans, and patrons (Antee & Swinburn, 1990);

23. Having participants engage in inappropriate or unsafe activities (Conn & Tompkins, 1994);

24. Allowing athletes or sport persons to play or participate while injured (Girvan & Girvan, 1993);

25. Travel injuries (Pittman, 1993; Neal, 1995).

Concept 413: Be Especially Cautious when Dealing with Injured Athletes lest Their Injuries Be Exacerbated and a Charge of Negligence Be Determined.

Sport managers must be especially concerned whenever there is a situation in which an athlete has been injured. Once injured, the athlete must be provided quality medical care (Gray, 1993). This includes immediate first aid, evaluation and treatment of the injury, as well as rehabilitation of the injury. An injury to an athlete also requires a careful evaluation of when the injured party may be allowed to return to practice and to actual competition. Far too often the athlete (as well as the coach) is anxious to return to action. Sometimes the athlete returns too soon and the consequence is that the injury is further aggravated and exacerbated.

Informing Participants as to the Potential Risks Involved in Any Activity

Those involved in the sport experience must be well acquainted with the potential risks and dangers involved in the activity. For competitive athletes, for members of a health or fitness club, or for individuals participating in a physical activity as part of a recreation program, this means that they must be adequately forewarned of what might happen to them even if they perform the activity in an acceptable fashion. This inherent danger or risk must be thoroughly explained to participants, and, if these individuals are minors, to their parents or guardians.

Concept 414: Fans, Volunteers, Patrons, and Participants Deserve to Be Warned of the Inherent Dangers and Risks Associated with the Activities in Which They Are to Be Involved.

If the individuals involved in the sport experience are fans or spectators, it is advisable that representatives of the sport organization adequately inform these individuals as to the inherent dangers or risks of their involvement. Such actions can have a significant impact on the incidents of accidents and injuries. "With the abundance of lawsuits, court decisions and payoffs taking place, a facility's signs and their placement take on added significance" (Turner, 1994).

This might mean placing appropriate signs and making timely announcements informing individuals of potential dangers. For example, those spectators arriving at an ice hockey game might be warned about the potential danger of being hit by a flying puck if their seats are located within a specific section of the arena. Similarly, baseball fans can be warned of possible foul balls being hit into certain sections of the stadium.

Concept 415: It Is the Responsibility of the Sport Managers to Provide Warnings of Risks to Those Involved in Activities Which Involve Significant Risks.

Failure to Warn Participants

The concept of "failure to warn" in sports-related injuries can be traced to the $6.4 million dollar judgment in 1982 against the Seattle school system (*Thompson v. Seattle School District*) in Washington state. The case resulted from a catastrophic injury to a high school football athlete. In this particular situation, the parents sued on behalf of their son who was paralyzed (quadriplegic) as a result of an injury while playing competitive football for a school team. The injury did not result from the athlete doing anything wrong or from the athlete failing to properly execute a skill. Rather, the youngster "sustained a neck injury from lowering his head to ward off the tackler..." (Leigh, 1988; Girvan & Girvan, 1993, p. 26, citing Lubell, 1989). Nevertheless, the athlete was paralyzed in an accident involving an activity that was part of the game of football.

Concept 416: Sponsors of Strenuous or Inherently Dangerous Physical Activities or Sports Must Adequately Warn Participants (and Parents if the Participants Are Minors) of the Risks Involved.

The parents in the Seattle, Washington case argued that they and their son had no idea that such a catastrophic and permanent injury would be possible as a consequence of performing normal football skills and tactics in practice or competition. The parents claimed that they should have been adequately forewarned of the potential dangers of such catastrophic and horrific injuries that accompany participation in such a violent and hazardous sport as football. The court, finding in favor of the plaintiffs, indicated that the school representatives had failed to warn the athlete and the parents in explicit terms that one of the risks of playing the sport of football was becoming paralyzed, that is, becoming a quadriplegic.

As a result, it is strongly recommended that individuals involved in activities that inherently involve some very real aspect of risk and potential peril to their persons be adequately informed (in writing) of such risks and possible consequences. This has severe repercussions for school-based athletic programs, recreation sport activities, as well as other organizations that sponsor vigorous physical activities or sports that can be considered inherently dangerous, i.e., ski resorts, sponsors of white-water rafting, and health and fitness clubs.

Use of a Risk Statement

A sample Risk Statement that is currently in use at the university level to warn participants who are involved in potentially dangerous or risky physical activities is provided in Box 12.1. A variation of this form was first utilized in 1989 at SUNY–Brockport when the

BOX **12.1**

Warning Notice or Risk Statement for Participation in Strenuous Activities

Risk Statement

Department of Physical Education and Sport
State University of New York, College at Brockport
Brockport, New York

This Physical Education Performance course requires vigorous activity that may be hazardous to your health. Especially at risk are those individuals with cardiopulmonary disease and those who have not recently engaged in strenuous exercise. There is a possibility of musculoskeletal injury, which may include paralysis or death. Any costs as the result of injury or illness connected with participation in this course or activity are solely the responsibility of the student. If you have a disability that you believe requires accommodation, please notify the instructor prior to participation in class activities.

AUTHORIZATION: I, ____________________ HAVE READ THE ABOVE AND AM AWARE OF THE INHERENT RISKS INVOLVED. MY SIGNATURE ALSO INDICATES THAT I HAVE RECEIVED A COPY OF THIS RISK STATEMENT.

____
Signature

____
Print Name

Date: ______________________

author, as Athletic Director, mandated its usage. The current version of this statement requires that the individual student sign the statement, acknowledging that the individual has read and understood the warning regarding the risks involved and the possible severe consequences of injury and illness. It is especially important that sport managers provide such warning statements to those individuals involved in competitive athletics or in strenuous recreational physical activities and sports.

Use of Waiver or Release Forms

Concept 417: Use of a Waiver Slip Can Help Protect the Sport Entity and Personnel in Selected Instances.

A charge of negligence can sometimes be successfully defended in a court of law by showing that the injured party (an adult) freely signed a written document waiving that person's right to sue for injuries that might result from their involvement in an activity or at a particular site (Berg, 1995d). Such forms require the person signing the document to acknowledge that they understand and accept the normal risks associated with the sport, activity, or program that they or their children are to be involved in.

Concept 418: Parents Cannot Waive the Rights of Their Children to Sue for Negligence.

However, not all states and courts treat such waiver or release forms the same. Some courts in some states have ruled the use of such forms invalid (Wong, 1988; Herbert, 1996). It is important to note that minors are not held accountable for signing such waivers because they cannot waive their rights to sue. Neither may parents nor guardians sign such a binding waiver on behalf of their minor children because parents–guardians cannot sign away the rights of minors to sue.

Use of a Permission Slip or Consent Form

The permission slip or consent form is a document created by the sport manager that is used to secure permission of the parents to allow their minor offspring to participate in a specific activity. This form simply gives the organization and its agents documentation that the participant has permission to be involved in the stated activity or sport. Frequently, the permission slip is piggybacked to the "warning statement" about the vigorous, strenuous, or dangerous activity and the risks involved in said activity.

Responding to Accidents and Injuries

How one responds to or reacts to an accident or injuries is of the utmost importance. For example, there must be both appropriate and timely responses made in such situations in terms of providing immediate and temporary first aid until qualified medical help arrives. However, it is equally important that sound steps be taken in terms of recordkeeping during and following accidents involving personal injuries.

For example, an accident report should be completed as soon as possible following an accident. The names, addresses, and phone numbers of all witnesses should be recorded as well as written statements regarding what each witness saw. Similarly, a written statement should be obtained from the injured party when deemed possible and appropriate.

Concept 419: Keeping Accurate and Detailed Records Will Significantly Aid in Defending the Sport Organization and Its Personnel against a Charge of Negligence.

Maintaining accurate records of all facts relating to personal injury situations cannot be overemphasized (Edwards, 1993). Keeping accurate and timely records of other pertinent factors throughout the calendar year is equally important. For example, being able to show that adequate warnings were given to parents and youngsters in a school setting can go a long way in defending the school district against charges of negligence (based on the "failure to warn" principle). Maintaining records indicating that a health and fitness club patron received personal instruction in terms of how to use each of the exercise machines in the club can be invaluable in showing that the patron, who was subsequently injured using one of the machines, was familiar with and knowledgeable in the use of the machines.

Similarly, having a physician's written statement giving the professional athlete the "all-clear" to participate in actual competition can stand the team owners and coaches in good stead against a charge of negligence. Finally, having records indicating that the class of beginning downhill skiers had been warned by their expert instructors to stay off of the advanced slopes will also help protect the ski operators and owners (against a charge of negligence) if an adult student from the class was subsequently injured attempting to ski down the forbidden advanced slope. The concept is simple: Establish clear-cut and intelligent policies, procedures, and practices, and document decisions made and actions taken before and after accidents and injuries. One must keep appropriate, accurate written records.

Product Liability

Many times sport organizations need to be concerned with product liability. So too do sport manufacturers. Product liability is a cross between tort and contract law and involves warranties, express or implied, that the product in question is good, safe, and appropriate when used for its stated purpose and under specific circumstances.

The phrase *warranty of merchantability* indicates that the burden of proof is on the manufacturer that the goods or products are safe and appropriate. When sport entities create, produce, sell, or give away items such as food, apparel, or premiums to spectators, the sport entities share responsibility with the manufacturers for the items sold and/or given away (The crisis continues, 1988; Liability/sports, 1988). Product liability also is involved when items of equipment (football, baseball, or ice hockey helmets, bats and balls, ski or exercise equipment, etc.) are sold to sport organizations as well as the general public. The manufacturer warrants that such equipment is safe to use under specified conditions and circumstances. It is imperative that sport managers pay particular attention to the quality of equipment and supplies used in the conduct of their programs and activities (Berg, 1995b).

Establishing Appropriate Policies Governing the Sport Activity or Program

One of the major challenges and responsibilities of sport managers today is to establish intelligent and appropriate policies, practices, and procedures as they relate to the sport organization and the various activities associated with the entity. These operational policies, procedures, and practices can relate both to internal as well as to external operations. They serve as a guide in terms of how the sport organization will be run and how its activities and programs are to be implemented and conducted. Some organizations have created a Risk Management Manual in which standard operating procedures (SOP) and operational activities that are applicable at various levels of the operation and can be carried out by employees, including managers and supervisors (Conn, 1993).

Concept 420: An Organization's Standard Operating Policies, Procedures, and Practices Should Play a Major Role in Preventing Situations in Which Negligence Results in Personal Injuries to Others.

There is a need to examine existing policies, procedures, and practices to insure that they are effective and efficient in terms of facilitating, in a safe manner, the operations of the sport entity. Additionally, they should be reviewed so that they do not put individuals (fans, patrons, and customers, as well as the organization's own personnel) or the sport entity itself at unnecessary and unacceptable risk.

Professional sports teams as well as collegiate teams and recreation entities must make decisions relative to crowd control. For example, how many security personnel will be present at specific contests? What will be their role, their authority and responsibility? Will they be stationed inside and outside of the actual playing facility? How will they react to specific types of situations? Will the concession stands sell alcoholic beverages at the contests? Will alcohol be served after a specific length of time (after halftime or after the sixth inning, for example)? What type of lighting will be available in the parking lots for the health and fitness club, for the athletic contest, or for the recreation event? Will fans or customers be allowed to carry bottles into the event? How will a restrictive policy be enforced? By whom?

Risk Management Audits

When a risk management audit is conducted, every aspect of the organization's operation is examined. The goal is to prevent injuries to and minimize risks (financial, public relations, and embarrassments) associated with the sport, recreation, or fitness operation. This necessitates looking at facilities, transportation, equipment and supplies, various operations, as well as all procedures, and policies, practices relating to all aspects of the entity (Olson, 1985, 1986; Cotten, 1993).

Such an audit or an assessment plan is a vital aspect of an organization's operation, one that can have a significant impact on the overall success or failure of the entity itself and its personnel (Edwards, 1993). Gray (1991, pp. 29–30) suggests that a quality risk management audit include identifying various risks associated with the activity or program or facility, making an assessment as to the probability and the significance of possible injuries, determining a method of negating or mitigating the risks involved, and instituting or implementing necessary and appropriate managerial practices, policies, and procedures.

Concept 421: A Risk Management Audit Involves a Close Inspection of All Standard Operating Policies, Procedures, and Practices as They Relate to Every Aspect of the Organization.

Assuming a Proactive Stance in Risk Management

Failure to be concerned about and alert to the potential dangers of being negligent in any sports operation invites disaster. Failure to take a proactive stance in the area of negligence and legal liability is indeed foolhardy in this litigious society. Adhering to the Boy Scout Motto, "Be Prepared," is a good and wise policy to follow. To do otherwise is to invite disaster and court adversity.

Conclusions

Sport managers who are active in conducting effective risk management programs are usually successful in diminishing their organization's potential for legal liability and exposure. Sport organizations and their personnel always face the risk of potential lawsuits based on negligence and other reasons from any number of sources, including their own employees, their customers, and the general public. If negligence is to be significantly reduced, sport managers need to assume a proactive approach in all aspects of their sport operation. Without such concerted efforts the consequences can be severe in terms of lost time, effort, and resources.

REFERENCES

Adams, S. H. (1993). Duty to properly instruct. *Journal of Physical Education, Recreation and Dance, 64*(2), 22–23.

American College of Sports Medicine. (1992). *ACSM's health/fitness facility standards and guidelines.* Indianapolis, IN.

Antee, A. and Swinburn, J. (1990). Crowd management: An issue of safety, security, and liability. *Public Management, 72*(1), 16–19.

Appenzeller, H. (1993). *Managing sports and risk management strategies.* Durham, NC: Carolina Academic Press.

Baley, J. A. and Matthews, D. L. (1989). *Law and liability.* Dubuque, IA: Wm. C. Brown.

Berg, R. (1993, December). The risk of not watching. *Athletic Business, 17*(12), 22.

Berg, R. (1994, July). How much injury care is enough? *Athletic Business, 18*(7), 20.

Berg, R. (1995a, March). California's immunity system breaks down. *Athletic Business, 19*(3), 19, 22.

Berg, R. (1995b, May). Soccer safety goal has not yet been met. *Athletic Business, 19*(5), 24.

Berg, R. (1995c, September). Feeling mistreated, injured athletes sue. *Athletic Business, 19*(9), 24.

Berg, R. (1995d, November). Grudging support for liability waivers in Florida. *Athletic Business, 19*(11), 24.

Berg, R. (1996, October). Advise and consent. *Athletic Business,* 20(10), 9.

Blauvelt, H. (1993, May 18). Safety worries hit titanium bats. *USA Today,* p. 10-C.

Borkowski, R. P. (1993a, May/June). Safety in football. *Scholastic Coach, 62*(10), 5, 6.

Borkowski, R. (1993b, October/November). Avoiding the gavel. *Athletic Management, V*(6), 22, 24–26.

Borkowski, R. P. (1996, December–January). Safety through supervision. *Athletic Management, VIII*(1), 12.

Brown, S. C. (1993). Selecting safe equipment—What do we really know? *Journal of Physical Education, Recreation and Dance, 64*(2), 33–35, 65.

Carpenter, L. (1994). Perfect or perilous: When is a teacher negligent? *Strategies, 7*(6), 23–25.

Clement, A. (1993). Civil rights—The first, fourth and fourteenth amendments. *Journal of Physical Education Recreation and Dance, 64*(2), 16–17, 62.

Cohen, A. (1996, August). Save situations. *Athletic Business, 20*(8), 33–38.

Conn, J. H. (1993). The litigation connection—Perspectives of risk control for the 1990s. *Journal of Physical Education, Recreation and Dance, 64*(2), 60–61.
Conn, J. H. and Tompkins, R. N. (1994, April–May). In the shadows. *Athletic Management, VI*(2), 18–22.
Cotten, D. J. (1993). Risk management—A tool for reducing exposure to legal liability. *Journal of Physical Education, Recreation and Dance, 64*(2), 58–61.
The crisis continues...Another manufacturer forced to cease production. (1988, August/September/October). *Sports Liability News,* p. 2.
Dropkin, B. (1996, October 29). CAPS: History and miscellaneous information. Personal Letter.
Edwards, K. (1993, August). Risk-management program. *Scholastic Coach, 63*(1), 5–6.
Gaskin, L. P. (1993). Establishing, communicating, and enforcing rules and regulations. *Journal of Physical Education, Recreation and Dance, 64*(2), 26–27, 63.
Girvan, G. and Girvan, J. T. (1993). Risk management practices in athletics—A content analysis. *Journal of Physical Education, Recreation and Dance, 64*(4), 26–28.
Gray, G. R. (1991). Risk management planning: Conducting a sport risk assessment to enhance program safety. *Journal of Physical Education, Recreation and Dance, 62*(6), 29–31, 78.
Gray, G. R. (1993). Providing adequate medical care to program participants. *Journal of Physical Education, Recreation and Dance, 64*(2), 56–57, 65–66.
Gray, G. R. (1995). Safety tips from the expert witness. *Journal of Physical Education, Recreation and Dance, 66*(1), 18–21.
Hart, J. E. and Ritson, R. J. (1993). *Liability and safety in physical education and sport.* Reston, VA: AAHPERD.
Herbert, D. L. (1995, November). The liability of off-premise activity. *Fitness Management, 11*(12), 18.
Herbert, D. L. (1996, April). Another release fails to bar suit against club. *Fitness Management, 12*(5), 20.
Kaiser, R. (1986). *Law and liability in recreation, parks and sport.* Englewood Cliffs, NJ: Prentice-Hall.
Kroll, B. (1990). Evaluating strength training equipment. *National Strength and Conditioning Association Journal, 12*(3), 56–65.
Lehr, C. (1993). Proper classification. *Journal of Physical Education, Recreation and Dance, 64*(2), 24–25, 63.
Leigh, P. (Ed.). (1988). A common sense of view of liability. *Parks & Recreation, 23*(9), 53–55.
Liability/sports—Rawlings: Helmets not worth the hassle. (1988, July). *Athletic Business, 12*(7), 16.
Lincoln, S. M. (1992). Sports injury risk management & the keys to safety—Coalition of Americans to Protect Sports (CAPS). *Journal of Physical Education, Recreation and Dance, 63*(7), 40–42, 63.
Lubell, A. (1987). Insurance, liability, and the American way of sport. *Physician and Sports Medicine, 15*(9), 192–200.
Lubell, A. (1989). Questioning the athlete's right to sue. *Physician and Sportsmedicine, 17*(24), 242–244.
Maloy, B. P. (1993). Legal obligations related to facilities. *Journal of Physical Education, Recreation and Dance, 64*(2), 28–30, 64.
Maloy, B. P. (1995, January). Dangerous base paths. *Athletic Business, 19*(1), 59–62.
Merriman, J. (1993). Supervision in sport and physical activity. *Journal of Physical Education, Recreation and Dance, 64*(2), 20–21, 23.
National Society to Prevent Blindness. (1981). *Eye protection recommendations for racquet sports players.* New York.
National Youth Sports Foundation for the Prevention of Athletic Injuries, Inc. (1993). *National youth sports—National youth sports injury-prevention month.* Needham, MA.
Neal, T. (1995, August–September). Anticipating away game injuries. *Athletic Management, VII*(5), 32–35.
Olson, J. R. (1985, November). Safety checklists: Making indoor areas hazard-free. *Athletic Business, 9*(11), 36–39, 42.
Olson, J. R. (1986, January). Are your gymnasts safe from injury? *Athletic Business, 10*(1), 38–39, 41.
Peterson, J. A. and Hronek, B. B. (1992). *Risk management for park, recreation, and leisure services* (2nd ed.). Champaign, IL: Sagamore.
Pike, L. L. and Rello, M. N. (1994, July). Training rules. *Athletic Business, 18*(7), 10, 13.
Pine, D. (1991). Preventing sports related eye injuries. *Physician and Sports Medicine, 19*(2), 129–130, 133–134.
Pittman, A. T. (1993). Safe transportation—A driving concern. *Journal of Physical Education, Recreation and Dance, 64*(2), 53–55.

Promote safer sports for youth. (1993). *Journal of Physical Education, Recreation and Dance, 64*(4), 12.
Rauschenbach, J. (1994). Effective supervision practices. *Journal of Physical Education, Recreation and Dance, 65*(5), 66–68.
Sharp, L. A. (1993). Employment of qualified personnel. *Journal of Physical Education, Recreation and Dance, 64*(2), 18–19, 62–63.
Sharp, L. A. (1996, September). Fault lines. *Athletic Business, 20*(9), 10, 14.
Siegenthaler, K. L. (1996). Supervising activities for safety. *Journal of Physical Education, Recreation and Dance, 67*(2), 29–30, 36.
Stier, W. F., Jr. (1994). *Successful sport fund-raising.* Dubuque, IA: Wm. C. Brown & Benchmark.
Stier, W. F., Jr. (1995). *Successful coaching—Strategies and tactics.* Boston, MA: American Press.
Turner, E. T. (1994, August). Vital signs. *Athletic Business, 18*(18), 65–67.
van der Smissen, B. (1990). *Legal liability and risk management for public and private entities.* Cincinnati, OH: Anderson Publishing.
Wolohan, J. T. (1995, January). Assume nothing. *Athletic Business, 19*(1), 10–11.
Wong, G. M. (October, 1988). Washington court says release forms invalid. *Athletic Business, 12*(10), 14.
Wong, G. M. (1989, July). Athletes aren't fair game for cheap shots. *Athletic Business, 13*(7), 16.
Wong, G. M. and Barr, C. A. (1993, July). Practice and malpractice. *Athletic Business, 17*(7), 16.
Wong, G. M. and Covell, D. (1995a, March). Duty-bound. *Athletic Business, 19*(3). 13, 14.
Wong, G. M. and Covell, D. (1995b, August). War of words. *Athletic Business, 19*(8), 10, 14, 20.

DISCUSSION AND REVIEW QUESTIONS

1. List the components of a sound risk management plan for a hypothetical sport entity.
2. What are some areas of concern that managers should pay special attention to in sport organizations, recreation programs, and fitness and wellness entities?
3. Provide examples that illustrate the differences between criminal law, contract law, and civil law for the sport manager and the sport organization.
4. Indicate how a sport manager might assume a proactive stance in terms of slander, libel, and defamation of character.
5. Cite examples in the fitness industry and in professional sports of negligence taking place as a result of acts of commission as well acts of ommission.
6. What are commonly used defenses against accusations of negligence?
7. Elaborate on the advantages and deficiencies of both waiver or release forms and permission slips/consent forms in terms of participants in sport, recreation, or fitness programs.
8. Explain why and how a sport organization and its personnel should be concerned with product liability in terms of the organization's and personnel's utilization of different products in the conduct of their day-to-day work.

APPENDIX A

The Managerial Continuum

(Managerial Contributions by Various Groups and Individuals

Approximate Year(s)	Individual or Ethnic Group	Major Managerial Contributions
5000 B.C.	Sumerians	Script; record-keeping
4000 B.C.	Egyptians	Recognized need for planning, organizing, and controlling
2700 B.C.	Egyptians	Recognized need for honesty or fair play in management; therapy interview—"get it off your chest"
2600 B.C.	Egyptians	Decentralization in organization
2000 B.C.	Egyptians	Recognized need for written word in requests; use of staff advice
1800 B.C.	Hammurabi	Use of witnesses and writing for control; establishment of minimum wage; recognition that responsibility cannot be shifted
1600 B.C.	Egyptians	Centralization of organization
1491 B.C.	Hebrews	Concepts of organization, scalar principle, and exception principle
1100 B.C.	Chinese	Recognized need for organization, planning, directing, and controlling
600 B.C.	Nebuchadnezzar	Production control and wage incentives
500 B.C.	Mencius	Recognized need for systems and standards
	Chinese	Principles of specialization and reorganization
	Sun Tzu	Recognized need for planning, organizing, and directing
400 B.C.	Socrates	Enunciation of universality of management
	Xenophon	Recognized management as a separate art
	Cyrus	Recognized need for human relations; use of motion study, layout, and materials handling
360 B.C.	Greeks	Scientific method applied; use of work methods and tempo
	Plato	Principle of specialization enunciated

Approximate Year(s)	Individual or Ethnic Group	Major Managerial Contributions
325 B.C.	Alexander the Great	Use of staff
175 B.C.	Cato	Use of job descriptions
50 B.C.	Marro	Use of job descriptions
284 A.D.	Diocletian	Delegation of authority
900 A.D.	Alferabi	Listed traits of a leader
1100 A.D.	Ghazali	Listed traits of a manager
1340 A.D.	L. Paccioli (Genoese)	Double-entry bookkeeping
1395 A.D.	Francisco DiMarco	Cost-accounting practiced
1410 A.D.	Soranzo Brothers	Use of journal entries and ledger
1418 A.D.	Barbarigo	Forms of business organization; work-in-process accounts used
1436 A.D.	Arsenal of Venice (Venetians)	Cost accounting; checks and balances; for control; numbering of inventoried parts; interchangeability of parts; use of assembly line technique; use of personnel management; standardization of parts; inventory control; cost control
1500 A.D.	Sir Thomas More	Called for specialization; decried sins of poor management and leadership
1525 A.D.	Niccolo	Reliance on mass consent principle
	Machiavelli	Recognized need for cohesiveness in organization; enunciated leadership qualities
1767 A.D.	Sir James Steurat	Source of authority theory; impact of automation
1776 A.D.	Adam Smith	Application of principle of specialization to manufacturing workers; control concepts; payment computations
1785 A.D.	Thomas Jefferson	Called attention to concept of interchangeable parts
1799 A.D.	James Watt Matthew Boulton Scho, England	Standard operating procedures; specifications; work methods; planning; incentive wages, standard times, standard data; employee Christmas parties; bonuses announced at Christmas; mutual employee's insurance society; use of audits
1810 A.D.	Robert Owen	Need for personnel practices recognized and applied
	New Lanark, Scotland	Assumed responsibility for training workers; built clean row homes for workers
1820 A.D.	James Mill	Analyzing and synthesizing human motions
1832 A.D.	Charles Babbage	Scientific approach emphasized; specialization emphasized; division of labor; motion and time study; cost-accounting; effect of various colors on employee efficiency
1835 A.D.	Marshall Laughlin, et al.	Recognition and discussion of the relative importance of the functions of management

Approximate Year(s)	Individual or Ethnic Group	Major Managerial Contributions
1850 A.D.	Mill, et al.	Span of control; unity of command; control of labor and materials; specialization–division of labor; wage incentives
1855 A.D.	Henry Poor	Principles of organization, communication, and information applied to railways
1856 A.D.	Daniel C. McCallum	Use of organization chart to show management structure; application of systematic management to railways
1871 A.D.	W. S. Jevons	Made use of motion studies; studied effect of different tools on worker; fatigue study
1881 A.D.	Joseph Wharton	Established college course in business management
1886 A.D.	Henry C. Metcalfe	Art of management; science of administration
	Henry R. Towne	Science of management
1891 A.D.	Frederick Halsey	Premium plan of wage payment
1900 A.D.	Frederick W. Taylor	Scientific management; systems applications; personnel management; need for cooperation between labor and management; high wages; equal division between labor and management; functional organization; exception principles applied to the shop; cost system; methods study; time study; definition of scientific management; emphasis on research, standards, planning, control, and cooperation
	Frank B. Gilbreth	Science of motion study
1901 A.D.	Henry L. Gantt	Task and bonus system; humanistic approach to labor; Gantt charts; management's responsibility for training workers
1910 A.D.	Hugo Munsterberg	Application of psychology to management and workers
	Harrington Emerson	Efficiency engineering; principles of efficiency
1911 A.D.	J. C. Duncan	First college text in management
1915 A.D.	H. B. Drury	Criticism of scientific management reaffirmed initial ideas
	R. F. Hoxie	Criticism of scientific management reaffirmed initial ideas
	Thomas A. Edison	Devised war game to evade and destroy submarines
1916 A.D.	Henri Fayol	First completed theory of management; functions of management; principles of management; recognized need for management to be taught in schools
	Alexander H. Church	Functional concept of management; first North American to explain the totality of managerial concepts and relate each component to the whole
	A. K. Erlang	Anticipated waiting-line theory
1917 A.D.	W. H. Leffingwell	Applied scientific management to office
1918 A.D.	C. C. Parsons	Recognized need for applying scientific management to offices
	Ordway Tead	Application of psychology to industry

Approximate Year(s)	Individual or Ethnic Group	Major Managerial Contributions
1919 A.D.	Morris L. Cooke	Diverse applications of scientific management
1921 A.D.	Walter D. Scott	Brought psychology to advertising and personnel management
1923 A.D.	Oliver Sheldon	Developed a philosophy of management; principles of management
1924 A.D.	H. F. Dodge H. G. Romig W. A. Shewhart	Use of statistical inference and probability theory in sampling inspection and in quality control by statistical means
1925 A.D.	Ronald A. Fisher	Various modern statistical methods, including chi square test, Bayesian statistics, sampling theory, and design of experiments
1927 A.D.	Elton Mayo	Sociological concept of group endeavor, "Hawthorne Effect"
	T. C. Fry	Statistical foundations of queuing theory
1930 A.D.	Mary Parker Follett	Managerial philosophy based on individual motivations; group process approach to solving managerial problems
1931 A.D.	James D. Mooney	Principles of organization recognized as universal
1938 A.D.	P. M. S. Blackett	Operations research
1943 A.D.	Lyndall Urwick	Collection, consolidation, and correlation of principles of management
1947 A.D.	Max Weber Rensis Likert Chris Argyris	Placed emphasis on psychology, social psychology, and research in human relations in organization theory; incorporation of an open-system theory of organization
1949 A.D.	Norbert Wiener Claude Shannon	Emphasized systems analysis and information theory in management
1951 A.D.	Abrams Benjamin M. Seleckman	Reintroduced managerial statesmanship into managerial thinking
1955 A.D.	Herbert Simon Harold J. Leavitt Robert Schlaifer	Placed emphasis on human behavior in decision-making, viewed as an identifiable, observable, and measurable process; increased attention given to managerial psychology

Additional updates below from: Bridges, F. J. & Roquemore, L. L. (1992). *Management for athletic/sport administration: Theory and practice*. Decature, GA: ESM Books. pp. 12–13. Reprinted by permission of ESM Books.

1957 A.D.	Northcotte Parkinson	Humorous look at administration; Parkinson's law; work expands to fill the time allowed for it
1960 A.D.	Douglas McGregor	Theory X and Theory Y views of workers and managers
1961 A.D.	Rensis Likert	Participative management

Approximate Year(s)	Individual or Ethnic Group	Major Managerial Contributions
1962 A.D.	Chris Argyris	Sensitivity training for managers
1964 A.D.	Victor H. Vroom	Expectancy theory of motivation
1969 A.D.	Laurence Peter	Peter Principle of promotion to level of incompetency; expressed dangers of preoccupation with growth; need for conservation
1971 A.D.	Ernest Dale	Empirical school of management theory
1981 A.D.	William Ouchi	Theory Z system of management
1985 A.D.	Gifford Pinchot, III	Coined term *intrapreneur* for new type of corporate manager who runs own business within framework of large corporation

Additions below provided by Stier, Jr., W. F. (1998, April 8). Fundraising, promotions, public relations and publicity for the 21st century. A presentation made at the national convention of the American Alliance for Health, Physical Education, Recreation and Dance, Reno, Nevada.

1900–1993	W. Edwards Deming	Total Quality Management (TQM); customer is most important; employers and employees work together as a team; decisions based on data
1909–present	Peter Druker	Modern expert on management
1942–present	Ken Blanchard	Modern author on management; wrote *The One-Minute Manager* as well as other popular works on management in the workplace

Adapted from: George, Claude S. (1972). *The History of Management Thought* (2nd ed.) pp. vii–xiii.

APPENDIX B

Sources of Information Pertaining to Facilities and Equipment

1. Amateur Softball Association of America, 2801 Northeast 50th Street, Oklahoma City, OK 73111 (405) 424-5266

2. Field Hockey Association of America, Inc., 1750 East Boulder Street, Colorado Springs, CO 80909–5764 (719) 578-4567

3. American Amateur Racquetball Association, 815 North Weber, Suite 101, Colorado Springs, CO 80903 (719) 623–5396; United States Handball Association, 930 North Benton, Tucson, AZ 85711 (602) 795-0434

4. American Youth Soccer Organization, 5403 West 138th Street, Hasthorne, CA 90250 (213) 643-8066

5. The Association for Higher Education Facilities Officers (APPA), 1643 Prince Street, Alexandria, VA 22314–2818 (703) 684-1446

6. The Association of Quality Clubs (IRSA; a not-for-profit trade association representing over 1600 clubs worldwide), 253 Summer St., Boston, MA 02222 (617) 951-0055 or (800) 228-4772

7. Athletic Equipment Managers Association (AEMA), 723 Keil Court, Bowling Green, Ohio 43402 (419) 352-1207 or Mr. Jeff Boss, Louisiana State University, P.O. Box 25095, Baton Rouge, LA 70894 (504) 388-1151

8. National Collegiate Athletic Association (NCAA), 6201 College Blvd., Overland Park, Kansas 66211–2422 (913) 339-1906

9. National Federation of State High School Associations, P.O. Box 20626, Kansas City, MO 64195 (816) 464-5400

10. The National Health Club Association, P.O. Box 2378, Corona, CA 92718–2378 (714) 371-0606, or 12596 West Bayaud Avenue, 1st Floor, Denver, CO (303) 753–6422 or (716) 467-4653

11. National Hockey League, Montreal Office, 1155 Metcalfe Street, Suite 960, Montréal, Québec H3B 2W2 Canada

12. National Junior College Athletic Association (NJCAA), P.O. Box 7305, Colorado Springs, CO 80933

13. National Spa and Pool Institute, 2111 Eisenhower Avenue, Alexandria, VA 22314–4678 (703) 838-0083

14. Nautilus Sports/Medical Industries (800) 628-8458

15. NIRSA, 850 S.W. 15th St., Corvallis, OR 97333 (503) 737-2088 or 737-2088

16. Sporting Goods Manufacturing Association, 200 Castlewood Drive, North Palm Beach, Florida 33408

17. Sports Turf Managers Association (STMA), 1455 E. Tropicana, Suite 390, Las Vegas, NV 89119 (702) 739-8052

18. Sportsplex Operators & Developers Association, P.O. Box 24263, Westgate Station, Rochester, New York 14624–0263 (716) 426-2215

19. StairMaster Sports/Medical Products, Inc., 12421 Willows Road, N.E., Suite 100, Kirkland, Washington 98034 (800) 635-2936

20. United States Badminton Association, 501 West Sixth Street, Papillion, NE 68046 (402) 592-7309

21. United States Soccer Federation, 1750 East Boulder Street, Colorado Springs, CO 80909 (719) 578-4678

22. United States Squash Racquets Association, Inc., 211 Ford Road, Bala-Cynwyd, PA 19004 (215) 667-4006

23. United States Swimming, Inc., 1750 East Boulder Street, Colorado Springs, CO 80909–5770 (719) 578-4578

24. United States Team Handball Federation, 1750 East Boulder Street, Colorado Springs, CO 80909 (719) 632-5551, ext. 4582

25. The United States Tennis Court and Track Builders Association, 3525 Ellicott Mills Drive, Suite N., Ellicott City, MD 21043 (410) 418-4875

26. Universal Gym Equipment, Inc., P.O. Box 120, Cedar Rapids, IA

27. W. A. Schmidt Corporation (manufactures, designs, and installs fitness facility mezzanines) (800) 523-6719

INDEX

PHOTO CREDITS

Pages 1, 2, 132, 139/courtesy of University of Tennessee Sports Information; page 22/courtesy of Kent Photographic Services; page 25/courtesy of Batavia Downs, Batavia, New York; pages 39, 215 (bottom), 251/courtesy of the Rochester Red Wings; pages 49, 52, 147, 214, 243, 304/courtesy of State University of New York, Brockport; pages 61, 84, 355/courtesy of the Buffalo Bills; pages 73, 210/courtesy of West Virginia University Sports Communications Office; page 76/courtesy of University of Tennessee Sports Information; pages 100, 193/courtesy of Midwest Athletic Club; pages 115, 167, 268/courtesy of Rochester Raging Rhinos; pages 126, 282, 298/courtesy of St. Lucie Mets, Port St. Lucie, Florida; pages 130, 291, 307, 360/courtesy of Washington State University Sports Information; page 136/courtesy of the University of Houston; pages 157, 205, 337/courtesy of Indiana University Sports Information; pages 203/courtesy of Ohio State University Sports Information; page 209/courtesy of Robert Rogers, Tampa Bay Devil Rays; page 215 (top)/courtesy of Messenger-Wolfe Publications, Robert Hanlon photographer; pages 217, 279/courtesy of Clemson University Sports Information; page 350/courtesy of Phyllis Salem, Gund Arena.